PRECEDENCE AND ARROW NETWORKING TECHNIQUES FOR CONSTRUCTION

PRECEDENCE AND ARROW NETWORKING TECHNIQUES FOR CONSTRUCTION

Robert B. Harris

Professor of Civil Engineering
THE UNIVERSITY OF MICHIGAN
Ann Arbor, Michigan

John Wiley & Sons
New York   Santa Barbara   Chichester   Brisbane   Toronto

Library of Congress Cataloging in Publication Data:

Harris, Robert Blynn, 1918-
   Precedence and arrow networking techniques
for construction.

   Includes bibliographies and indexes.
   1. Construction industry—Management.
2. Network analysis (Planning)   I. Title.
TH438.H37   658.4′032   78-5786
ISBN 0-471-04123-8

Printed in the United States of America

10 9 8 7 6 5 4 3

PREFACE

This book developed out of the experience gained during several years of teaching courses in networking techniques to students of construction. During that period it became clear that the precedence, or activity on the node, diagraming technique must form a major part of any course dealing with this subject area. The precedence technique's flexibility in expressing the project constraints, its ease in diagram construction, its computational efficiency in both manual and computer calculations, and its ability to accommodate a variety of extensions to the basic schedule are benefits that the modern manager of construction would not wish to be without. Yet, it also became clear that the arrow diagraming technique, first introduced for CPM and PERT, must be included in these courses because of its popularity among some project managers, its well-established use in the construction industry, and the availability of the large numbers of computer programs that have been written for it. To satisfy the instructional needs for these courses a textbook on networking for management based upon a parallel treatment of these two techniques appeared to be required.

The aim of this book is to provide such a parallel treatment while avoiding the oversimplification found in some works, and to present the discussion in language that a beginner in this subject can readily comprehend. The student should acquire a sound basis for the practical application of each method after a careful reading of the text.

Chapter 1 presents background information applicable to networking techniques in general, and introduces the student to the concept that the creation of the scheduling plan is a design process in which assumptions are made, calculations are performed, results are tested against desired criteria, adjustments are made to the assumptions, and calculations are repeated. This procedure is reiterated as often as is needed to obtain a solution which in the planner's view is final.

In Chapter 2, steps for creating the list of activities comprising the project are developed. Such a list forms the basic input needed for any networking technique.

Chapter 3 discusses the construction of the arrow diagram, and Chapter 4 details the procedures for creating the precedence diagram. Both these chapters treat only the logic relationships in the network that are independent of the duration of the individual activities. Background for the establishment of activity durations and the manner for handling time allowances is presented in Chapter 5.

Computations for arrow diagrams are detailed in Chapter 6. Both the activity time and event time approaches for float values are discussed. Procedures are given for calculations made directly in a table or on the diagram.

Precedence network computations are discussed in Chapter 7. Formulas for the calculation of float values are based upon the concept of link lag. A new procedure is presented for the calculation of schedule values using tabulated data taken directly from the activity list without reference to a drawn diagram. Procedures for calculating values on the diagram are given, and a unique method is demonstrated for making the calculations on a matrix.

Chapter 8 discusses the communication of the schedule derived from either of the two networking bases and forms the background for the project monitoring and control phase presented in Chapter 9. Procedures for documenting the progress of the project are treated in Chapter 9 also.

The student will find in Chapter 10 practical techniques for making time-cost adjustments to the early start schedule, and will be provided with insight as to the means for controlling the work when time and cost are of major importance.

The establishment of limits for resources by the process of leveling the early start schedule is presented in Chapter 11. Leveling by use of the traditional maximum resource limit is given first in the chapter, and is followed by a procedure based upon the concept of the minimum moment of the resource histogram and the use of an improvement factor to more completely satisfy the needs of the manager of construction.

Chapter 12 reviews the PERT method and introduces the student to the use of probability in the planning, scheduling, and control phases of networking. Particular applications to the construction industry are discussed.

Overlapping precedence networking is the topic for Chapter 13. Complete coverage of all overlapping relationships is presented, allowing the planner and scheduler almost unlimited freedom of expression for modeling complex projects. Overlapping networks have particular use in the development of summary networks for upper levels of management control.

The book concludes with Chapter 14 in which some particular applications of networking techniques are discussed. Study of these cases will enable the practitioner to apply the theory to the particular needs of real-life projects.

Instructors will find that the chapters as outlined above allow for the development of several possible courses of varying length and emphasis. Although the emphasis throughout the book is upon construction work, the methods and procedures are easily adaptive and can be applied to any project where there is a sequence of time-dependent tasks to be performed. In most commercial or manufacturing applications the same elements are present, and nomenclature becomes the only stumbling block to their utilization. For instance, These procedures have been applied to a number of plant engineering situations that involved assembly line changeover, remodeling of work areas, payroll scheduling, and the like.

Where the instructional emphasis is to be on arrow networking alone, Chapters 1 to 3, 5, 6, 8, and 9 form a short but basic course. If the emphasis is to be on the precedence technique alone, Chapters 1, 2, 4, 5, 7, 8, and 9 form another basic course independent of the arrow technique. A third somewhat longer course involving both the above techniques may be assembled from Chapters 1 to 9; Chapters 10 to 14 may be added as desired.

To assist the instructor and to provide the student with practice in using these methods, typical exercises are given at the end of each chapter. References are also included at the ends of the chapters to allow serious readers to increase the depth of their knowledge of these important scheduling techniques.

The contributions of many students, faculty, and practitioners are so numerous that it is impossible to acknowledge each individually. Without these persons this work could not have been prepared. It is to these persons, particularly the students, that this volume is dedicated.

Robert B. Harris

CONTENTS

1

INTRODUCTION

1.1 INTRODUCTION

No one knows for sure when the concept of scheduling time begins. Perhaps some prehistoric man decided to return to the comfort of his cave and the companionship of his mate at the end of the day instead of curling up on the ground in a forest. No doubt he chose sundown as an appropriate target for returning, thus setting a schedule for himself. When he told his mate that she could expect him at that time, he communicated his schedule and made it possible for others to plan their activities to coincide with his plan.

Today all of us continue to follow this same routine of scheduling our lives and communicating our plans to others about us. In fact, we are forced by the complexities of modern living to establish very elaborate schedules in order that we can carry out the functions of society.

With the advent of the written word and the development of numbering systems the communication of time information was greatly facilitated. It became possible to make lists and to set specific times for events to occur. In the construction process this meant that arrangements could be made for materials before the actual construction was to take place and tradesmen could be grouped together to speed the work. The listing of items and human resources prevailed for many years until the period now known as the industrial revolution.

By the middle of the nineteenth century industrial shops found that it was essential to do more and more scheduling of the jobs passing through their factories if demands of quantity and delivery were to be met. The emphasis was upon the continuous utilization of the machinery, and little attention was paid to the scheduling of human resources because in most cases there was a one-to-one correspondence between machines and operatiors. Lists of start and completion times were the main vehicles of communication. As shops became more complicated there was a need for a more rapid method of schedule expression, and managers turned to graphical representations.

During World War I, Henry L. Gantt developed a display for production control which was basically a bar chart upon which specific time points were indicated.[1.6, 1.7, 1.8] This device has continued to be one of the most direct and easily understood methods for expressing project plans.

Because the emphasis in the construction field has always been on the utilization of human resources rather than on machinery, scheduling by list for the employment of the various construction craftsmen prevailed well into the present century. Construction was considered a trade and not an industrial process; however, the bar chart did become an accepted scheduling technique for construction work because it depicted the tasks to be done and made the creation of the human resources list an easier task. Control of the work was exercised by marking off the work completed on the chart, and some idea of progress was obtained by observing the amounts so marked.

As construction began to use the products of industry, new materials, and new equipment demanded by advances in lighting, power, and climate control, the construction manager found it increasingly difficult to maintain the schedule. It became evident that some of the tools being used by industry could apply, and the bar chart began to change significantly. Schemes were devised to show more of the interaction between the elements of the work and attempts were made to show more accurate rates of completion. Some charts depicted the bars as triangles or other geometric shapes to show that construction tasks are frequently more than simple production processes.

By 1956 the complexities of construction work for chemical plants led the E. I. du Pont de Nemours & Company to study this problem in detail. A team with the objective of improving the planning and scheduling of engineering design and construction was formed with Morgan Walker of du Pont and James E. Kelley, Jr. of Remington Rand Corporation directing the work.[1.7,1.8] This team presented their concept of network planning and developed the initial mathematical theory upon which the Critical Path Method of analysis is based.[1.4] It soon became apparent that these network-based systems would require a greatly increased capacity for computation over those that used the traditional hand methods if they were to be of major success in the handling of even moderately sized projects. Dr. John W. Mauchly, a director of UNIVAC at that time, joined with Kelly and Walker to adapt the technique to the digital computer.

At the same time that Du Pont was experiencing difficulties with construction, the U.S. Navy was searching for better techniques to manage its large projects. A Program Evaluation branch of the Special Projects Office, Bureau of Naval Weapons, was set up in mid-1956 and Willard Fazar was placed in charge.[1.2] This group had the responsibility of providing its top management with continuous appraisals of overall performance and progress measured against the major end objectives of the Fleet Ballistic Missile (POLARIS-Submarine) Program. By the fall of 1957 a decision was made to seek proposals from outside organizations to design a system for program evaluation which would provide information that was not being obtained from the various management tools then available for the POLARIS Project. In December 1957 contracts were arranged with Booz, Allen & Hamilton, Management Consultants, and the Lockheed Missle and Space Division, prime contractor for the POLARIS Missile Subsystem of the Fleet Ballistic Missile System. The code name selected for this effort was PERT, derived from the first letters of the title "Program Evaluation Research Task." Dr. Charles E. Clark of the Booz, Allen & Hamilton organization initiated the concept of a network with three time estimates for each activity, and developed the logic and mathematics that formed the basis of PERT.[1.5] In July 1958 the Special Projects Office published their report on Phase I[1.1] and identified the procedure as PERT—Program Evaluation and Review Technique—the name by which it is presently known.

In 1961, John W. Fondahl of Stanford University published a report[1.3] prepared for the U.S. Navy Bureau of Yards and Docks which presented a noncomputer approach to scheduling. It is a critical path method but uses a different technique for expression than that originally proposed by Walker and Kelly. Fondahl's procedure has since become a major technique for project analysis.

Although both the Critical Path Method (CPM) and the Program Evaluation and Review Technique (PERT) were developed independently, they both made use of the network as the graphical model and their solutions identified the longest, or critical, path. Over the years both names have been used in a generic sense even though the time estimates for the activity durations are distinctly different. CPM assumes that the duration of each activity can be established with reasonable accuracy, that is, that the variation in the duration time is very small. PERT on the other hand makes the assumption that the duration times have a fairly large variation. These two viewpoints have naturally arisen from the construction background of CPM, in which activity durations are set by the experience of the contractor, and from the research and development background of PERT, in which the details of the activities are largely unknown. In both cases the solution of the network follows the same pattern once the durations have been established.

1.2   THE FIVE RESOURCES FOR PLANNING

There are numerous methods being used to plan projects, many of which are very old in origin. Most persons are acquainted with the type of schedule referred to above which is prepared by management and consists basically of a list of dates on which certain items are to take place or to be completed. Most are familiar with the Gantt chart, developed in the early 1900s which supplies additional information by showing the beginning and ending of each portion of the work as well as the total scope of the project. Not so many are knowledgeable about more recent networking techniques, however.

The decision concerning the method to be used for the planning of a project rests with the project manager, or planner, and the supporting staff. Success or failure depend in large part upon the knowledge of available procedures and the ability to choose the method which will be of maximum benefit to the company. Whatever choice is made for planning the project, the decision will involve gathering as much information as possible (within the limits of practicality) on the following items; materials, machines, manpower, money, and time.

The material takeoff prepared by the estimating department from the plans and specifications can be summarized to determine the quantity and type of material that will be needed to perform the work. The availability and the probable delivery time for these materials must be derived from prior knowledge or from the supplier's information. In many instances, several months may be needed to obtain the material. For example, steel shapes may depend upon the next available rolling by the manufacturer, or a particular type of glazed brick may depend upon the next firing by the brick company.

Equipment needed to complete a construction project is of course dependent upon the kind of material that is to be used and the placement method that is anticipated. After the selection of a suitable type of equipment, the availability and delivery prospects must be ascertained. In heavy and highway construction this determination may be extremely important in establishing the time for project completion. If scrapers and bulldozers are not available from the company fleet, purchase or rental may require a considerable amount of time; and should special equipment need to be created, even longer waits may be anticipated.

Most projects require the employment of a number of different classifications of human resources. A clear understanding of labor requirements by the planner is essential to the determination of the performance time of the various activities to be undertaken during the construction process. Special skills may be needed, which may involve the training of manpower or the assembly of skilled labor from distant areas, or both. The importance of the geographical location of the work and its influence on the labor pool cannot be underestimated. When an adequate review of this factor has not been made, subsequent delays in the schedule can be expected.

No project can survive for long without the application of funds to pay for the materials, the machinery, and the labor. This need demands a budget and requires the determination of a feasible cash flow because a construction company must use its own money to build a project. It receives funds from the client only after portions of the work have been completed. In short, the company builds and sells the project to the owner on a piecemeal basis. This procedure requires that adequate funds be available to begin the work and meet immediate bills. In most instances the company is not in a position to obtain these funds from its own resources but must borrow from some lending institution. The time required to arrange for this financing needs to be determined at the outset if the success of the total plan is to be assured.

It will be recognized that four items: materials, machines, manpower, and money, are the common resources which need to be evaluated for the planning of any project. To these should be added the additional resource, time. The owner frequently desires particular beginning, ending, and other milestone dates and these usually appear in the bidding documents. There are also time limits imposed by the overall needs of the construction organization and these must be taken into account as the planning proceeds.

It will be evident from the above discussion that the availability of the resources needed for the project and the time constraints placed upon them constitute the basic framework from which the planner must work. Whereas much of the detail that needs to be completed to create successful schedules for bidding and execution can be entrusted to office personnel and field technicians, the initial input from the top management of the firm sets the boundaries that determine the quality of the company's performance.

1.3 THE HIERARCHY OF SCHEDULES

A well-planned construction project will use a series of schedules that depict the utilization of each of the five main resources. In addition, there may be other special schedules set up to allow the company to anticipate particular needs and to see that these are controlled as the work progresses. None of these schedules are independent of each other, however.

The lack of independence among the resource schedules would at first seem to be an insurmountable difficulty. This is not the case if the time schedule is prepared first. This basic construction schedule thereby becomes the most important element in the planning process. Its development and refinement are worth more attention than is frequently given to these efforts.

Materials and their needed quantities are frequently obtained from the take-off prepared for the bidding process. If instead, these materials are related to the timing of the activities given by the basic construction schedule, ordering and delivery demands can be met more easily. In turn, this materials schedule also sets the groundwork for the timed use of other resources.

The equipment use schedule follows the preparation of the basic construction schedule and the materials schedule. Because it naturally relates to time, its development and use can facilitate decisions on such questions as whether to rent or purchase machinery. The schedule can also lead to efficiency in equipment allocation and operation, and further serves as an additional information base for the estimation of cash flow and capital expenditure.

Construction equipment requires the application of skilled labor for its operation. The emplacement of materials uses both skilled and unskilled workers. It is therefore evident that labor demands may be met by the creation of a labor schedule after the material and equipment schedules have been formulated. A satisfactory labor schedule can serve to reduce the costs of hiring and firing of employees and can enhance the acquisition of skilled mechanics. It also makes it possible to properly assign and evaluate both skilled and unskilled personnel.

The establishment of cash flow budgets are commonly depicted in a financial schedule. Naturally, these cash requirements depend on the material, equipment, and labor demands. The more complete and exact the schedules, the more accurate the financial plan.

As stated before, these schedules are not independent of each other, and in actual practice their preparation may not follow exactly the order given. In most cases all are being created at about the same time and adjustments are made to each as the need arises to provide a workable construction plan. The basic construction schedule serves as the control in these preparations. The better the basic schedule, the better and more easily prepared the following schedules. Properly performed network planning can provide this high-quality basic construction schedule.

1.4   THE BAR CHART

It has been pointed out that the bar chart is one of the oldest methods for scheduling and controlling construction projects. However, severe limitations in its creation are imposed when a modern complex structure is being planned. These limits arise from the difficulties faced by the planner who decides the order for the activitites. The operations frequently selected tend to be large in scope, forcing the decision as to which activity to schedule first, which second, and so on: thus it becomes clear that among these large activities there is a great deal of overlap in possible performance times. Further, the relationships that exist between the operations cannot be shown with a sufficient degree of accuracy even if they are completely known by the planner.

The bar chart has found wide acceptance despite its limitations because it is readily understood by almost everyone, it shows the total program in a compact format that is easy to use in the office and field, and it affords an opportunity to show visually the plan and the progress of the project. These advantages should not be set aside; rather, the application of network planning should enhance the communications aspect of these charts. It will be shown in a later chapter that this can be done if the ordering and timing of the activities are separated initially and if the chart is constructed from the resulting schedule computations.

A bar chart of a typical construction schedule is shown in Figure 1.1. The chart represents the plan for constructing a small building addition to an existing manufacturing plant consisting of two floors with a steel frame. The work has been broken into 12 operations, some of which are let as subcontracts. Note that the status of the work at the beginning of May is indicated. It can be inferred that this project is somewhat behind in schedule, but not so much that the finish date of June 15 could not be met.

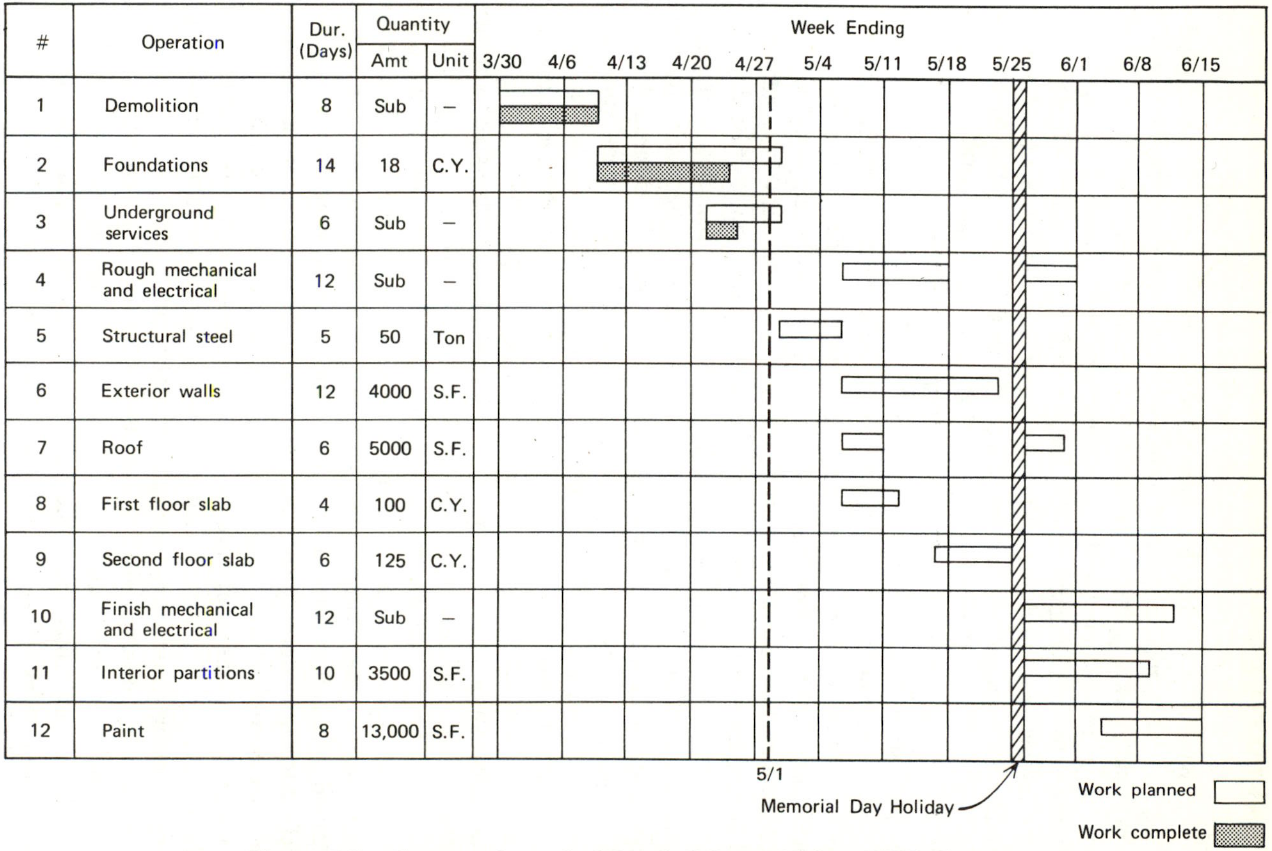

#	Operation	Dur. (Days)	Quantity Amt	Unit
1	Demolition	8	Sub	–
2	Foundations	14	18	C.Y.
3	Underground services	6	Sub	–
4	Rough mechanical and electrical	12	Sub	–
5	Structural steel	5	50	Ton
6	Exterior walls	12	4000	S.F.
7	Roof	6	5000	S.F.
8	First floor slab	4	100	C.Y.
9	Second floor slab	6	125	C.Y.
10	Finish mechanical and electrical	12	Sub	–
11	Interior partitions	10	3500	S.F.
12	Paint	8	13,000	S.F.

Week Ending: 3/30, 4/6, 4/13, 4/20, 4/27, 5/4, 5/11, 5/18, 5/25, 6/1, 6/8, 6/15

Work planned

Work complete

5/1

Memorial Day Holiday

Figure 1.1   Construction schedule—building addition, XYZ Company.

7

1.5 NETWORKS

The term *systems* is not uncommon to a modern person, who is acquainted with electrical systems, piping systems, water systems, highway systems, mechanical systems, and sewage systems, to name but a few of many encountered in the course of everyday activity. In fact, one can hardly read a newspaper or a magazine without seeing an article dealing with one of them. Generally these discussions center around one aspect of the particular system under examination and make the assumption that the reader has in mind some abstractions about the characteristics of the system. These abstractions are not sufficient, however, to make detailed value judgments about the system or to use the system to accomplish some objective.

If one is to travel to a distant city by automobile, an assumption is made that there is a highway system connecting the person's place of residence and the objective city. Several routes may be evident. It is only when a highway map is examined that the route which best meets one's needs in terms of distance, time, road condition, scenic values, points of interest, and so on, can be determined. The map provides a model of the real system and contains a quantity of information that allows a decision. Yet it may even be necessary to examine several maps to assemble all the information that may be desired, for no one map can contain all possible detail. The map model is a graphical representation of the system and depicts the network of highways joining many cities, of which our traveler's destination is but one. It may be concluded that the highway map is a network that can be used in the decision-making process.

The construction of a building can be thought of as an objective to be met by a contractor in much the same way that the distant city was the objective of our traveler. Similarly, there are many ways that a building can be constructed, and many routes that can be taken to produce the completed product. The difficulty is that there are no "road maps' which can be taken out of the rack and examined. The contractor must create a map, or network, to follow.

Before trying to develop such a network, a more formal definition is in order. *A network consists of two basic elements, nodes and links between these nodes.* In the highway map the nodes are the cities or intersections and the links are the highways. A map of a water distribution system would present a network of pipe intersections or service taps connected by the pipes.

It should be observed that the above definition of a network—nodes and connecting links—does not mention the element to be emphasized. Thus, it would be just as proper from the network standpoint to think of the highway network as a collection of cities connected by highways as it would be to think of it as a collection of highways connected through the cities and towns.

It also should be observed that the network definition does not include anything about the nature of the interaction between the elements through their connections. In the highway analogy, nothing about the map dictates the

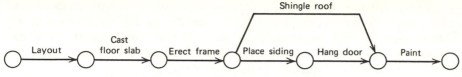

Figure 1.2   *Arrow diagram for a small garage.*

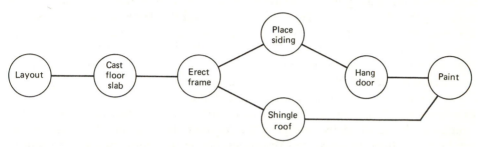

Figure 1.3   *Precedence diagram for a small garage.*

direction of travel unless one-way roadways are involved (and these are usually paired). The flow of traffic can proceed in any direction desired. All that is known is that several highways enter a city from several directions and a number of them exit to several destinations.

Applying the above concepts to the construction of a building leads to two different types of network expressions. The various building activities can be conceived as the links of the network and the relationships between them expressed by the connecting nodes. The result is an "Arrow Diagram" (Figure 1.2). If the construction activities are thought of as the nodes of the network, the links then become the relationships and the resulting diagram is termed a "Activity on the Node Diagram" or "Precedence Diagram" (Figure 1.3). Both types of network serve as models of the building process and show the same relationships among the activities, hence it is the planner's decision as to which type is used. The following chapters will discuss these two types in detail.

1.6   DESIGNING THE SCHEDULE PLAN

The word *design* has a number of different meanings that are dependent on the context of the discussion. The design of a work of art presents images of the artist. The design of an automobile engine is conceived by the mechanical engineer; the design of a building, the architect; the design of a chemical process, the chemical engineer; and so forth. Whatever the object being designed, all these designers employ a common procedure. They begin with a concept of the item to be designed, develop the concept with the tools of their specialty, evaluate the results against some criterion, modify the design where it fails to measure up, and reappraise their effort. The number of iterations needed for modification and reappraisal is a function of a subjective, preconceived idea as to the satisfaction and quality of the result desired.

In the same way, the development of a satisfactory system for the construction of a project may be viewed as a design. Beginning with the contract documents, an activity list is prepared which details the many items that will be needed to build the project. To this list are applied the demands of the resources that are required by each activity. If there are resource needs that have been overlooked, the list is revised. When this initial list is declared to be adequate, the planning network is assembled. The creation of this network can be considered as the end of the basic planning phase.

Preliminary scheduling computations are then made for the network. An examination of the schedule thus created will reveal any glaring discrepancies which can be rectified by changing the logic of the plan or by adjusting the resources, in turn changing the durations of the activities. In some instances activities will have to be added to the list or removed or consolidated with other activities The recomputation of the network provides a schedule that can serve as the basic plan for the work.

Although this schedule serves many useful purposes, the total planning and scheduling process is not complete. When costs associated with the methods to be used are an important factor, further analysis is employed, resulting in still further adjustments. The time of performance of an activity is more or less directly related to the amount of the resources needed. The shorter the time for performance, the greater the resource requirement. High cost activities may therefore be extended in time with a consequent reduction in cost and a lower level of resource. These time extensions, of course, are made at the expense of scheduling freedom. In instances where the resource levels are excessive even after extending the activity durations to their practical limits, a revision in the activity list and the network logic may be required.

Another adjustment in the schedule plan is frequently required. Because the above schedules and adjustments assume that all the activities are to start at the earliest possible time, they tend to cause a build-up in the resource demands on a day-to-day basis. This build-up would seem to indicate that the required resource levels are higher than is actually the case. The successful plan recognizes this difficulty and reschedules certain activities to later times within the freedom of the network computations, a process that is called resource leveling. Leveling adjustments revise the start and finish times of the activities and may require that the activity list be revised and the cycle repeated.

Only after the schedule has undergone these changes and has been declared satisfactory can it be said that the plan is ready for the construction process. This design of the schedule plan with its two phases, planning and scheduling, is illustrated in Figure 1.4.

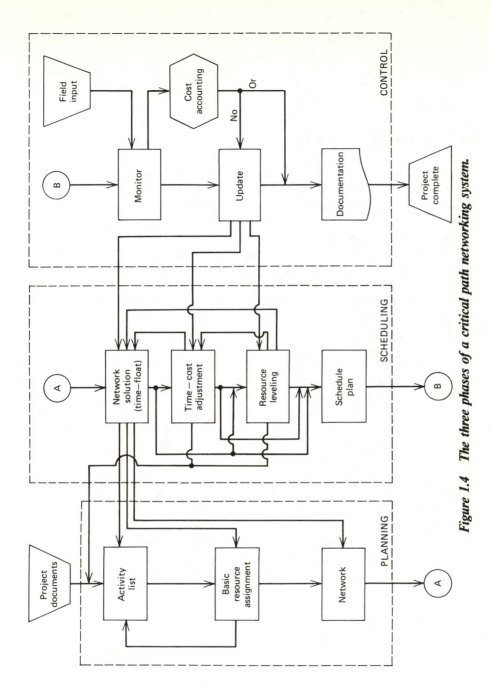

Figure 1.4   The three phases of a critical path networking system.

11

It should be clear to the reader that because the creative process described above is subjectively dependent, the construction plan formulated by one planner or group will not be the same plan as that designed by another. In essence, there is no "one best plan." As a corollary, there is no plan that cannot be improved in the eyes of an analyst.

1.7 PROJECT CONTROL

The creation of a schedule plan using networking techniques provides a sound base for good project management. However, the two phases of planning and scheduling cannot of themselves be considered as an adequate set of tools to insure the greatest benefits to the contractor. They provide only a plan, and do not deal with the operation of the project. They fail to recognize that the construction process is dynamic and that changes in the plan are necessary and normal functions. A third phase—control—is required to allow for these changes.

Typical project control procedures include two major functions, monitoring and updating. Monitoring allows the construction manager to determine the progress of the work and to predict the likelihood of meeting the planned schedule. When it is determined that these prospects will result in overruns in cost or time, the schedule plan is altered, or updated, to meet contract requirements. Figure 1.4 illustrates these feedbacks. Monitoring and updating details will be discussed more fully in Chapter 9.

Project control is an active process which all contractors practice whether or not they are using a network technique. In instances where the control phase of network planning has not been utilized, there is usually only a scattered record of how the project has been managed. The control phase enables the recording of the actual decisions that were made during the life of the work. This documentation can provide an excellent source of information for the planning of future projects of similar nature. It can also be used for compensation of extras authorized by the owner or owner's representatives and for evidence in the settlement of legal disputes. The contractor's organization thus protects both itself and the client from misunderstandings. This in turn leads to better contractor-client relations and the possible repeat of contract awards.

REFERENCES

1.1 Anonymous, *PERT Summary Report, Phase I*, Special Projects Office, Bureau of Naval Weapons, Department of the Navy, Washington, D.C., July 1958.

1.2 Fazar, Willard, "The Origin of PERT," *The Controller*, Vol. 30, December 1962, p. 598.

1.3 Fondahl, John W., "A Non-computer Approach to the Critical Path Method for the

Construction Industry," Technical Report No. 9, The Construction Institute, Department of Civil Engineering, Stanford University, Stanford, CA, 1961 (Second Edition 1962).

1.4 Kelley, James E., Jr., "Critical Path Planning and Scheduling: Mathematical Basis," *Operations Research*, Vol. 9, No. 3, 1961, pp. 296–320.

1.5 Malcolm, Donald G., John H. Roseboom, Charles E. Clark, and Willard Fazar, "Applications of a Technique for R and D Program Evaluation (PERT)," *Operations Research*, Vol. 7, No. 5, 1959, pp. 646–669.

1.6 Miller, Robert W., *Schedule Cost and Profit Control with PERT*, McGraw-Hill Book Co., New York, 1963.

1.7 O'Brien, James J., *CPM in Construction Management*, McGraw-Hill Book Co., New York, 1965.

1.8 O'Brien, James J., (ed.), *Scheduling Handbook*, McGraw-Hill Book Co., New York, 1969.

EXERCISES

1.1 Draw a bar chart for the preparation and serving of a meal for eight persons with the following menu: soup, salad, relishes, roast beef, baked potato, green peas, apple pie, rolls, wine, coffee, and tea. Assume all ingredients are on hand before preparation begins.

1.2 Draw a bar chart for the preparation and serving of the meal in Exercise 1.1 but assume that the project is to begin with the time of purchase of each item from the grocery store.

1.3 A small bus stop project is to be constructed at one side of a street. It consists of a stopping area for busses and a small shelter approximately 8'-0 by 16'-0 in plan (see Figure Ex. 1.1). The floor is to be a concrete slab and the walls are to be brick. There is a timber beam across the front to support a laminated timber roof. The structure is lighted by two light fixtures, one on each end wall. The existing curb and sidewalk are to be removed and replaced as shown to give stopping space for the busses out of the traffic lane. This stopping space will need to be repaved. The project has been broken down into steps and a construction time estimate has been made for each as follows. These steps are not in any particular order. Draw a bar chart for this project.

1. *Shelter Slab*: Includes the fine grading, casting of concrete, and finishing. Time: 2 days.
2. *Shelter Walls*: Includes the laying of the brick for the walls and the inclusion of electrical conduit for the lighting. Time: 3 days.
3. *Shelter Roof*: Includes the construction of the laminated roof, the covering with a built-up roofing, and the trimming of the edges. Time: 2 days.
4. *Roof Beam*: Includes the cutting and erection of the beam. Time: 1/2 day.
5. *Cut Curb*: Includes the cutting of the existing curb and breaking up of the existing curb and sidewalk. Time: 1 day.
6. *Excavation*: Includes the removal of broken concrete curb and sidewalk, the excavation of the parking space, the excavation of the space for the shelter slab and sidewalk. Time: 2 days.

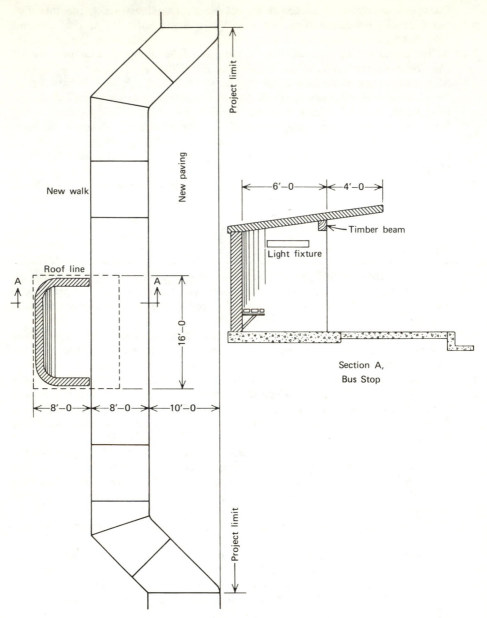

New walk

New paving

Roof line

A

A

Project limit

16'-0

8'-0   8'-0   10'-0

6'-0   4'-0

Timber beam

Light fixture

Section A,
Bus Stop

Project limit

Figure Ex. 1.1

7. *Curb and Gutter*: Includes the forming, casting, and finishing of the new curb and gutter. Time: 2 days.
8. *Sidewalk*: Includes the forming, casting, and finishing of the new sidewalk. Time: 2 days.
9. *Shelter Seat*: Includes the attachment of seat brackets to the wall and the construction of the seat. Time: 1 day.
10. *Lights*: Includes the wiring and attachment of the light fixtures. Time: 1 day.
11. *Paint*: Includes putting a natural stained exterior finish on the edges of the roof, the roof beam, and the shelter seat. Time: 1 day.
12. *Paving*: Includes the laying of the finished paving in the parking strip. Time: 1 day.

1.4 A small one-story commercial building is to be constructed on the site of an existing small frame structure. It is 30 ft by 60 ft in plan (see Figure Ex. 1.2). The exterior and interior walls are of concrete block. The roof is comprised of bar joists on long-span bar joists covered with a steel roof deck, rigid insulation, and built-up roofing. The ceiling is a suspended accoustical tile. The floor is a concrete slab on grade with an asphalt tile finish. Interior finish on all walls is paint. The project has been broken down into 18 steps and a construction time estimate has been made for each as follows. These steps are not in any particular order. Draw a bar chart for this project.

1. *Demolition*—Including the demolition of the present structure, removal of debris, and rough grading of the site. Time: 2 days.
2. *Foundations*—The construction of the foundation for the new structure. Time: 3 days.
3. *Underground Services*—The installation of water and sewer service from mains in the street. It is assumed that these services will be brought in under the structure within 30 ft width. Time: 1 day.

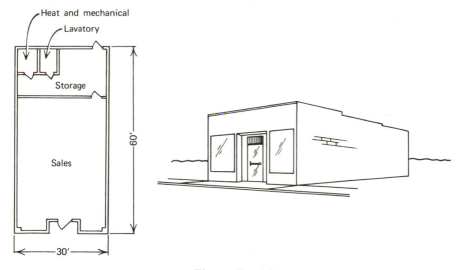

Figure Ex. 1.2

4. *Exterior Walls*—The construction of the exterior block walls. Time: 6 days.
5. *Interior Walls*—The construction of the interior block walls. Time: 3 days.
6. *Roof Steel*—Includes the installation of the long-span joists, the bar joists, and the steel roof deck. Time: 2 days.
7. *Roof Finish*—Includes the installation of the rigid insulation on the steel deck and the installation of the built-up roofing. Time: 2 days.
8. *Floor Slab*—Assumed to include fine grading, sand fill and compaction, membrane waterproofing, casting and finishing of the floor slab. Time: 3 days.
9. *Floor Finish*—Includes the installation of asphalt tile and base mold. Time: 2 days.
10. *Rough Plumbing and Heating*—Includes the setting of the heating unit and rough ductwork, the installation of rough plumbing above the floor slab, vents, and so on. Time: 3 days.
11. *Finish Plumbing and Heating*—Includes the final installation of the heating radiators, controls, and so on, and the installation of the sink and water closet. Time: 4 days.
12. *Rough Electrical*—The installation of conduit, service inlet and meter box, and so on. Time: 3 days.
13. *Finish Electrical*—The installation of wire and fixtures. Time: 3 days.
14. *Rough Carpentry*—The installation of rough door frames, display window framing, and so on. Time: 2 days.
15. *Finish Carpentry*—The installation of door trim, hanging of doors, and so on. Time: 4 days.
16. *Ceiling*—The installation of the suspended acoustic ceiling. Time: 3 days.
17. *Display Windows*—The installation of the display window glass and metal trim. Time: 1 day.
18. *Paint*—Painting of interior walls and trim. Time: 3 days.

1.5 Although the bar chart has achieved wide acceptance as a planning tool, it still has limitations. Discuss these limitations and describe the objectives that a good scheduling system should achieve.

2

PROJECT BREAKDOWN

2.1 PROJECT ORGANIZATION

Having decided to use a network technique for the construction of a project, the planner faces the first set of decisions centering upon the question: How is this project to be organized? An examination of the contract documents will reveal many natural divisions of the work but these may be neither convenient nor sufficient for the person who will be using the schedule.

Very large projects usually contain a series of construction stages which are to be built. For example, if the project is to construct a multipurpose dam for flood control, water supply, power, and recreation, the staging might be:

Clear the reservoir site

Construct the dam

Relocate the highway in the reservoir area

Relocate the area residents as needed

Relocate the railroad

Construct the power house

Construct the power distribution lines

Construct the water conduit

Construct the recreation facilities

Each of the above stages could be a separate project in its own right, even though it is a part of the whole.

Construction stages can be broken down into many operations that define the major elements to be performed. In thinking about the construction of the power house, the planner may be concerned about building the foundation, erecting the structural frame, casting the floor slabs, placing the roof and roofing, and installing the turbines and generators. Again, all these operations appear to be quite large in scope and require many separate activities. Operations, in turn, may be broken down into suboperations which may be further refined into sub-suboperations, or activities.

2.2   THE SINGLE RELATIONSHIP

Network planning can be used to represent a project at every level of organization. The more sophisticated the project the more sophisticated will be the resulting network and schedule. At the stage level the various stages are clearly interdependent and the technique must reflect these multiple relationships. At the lowest level the interrelationships are minimized and the construction of the network becomes an easier task.

In the discussions that follow it is assumed that *only one relationship can exist between any two activities*. This assumption places a restriction upon the planning in that each activity must be selected so that all previously required activities must be completed before the chosen one can begin, and all following activites cannot be started until the chosen one is complete. In the case where an activity must start after some portion of another activity has been completed, the earlier starting activity must be divided into two parts so that this assumption can be met.

2.3   ACTIVITY DEFINITION

It has been suggested that sub-suboperations are activities and also that networks can be constructed for all levels of project organization. A precise definition of the term *activity* is therefore in order to remove any apparent confusion. Simply stated,

> **An activity is a unique unit of the project which can be described within prescribed limits of time.**

In other words, it is any task, function, or decision that consumes time. It does not need to cost anything nor does it need any resource other than time. Conversely, it may require many resources, may be very expensive, and take a great deal of time. As a generic term, *activity* can be equated to project, stage, operation and suboperation if these are sequentially related and assembled into a network.

In network diagraming of both the arrow and precedence types it is sometimes desirable or necessary to use an activity having a zero duration time. These activities, often called "dummy activities," may appear to be in conflict with the activity definition stated above. They may readily be included, however, if each is thought of as representing the lowest time limit that the activity may have. The activity definition includes no notion as to the magnitude of the duration time of any activity, but requires only time limits. When an activity's duration time is extremely small in comparison with the durations of other activities in a network, it may then be considered to have a zero value for practical purposes. Dummy activities, whether used to establish proper logic, to maintain a numbering system, or to mark milestone events, may thus be considered as having extremely small durations and hence may be called activities under the definition in the previous paragraph. By a similar reasoning dummies require no resource usage.

2.4 TYPES OF ACTIVITIES

Although the definition of an activity given above is a good general one, it lacks the necessary detail to be satisfactorily applied to most projects. It is necessary therefore to describe more clearly the types of activities that can be included in the network diagram. Shaffer, Ritter, and Meyer[2.1] have considered this need. They have categorized the activities that might appear in a network and this section is based largely upon their work.

An initial look at the estimator's bid list will provide some guidance as to the kinds and types of activities that are to be included in the project. These bid items, however, are not satisfactory for use in network diagramming because they tend to be operations of rather large scope rather than being activities. As an example, "Footings" might include abutment footings, column footings, and machine footings; or "Columns" might include first floor, second floor, or third floor columns. There is no way to identify the subitems from such a list, yet a satisfactory network requires their identification.

Bid items also are inadequate because they are frequently material designators. For example, an item might be "Sand and gravel backfill," or "Class A concrete." There is no clue as to where the item is used in the project nor with what construction activity it is associated.

A perusual of the construction estimate does reveal that there are items which if identified and broken down into activities, will group themselves into categories. It appears that there are three such groups: production activities, procurement activities, and management decision activities.

Production Activities

Production activites are those that can be taken directly from the plans and specifications. They involve the application of resources—materials, labor, or equipment. Such activites are the most obvious and consume the greatest amount of time for completion of the project. Some examples are: excavating, forming, setting reinforcing steel, placing concrete, building the west wall, installing the crane, and so on. Production activities must always be completely shown on any construction project network. The omission of a production activity from the activity list and out of the network might result in failure to fulfill the contract.

Procurement Activities

One of the most difficult, and indeed frustrating, aspects of any construction project is the procurement of material that must enter the construction. This material may be the routine brick, block, concrete, and so on, or it may be specialty items or particular items that must be purchased and installed as the construction progresses. All of these are appropriate for entry into the network. Ordinarily, the common materials with which the builder is acquainted and which can be procured on a day-to-day basis are omitted. Agreements with suppliers are made in advance of the work and the materials are delivered on demand. However, Those items that must be bought in advance for later installation should be included. Because it takes time to place an order and have items such as windows delivered to the site, the procurement activities appearing on the diagram might be "Order windows" and "Window delivery." The effect of these would be to restrain those production activities that are dependent upon windows. The inclusion of special material purchases should always appear in the network, for if the material is not present, the dependent activity cannot proceed. Many procurement activities for materials therefore begin at or near the beginning of the project and terminate immediately before the installation activity for the material.

As in the case of material resources, the procurement of specialized labor is sometimes a determining restraint on a project, and if so, it should be included in the network. It takes time to obtain the labor necessary for specialty jobs and the project could be delayed if this time has not been anticipated properly. The time to have steel erectors available for certain steel erection, or for riggers to be on hand for installing heavy equipment, or for the plumbing contractor to be mobilized on the site, are typical of labor procurement. In one instance of record it took approximately 30 days to qualify welders to make some multipass welds of special design in a bridge girder. Training functions are always appropriate procurement of labor activities.

It also takes time to procure equipment and have it ready for installation or use at the site. One obvious example is the time necessary to obtain a crane to lift heavy equipment into place. In most instances a crane is not operable on the day that it is rented and it may take two to four days for its erection at the site before it can be used. If it is to be moved from one location to another at the site, this again may involve a time interval which in a sense is also a procurement of equipment. Appropriate activities should appear on the network to reflect these time intervals. Often there is a need to purchase equipment and have it delivered before it can be used. A contractor may decide to purchase a new bulldozer for excavating and grading around the outside of the building that is being erected. Delivery time for the machine must be anticipated, because if the purchase order is not issued soon enough, the project may be delayed. The appearance of the activity "Purchase bulldozer" on the network will alert the contractor and all the organization of this need.

Another time-consuming item for many construction projects is the securing of adequate funding. Finances are commonly obtained from various outside agencies and a contractor, in particular, must make arrangements for day-to-day financing of the project. In those projects that are divided such that various portions are funded separately, it may be necessary to wait until certain allocations are made, either by legislative appropriation or by a release of funds from some corporation financial officer. Loans, budget approvals, and transfers of funds all have appropriate spots in a network and represent a time interval for the procurement of this financing.

Another procurement area which is frequently encountered is that for permits and licenses. Again, outside agencies are being dealt with and it is reasonable to expect that it will take time for them to issue a permit or license to perform certain types of work. Failure to allow sufficient time to obtain a permit to use radiographic equipment for field-weld inspection, or for a building department to review the building plans before a final building permit is issued, could result in serious delays should it be overlooked. The inclusion of such time intervals as activities in the network will permit the uninterrupted execution of the project.

Closely allied to permits and licenses are engineering approvals and inspections. Frequently, intermediate inspections are necessary for such items as rough plumbing, rough electrical work, and so on, before subsequent work can proceed. Unless the appropriate inspectors are constantly at the site, they must be given advance warning of the desired approval, which in most instances may require a week to ten days. By including such items as activities in the network, the inspection can be anticipated by all concerned. Approvals of shop drawings are called for by engineering and architectural firms, and there are numerous instances where the failure to include this kind of procurement activity has resulted in project delays far beyond the anticipation of the owner or the contractor.

Another type of procurement restraint which is frequently overlooked in preparing a network is that related to the work site. Good project planning and efficient resource utilization require avoidance of having two major crews in a workspace at the same time. In many cases this is a necessity when two separate trades are involved. Further, two physical activities may not be compatible. For example, it may be physically possible to cast pile caps in a pile cluster at the same time that pile driving is proceeding. However, this generally would not be done because the vibration from the pile driving might cause several possible kinds of damage to the caps before their concrete has the opportunity to reach its proper strength. In addition, near the beginning of the project it may be necessary to relocate various utilities; gas, water, electricity, and so on. In most instances the utility companies prefer to make the relocation themselves, and a proper amount of time must be provided for them to carry out this function.

Management Decision Activities

Construction management must continually exercise its prerogative to see that its total organizational functions are carried out to the best of its ability, and the decisions made can be expected to occasionally adversely affect some one part of the total effort of the company. Many of these decisions will affect the completion time of a given project, and it is appropriate that activities be entered into a network which will reflect these choices. If a contractor's manager decides to avoid heating and housing of concrete, an activity "Concrete delay" may be created to begin at the project start and terminate before the concreting activity. The result of including this delaying activity would be to hold off all concrete work until after the delay period has passed. It can be seen that this management decision directly affected the production activities of the project. As a further example, it is not uncommon for the management of a small organization to set aside a definite time period for company vacations. A simple activity reflecting this condition might be entered on the network where it would appear as a 14-day activity called "Vacations."

Management decision activities usually appear to be quite arbitrary and may not seem to bear any direct relationship to the project at hand. Their skillful use in a project network can greatly enhance the effectiveness of the plan in its relationship to the other projects of the company.

2.5 DEGREE OF PROJECT BREAKDOWN

Although all project networks contain activities representative of the three basic types discussed in Section 2.4, refinement, or degree of breakdown of the project within these types, is controlled by the intended purpose of the schedule. The project planner must ask such questions as; Who will use this network?, What are the user's interests? What is the management span of control over which this network will be used?, and so on. At the working or production level the detail must be extensive. Upper levels of management, on the other hand, wish to know schedules in larger blocks of time and will find rather gross networks acceptable.

It frequently happens that networks must be destined for several levels of management. No one network will serve these needs, and the planner finds that two or three addtional networks must be created to satisfy these demands. The planner may begin by assembling the upper level network first and then breaking down the activities into their components, or may begin at the lowest level desired and assemble the upper level networks by composing several activities into one of larger scope. The latter procedure is generally the easier one to follow and is recommended here, although in practice the planner will find it necessary to do some of both procedures so that the logic of the plan can be properly expressed.

There are no firm rules to be followed to determine the level of detail for a network. Planners must decide for themselves what is and what is not appropriate. There are, however, some guidelines which might be used to assist in the choice. One such guide is to select the type of work or the job classification of the human resource, or both, as the basis when establishing the activity list. For instance, activity titles such as "Concrete block masonry" and "Exterior brick masonry" might represent two activities. In the first case the activity would imply semifinished work and in the second, finished work. Also titles such as "Masonry," "Electrical conduit," "Plumbing," and so on, clearly reveal the trades involved in these particular areas.

Another widely accepted procedure is to break down a project according to its various elements. Here some of the activity titles might be: "Construct footings," "Construct columns," "Install machine base," "Design field data card," or "Prepare budget." The reason for the popularity of this procedure is that most projects contain readily identifiable elements to which times can be assigned. Such elements also coincide with traditional ideas about a project often expressed in the bar chart method of scheduling. It may be noted that when construction elements are selected, more than one type of work might be involved and even several labor classifications might be included in an activity. Needless to say, if it is necessary to determine the amount of work for any given trade, this would not be a convenient breakdown. The obvious solution to this dilemma is to choose a combination of both the labor classification and the work element as the basis for the detail.

There are some projects, particularly those destined to be used by upper level management, in which the detail may be assigned according to the work responsibility of various groups within the organization. In this case one or more projects might actually be handled by the same group at a given time. In the construction area this kind of division is frequently used when dealing with subcontractors who have particular responsibilities. An example might be "Elevators," which would be installed by the elevator subcontractor. There are many activities involved in installing an elevatror, but this detail would not be necessary on the general contractor's network.

On extensive projects the location of the work is often taken as a delineator for the degree of breakdown. Typical examples might be: "Construct front wall," "Construct rear wall," "Test fan no. 1," "Test fan no. 2," and simialr arrangements. Here again, it should be pointed out that this breakdown might also result in activities which involve the type of detail indicated in the previous paragraphs.

Equipment availability and usage also tend to serve as a focus, and the planner is frequently led to establish activities that utilize a particular piece of equipment for a particular job.

Quantity alone may serve as a guide to the breakdown of a project into activities, which is similar to making the selection on the basis of location. It usually involves an arbitrary division based upon a reasonable amount of work, and the aim is to shorten the overall project time by causing an overlap in certain physical elements. Consider a contractor who has to cast a large number of concrete columns, all of which are on the same floor. This might be entered in the acitivity list as "Cast second floor columns." It would probably become obvious, however, that this would take a considerable amount of time and that the construction of the second floor could start after casting some of the second floor columns. The contractor might then choose to divide the second floor columns into two groups. On further examination, it might be decided to break them into three, four, or even more groups. Yet, there is a limit in the amount of time that can be saved in this way. For most projects this limit in division is about six and it may be even less when other factors are involved.

In establishing detailed breakdowns it is usually good practice to include not more than one major labor or equipment resource per activity. Material and labor resources are often used in combination as are combinations of material and equipment. In some instances it is possible to include labor and equipment together, but usually the only labor required is the equipment operator.

2.6   CREATING THE ACTIVITY LIST

It has been shown that the creation of the activity list is dependent upon many factors that must be evaluated by the planner. No two planners will make the same judgments when they review the plans and specifications, and it would not be surprising to find that they created different lists. Further, even if the lists were identical, they might establish different dependencies among the various items. This section will demonstrate the process followed by a planner in establishing a satisfactory set of activities with their corresponding dependencies.

For the purpose of this demonstration, consider the following project: A contractor has the bidding documents, including the plans and specifications, for the remodeling of a chemical laboratory. The present room contains some outmoded laboratory equipment thay has been deemed unsatisfactory for future use. The plans call for the contractor to remove this old equipment and replace it with new laboratory benches along three walls of the room. Around the room there are wall-mounted cabinets above the base cabinets and a few wall cabinets that extend from the floor to near the ceiling. The present plans call for all these cabinets to be purchased preassembled, but they must be finished on the site.

The new laboratory benches will have electrical outlets and taps for hot and cold water, compressed air, negative pressure air, and gas. These services will require the plumbing and electrical work to be redone in its entirety. The contractor has decided to obtain subcontracts for this work. There is to be a new fume hood installed above one of the base units, and this must be connected to a new duct because the old one has holes in it and must be removed. It is evident that when the new duct has been installed and the plumbing and electrical work have been roughed-in, the walls, ceiling, and floor must be repaired. There is also a special chemical sink that is to be installed in the base cabinet below the fume hood. The walls and ceiling will require repainting and the floor will have a vinyl floor covering applied. The specifications indicate that

TABLE 2.1

Initial Activity List—Remodeling Chemical Laboratory

Activity List

Strip room
Repair walls and ceilings
Repair floor
Lay vinyl floor
Rough-in plumbing and electrical
Finsih plumbing and electrical
Replace existing fume duct
Install new fume hood
Install base cabinets
Install wall cabinets
Install chemical sink
Paint cabinets
Paint walls and ceiling

the present heating and ventilating system, apart from the fume hood, is to be maintained.

The first list of activities that might be put together is shown in Table 2.1. Notice that each activity description contains an active verb. Strip, repair, lay, rough-in, finish, replace, install, and paint all call to mind the actual performance of some part of the project. They are therefore activities representative of the production activity category.

This list of production activities should next be reviewed to deterime if it adequately depicts the project as it was conceived. The activity "Lay vinyl floor" suggests that there will be some flooring to lay. An additional activity, "Obtain vinyl floor covering," is therefore added to the list. In a similar manner, the activities "Obtain cabinets," "Obtain fume hood," and "Obtain chemical sink" are added. All of these activities are of the "procurement" variety.

The contractor may also realize when analyzing the preliminary list that all of the painters are occupied on another project for at least four weeks after this one is to begin. Another activity "Painter availability" is also added representing a labor procurement. Table 2.2 shows the revised list after these changes.

Many contractors feel that the creation of the activity list is the most important step in using network techniques. It follows that if the list is not complete, the resulting network and computations will not reflect this importance, nor be realistic and usable for carrying out the work. The list at this point, however, should not be considered final because there will be changes made in it as the design proceeds.

Thus far the relationships among the activites have not been considered.

TABLE 2.2

Preliminary Activity List—Remodeling Chemical Laboratory
Activity List

Strip room
Repair walls and ceilings
Repair floor
Lay vinyl floor
Rough-in plumbing and electrical
Finsih plumbing and electrical
Replace existing fume duct
Install new fume hood
Install base cabinets
Install wall cabinets
Install chemical sink
Paint cabinets
Paint walls and ceiling
Obtain vinyl floor covering
Obtain cabinets
Obtain fume hood
Obtain chemical sink
Painter availability

Probably it has been tacitly assumed that stripping the room is the first thing that must be done, but to what does the repair of the walls and ceiling relate? The question that must be asked of every activity in the list must be "*What does this activity depend upon?*" In other words, what activities must be *finished* before this one can start?

Earlier in this chapter it was stated that this single relationship is assumed to be the only one that can exist. It may seem that the questions "What activity may be done at the same time as this one?" and "What activity must follow this one?" should be asked. These questions may imply that additional relationships link the activities. Although the answers to these questions may be helpful in establishing the activity interdependencies, only the basic question must be asked and it must always be answered.

If the preliminary activity list is numbered, the dependencies for each activity can be easily expressed. For example, in Table 2.3, Activity 2, "Repair walls and ceiling," certainly cannot start until the stripping of the room has been completed. It also cannot begin until the plumbing and electrical work has been roughed-in and the new fume duct has been installed. The numbers of these preceding activities—1, 5, and 7—are thus inserted after Activity 2 in the list. This process continues until the dependency for each item has been stated.

TABLE 2.3

Activity List with Dependencies—Remodeling Chemical Laboratory

Activity List

No.	Activity	Depends Upon
1	Strip room	—
2	Repair walls and ceiling	1, 5, 7
3	Repair floor	1, 5
4	Lay vinyl floor	3, 12, 13, 14
5	Rough-in plumbing and electrical	1
6	Finish plumbing and electrical	2, 3, 5, 9, 10, 11, 19
7	Replace existing fume duct	1
8	Install new fume hood	2, 3, 16
9	Install 1/3 base cabinets	2, 3, 8, 15
10	Install wall cabinets	2, 3, 7, 15
11	Install chemical sink	2, 3, 5, 9, 17
12	Paint cabinets	6, 8, 9, 10, 11, 18
13	Paint walls and ceiling	2, 3, 6, 8, 9, 10, 18
14	Obtain vinyl floor covering	—
15	Obtain cabinets	—
16	Obtain fume hood	—
17	Obtain chemical sink	—
18	Painter availability	—
19	Install 2/3 base cabinets	2, 3, 9, 15

Table 2.3 illustrates these relationships. Notice that Activity 9 has been altered. The contractor has decided that there is no reason to wait until all of the base cabinets have been installed before installing the chemical sink; for as soon as the base that will receive the sink is in place, the sink can be set. On the other hand, the installation of the sink would be difficult if the adjacent cabinets are being worked upon. It may be assumed that the base cabinets along the other walls can be placed with the sink without difficulty, and the base cabinet activity has therefore been divided into two parts, one being the installation of one third of the base cabinets and the other being the installation of the remaining two thirds. Thus, the original activity has been changed to "Install 1/3 base cabinets," and a new activity "Install 2/3 base cabinets" has been added.

2.7 THE PLANNERS' ATTITUDES AND ASSUMPTIONS

Before actually starting to assemble a network diagram for a project there are some attitudes and assumptions which the planner must adopt if an efficient plan is to be created. The planner should be prepared for the task, and should have as open a mind as possible with regard to construction methods. Arbitrary restrictions on the activities must not be imposed, and unlimited resources should be assumed.

There is an axiom frequently used among those engaged in computer activities —"garbage in, garbage out (GIGO)"—referring to the fact that computations are no better than the basic material from which they are derived. In planning a network the axiom holds. In the construction industry more failures of network planning owe their origin to the lack of realistic and valid information than to any other source. An efficient network diagram cannot be put together by a someone who is totally not prepared to meet the demands of the project. Even though the activity list has been assemled with a great deal of care and has been reviewed by the personnel charged with the construction, a planner who does not understand the methods to be used will be unable to draw a good network. As was the case in creating the activity list, the methods to be used and the idiosyncrasies of the construction superintendent must be known, otherwise the logic of the network will bear little resemblance to the actual work as performed at a later date.

A word of caution is in order here; the planner must not only ask the field personnel *how* they plan to do the job, but must be able to raise questions as to *why* things should be done the way proposed. He or she must accept the methods to be employed and also seek the various alternatives. Just because the planner is told "that is the way we do it," he or she should not accept this statement as the only answer to the question "Why?". This open-minded stance on the part of the planner will reveal many unexplored techniques and procedures to the construction team and lead to cost savings, sometimes of considerable magnitude.

Restrictions of time and space are not a proper consideration when constructing the initial network. It may be perfectly evident that the chief finish carpenter will be needed on two separate activities, but the planner must not decide that one of these activities must precede the other just to meet a preconceived idea. The time to decide which activity to schedule first comes later after preliminary computations of the network have been run out, for the interactions of the network may have already spaced the two tasks so that no conflict is present. If not, then the computed figures will indicate the most desirable way to make this resolution. The only restrictions that are to be imposed while constructing the diagram are those forced by the plans and specifications or the method chosen by the field personnel.

Closely related to the tendency to impose undue restraints is the planner's assumption that known resource demands must be met. As will be shown later, required resource levels can be satisfied after the analysis has been made. The planner should assume that *if a resource is needed, that resource can be made available*. This is the *assumption of unlimited resources*, one of the basic assumptions that every planner should always make and which is a cardinal rule of efficient networking.

REFERENCE

2.1 Shaffer, L. R., J. B. Ritter, and W. L. Meyer, *The Critical Path Method*, McGraw-Hill Book Co., New York, 1965, pp. 63, 64.

EXERCISES

2.1 Determine the major stages you would have to consider in planning for next year's budget for an engineering consulting firm.

2.2 Identify the major stages to be considered in the building of a house.

2.3 Identify the major stages to be considered in the planning and construction of a 5-mile stretch of interstate highway.

2.4 Categorize each of the following activities for the construction of a highway grade separation bridge according to production, procurement, and management decision activities.

Set up traffic detour.

Order and deliver piles.

Excavate for Abutment A.

Excavate for Abutment B.

Drive piles for Abutment A.

Move pile driver to Abutment B.

Drive piles for Abutment B.

Construct footings for Abutment A.

Construct footings for Abutment B.

Construct Abutment A.

Construct Abutment B.

Place backfill for Abutment A.

Place backfill for Abutment B.

Construct bridge deck.

Fabricate structural steel.

Erect structural steel.

Place backfill for approaches.

Order and deliver bridge railing.

Order and deliver guard rail.

Erect bridge railing.

Erect guard rail.

Construct concrete curb and gutter.

Set up paving train.

Pave approach roadways.

Delay seeding of slopes until April 1.

Seed and sod approach slopes.

Final inspection.

2.5 From your experience select a project containing at least 10 activities. Create an activity list for this project and establish the dependencies.

2.6 List the activities of Exercise 2.4 and establish the dependencies for each.

2.7 Break down the activity list for the bridge project of Exercise 2.4 to clearly identify the work to be performed by the following three trades: Rough Carpenters, Reinforcing Steel Ironworkers, and Concrete Finishers.

2.8 Prepare an activity list for the bridge project of Exercise 2.4 that will be suitable for the upper levels of management of the construction contractor.

3

BASIC ARROW DIAGRAMING

3.1 CHARACTERISTICS

Critical path methods of both the CPM and PERT types in the late 1950s used the arrow diagram technique for constructing the graphical model of the project. The analytical procedures which were followed required that the graphics be depicted in terms that could be mathematically expressive. The most likely way to represent a network of nodes and links was to assign to the node an identifying number and to denote the link by referring to the numbers at each extremity.

Because the CPM model placed great emphasis upon the task to be accomplished (i.e., the activity), it was natural to use the two number concept to refer to the activity. Thus, the activities fell on the links and the interrelations between the activities were assigned to the nodes.

In contrast to a network of wires or pipes as might be used in modeling an electrical or water system, the network describing a construction project (or any project that has a sequence of activities), has the interactions at the nodes related in only one direction. That is, activities following a node are dependent upon the activities that enter a node, and the reverse is not true. It is therefore analogous to a piping system which will permit a flow in one direction but not in another. An arrowhead added to the link thus serves to point out this unidirectional feature.

Arrow diagraming has remained a popular technique since network planning began. It has proven to be easily computerized, which is advantageous when dealing with projects having many activities. Further, the two number scheme for identification of the activity provides a convenient reference when the computations of the schedule are made either manually or by computer. The diagram is easily converted to a time-scaled representation that is similar to the familiar bar chart and this appears to be advantageous to many users.

The dummy is one feature of the arrow diagram with which most planners have difficulty in the early stages of network construction. It is required to insure proper interrelationships, but unless care is taken, it can easily yield misrepresentations and redundancies.

3.2   BASIC LOGIC PATTERNS

As indicated in the previous section, the graphical representation of an activity is an arrow. These arrows should not be confused with vectors as used in many engineering disciplines. The length of the arrow has no significance and the arrow may assume any form. It may be straight, curved, bent, or wavy to suit the needs of the model.

Each activity has a definite beginning and end and these conditions are represented by the nodes that occur at each end of the arrow. These nodes are commonly called "events." They mark points in time and have no time durations themselves. With respect to a given activity, the event at the head of the arrow is called the "j event" and that at the tail of the arrow is the "i event." These representations are shown in Figure 3.1a.

Two activities that are independent of each other will be indicated as two separate arrows having no connection. Figure 3.1b shows an example of this condition.

When one activity is dependent upon another, they appear in the diagram as two arrows having a common node. Figure 3.1c illustrates this logic. Note that node number 6 serves as the i node of Activity B at the same time as it serves as the j node of Activity A.

It frequently happens that there is an activity that cannot start until two or more activities have been completed. This appears in the diagram as a "merge" and is shown in Figure 3.1d. Similarly, when two or more activities cannot be started until a third activity is completed, the diagram will contain a "burst" as illustrated in Figure 3.1e.

If two or more activities must be completed before two or more activities can start, then the resulting diagram is said to contain a "cross" illustrated by Figure 3.1f. It should be noted that in this situation neither Activity C nor D can start until both Activity A and Activity B have finished.

When one activity is dependent upon both the preceding activities and another is dependent upon only one of the preceding activities, then the cross is not an accurate representation of the logic. Assume that Activity C depends upon the completion of Activities A and B, but that Activity D depends only upon Activity B. The cross diagram as shown in Figure 3.2a is inaccurate. To remove this logic error, Event 6 can be divided into two events numbered 5 and 6, and a dummy activity inserted between them. (The dummy activity is a fictitious activity that has no time duration and requires no resource utilization, as pointed out in Section 2.3.) The correct solution is shown in Figure 3.2b.

While constructing an arrow diagram, there will be a number of situations wherein there are two or more activities that depend upon the same preceding activities and have the same following activities also. If each activity is to be described by its event numbers, then these numbers must be unique if confusion is to be avoided. Figure 3.3a shows two activities A and B that begin and end on

(a) *Basic activity*

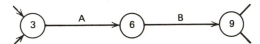

(b) *Independent activities*

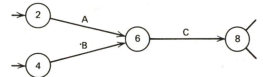

Activity B depends upon the completion of Activity A

(c) *Dependent activities*

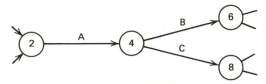

Activity C depends upon the completion of both Activities A and B

(d) *A merge*

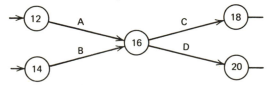

Activities B and C both depend upon the completion of Activity A

(e) *A burst*

Activities C and D both depend upon the completion of Activities A and B

(f) *A cross*

Figure 3.1   Basic logic patterns for arrow diagrams.

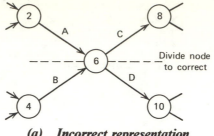

(a) Incorrect representation

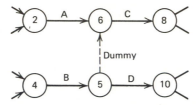

(b) Correct representation

Figure 3.2 The use of the dummy to define correct logic in an arrow diagram. (Required: Activity C depends upon Activities A and B. Activity D depends upon Activity B only.)

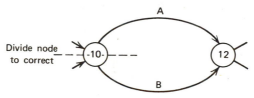

(a) Incorrect representation

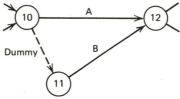

(b) Correct representation

Figure 3.3 The use of the dummy to maintain unique numbering of activities.

common events numbered 10 and 12. To describe both Activities A and B by the numbers 10–12 is clearly ambiguous. The removal of this error is accomplished by again dividing the node at the tail of the arrow and establishing a new event with a dummy activity connecting the new and original events. Figure 3.3b illustrates this correction in logic. It must be emphasized that the node to be divided is the one at the tail of the arrow. This is necessary for the correct solution of the schedule, as will be discussed in a later chapter.

It will be found that, in constructing the arrow diagram initially, a number of dummies are included to ensure that the logic is expressed correctly. Many of these dummies can and should be eliminated, for it must be remembered that each dummy is an activity even though it has no duration time. As such, it requires the same treatment as any other activity in the network. It must be

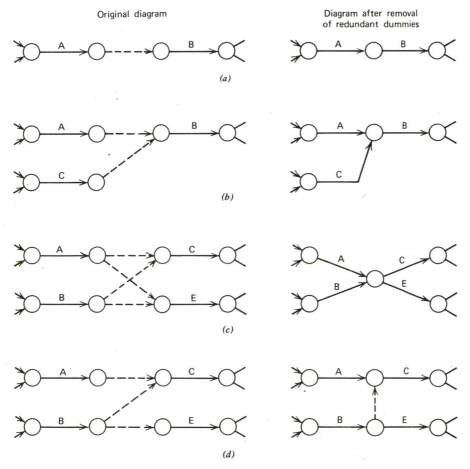

Figure 3.4   *Removal of redundant dummies.*

represented on the drawing, must be considered in the computations, and must be evaluated in the analysis after the computations have been made. The elimination of unnecessary dummy activities therefore saves much time and expense whether the computations are to be made manually or with the computer.

Figure 3.4 shows four typical cases of redundant dummies and their resolution. The most common redundancy is illustrated in Figure 3.4*a* where the dummy between Activity A and Activity B is clearly unnecessary. It is also fairly obvious that the two dummies in Figure 3.4*b* are extra, but it is not quite so clear that the four dummies in Figure 3.4*c* are not needed. Because both Activities C and E are dependent upon both Activities A and B, however, the proper pattern is the cross as shown. In Figure 3.4*d* it is not possible to eliminate all three dummies because in this case Activity E is dependent only upon Activity B. However, the dummy between Activities A and C and the one between Activities B and E can be removed.

There is a tendency to remove dummies when there appears to be two of them entering the tail node of an activity. Caution should be exercised in these situations because they both may be needed. Figure 3.5 illustrates a case wherein both are needed because Activity E is dependent upon both Activities A and B, whereas Activity C depends on only Activity A and Activity F depends only on Activity B.

In Chapter 2 it was pointed out that every activity in the network must have a dependency except those that start the project. Taken at face value, this would mean that if there are several beginning activities, each would have a unique starting node. It is evident, however, that the event which each of these beginning nodes represent is the initial event, the beginning of the project. These nodes should therefore be combined into a single one. Not only is this practice desirable from the standpoint of proper logic, it also helps to prevent the creation of accidental logic loops, and it will be found later that this procedure aids greatly in making the computations. It also makes computation time more efficient, and in some computer programs it is a necessity.

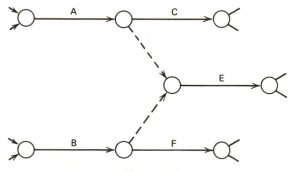

Figure 3.5

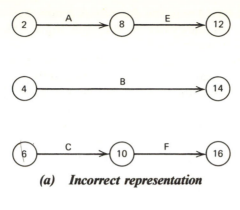

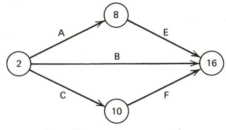

(a) Incorrect representation

(b) Correct representation

Figure 3.6 Combining beginning and ending nodes.

A small project of five activities is diagramed in Figure 3.6. Activities A, B, and C can start at the same time and start the project. Activity E depends upon A, Activity F depends upon C, and when Activities B, E, and F are complete, the project is finished. Figure 3.6*a* shows a diagram of this logic with the beginning and ending nodes considered independently. The correct diagram is shown in Figure 3.6*b*.

3.3 NUMBERING THE NETWORK

Event numbering ordinarily is not done until the diagram is essentially complete. The numbers "i" and "j" are arbitrarily assigned; however, it is common practice to assign them in such a way that the number at the tail of the arrow is smaller than that at the head. Because the arrow diagram is unidirectional, this practice insures that this property is maintained; however, it does not provide a unique pair of numbers to depict each activity. Figure 3.6*b* has the events numbered according to this convention. Note that Activity A may be referred to as Activity 2–8 also. If it is assumed that the event numbers 8 and 10 are interchanged, the activities are still defined with small numbers at their tails and the larger numbers at their heads, but Activity A is now Activity 2–10. Either set of numbers is correct for they establish the same logic. The computations will reflect this difference, however.

Care must be exercised to make sure that each event in the network has a unique number. If duplicate numbers occur, an ambiguity exists which will result in erroneous computations even though the network has been drawn correctly.

Consecutive numbering, of course, satisfies the requirements of directionality and uniqueness but does not permit the addition of future activities. It is a rare network, indeed, that can be put together with all needed activities known at the beginning of diagraming. By choosing some numbering pattern, such as even numbers, odd numbers, numbers in fives or tens, and so on, additional events can be inserted without renumbering the entire network.

When activities are to be identified with certain portions of the project or when they are to reflect material, labor, or equipment accounts, code numbers may be used. The major difficulty in using accounting codes is the inability to keep the uniqueness concept. Usually, the addition of a sequential number before or after the account code will satisfy this need.

3.4   CONSTRUCTING THE DIAGRAM

There are no easy direct approaches to the process of actually drawing the arrow diagram. The need for dummy activities introduces conditions which are so variable that they seem to defy any formalized technique, yet there are three approaches which network planners find acceptable. Each individual planner uses the scheme which he finds to be the best for his own needs.

The first of these methods might be called the "start event approach."[3.1] The planner begins by putting down the first event and the activities that burst from it. He then adds the *j* events for these activities. For each of these events he adds the bursting activities and continues in this manner until the last event is reached. This procedure soon requires correcting the position of the activities when the need for dummies is encountered.

A variation of the "start event approach" is the "finish event approach."[3.1] Here the planner begins by putting down the terminal event and the activities that merge to it. After placing the *i* events, he adds their merging activities and continues in this manner until the initial event is reached. This method does not require as much changing, but is satisfactory only if the activity list is complete. It clearly will not work if the activity list is still being developed, a condition that is frequently found in actual practice.

The third approach, which might be termed the "independent activity approach,"[3.2] begins with the planner putting down the activities in an approximate order. Both the *i* and *j* events are added for each activity. The dependencies are then established by connecting all related events with dummies. The resulting

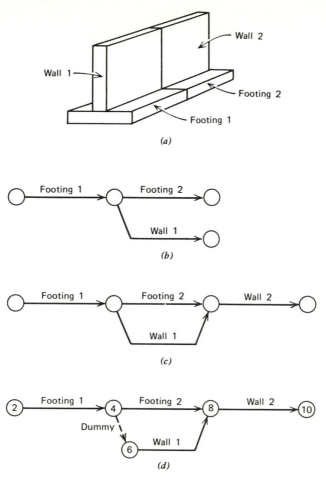

Figure 3.7 Retaining wall arrow diagram—start event approach.

diagram is then reviewed and all unnecessary dummies and events are removed.

Figure 3.7 illustrates the start event approach used to construct an arrow diagram for a small retaining wall. Assume that both the wall and the footing have a construction joint at mid-length resulting in four parts to be built as shown in Figure 3.7a. Also assume that it is desired to start with the first half of the footing. In Figure 3.7b the initial event is shown with the activity Footing 1 following it. The second event and the two succeeding activities, Footing 2 and Wall 1, are also given. Wall 2 is added in Figure 3.7c. Note that this has created a need for a dummy in order to preserve the numbering uniqueness for the activities. Figure 3.7d shows the final diagram with this correction and with the events properly numbered.

TABLE 3.1

Activity List with Redundant Dependencies Removed—Remodeling
Chemical Laboratory

Activity List		
No.	**Activity**	**Depends upon**
1	Strip room	—
2	Repair walls and ceiling	1̸, 5, 7
3	Repair floor	1̸, 5
4	Lay vinyl floor	3̸, 12, 13, 14
5	Rough-in plumbing and electrical	1
6	Finish plumbing and electrical	2̸, 3̸, 5̸, 9̸, 10, 11, 19
7	Replace existing fume duct	1
8	Install new fume hood	2, 3, 16
9	Install 1/3 base cabinets	2̸, 3̸, 8, 15
10	Install wall cabinets	2, 3, 7̸, 15
11	Install chemical sink	2̸, 3̸, 5̸, 9, 17
12	Paint cabinets	6, 8̸, 9̸, 1̸0̸, 1̸1̸, 18
13	Paint walls and ceiling	2̸, 3̸, 6, 8̸, 9̸, 1̸0̸, 18
14	Obtain vinyl floor covering	—
15	Obtain cabinets	—
16	Obtain fume hood	—
17	Obtain chemical sink	—
18	Painter availability	—
19	Install 2/3 base cabinets	2̸, 3̸, 9, 1̸5̸

The sample project of Chapter 2 has been selected to illustrate the independent activity approach. It will be recalled that the project consists of the activities needed to remodel a chemical laboratory. The activity list from Table 2.3 is reproduced in Table 3.1 together with some corrections.

A quick review of the dependencies in Table 2.3 reveals that some of them are not needed. For example, Activity 2 does not need the dependency of Activity 1, because Activity 5, which is also Activity 2's dependency, is dependent upon Activity 1. The first step in this approach is therefore to eliminate these obvious redundancies because they contribute nothing to the logic of the diagram, cause additional effort, and clutter the drawing.

The procedure for removing redundant dependencies is rather simple. Each project activity is considered in turn, and an activity number from its dependency list is selected. If the dependency list for this selected activity number contains a dependent activity which is the same as one of the activities in the dependency list of the original activity, then that number is removed from the

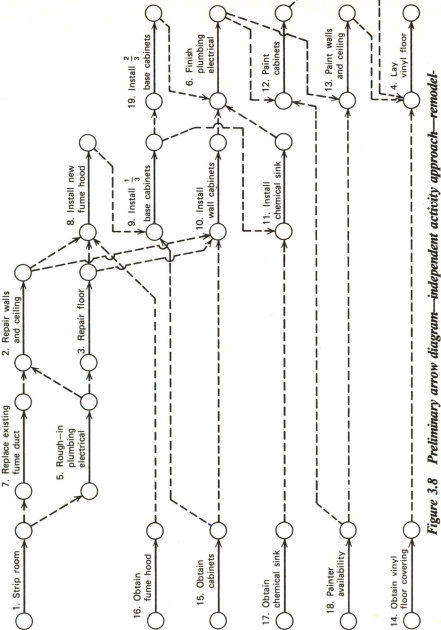

Figure 3.8 *Preliminary arrow diagram—independent activity approach—remodeling chemical laboratory.*

Diagram labels:
1. Strip room
2. Repair walls and ceiling
3. Repair floor
4. Lay vinyl floor
5. Rough—in plumbing electrical
6. Finish plumbing electrical
7. Replace existing fume duct
8. Install new fume hood
9. Install ⅓ base cabinets
10. Install wall cabinets
11. Install chemical sink
12. Paint cabinets
13. Paint walls and ceiling
14. Obtain vinyl floor covering
15. Obtain cabinets
16. Obtain fume hood
17. Obtain chemical sink
18. Painter availability
19. Install ⅔ base cabinets

42

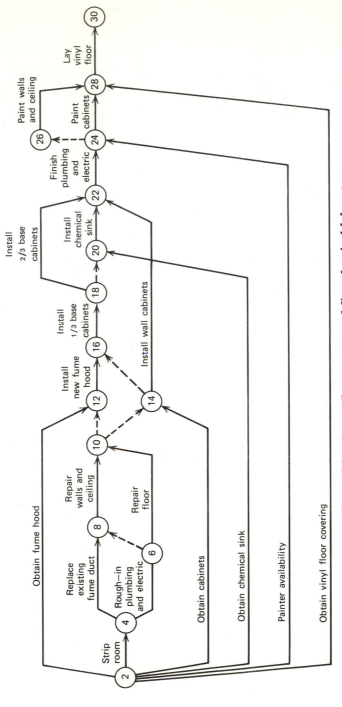

Figure 3.9 Arrow diagram—remodeling chemical laboratory.

original activity's dependencies. The next number is then chosen and the process repeated until the dependency list of the original activity is depleted.

To illustrate, consider Activity 2 in Table 3.1. Its dependency list has three numbers, 1, 5, and 7. Select one of these, say number 7. The dependency list for Activity 7 is examined, and it is found to have a dependency on Activity 1. This number is then crossed out where it appears in Activity 2's dependency list. Activity 5 is the next number in the list and it also is dependent upon Activity 1. This requires the elimination of Activity 1 as before. Activity 1 is the next selection. Even though it has been crossed out, its list must be considered. In this instance, Activity 1 has no dependency so no further elimination occurs.

The rest of the project's activity list has been adjusted in the same manner. Special attention should be paid to Activity 11. In this case Activities 2 and 3 have been removed because Activity 9's list contained them as dependencies, but their elimination from this list does not restrict their consideration for removal while dealing with Activity 11.

Figure 3.8 is the diagram that results when the activities of the project are independently positioned and connected by dummies representing the dependencies given in Table 3.1. It may be observed that there are many redundant dummies and events which must still be removed. For example, the three events connected by the two dummies relating Activities 1, 5, and 7 can be combined into a single event and the two dummies eliminated.

When all the redundancies have been eliminated, the diagram becomes an efficient arrow network. An examination of Figure 3.9 will reveal that the number of dummies has been reduced to six, thus making a network of 25 activities. This diagram expresses only the logical relations which make up the project. No times are shown and no consideration has been given to the scheduling of the activities in time. It must not be assumed that because two activities can start after the finish of another that they must start then. The determination of these starting times will be discussed later in the book.

REFERENCES

3.1 Moder, Joseph J. and Cecil R. Phillips, *Project Management with CPM and PERT*, Reinhold Publishing Corp., 1964 (Second Edition, Van Nostrand Reinhold Co., New York, 1970).

3.2 Radcliffe, Byron M., Donald E. Kawal and Ralph J. Stephenson, *Critical Path Method*, Cahners Publishing Co., Inc., Chicago, 1967.

EXERCISES

3.1 Construct the arrow diagram for the following sequence of activities. Label the activities in the network by activity letter and also by *i* and *j* number. Remove any redundancies. Label any dummies D–1, D–2, and so on.

    1.   Activities A and P start the project.
    2.   When Activities F and G are finished the project is complete.
    3.   Activities C, B, and N must be complete before Activity E can start.
    4.   Activity G cannot start until Activity M is finished.
    5.   Activities H and K can be done at the same time.
    6.   Activity P immediately precedes Activities N, M, and L.
    7.   Activities B and C immediately follow Activity A.
    8.   Activity H depends upon the completion of Activities B, C, L, M, and N.
    9.   Activity F cannot start until Activities A, B, and E have ended.
   10.   The finish of Activities H and K controls the start of Activity G.
   11.   Activities P and L must be finished before Activity K can start.

3.2 Establish the dependencies for the activities of the bus stop project of Exercise 1.3 and draw the arrow diagram.

3.3 Establish the dependencies for the small building activities given in Exercise 1.4 and draw the arrow diagram.

3.4 Use the activities of the bridge project of Exercise 2.4 and the dependencies established in Exercise 2.6 and draw the arrow diagram.

3.5 Draw an arrow network that will represent the overlapping relationships between the activities of the following project.

After the first 30 percent of Activity A has been done Activity C may begin; however, the last 15 percent of Activity C must remain after Activity D is started. Activity B cannot start before Activity A is finished. Activity D is directly dependent on Activity A, but Activity D must be completed before the last 40 percent of Activity B is done.

3.6 Draw an arrow network that will represent the overlapping relationships between the activities of the following project.

After the first 40 percent of Activity A has been done Activity B can be started. Once Activity A is done 25 percent of the work of Activity C must be remaining. After the first 75 percent of Activity C is completed 50 percent of Activity D must remain and Activity D must follow the completion of Activity B.

3.7 Assume that the logic in the diagram of Figure Ex. 3.1 is correct. Locate and correct any diagraming errors. Redraw the arrow diagram in its correct form.

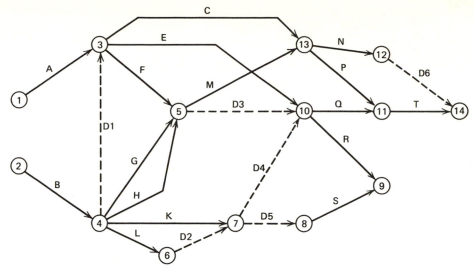

Figure Ex. 3.1

4
BASIC PRECEDENCE DIAGRAMING

4.1 INTRODUCTION

While the early developments of CPM were rooted in the use of the arrow diagram, the contributions of Professor John W. Fondahl[4.3] (of Stanford University) in 1961 laid the foundation for the precedence diagraming technique. Fondahl accepted the activity emphasis that existed in the earlier CPM model but instead of assigning the activity to the link, he placed the activity on the node. This then required that the links between the nodes of the network represent the relationships among the activities.

This type of modeling was originally termed "circle and connecting line" by Fondahl. It has also been referred to as the "activity on the node" technique,[4.4,4.5] and more recently J. David Craig has called it a "precedence diagram" with only the finish-to-start relationship identified.[4.1,4.2] This book chooses the precedence diagram term and considers this single relationship initially. There are four possible precedence linkages. The three additional linkages are discussed in Chapter 13.

A number of advantages result from Fondahl's change in representation. No fictitious, or dummy, activities are required to define network logic and a single number can be assigned to identify each activity, thus simplifying the construction of the model. The analytical procedures are no more difficult to carry out on the computer and are simpler if the solution is done manually.

Another concept introduced by Fondahl is the sequence step arrangement for the activities of the network. This scheme, based upon the logical relationships between the activities, allows ready discernment of mutually independent activities. Arranging the diagram in sequence steps permits computations to be made without their being dependent upon any arbitrary numbering pattern. Also, sequence step identifications are helpful aids in drawing and numbering the network and permit greater clarity of the diagram as a whole.

4.2 LOGIC PATTERNS

An activity in a precedence diagram is represented by an identifying name and corresponding number enclosed in some kind of symbol. Usually, these symbols are circular but they may be square, hexagonal, or any other convenient shape.

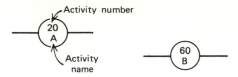

(a)   Independent relationships

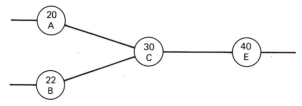

Activity B depends upon the completion of Activity A

(b)   Dependent relationships

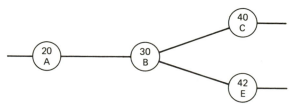

(c)   Merging relationships

(d)   Bursting relationships

Figure 4.1   Basic logic patterns for precedence diagrams.

As pointed out in the previous section, the relationships among the activities are expressed by a connecting line or link from one symbol to another. The total set of these symbols and lines makes up the network.

When two activities are independent of each other, each will appear on the diagram as a separate symbol without a connecting linkage. This condition is shown in Figure 4.1*a*. If the two activities are related so that one must be completed before the other can begin, then the symbols are linked. Figure 4.1*b* illustrates the case where Activity A is to be completed before Activity B can be started.

When two or more activities must be completed before a common activity can start the diagram will contain a "merge" relationship. An example of this situation is pictured in Figure 4.1c where Activity A and Activity B both must finish for Activity C to begin. In a similar manner, when two or more activities depend upon the completion of a common one, a "burst" relationship is said to exist. Figure 4.1d delineates this case for the linkages between Activity B and Activities C and E.

It frequently happens that an activity is known to be related to two activities which at the same time are related to each other. This situation creates a redundancy in the network which should be removed. For example, in Figure 4.2a Activity C is known to be related to both Activities A and B whereas Activity B depends upon Activity A. The connecting link between Activities A and C is not needed to satisfy the logic of these relationships, for if Activity C depends upon the completion of Activity B, and Activity B depends upon the completion of Activity A, then Activity A must surely be complete before Activity C can start. Such redundancies are easy to detect in a precedence network because they always form a triangle in the linkage pattern. Figure 4.2b shows the correct representation.

Redundancies should always be removed unless there is a special reason as to why the extra relationship should be pointed out to the user of the diagram. As extra activities, redundancies result in needless computations and added diagraming effort. They do not cause any difficulty in the subsequent computations, however.

In most projects there will be several activities that logically can be considered as starting activities. Also, there are usually a number of activities that upon

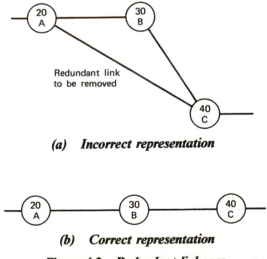

(a)   Incorrect representation

(b)   Correct representation

Figure 4.2   Redundant linkages.

completion signify the termination of the work. The resulting diagram will therefore contain several nodes without links to preceding activities and several without links to succeeding activities even though it is clear that there should be some one activity that starts the project and one that ends it. To correct this error in the logic, a dummy activity, or "event node," can be introduced to close the network. Figure 4.3*a* represents a network of five activities. Activities A, B, and C are independent of each other, whereas Activity E depends upon the completion of Activity A and Activity F depends upon the completion of Activity C. As expressed, the logic among the activities is correct but there are open beginning nodes (A, B, and C) and open ending nodes (E, B, and F). The logic representation for the start and finish is not correct. The correct representation is shown in Figure 4.3*b* where the start and finish event dummies have been added. It will become clear in following chapters that it is essential that a single beginning and ending node be used if the computations are to be properly done.

A simple example will serve to summarize the logic patterns discussed. Assume that a retaining wall is to be built consisting of a spread footing and

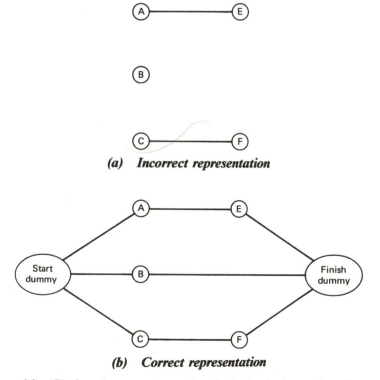

(a)   Incorrect representation

(b)   Correct representation

Figure 4.3   Closing the network to give single beginning and ending nodes.

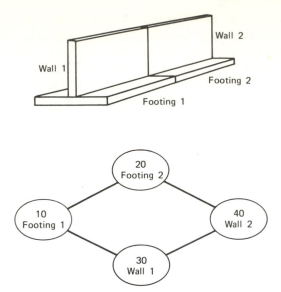

Figure 4.4   Retaining wall precedence diagram.

vertical stem. The wall and footing each have a construction joint at mid-length so that there are four portions to consider. Also assume that it is desired to start the construction with the first part of the footing and that the second part of the wall is to be cast against the first part of the wall.

Figure 4.4 shows the precedence diagram for this project. Note that Activity 20 (Footing 2) and Activity 30 (Wall 1) are independent; that is, either could be cast after Footing 1 is completed but they are not dependent upon each other. A burst relationship is formed by the links between Activity 10 and Activities 20 and 30, and a merge relationship is set up by the two links between Activities 20 and 30 and Activity 40. In this simple diagram there is no need for the use of dummies at the start and finish because the diagram naturally closes with single nodes.

4.3   SEQUENCE STEPS AND NETWORK NUMBERING

With every activity enclosed in a symbol and the connecting links representing the dependencies, some kind of ordering becomes necessary if a clear under-standing of the logic of the network is to be obtained. Also the computations to be made using the precedence diagram require that a numbering scheme be set up so that network directionality can be maintained. These objectives are met by placing the activities in sequence step order.

A sequence step may be defined as the earliest logical position in the network that an activity can occupy while maintaining its proper dependencies.

This definition can be more fully understood by referring to Figure 4.5. The beginning activity, Activity Start, has been placed on Sequence Step 1 and Activities A, B, and C, each of which are dependent upon Activity Start, have been placed one step to the right and appear on Sequence Step 2. Activities E and F are positioned on the step following their dependencies, that is, on Step 3. Finally, Activity Finish is on Step 4, one step from its dependent Activities E and F, and two steps from Activity B as shown. It should be noted that Activity B is at the earliest of its two possible logic steps in accordance with the sequence step definition.

Each activity shown in the network should carry a unique identifying number. The numbers arbitrarily assigned during the creation of the activity list can be used by some computer programs, but this practice generally is not satisfactory. Ordinarily, the activities are given their numbers after the diagram has been essentially completed and arranged in sequence step order. To meet the directional requirements of the network, it is the practice to assign to the activity that appears at the left end of a link a smaller number than the one assigned to the right end.

Consecutive numbering, of course, satisfies the requirements of directionality

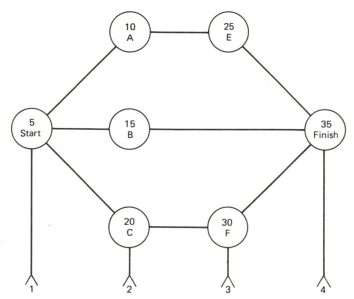

Figure 4.5   Precedence diagram—sequence stepped and numbered.

and uniqueness but does not permit the addition of future activities without renumbering the entire network. Instead, a numbering pattern may be chosen, such as even numbers, odd numbers, numbers by fives or tens, and so on. It is doubtful that any network can be constructed where every activity is known before diagraming begins, hence, the numbering pattern chosen should reflect the quantity of anticipated additions.

Care must be exercised to make sure that each activity has a unique number. If duplicate numbers occur, an ambiguity exists that will cause the computations to give erroneous results.

When activities are to be identified with certain portions of the project or when they are to reflect material, labor, or equipment accounts, code numbers may be used. The major difficulty in using accounting codes is the inability to keep the uniqueness concept. Usually, the addition of a sequential number before or after the account code will satisfy this need.

Activity numbering may be done easily if the lowest number is assigned to the starting activity and the next number of the chosen pattern is assigned to the activity at the top of the next sequence step. Numbering continues to the bottom of the step and then to the top of the following step, and so forth, until the terminal activity is reached.

The activities of Figure 4.5 have been numbered in intervals of five. Activity Start was assigned the number 5; Activity A was numbered 10; Activity B, 15; and so forth. These same numbers can serve to identify the links in the diagram, and may be referred to as activity numbers for the link's I and J activities, respectively. This two number representation will become increasingly important in making the schedule computations as discussed in a later chapter.

4.4   DRAWING THE DIAGRAM

There are two stages for drawing the precedence diagram. The first is to construct a rough diagram with all the dependencies from the activity list. From this drawing the sequence step numbers for each activity are determined. The second stage is to assemble the finished drawing with the activities arranged in sequence step order, with all redundant links removed and with the activities given their final numbers.

The sample project of Chapter 2 will be used to illustrate the process. It will be recalled that the project consists of the activities needed to remodel a chemical laboratory. An augmented activity list is given in Table 4.1.

A brief examination of the original dependencies in Table 2.3 will reveal that some are not needed. For example, Activity 2 does not need the dependency of Activity 1, because Activity 5, which is also a dependency for Activity 2, is dependent upon Activity 1. The removal of these obvious redundancies is desirable because they contribute nothing to the logic of the diagram, cause additional effort, and clutter the drawing.

TABLE 4.1

Augmented Activity List with Redundant Dependencies Removed—
Remodeling Chemical Laboratory

Activity List

No.	Activity	Depends upon
1	Strip room	—
2	Repair walls and ceiling	~~1~~, 5, 7
3	Repair floor	~~1~~, 5
4	Lay vinyl floor	~~3~~, 12, 13, 14
5	Rough-in plumbing & electrical	1
6	Finish plumbing & electrical	2, ~~3~~, ~~5~~, ~~9~~, 10, 11, 19
7	Replace existing fume duct	1
8	Install new fume hood	2, 3, 16
9	Install 1/3 base cabinets	2, ~~3~~, 8, 15
10	Install wall cabinets	2, 3, ~~7~~, 15
11	Install chemical sink	2, ~~3~~, ~~5~~, 9, 17
12	Paint cabinets	6, ~~8~~, ~~9~~, ~~10~~, ~~11~~, 18
13	Paint walls and ceiling	2, ~~3~~, 6, ~~8~~, ~~9~~, ~~10~~, 18
14	Obtain vinyl floor covering	—
15	Obtain cabinets	—
16	Obtain fume hood	—
17	Obtain chemical sink	—
18	Painter availability	—
19	Install 2/3 base cabinets	2, ~~3~~, 9, ~~15~~

The process for making this adjustment is rather straightforward. Each project activity is considered in turn and an activity number from its dependency list is selected. If the dependency list for this selected number contains a dependent activity that is the same as one of the activities in the dependency list of the original activity, then that number is removed from the original activity's dependency list. The next number is then chosen and the procedure repeated until the original activity's dependency list is depleted.

To illustrate, consider Activity 2 in Table 4.1. Its dependency list originally had three numbers, 1, 5, and 7. Select one of these numbers, say number 7. The dependency list for Activity 7 is searched and it is found that Activity 7 has a dependency of Activity 1. This number has therefore been crossed out in the list of the original activity's dependencies. Activity 5 is the next number on the list and it also is dependent upon Activity 1, thus requiring the elimination of Activity 1 as before. Activity 1 would be the next selection, but even though it has been crossed out it must be considered. In this instance, Activity 1 has no dependency so no further elimination takes place.

The remainder of the project's activity list has been adjusted in the same manner. Special attention should be paid to Activity 11. In this case Activities 2 and 3 have been removed because Activity 9 contained them in its dependency list. Their removal from Activity 9's list does not restrict their consideration for removal while dealing with Activity 11.

The rough diagram, sometimes called the "ball-of-string" diagram, is drawn from the augmented activity list. Figure 4.6 shows such a diagram for the example project. The activities from the activity list in Table 4.1 that have no dependencies are arranged toward the left of the drawing and the other activities are arranged in the order that they appeared on the list. Because there are several activities without dependencies in Figure 4.6 an initial dummy activity representing the start event of the project and called "Contract Award" has been added to their left for the purpose of providing a single initial activity as discussed in Section 4.2. A connecting line has been drawn between each related pair of activities and an arrowhead has been added to show the proper dependency. For illustration, consider Activity 2. Its dependence upon Activities 5 and 7 is shown by the lines connecting Activities 5 and 7 to Activity 2 and having the arrowheads at the Activity 2 end. When all the activities are related to each other in this way, the diagram resembles a mass of tangled yarn, hence its ball-of-string name.

The ball-of-string diagram not only shows every relationship that is listed in the augmented activity list, but provides the means to determine the sequence steps for each activity. The initial activity is assigned to Sequence Step 1. Because all activities that are to follow are to be at least one sequence step away, the step number is increased by one and the ends of the links leaving the activity are labeled with this number. Successive activities are examined, and when it is found that all the links entering an activity have been labeled, the largest step number from the entering links is chosen as the sequence step number for that activity.

In the example ball-of-string diagram, Figure 4.6, Sequence Step 1 is assigned to the Contract Award Activity. This is indicated by the small circled 1 inside the symbol. The small numbers at the arrowhead ends of each of the following links are the possible sequence step numbers for the following activities. Thus, the small 2 at the end of the link between the Contract Award and Activity 1 becomes the sequence step for Activity 1, and the label 3 at the end of the link between Activities 1 and 7 is the sequence step for Activity 7. Note that links from Activities 2 and 3 to Activity 8 are labeled 5 and the link from Activity 16 to Activity 8 is labeled 3. The 5, being the largest, is the sequence step number for Activity 8 and is circled in the symbol. Each activity in the network has been examined in a similar manner until all have had their sequence step numbers determined.

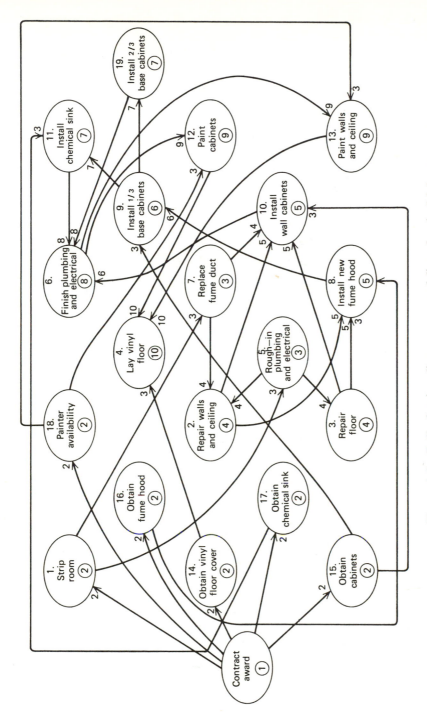

Figure 4.6   Ball-of-string diagram—remodeling chemical laboratory.

56

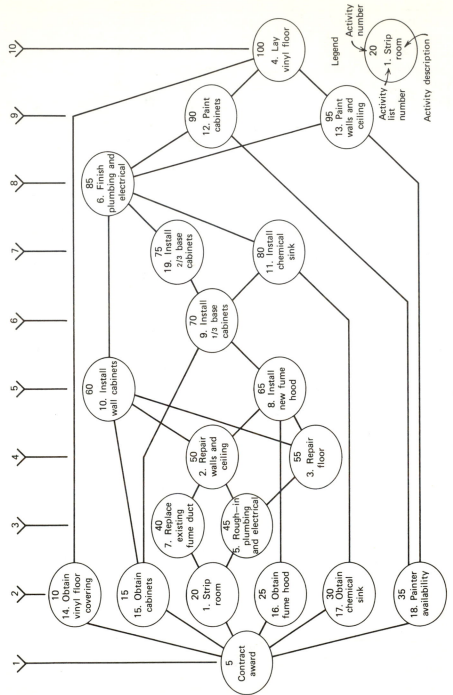

Figure 4.7 Precedence diagram—remodeling chemical laboratory.

After all the sequence step numbers have been assigned, the final precedence diagram can be assembled and permanently numbered. In Figure 4.6 the largest sequence step number was 10 which was assigned to Activity 4, "lay vinyl floor"; therefore, the diagram is arranged in ten vertical columns, one for each sequence step. Each activity is positioned on its individual sequence step such that it is convenient to draw the connecting links with as few crossed lines as possible. There is no need to add the arrowheads to the links because the diagram is to be read from left to right and the directionality is established by the sequence steps.

The removal of the redundancies from the initial activity list does not ensure that there will be no redundancies in the network. Hence, care must be exercised in transferring the links from the ball-of-string diagram to the final diagram to make sure that all dependencies are represented and that any remaining redundancies are removed. Consider the activity, Install Wall Cabinets, which is Activity 10 in the ball-of-string diagram with links from Activities 2, 3, and 15. The link from Activity 7, Replace Existing Fume Duct, was inadvertently shown in Figure 4.6 and is a redundancy because Activity 7 is followed by Activity 2, Repair Walls and Ceiling, which in turn is followed by Activity 10. Had the link also been shown in Figure 4.7, a triangular pattern would have been set up as mentioned earlier.

The last step in completing the precedence diagram is to assign the permanent activity numbers that will be used in the future for reference and computation. In Figure 4.7 they are shown to have been assigned in intervals of five in the manner discussed above.

4.5   SEQUENCE STEPS FROM THE ACTIVITY LIST

It is sometimes desirable to be able to ensure that a network has but one beginning and one ending node and also to determine the sequence step number for each activity without drawing the precedence diagram. At first this may seem like an impossible task, yet the procedure for establishing these values is rather simple. The technique can be illustrated by determining these values for a sample set of activities and their dependencies.

Table 4.2 is an activity list for a small project consisting of six activities. Note that Activities A and F are not dependent upon any other activity. Because there is to be only one beginning, neither of these activities can logically be the starting node, hence, an additional node must be created. In Table 4.3 this created activity, called ST, was added to the activity list and the dependency for Activities A and F was changed to ST.

The establishment of the single terminal node begins by selecting an activity from those listed and checking to see whether or not it appears as any activity's dependency in the dependency list. If it does not appear there and it is not the starting activity determined above, then it is added to the dependency list and a terminal activity is added to the activity list.

TABLE 4.2

Activity	Depends upon
A	—
B	A
C	E, F
D	E
E	A
F	—

TABLE 4.3

Activity	Depends upon
A	≠ST
B	A
C	E, F
D	E
E	A
F	≠ST
ST	—
FIN	B, C, D

The activities of the sample network have been considered in the order shown in Table 4.3. Activity A appears on the dependency list and, hence, must not be a terminal activity. Activity B does not appear there and has been added to the foot of the dependency column. Similarly, Activities C and D also have been added. The closing activity, Activity FIN, has been listed in the activity column opposite the dependencies B, C, and D.

The determination of sequence step numbers is started by assigning Sequence Step 1 to the beginning activity. Each succeeding activity is selected in turn and its sequence step number is set one greater than the sequence step number of any of its dependencies. When every activity in the list has been considered, the process is repeated. Several repeat cycles may be needed to ensure that no further changes in number will occur. The correct sequence numbers have then been found.

In Table 4.4 the activities have been listed with Activity ST first. This activity has been assigned to Step 1 at the beginning of Cycle 1. Activity A was considered next and from Table 4.3 was found to be dependent upon Activity ST. It was therefore assigned to Step 2, one greater than the step of Activity ST. Similarly, the sequence step number for Activity B was found to be 3. The third activity selected, Activity C, depends upon both Activities E and F, which have not as yet had step numbers determined, and the assignment for Activity C was not made.

TABLE 4.4

Activity	Sequence steps	
	Cycle 1	Cycle 2
ST	1	
A	2	
B	3	
C	~~4~~	4
D	~~4~~	4
E	3	
F	2	
FIN	~~4~~	5

After all the activities were considered as above the second cycle was begun. The assignments for Activities ST, A, and B remain as in Cycle 1 so no entries appear in the Cycle 2 column. Activitiy C now has been assigned to step 4 because Activity E was found to have a step number of 3 in Cycle 1. Activity D was assigned to step 4 also and the terminal activity, Activity FIN, had its step number changed from 4 to 5 to agree with its dependency upon Activity C. A third cycle would show no change in the sequence step numbers and those thus determined may be taken as the final sequence step values.

REFERENCES

4.1   Anonymous, *Project Control System/360 (360A-CP-06X) Program Description and Operations Manual No. H20-0376-3*, IBM Corporation, White Plains, N.Y., 1967.

4.2   Archibald, Russell D. and Richard L. Villoria, *Network-Based Management Systems (PERT/CPM)*, John Wiley & Sons., Inc., New York, 1967 (Appendix B).

4.3   Fondahl, John W., *A Non-Computer Approach to the Critical Path Method for the Construction Industry*, Technical Report No. 9, The Construction Institute—Department of Civil Engineering, Stanford University, Stanford, Calif., 1961 (Second Edition, 1962).

4.4   Moder, Joseph J. and Cecil R. Phillips, *Project Management with CPM and PERT*, Reinhold Publishing Corp., New York, 1964 (Second Edition, Van Nostrand Reinhold Co., 1970).

4.5   Muth, John F. and G. L. Thompson, *Industrial Scheduling*, Prentice-Hall, Englewood Cliffs, N. J., 1963.

EXERCISES

4.1   The network logic for a project is given by the statements below. Construct the precedence network. Arrange the network by proper sequence step and remove any redundancies. Number the nodes.

   1.   Activities A and P have no predecessors.

2. Activities B, C, and N must be complete before Activity E can start.
3. Activity G cannot start until Activity M is finished.
4. Activities H and K can be done at the same time.
5. Activity P immediately precedes Activities L, M, and N.
6. Activities B and C immediately follow Activity A.
7. Activity H depends upon the completion of Activities B, C, L, M, and N.
8. Activity F cannot start until Activities A, B, and E have ended.
9. The finish of Activities H and K controls the start of Activity G.
10. Activities P and L must be finished before Activity K can start.
11. Activity G must follow the completion of Activity A.

4.2 Establish the dependencies for the activities of the bus stop project of Exercise 1.3 and draw the precedence diagram. Place the activities on the correct sequence step and number each one.

4.3 Establish the dependencies for the small building activities given in Exercise 1.4 and draw the precedence diagram. Place the activities on the correct sequence step and number each one.

4.4 Use the activities of the bridge project of Exercise 2.4 and the depenedencies established in Exercise 2.6 and draw the precedence diagram. Place the activities on the correct sequence step and number each one.

4.5 Draw a precedence network that will represent the overlapping relationships between the activities of the following project.

After 20 percent of Activity A has been completed Activity B can be started, however, 75 percent of Activity C must be reamining; 40 percent of the work in Activity B must precede the start of Activity D; 60 percent of Activity B must remain after the completion of Activity A. Activity D must be completed before the last 40 percent of Activity C can be started.

4.6 Draw a precedence network that will represent the overlapping relationships between the activities of the following project.

When 50 percent of Activity A is completed Activity B can be started. Activity C can be started as soon as the first half of the work in Activity B has been completed, but at least 25 percent of the work in Activity C cannot be completed until Activity A is completed entirely. Finally, Activity D cannot be started until Activity B is completed and it must precede the last 15 percent of Activity C.

4.7 The ten activities of a project and their dependencies are given below. Without constructing the network determine the sequence step for each activity.

Activity	Depends Upon
A	S
B	A, K
C	B, H
D	H
E	G, K
F	C, D, E
G	S
H	K
K	S
S	—

4.8 Transform the arrow network shown in Figure Ex. 4.1 into a proper precedence network. Label and number each activity and arrange the network on the proper sequence steps.

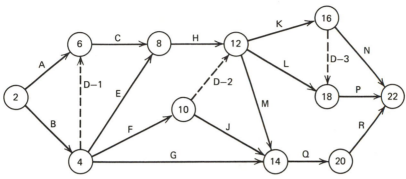

Figure Ex. 4.1

5

ESTABLISHING ACTIVITY DURATIONS

5.1 INTRODUCTION

The second phase of project management, the scheduling phase, depends upon having proper time durations for each activity if success is to be achieved. At times these durations are easy to establish but more often their formulation is complex and time consuming. The time interval to be used as a basic measure must first be selected. Then an estimate of the time duration for each activity must be made based upon the methods to be used and the resources to be applied. These durations may be established from the company's historical data file or may be obtained from direct interviews with the field forces. Finally, considerations of contingency and other time allowances must be reflected in the durations finally chosen.

5.2 TIME INTERVALS FOR NETWORK SCHEDULING

There are many time intervals that can be selected for the management of projects, and any convenient one may be used as a base; seconds, minutes, hours, days, weeks, months, years, decades, and so on—all are acceptable. The choice may be natural or may derive from customary practice.

The amount of time needed to perform the representative activities of the project may give rise to such a natural selection for the basic interval. It would make little sense to use days as the base if most of the activities require only an hour or two, or to choose hours if most activities are to extend over several days.

In the commercial domain it is the usual practice to select the calendar day as the basic interval for the project. Networks that are composed mostly from procurement activities will be observed to follow this scheme.

The customary employment period of the activity resource is probably the most frequently adopted basic time interval for the schedule. In the construction industry manpower is usually paid an hourly wage, but the employment period is commonly the 8-hour working day. The working day thus becomes the basic scheduling interval. Similarly, the 5-day, 40-hour work week is often used as the base for large projects.

Whatever time interval is chosen for network activity durations, it must be followed consistently throughout the diagram. If the working day is adopted as the basic interval and there are several procurement activities with durations expressed in calendar days, the procurement durations will have to be adjusted. Thus, an item that has a 30-day delivery will actually consume only 22 working days if a 5-day week is being followed and 26 days if a 6-day week is the pattern.

Occasionally there are activities that must take longer than the usual work day. For example, there may be an activity in a network drawn for the construction of a water treatment plant that is entitled "Pipe Cutover" representing the interruption of flow in an existing pipe, the removal of a section of it, the installation of a new section of pipe, and the resumption of flow through a new part of the system. This activity is estimated to take 12 hours to accomplish. Because the task must be done without interruption, however, it will appear on the network as a 1-day activity even though the basic time interval has been chosen as a working day 8 hours long.

5.3 ESTIMATING ACTIVITY DURATIONS

The time duration for each activity in the network deserves a sound analysis if the schedule to be subsequently derived is to become an accurate representation of the project. Off-hand estimates of activity times have not proven satisfactory. The planner may be tempted to take the initial time casually offered by the company estimator as the most probable duration for an activity, but unless the estimator has recorded time durations from past projects, the statement may be off the true value by as much as 100 percent or more.

Typical estimating guides[5.1,5.2,5.3] currently in use give the costs to perform work in terms of dollars per unit of material, such as "$50 per cubic yard" or "$20 per square foot." Such figures are based on the tacit assumptions of a commonly used method and a customary utilization of human resources and equipment. Adjustments to these figures are made on a subjective basis by the estimator to account for job conditions and other factors. The published figures do not account for such things as overtime charges, quality of workmanship required, size of project, geographical location of the work, height above ground, season of the year, general business conditions, and other similar factors that affect the production rate and, hence, activity costs.

In most construction company offices records are not kept in a manner that will allow the planner to determine the time it takes to do a particular task, although the cost of doing so may appear to be assessed with a fair degree of certainty. Because the duration time is essential to the use of the CPM technique, it becomes clear that steps must be taken by the planner to derive the activity times from additional sources other than from the estimating department or from company history.

Probably the most direct additional source for the needed time information is to be found from interviewing the field forces that are actually to perform the work. These persons must be brought into the scheduling process as well as into the planning procedure mentioned earlier. In addition to their input about the logic to be followed, their ideas regarding the methods they propose to use must be added. The project superintendent can supply much of this information, but personnel at the foreman level may provide many helpful insights leading to improved efficiency of the method proposed, thereby lowering costs and providing more accurate duration times.

This procedure is a very informal one if the company is relatively small, because the management of the company is closely associated with the work force. As company size increases this process must become more formalized because the office and field forces probably lose contact with each other. A prescheduling conference may be needed to bring together both the field and office forces to facilitate a common understanding.

5.4   WEATHER AND CONTINGENCY ALLOWANCES

Closely associated with the determination of activity duration times is the consideration of weather allowances and other adjustments to account for known contingencies generally present in any project. The method for assigning such allowances is chosen after an examination of the kinds of activities comprising the network and the expected durations of the activities that may be affected by the contingency.

Weather factors, always present in construction projects, are the most frequently cited cause for project delay; yet there is reason to believe that weather is not always the culprit, but rather mismanagement is the true cause. Even in the best of organizations delaying situations develop where there appears to be no other possible cause than the weather. But, when weather factors have been included in the network, many of these delays are brought into proper perspective and the true cause becomes evident to the advantage of the company's managing personnel. It is better for the project manager to know that one employee has made a mistake than to blame the rain that fell the day before yesterday.

Moder and Phillips[5.4] suggest two basic approaches to the assignment of weather allowances. One is to make the assignment by adding a weather activity at the end of the project network and the other is to make the assignment by increasing the duration of each affected activity. In some cases the allowance can be applied to certain segments of the project instead of the total.

When the allowance is assigned to a weather activity at the end of the network, the effect is to distribute the allowance to the individual activities in proportion to the time duration of each. This assignment method is especially good if the bulk of the activities may be affected by the weather. Representative projects of this type are highway and street improvements, curb and gutter constructions, and underground pipeline installations. This procedure may also be effective if many of the activities that establish the project's time length have long durations and are weather dependent. The procedure tends to be inaccurate if the longest duration activities are not weather dependent, if there are relatively few of them in number, or if they do not enter into setting the project time length.

When the weather allowance is assigned as a single activity it may appear as the project proceeds that the allowance is not enough. This feeling is brought about by the need to start activities later than the earliest starting date and the build-up of material at the site. Material that arrives before it is to be used can cause storage problems and can create the need for additional protection from future weather, vandalism, and theft.

If the project will permit, the weather allowance activity may be placed at the end of a certain segment of the project. For instance, it might be assigned at the end of the site preparation activities or at the end of the foundation installation group. This plan reduces the amount of misassignment to unaffected activities and helps to reduce material losses as well as being more accurate for the total project duration.

When the weather allowance is assigned to the activities most affected by weather a still better representation of the time effect of the weather is established. This method is most successful for building projects, where a great many of the activities can proceed after the building is under cover and are not weather dependent. However, there can be difficulties in material handling with this assignment method also. If the weather that was expected by the allowance does not materialize, delays may occur because the needed equipment and material is not on the site. On the other hand, there may be an advantage to this assignment procedure in that it permits extensions to the CPM technique.

Known contingency allowances can be treated in the same manner as weather allowances. It is not uncommon for certain material orders to be accepted with a known contingency. Fabricated steel sections may have a stated delivery of 30 days after receipt of the steel from the rolling mill, with a mill rolling to be expected in one or two months. This variation of one month can be accommodated by an allowance assigned to the steel delivery activity. Similarly, if a particular supplier has had a history of late deliveries, a contingency activity allowance may be introduced into the network to recognize this probability.

Strikes, which are so much a part of the labor scene, can frequently be handled in the same way. If there is a probability of a strike occurring at the end of the labor contract period, it will usually be known to the contractor as much as four to six months in advance of the contract deadline, and this allowance may be entered on the diagram as a contingency activity after the most likely affected segment of the project. It should be kept in mind that unknown crises are not subject to the contingency allowance procedure. Such happenings can best be handled by an updating process to be discussed later. Only those events that have a real possibility of occurrence should be included as contingencies.

5.5 TIME ZERO

Because all schedules are dependent upon the measurement of time along some scale it is necessary to have a clear understanding of the beginning point in time or "time zero." It is also evident that as activity durations are to be added to obtain project durations, the time zero must be set to facilitate this addition without ambiguity.

The commonly accepted *zero point is the close of the work period immediately preceding the start of the project*. Assuming that the working day has been chosen as the time interval, the time zero for the project will be at the end of the work day before the first activity begins.

This position of the time zero allows the emphasis to be placed upon the completion of each activity. If the first activity is to take five days to accomplish, the start of the project is set to zero and the first activity will be expected to finish at the *end* of the fifth day.

Of course, other time zeros could be selected and another emphasis given. The start of the day might be chosen and the emphasis would then shift to the beginning of the activity, for example.

It should be kept in mind that this definition means that weekends and holidays do not appear in the computations that follow. Activities that use these periods as a part of their duration times will therefore have to have their durations adjusted. Concrete curing activities are examples where this condition is exhibited. The usual practice is to enter such activities into the network with their required curing durations and after the preliminary schedule has been computed, to reduce their times to account for these extended periods.

REFERENCES

5.1 Anonymous, *The Building Estimator's Reference Book*, Frank R. Walker Co., Chicago, Nineteenth Edition, 1977.

5.2 Anonymous, *Building Construction Cost Data 1977*, Robert Snow Means Co., Inc., Duxbury, Mass., Thirty-Fifth Edition, 1977.

5.3 Dallavia, Louis, *Estimating General Construction Costs*, McGraw-Hill Book Co., New York, Second Edition, 1957.

5.4 Moder, Joseph J. and Cecil R. Phillips, *Project Management with CPM and PERT*, Second Edition, Van Nostrand Reinhold Co., New York, 1970, p. 45.

EXERCISES

5.1 A contractor has obtained the contract for a large project which is expected to last for five years. As a scheduling consultant what time interval might you suggest for the CPM network? Discuss the reasons for your choice.

5.2 A school project requires the use of epoxy paint on the underwater surfaces of the swimming pool. To insure a continuous waterproof membrane, the paint must be continuously applied once painting is started. It has been estimated that this job will require 16 hours of work. The CPM network is constructed using 8-hour working days. Discuss the time duration that should be used for this activity in the network.

5.3 Indicate the method of treating weather contingency that should be used for each of the following projects. Discuss your reasons for making each choice.

(a)   The installation of a gas main in a city street.

(b)   The construction of a high school.

(c)   The construction of a small dam.

(d)   The construction of a water treatment plant.

(e)   The building of an apartment project consisting of 75 units in one building.

6

SCHEDULING COMPUTATIONS FOR ARROW NETWORKS

6.1 OBJECTIVES

The objective of the scheduling phase of any networking technique is to provide the manager with detailed information from which to make decisions during the conduct of the project. This chapter develops procedures, based upon the arrow diagram, that furnish two major items of information about the project and three concerning the individual activity.

The computations will reveal the project's duration and will differentiate between those activities that establish this time interval and those that do not. In addition, they will identify the points in time when each activity can begin and when each must end if the project completion is not to be delayed. The amount of scheduling leeway that every activity possesses also will be made evident.

Forward pass calculations supply the earliest times for the start and finish of the activities and also the total time necessary for the completion of the project. Backward pass calculations give the latest times for every activity's beginning and ending. The amount of leeway for the activities results from the manipulation of the values from the forward and backward passes.

6.2 THE FOUR ACTIVITY TIMES

Each activity in the network has associated with it on the time scale four values than can be identified as follows:

ESD—Early start date

EFD—Early finish date

LSD—Late start date

LFD—Late finish date.

It will be recalled that each activity has a definite beginning and end and that these conditions are represented by the nodes at the tail and head of the activity arrow. These nodes are identified by i and j numbers, which can serve as subscripts in discussing the four dates above and other activity related values.

The early start date, ESD, for an activity is the earliest point in time that any activity bursting from its beginning node can start. Similarly, the late finish date, LFD, is the latest point in time that any activity which merges at the activity's

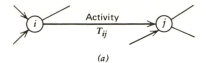

(a)

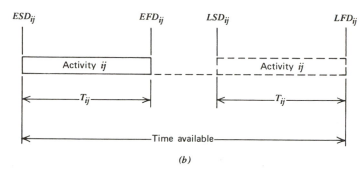

(b)

Figure 6.1   The four activity times—arrow diagram notation.

ending node can finish. The early finish date, *EFD*, is dependent upon the determination of the early start date, and the late start date, *LSD*, is related to the late finish date.

Figure 6.1 illustrates these relationships for a single activity. A part of an arrow diagram containing the activity is pictures in Figure 6.1*a* and in Figure 6.1*b* the same activity is shown as a time scaled bar. The time duration of the activity is denoted as T_{ij}. Based on the definitions of *LFD* and *ESD* above the total time available is given by the difference in time between the LFD_{ij} and the ESD_{ij}. The activity is shown in two possible schedule positions within this time range, one at the earliest point and the other at the latest point. Note that there is no relationship directly linking the *LSD* and the *EFD* of the activity. The schedule that results when all activities of the network are positioned in the early start location is termed an early start schedule. Similarly, when every activity is in the late position, the resulting schedule is a late finish schedule. It should be clear that other scheduling possibilities can be chosen for the benefit of the user. These will be discussed in later chapters.

6.3 FORWARD PASS COMPUTATIONS

The main objective of forward pass computations is to determine the duration of the project. This time span is found by searching through the network for a continuous chain of activities beginning at the initial node, ending at the terminal node, and having the greatest total time duration.

The most common procedure for finding this duration is to successively add activity durations along chains of activities until a merge node is found. At the merge node the largest value of the sum of the activity times from each path entering the node is taken as the start of the succeeding activities. Addition continues to the next merge point, and these steps are repeated until the terminal node is reached.

This merge node decision-making procedure does not allow for the identification of the activities that determined the start of any activity following the merge. This may be done, however, and Moder[6.1] presents a scheme for making this identification.

Activity early start and finish values become apparent from the additions made while finding the project duration and can be tabulated as they are found. Figure 6.2 is the project network developed in Chapter 3 with the activity durations added below each activity arrow. Table 6.1 lists these activities and their durations. For convenience, the activities are arranged in Table 6.1 according to their ij numbers, primarily by ascending i number and secondarily by ascending j number. Although computations can be carried out with the activities listed in any order, the above arrangement makes for easier manual calculation and saves considerable time in the computer application.

The scheduling computations begin by assigning to the ESD values of the activities that begin at the initial node the value of "time zero." This will usually be a zero but may be another number that may relate the project to other company operations or to the updating period, as will be seen later. In Table 6.1 the first six activities have i numbers of 2, corresponding to the initial node, and hence have ESD values equal to 0.

The early finish date, EFD_{ij}, for any activity, ij, is found by adding the activity duration, T_{ij}, to the ESD_{ij}. In equation form the expression is

$$EFD_{ij} = ESD_{ij} + T_{ij} \qquad (6.1)$$

Applying this equation to the first six activities in Table 6.1 yields the EFD values shown. The seventh activity, Activity 4–6, depends upon the completion of Activity 2–4; therefore, the earliest that Activity 4–6 can start is the earliest that Activity 2–4 can finish. The EFD of Activity 2–4 was found to be 3 days; hence, the ESD of Activity 4–6 becomes 3 days. Applying Equation 6.1 again results in the EFD for Activity 4–6, being 8 days. This process continues activity by activity until the EFD of the last activity has been found.

Note should be taken of the choice for the ESD of Activity 8–10. This activity has a dependency upon both Activities 4–8 and 6–8 which merge at node 8 and which have EFD values of 6 days and 8 days, respectively. Because the longest time path is being sought, the choice for the ESD of Activity 8-10 is taken as the greatest of these two values, or 8 days. Similar decisions are made for all other activities exiting from merge nodes.

The early finish day for the last activity in the network, Activity 28–30, is found to be 27 days, which is the project duration. The determination of this

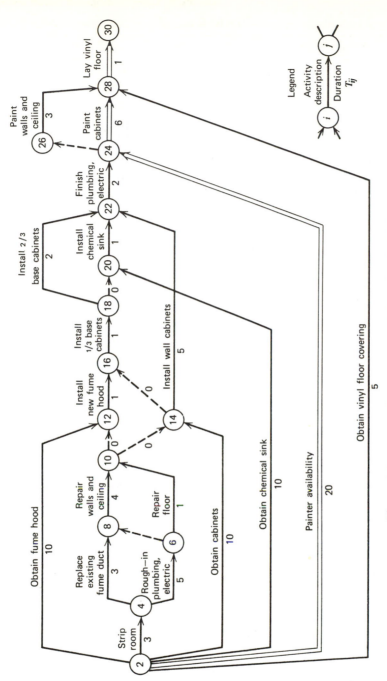

Figure 6.2 Arrow diagram—remodeling chemical laboratory.

71

TABLE 6.1

Forward Pass Computations—Remodeling Chemical Laboratory

i	j	Activity Description	T (Days)	ESD	EFD
2	4	Strip room	3	0	3
2	12	Obtain fume hood	10	0	10
2	14	Obtain cabinets	10	0	10
2	20	Obtain chemical sink	10	0	10
2	24	Painter availability	20	0	20
2	28	Obtain vinyl floor covering	5	0	5
4	6	Rough-in plumbing and electrical	5	3	8
4	8	Replace existing fume duct	3	3	6
6	8	Dummy	0	8	8
6	10	Repair floor	1	8	9
8	10	Repair walls and ceiling	4	8	12
10	12	Dummy	0	12	12
10	14	Dummy	0	12	12
12	16	Install new fume hood	1	12	13
14	16	Dummy	0	12	12
14	22	Install wall cabinets	5	12	17
16	18	Install 1/3 base cabinets	1	13	14
18	20	Dummy	0	14	14
18	22	Install 2/3 base cabinets	2	14	16
20	22	Install chemical sink	1	14	15
22	24	Finish plumbing and electrical	2	17	19
24	26	Dummy	0	20	20
24	28	Paint cabinets	6	20	26
26	28	Paint walls and ceiling	3	20	23
28	30	Lay vinyl floor	1	26	27

value meets the objective of the forward pass computations and brings these calculations to a close.

6.4 BACKWARD PASS COMPUTATIONS

Backward pass computations provide the latest possible times of occurrence for the start and finish of each activity. These values are derived by finding the path with the greatest time duration extending from the terminal node back to the initial node of the project network.

The calculations are started by assigning a late finish date to all the activities merging at the last node in the project and then successively subtracting activity durations along chains of activities until a burst node is found. At the burst node the smallest value of late starting dates calculated for each path leaving that node is taken as the late finish date for all activities that enter the burst node. Once this decision is made, subtractions continue until the next burst point is met. A new decision is then made and the process continues in like manner until the initial node is reached. As in the forward pass computations,

TABLE 6.2

Backward Pass Computations—Remodeling Chemical Laboratory

i	j	Activity Description	T (Days)	ESD	EFD	LSD	LFD
2	4	Strip room	3	0	3	1	4
2	12	Obtain fume hood	10	0	10	4	14
2	14	Obtain cabinets	10	0	10	3	13
2	20	Obtain chemical sink	10	0	10	7	17
2	24	Painter availability	20	0	20	0	20
2	28	Obtain vinyl floor covering	5	0	5	21	26
4	6	Rough-in plumbing and electrical	5	3	8	4	9
4	8	Replace existing fume duct	3	3	6	6	9
6	8	Dummy	0	8	8	9	9
6	10	Repair floor	1	8	9	12	13
8	10	Repair walls and ceiling	4	8	12	9	13
10	12	Dummy	0	12	12	14	14
10	14	Dummy	0	12	12	13	13
12	16	Install new fume hood	1	12	13	14	15
14	16	Dummy	0	12	12	15	15
14	22	Install wall cabinets	5	12	17	13	18
16	18	Install 1/3 base cabinets	1	13	14	15	16
18	20	Dummy	0	14	14	17	17
18	22	Install 2/3 base cabinets	2	14	16	16	18
20	22	Install chemical sink	1	14	15	17	18
22	24	Finish plumbing and electrical	2	17	19	18	20
24	26	Dummy	0	20	20	23	23
24	28	Paint cabinets	6	20	26	20	26
26	28	Paint walls and ceiling	3	20	23	23	26
28	30	Lay vinyl floor	1	26	27	26	27

this decision-making procedure does not reveal the activities that lie on the longest time path.

When assigning the late finish date for the project, an assumption must be made regarding its value. Usually this is that the late finish date for the activities merging at the terminal node is to be taken as the project duration found from the forward pass calculations, for if the project can be finished within a given time duration, there is no reason to believe that it should not do so. Other assumptions may be appropriate under some conditions. These will be discussed in a later chapter.

Activity late start and finish values are tabulated as they are found during the process of finding the longest backward path. Table 6.2 shows the backward pass figures for the network of Figure 6.2. The early finish for Activity 28–30 was found to be 27 days in the forward pass computation. This value is therefore assumed to be the greatest amount of time that the project should require and is taken as the late finish date, LFD, for Activity 28–30. These values are circled in Table 6.2.

The late start date, LSD_{ij}, for any activity, ij, is found by subtracting the activity duration, T_{ij}, from the late finish date, LFD_{ij}. The equation for this operation is

$$LSD_{ij} = LFD_{ij} - T_{ij} \qquad (6.2)$$

By applying Equation 6.2, Activity 28–30 is found to have an LSD of 26 days.

Activity 26–28 is considered next and its LFD is the latest point in time that its following activity can start. In this case it is the latest that Activity 28–30 can start, or 26 days. Equation 6.2 is again applied to find the LSD of Activity 26–28 as 23 days. This procedure continues activity by activity until the LSD value for Activity 2–4 has been found.

Observe that the LFD for Activity 22–24 has been taken as 20 days, which is the minimum of the LSD values of its successors: Activities 24–26 and 24–28 which burst from node 24. Similar choices were made when determining the LFD values for all other activities entering nodes where there is a burst.

6.5   FLOAT DERIVED FROM ACTIVITY TIME VALUES

The amount of scheduling leeway that a network activity has is called its float. For each activity of the project it is possible to calculate four float values from the results of the forward and backward pass computations. These are total float, free float, interfering float, and independent float.

Total Float

> **Total float may be defined as that time span in which the completion of an activity may occur and not delay the termination of the project.**

From the forward and backward pass figures this time span must then be bounded by the latest that the activity must finish and the earliest that it can finish. For any activity, *ij*, this may be written as

$$TF_{ij} = LFD_{ij} - EFD_{ij} \tag{6.3}$$

where TF_{ij} is the total float.

The choice of maximum *ESD* values at merge nodes in the forward pass computations resulted in the longest path from the initial node of the project to the terminal node. Similarly, the choice of minimum *LFD* values at burst nodes in the backward pass resulted in the longest path from the terminal node to the initial node. Activities found to have the same start and finish dates from either determination must therefore lie on the longest time path between these nodes and be restricted to these computed schedule times if no delays are to be permitted. This path is called the *critical path* because any slippage in duration time of the activities comprising it will cause the project to be delayed. Such activities are termed the *critical activities* of the network.

Any activity, *ij*, having a late finish date the same as its early finish date will have a total float equal to zero when these values are substituted into Equation 6.3. It can therefore be said that *an activity is a critical activity if its total float is zero*.

Table 6.3 contains the float computations for the project used to illustrate the forward and backward pass calculations. Equation 6.3 has been applied to each activity in the list and the results are given in the column headed *TF*. Only three activities have total floats of zero: Activities 2–24, 24–28, and 28–30. They are starred on the left of the table to indicate their critical nature and the arrows forming the critical path are emphasized in Figure 6.2.

Free Float

There are activities that possess total floats and that may be completed in the time span represented by these values without delaying the project's termination; however, their completion may delay the start of succeeding activities. It is therefore important to know whether a slippage past the early completion of an activity will actually cause a following activity to be postponed. This information is provided by the free float.

> **Free float may be defined as the time span in which the completion of an activity may occur and not delay the finish of the project nor delay the start of any following activity.**

The boundaries of this time span are the early start date for the immediately following activities and the early finish date of the activity itself. In general terms, for any activity, *ij*, the expression is

$$FF_{ij} = ESD_{jk} - EFD_{ij} \tag{6.4}$$

TABLE 6.3

Float Computations—Remodeling Chemical Laboratory

i	j	Activity Description	T (Days)	ESD	EFD	LSD	LFD	TF	FF	INTF	INDF
2	4	Strip room	3	0	3	1	4	1	0	1	—
2	12	Obtain fume hood	10	0	10	4	14	4	2	2	2
2	14	Obtain cabinets	10	0	10	3	13	3	2	1	2
2	20	Obtain chemical sink	10	0	10	7	17	7	4	3	4
*2	24	Painter availability	20	0	20	0	20	0	—	—	—
2	28	Obtain vinyl floor covering	5	0	5	21	26	21	21	0	21
4	6	Rough-in plumbing and electrical	5	3	8	4	9	1	0	1	—
4	8	Replace existing fume duct	3	3	6	6	9	3	2	1	1
6	8	Dummy	0	8	8	9	9	1	0	1	—
6	10	Repair floor	1	8	9	12	13	4	3	1	2
8	10	Repair walls and ceiling	4	8	12	9	13	1	0	1	—
10	12	Dummy	0	12	12	14	14	2	0	2	—
10	14	Dummy	0	12	12	13	13	1	0	1	—
12	16	Install new fume hood	1	12	13	14	15	2	0	2	—
14	16	Dummy	0	12	12	15	15	3	1	2	0
14	22	Install wall cabinets	5	12	17	13	18	1	0	1	—
16	18	Install 1/3 base cabinets	1	13	14	15	16	2	0	2	—
18	20	Dummy	0	14	14	17	17	3	0	3	—
18	22	Install 2/3 base cabinets	2	14	16	16	18	2	1	1	0
20	22	Install chemical sink	1	14	15	17	18	3	2	1	0
22	24	Finish plumbing and electrical	2	17	19	18	20	1	1	0	0
24	26	Dummy	0	20	20	23	23	3	0	3	—
*24	28	Paint cabinets	6	20	26	20	26	0	—	—	—
26	28	Paint walls and ceiling	3	20	23	23	26	3	3	0	30
*28	30	Lay vinyl floor	1	26	27	26	27	0	—	—	—

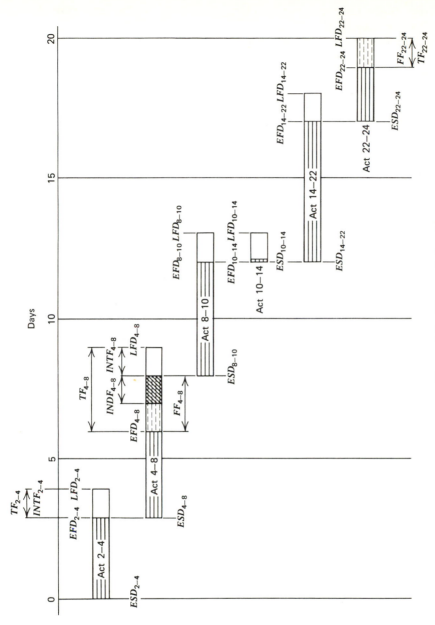

Figure 6.3 Float relationships.

77

where FF_{ij} is the free float of the activity and ESD_{jk} is the early start date for any following activity, jk.

Free float may be thought of as the amount of leeway of an activity if all the activities of the project are to be started at their earliest possible time. As such, it can never be greater than the total float but may be equal to it if the activity ESD_{jk} and LFD_{ij} coincide. This condition is found only when the activity is followed by a critical activity or the j node is an event on the critical path.

A chain of activities whose floats were computed in Table 6.3 and that form a path from Node 2 is shown in bar chart form in Figure 6.3. This is only one of 15 such paths between these two nodes and has been chosen to illustrate the float relationships. Activity 4–8 has a total float of 3 days and a free float of 2 days as shown. The only other activity in this chain that has free float is Activity 22–24. Here the total float and free float are the same because Node 24 is a critical node.

Interfering Float

That part of the total float which remains after free float has been deducted is the interfering float.

> **It may be defined as: The time span in which the completion of an activity may occur and not delay the termination of the project but within which completion will delay the start of some other following activity.**

Its boundaries are of course, the latest that the activity must be completed and the earliest that the following activity can start. It may be found as follows:

$$INTF_{ij} = TF_{ij} - FF_{ij} \qquad (6.5)$$

where $INTF_{ij}$ is the interfering float. An alternate expression using activity early and late dates may be derived from Equations 6.3 and 6.4.

$$TF_{ij} = LFD_{ij} - EFD_{ij}$$
$$\underline{-[FF_{ij} = ESD_{jk} - EFD_{ij}]}$$
$$INTF_{ij} = LFD_{ij} - ESD_{jk} \qquad (6.6)$$

where jk refers to the following activity as before.

These interfering float values computed by Equation 6.5 are tabulated in Table 6.3 and those in the illustrative chain are diagramed in Figure 6.3. Note that the interfering float is never greater than the total float but is frequently equal to it. Any slippage in the completion of Activity 2–4 without delaying the project will delay Activity 4–8. Also, a delay in finishing Activity 8–10 will delay the dummy Activity 10–14, Activity 14–22, and Activity 22–24.

Independent Float

The fourth float, independent float, is the amount of scheduling leeway of an activity that is independent of the early starts and late finishes of any other activity. It may be formally defined as:

The time span in which the completion of an activity may occur and not delay the termination of the project, not delay the start of any following activity, and not be delayed by any preceding activity.

By the above definition, in order for an activity to have independent float, every following task must start as soon as possible and every preceding task must finish as late as possible, thus defining the minimum time span in which to perform the activity. In many cases this amount of time is not sufficient to allow for the accomplishment of the activity and there is no independent float. In fact, the computation may frequently result in a negative value. When this is the situation, the value is listed as zero, for no time interval may ever be less than this amount.

An expression for independent float in terms of the activity early and late start and finish times may be derived by utilizing this minimum time concept. The earliest that a following activity, jk, can start is its ESD_{jk}. The latest that a preceding activity, hi, can encroach upon activity, ij, is the latest that it can end, or LFD_{hi}. From this minimum time span the activity duration must be deducted. These statements can be written in equation form as

$$INDF_{ij} = ESD_{jk} - LFD_{hi} - T_{ij} \qquad (6.7)$$

The values of independent float computed from Equation 6.7 are tabulated in Table 6.3. Note that these values are never more than the free float and that when the free float is zero, they have not been calculated.

As a sample computation, consider the independent float for Activity 4–8.

$$INDF_{4-8} = ESD_{8-10} - LFD_{2-4} - T_{4-8}$$

Substituting the tabulated values

$$INDF_{4-8} = 8 - 4 - 3 = 1$$

A similar computation for Activity 18–22 results in a value of -1. This has been listed in the table as a 0. Likewise, Activity 20–22 has a calculated independent float of -1 which has been changed to 0 before tabulation.

The activities that begin at the initial node do not have LFD_{hi} values. In this instance, the value for substitution in Equation 6.7 is taken as if there were a virtual activity preceding the initial node. Hence, the LFD_{hi} is the value given for the early start of the network, or zero in this case. Activities that end at the terminal node likewise do not have ESD_{jk} values. Here the value of the ESD_{jk} is taken as the project duration, which would be the ESD_{jk} if there were a virtual activity following the terminal node of the network.

There is one condition that may exist in an arrow network in which the value of independent float as computed by Equation 6.7 is not correct. This condition can be recognized if all the activities merging at the i event of an activity, ij, are dummies.

It may be recalled that the dummy, a virtual activity, is created by the splitting of an event at the tail of the real activity in order to properly express logic or to maintain a unique number pair for the activity. Also, the dummy is treated in the computations as though it were a real activity. The resulting computations then show that the dummy will interfere with the real activity.

In order to correctly compute the independent float of an activity immediately preceded only by dummies, the event at the tail of the real activity is ignored. The activity is then assumed to originate at one of the tail events of the dummies. The particular tail event to be chosen is the one having the maximum LFD value for the activities entering it. Equation 6.7 is then applied.

To illustrate this correction consider the computation for the independent float by Activity 26–28. This activity is preceded by the Dummy 24–26 and its independent float calculated by Equation 6.7 is zero. This value is incorrect and is caused by the interference of the dummy which, in actuality, is only a computing device and not a real activity. The correct calculation can be made by ignoring Event 26 and considering the activity to actually extend from Event 24 to Event 28. Thus by Equation 6.7,

$$INDF_{26-28} = ESD_{28-30} - LFD_{22-24} - T_{26-28}$$
$$INDF_{26-28} = 26 - 20 - 3 = 3$$

In Table 6.3 the previously computed value for the independent float of zero has been crossed out and the correct value of 3 has been entered.

6.6 THE TWO EVENT TIMES

In the forward pass computations the maximum of the EFD values for all activities merging at a node was taken as the single ESD value for all the activities that burst from the same node. This fact allows the assignment of this maximum number to the node itself as the early time of occurrence for the event that marks the beginning of the following activities.

A parallelism exists with respect to the backward pass computations wherein the minimum of the LSD values was taken as the latest finish time for all activities that enter the node. An assignment can then be made to the node to represent the latest time of occurrence for the event that marks the finishing of all its merging activities.

Each event node can thus be said to have two event times that can be identified as follows:

TE—Early event time

TL—Late event time

For any node, i, the early event time, TE_i, is identical to the early start date of the activity following, or ESD_{ij}. Also, the late event time, TL_j, is identical to the late finish date of the preceding activity, or LFD_{ij}. There are therefore two identities that relate the values between the two sets of notation.

$$TE_i \equiv ESD_{ij} \qquad\qquad (6.8)$$

$$TL_j \equiv LFD_{ij} \qquad\qquad (6.9)$$

where the i and j refer to the events at the start and finish of the activity.

6.7 CRITICAL PATH COMPUTATIONS ON THE NETWORK

Many planners prefer to make forward and backward pass computations directly on the network diagram by computing the early and late event times for each node of the project. This is a rapid method that is especially useful for small projects, or even for larger projects where a preliminary determination of the critical path is desired.

Early event times are computed by assigning the starting date of the project as the TE for the initial node of the network. Usually this assignment is a zero as was the case in the forward pass computations made in Table 6.1. To this number is added the activity duration for all activities that burst from the initial node. The TE for the next node is taken as the sum just found as long as there is only one activity that enters this node. This additive process continues, node by node, until the final node has been reached.

If more than one activity enters any node, j, then a decision must be made as to the value of the TE_j. This is to be taken as the greatest of the sums calculated as above for all the activities that merge to the node. An expression may be written to represent these statements as

$$TE_j = \mathop{\text{Max}}_{\forall i} (TE_i + T_{ij}) \qquad\qquad (6.10)$$

where the symbol, $\text{Max}_{\forall i}$ indicates that the maximization is to be taken from all sums wherein the value of i is used such that ij is an activity ending at node j.

The result of the application of Equation 6.10 to every node in the network of Chapter 3 is shown in Figure 6.4 where the figures in the small flaglike symbols pointing to the right are TE values for the adjacent nodes.

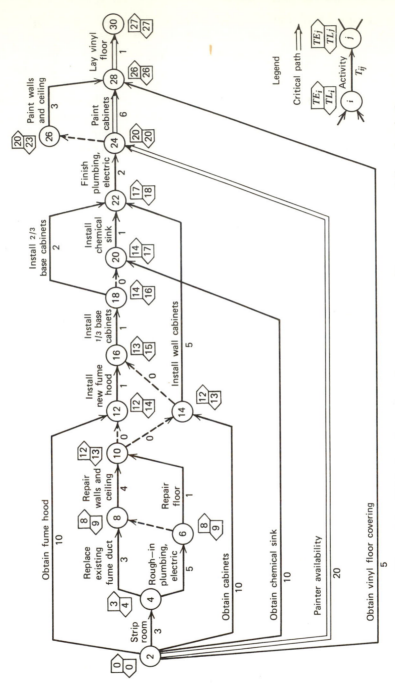

Figure 6.4 *Critical path computations on an arrow diagram—remodeling chemical laboratory.*

82

For example, the *TE* for Node 8 is found as follows:

$$TE_8 = \underset{\forall i}{\text{Max}} \left\{ \begin{array}{l} (TE_4 + T_{4-8}) = (3+3) = 6 \\ (TE_6 + T_{6-8}) = (8+0) = 8 \end{array} \right\}$$

$$TE_8 = 8$$

An 8 is therefore recorded in the right-pointing flag symbol above Node 8.

The computation of the late event times for each node begins by assigning to the terminal node of the project a suitable late event time. As in the backward pass computations made in Table 6.2, this time is commonly set as the latest that any activity merging at the terminus can be finished. Once this value has been chosen, the activity duration is subtracted from it for all activities merging to the terminal node. The *TL* for the next earlier node is taken as the value of the subtraction just performed as long as there is only one activity exiting from this node. These subtractive calculations proceed, node by node, until the initial node is reached.

If more than one activity exits from a node, *i*, then a decision must be made as to the value to use for the TL_i. This is taken as the smallest of the values found as above for all activities that merge at node *i*. The mathematical expression is

$$TL_i = \underset{\forall j}{\text{Min}} \left(TL_j - T_{ij} \right) \qquad (6.11)$$

where the symbol, $\text{Min}_{\forall j}$, is to say that the minimumization is to be taken from all differences wherein the value of *j* is used such that *ij* is an activity beginning at node *i*.

The figures in the small flaglike symbols pointing to the left in Figure 6.4 are the *TL* values of the adjacent nodes computed from Equation 6.11.

For an example of these calculations, consider the *TL* for Node 24. The application of Equation 6.9 is as follows:

$$TL_{24} = \underset{\forall j}{\text{Min}} \left\{ \begin{array}{l} (TL_{26} - T_{24-26}) = (23-0) = 23 \\ (TL_{28} - T_{24-28}) = (26-6) = 20 \end{array} \right\}$$

$$TL_{24} = 20$$

A 20 is therefore recorded in the left-pointing flag below Node 24.

It will be noted that the maximum choice made for the early event time, *TE*, is the same choice that was made during the forward pass computation when the early start date, *ESD*, of the activity was determined. Similarly, the minimum choice made for the late event time, *TL*, is the same as that made during the backward pass computations when the late finish date, *LFD*, was established.

Only the two activity times above are thus directly related to the event times. The other two, the EFD_{ij} and LSD_{ij}, must be found from the application of Equations 6.1 and 6.2, respectively.

6.8   FLOAT DERIVED FROM EVENT TIMES

Section 6.5 discussed the computation of float values from the early and late start dates of the activities. Four floats were defined and equations were derived from which these calculations could be made. The objective of this section is to derive equations for and to illustrate the calculation of these same float values from the early and late event times discussed in Section 6.7.

The total float represents the total time span available for performing the activity, less the activity duration. Equation 6.3 gives this value as

$$TF_{ij} = LFD_{ij} - EFD_{ij}$$

If the value for the EFD_{ij} from Equation 6.1 is substituted in the expression, it becomes

$$TF_{ij} = LFD_{ij} - (ESD_{ij} + T_{ij})$$

Substituting the identities for ESD_{ij} and LFD_{ij} from Equations 6.8 and 6.9 results in

$$TF_{ij} = TL_j - TE_i - T_{ij} \qquad (6.12)$$

This equation is illustrated graphically in Figure 6.5.

The identity of Equation 6.8 allows one to obtain the early event time, TE, values from the early start date, ESD, values in Table 6.3 when the i column is

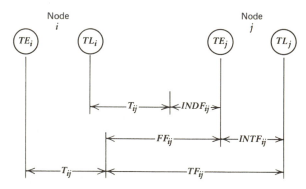

Figure 6.5   Float relationships in event time notation.

used as the reference for the index. Thus, the value of TE_4 is found in the ESD column opposite Activities 4–6 and 4–8, each of which have a 4 in the i column; TE_6 is found opposite Activities 6–8 and 6–10, and so forth.

In a similar manner, the identity of Equation 6.9 allows for the identification of the late event time, TL, values from the late finish date, LFD, values in Table 6.3 when the j column is used as the index reference. Thus, the value of TL_8 is found in the LFD column opposite Activities 4–8 and 6–8, each having an 8 in the j column; TL_{10} is found opposite Activities 6–10 and 8–10, and so forth.

The following is an example of the computation of total float for Activity 2–20, using the TE values from either Table 6.3, or Figure 6.4, and Equation 6.12.

$$TF_{2-20} = TL_{20} - TE_2 - T_{2-20}$$
$$TF_{2-20} = 17 - 0 - 10 = 7$$

which is the same value found from previous computations.

The free float represents the leeway of an activity if all activities are started as soon as they can. Equation 6.4 states this as

$$FF_{ij} = ESD_{jk} - EFD_{ij}$$

Substituting the EFD_{ij} value from Equation 6.1 results in

$$FF_{ij} = ESD_{jk} - (ESD_{ij} + T_{ij})$$

Applying Equations 6.8 and 6.9 yields

$$FF_{ij} = TE_j - TE_i - T_{ij} \qquad (6.13)$$

Figure 6.5 supplies a graphical representation of this expression.

For a sample computation using Equation 6.13, consider the calculation of the free float for Activity 2–20.

$$FF_{2-20} = TE_{20} - TE_2 - T_{2-20}$$
$$FF_{2-20} = 14 - 0 - 10 = 4$$

which is again the same value as found earlier.

It has been shown previously that the interfering float is the difference between the total float and the free float. Equation 6.5 stated it as

$$INTF_{ij} = TF_{ij} - FF_{ij}$$

Performing the indicated subtraction using Equations 6.12 and 6.13 results in

$$
\begin{aligned}
TF_{ij} &= TL_j - TE_i - T_{ij} \\
-[FF_{ij} &= TE_j - TE_i - T_{ij}] \\
\hline
INTF_{ij} &= TL_j - TE_j
\end{aligned} \tag{6.14}
$$

An alternate expression for interfering float was given by Equation 6.6 as

$$
INTF_{ij} = LFD_{ij} - ESD_{jk}
$$

An application to this statement of the identities for *ESD* and *LFD* from Equations 6.8 and 6.9 finds

$$
INTF_{ij} = TL_j - TE_j \tag{6.14}
$$

which is the same as derived above. Figure 6.5 graphically shows this subtraction.

Consider the computation of this float value for Activity 2–20 using Equation 6.14:

$$
INTF_{2-20} = TL_{20} - TE_{20}
$$
$$
INTF_{2-20} = 17 - 14 = 3
$$

This is the value found in Table 6.3, as may have been anticipated.

The fourth float, independent float, also has early and late event time expressions which are derived in a fashion similar to that of the others. Equation 6.7 gave the following statement:

$$
INDF_{ij} = ESD_{jk} - LFD_{hi} - T_{ij}
$$

When the identities of Equations 6.8 and 6.9 are applied to this expression it becomes

$$
INDF_{ij} = TE_j - TL_i - T_{ij} \tag{6.15}
$$

An examination of Figure 6.5 will reveal that this float is a part of the free float. It will also be recalled that this float, unlike the others, can have a negative result from the equation. When this is the case, the value is automatically set to zero as no time span may be less than this amount.

A sample computation illustrates how the independent float is calculated. Consider Activity 2–20, which has been used before:

$$
INDF_{2-20} = TE_{20} - TL_2 - T_{2-20}
$$
$$
INDF_{2-20} = 14 - 0 - 10 = 4
$$

This is also the same figure that was found in Section 6.5.

In Section 6.5 it was pointed out that in an arrow network the independent float for an activity will not be correctly computed if that activity is preceded only by dummy activities. As was stated there, the correct value for the independent float in such a case may be calculated by ignoring the event at the tail of the real activity. The activity is then assumed to begin at one of the events from which the dummies burst. The particular event to be selected is the one having the maximum TL value. Equation 6.15 may then be applied and the correct value of the independent float will be found.

To illustrate this correction consider the calculation for the independent float for Activity 26–28. This is the only activity in the diagram of Figure 6.4, which is precede only by dummies, in this case by Dummy 24–26. Activity 26–28 may therefore be considered as originating at Event 24 and ending at Event 28, ignoring Event 26. Thus, by Equation 6.15,

$$INDF_{26-28} = TE_{28} - TL_{24} - T_{26-28}$$

$$INDF_{26-28} = 26 - 20 - 3 = 3$$

This is the same value as found in Section 6.5.

The four float values just discussed have not been shown on the diagram of Figure 6.4. The reader should make the remaining calculations and compare them with those tabulated in Table 6.3 to verify the validity of the above event time expressions.

6.9   FLOAT ALONG SIMPLE ACTIVITY CHAINS

In the early sections of this chapter, float was treated only in its relationship to the activity. Activities are arranged naturally in chains throughout the network, however, and there are float relationships that may be observed which apply to chains themselves.

A chain may be defined as two or more activities in series extending from one event node to another. It is called a simple chain if every intervening node has only one activity entering it and only one leaving it. When more than one activity enters or leaves an intervening node, the chain is said to be compounded or branched. In the project of Chapter 3, which is illustrated by Figure 6.4, Chain (24–26, 26–28) is the only simple chain in the network. The others have varying degrees of compounding and branching.

Zimmerman and Shaffer[6.3] define a simple chain as a series of activities wherein each activity in the series has the same total float and the head and tail nodes of the series must be critical nodes. By this definition, Chain 2–4, 4–5, 6–8, 8–10, 10–14, 14–22, and 22–24 is also a simple chain having a total float of one, even though there are a number of branches.

Chains that begin at the initial node and end at the terminal node of the network are called paths. In Figure 6.4 there are 45 such paths through the network, only one of which is the critical path.

It may seem to the reader that an easy way to find the critical path would be to systematically determine all the possible paths in the network and then select the one with the greatest time duration. It should be clear, however, that this procedure would become unwieldy for most purposes and would not provide sufficient information about individual activity interrelationships. Therefore this procedure is not followed except in some particular computer applications of the CPM method.[6.2]

Figure 6.6a represents a simple chain consisting of four activities, which has been removed from a larger network. This chain is shown to begin and end at Nodes 7 and 15, respectively, and in a sense, these nodes may be thought of as the i and j nodes of the chain. It may be anticipated that if between these nodes the chain is replaced by a virtual activity having a duration equal to the sum of the durations of the activities along the chain, the total and free float of the

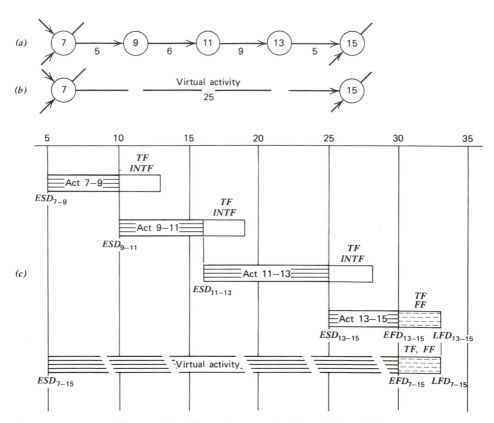

Figure 6.6   Float along a simple activity chain.

virtual activity will correspond to the total and free float for the chain. This virtual activity is shown in Figure 6.6b, and both the chain and the virtual activity are diagramed in bar chart form in Figure 6.6c.

It should be evident that because of the duration condition imposed, the EFD for the virtual activity would need to be the same as the EFD of the last activity in the chain, Activity 13–15. The LFD would, of course, be the same as the ESD of the activities following Node 15 whether either the virtual activity or the last activity of the chain were being considered. The application of Equation 6.3 to the virtual activity gives

$$TF_{7-15} = LFD_{7-15} - EFD_{7-15}$$
$$TF_{7-15} = 33 - 30 = 3$$

The same computation for the last activity, Activity 13–15, is

$$TF_{13-15} = LFD_{13-15} - EFD_{13-15}$$
$$TF_{13-15} = 33 - 30 = 3$$

which is an identical result.

In a similar manner the free float of the virtual activity and the last activity can be demonstrated to be identical.

In making float computations there is an implied assumption that each activity is to begin at its early start date. Also, because of the definition of a simple chain, the early start date for any activity in such a chain is set by the early finish date of the preceding activity.

Computation of the total float for each of the other activities in the chain from Nodes 7 to 15 yields a value equal to three days. The value of the free float will be zero for each one of these activities because of the implications above, and it will be observed that the interfering float for each is three days, as may have been anticipated. Notice that any slippage in completion of any activity in this simple chain, except the last activity, will cause all of the following activities to be delayed and the free float of the last activity to be used up.

It may be concluded then, that in simple chains the total float may be considered to belong to the chain itself, whereas the free float belongs to that activity which is last in the chain; and further, that all other activities along the chain will have interfering float of the same value as the total float of the last activity.

Compound chains cannot be said to have so clearly defined float relationships because the compounding activity or chain may alter the early or late finish dates of one of the chain's activities. Compound chains frequently may be considered merging or bursting simple chains, and the float values may be analyzed by applying the virtual activity concept used above.

REFERENCES

6.1   Moder, Joseph J. and Cecil R. Phillips, *Project Management with CPM and PERT*, Second Edition, Van Nostrand Reinhold Co., New York, 1970, p. 76.
6.2   Ponce-Campos, Guillermo, "Extensions to the Solutions of Deterministic and Probabilistic Project Network Models," Ph.D. Dissertation, The University of Michigan, Ann Arbor, 1972.
6.3   Zimmerman, Lawrence S. and L. R. Shaffer, *A Network Approach to Resource Scheduling*, Civil Engineering Construction Research Series, No. 10, University of Illinois, Urbana, June 1967.

EXERCISES

6.1   Set up a table and compute the early and late activity dates for the activities whose arrow network data is shown below. Compute the four float values from these activity dates and show them in the table. Star the critical activities.

i	j	Activity	T
2	4	A	2
4	6	B	6
4	8	C	3
6	8	D–1	0
6	12	E	1
8	10	K	5
10	12	D–2	0
10	14	F	7
12	14	G	4
14	16	H	5

6.2   Set up a table and compute the early and late activity dates for the activities whose arrow network data is shown below. Compute the four float values from these activity dates and show them in the table. Star the critical activities.

i	j	Activity	T	i	j	Activity	T
1	2	A	4	7	8	D–2	0
1	3	B	2	7	11	P	4
2	4	C	2	8	12	Q	6
2	5	E	2	9	14	R	4
3	5	F	5	10	13	S	3
3	6	G	4	11	15	T	5
3	9	H	9	12	14	D–3	0
4	7	K	3	12	15	D–4	0
5	8	D–1	0	13	14	U	1
5	9	L	7	13	16	V	6
6	9	M	4	14	16	W	7
6	10	N	2	15	16	X	1

6.3 The activities of the bus stop project of Exercise 1.3 have been arrow diagramed. The network data is given below. Set up a table and compute the early and late dates and the four floats for each activity. Star the critical activities.

i	j	Activity	T (days)
1	3	Cut curb	1
3	5	Excavation	2
5	7	Shelter slab	2
5	9	Curb and gutter	2
7	9	Dummy 1	0
7	13	Shelter walls	3
9	11	Dummy 2	0
9	21	Sidewalk	2
11	21	Paving	1
13	15	Roof beam	1/2
13	21	Lights	1
15	17	Shelter roof	2
17	19	Shelter seat	1
19	21	Paint	1

6.4 The activities of the small building project of Exercise 1.4 have been arrow diagramed. The network data is given below. Set up a table and compute the early and late dates and the four floats for each activity. Star the critical activities.

i	j	Activity	T (days)
1	3	Demolition	2
3	5	Foundations	3
3	7	Underground services	1
5	9	Exterior walls	6
5	11	Floor slab	3
7	15	Rough plumbing and heating	3
9	13	Interior walls	3
9	17	Roof steel	2
11	21	Rough carpentry	2
11	29	Floor finish	2
13	15	Dummy 1	0
13	19	Dummy 2	0
15	29	Finish plumbing and heating	4
17	19	Roof finish	2
19	25	Rough electrical	3
21	23	Finish carpentry	4
23	29	Display windows	1
25	27	Dummy 3	0
25	29	Finish electrical	3
27	29	Ceiling	3
29	31	Paint	3

6.5   From the data given in Exercise 6.1 draw the arrow network and compute the early
       and late event times on the diagram. From these event times compute the four float
       values for each activity and show them on the diagram. Indicate the critical path.

6.6   Solve Exercise 6.5 using the network data from Exercise 6.2.

6.7   Solve Exercise 6.5 using the network data from Exercise 6.3.

6.8   Solve Exercise 6.5 using the network data from Exercise 6.4.

6.9   Figure Ex. 6.1 represents an activity that has been removed from an arrow
       network. Compute the four float values for Activity X.

Figure Ex. 6.1

6.10   Figure Ex. 6.2 represents an activity that has been removed from an arrow
       network. Compute the four activity dates and the four float values for Activity Y.

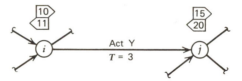

Figure Ex. 6.2

6.11   Figure Ex. 6.3 represents a portion of an arrow network. Compute the remaining
       total float, free float, and interfering float values for Activities G, H, K, L, M, N,
       P, R, S, T, and U.

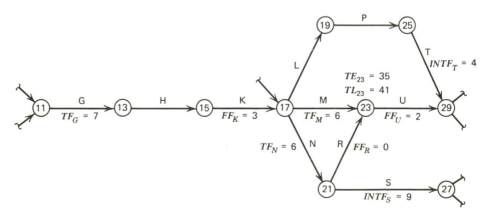

Figure Ex. 6.3

7

SCHEDULING COMPUTATIONS FOR PRECEDENCE NETWORKS

7.1 INTRODUCTION

It was pointed out in Chapter 1 that the scheduling of the activities in some time sequence is the second phase in the use of networking techniques. This implies that there be a systematic solution to the network which will yield information concerning the earliest and latest points in time that activities may have as well as the amount of leeway that each might posses. This is the kind of information needed to enable the planner to make those decisions that influence both the project and the overall operations of the company. This chapter develops mathematically based procedures that provide this information from the precedence diagraming model.

The computations reveal the total duration of the project and the early start and finish dates of each activity. Four different kinds of leeway, or float, are calculated, and the activities that established the project duration are identified. Finally, the late start and finish dates for every activity are obtained.

Three approaches are demonstrated for making these computations. A procedure for calculating the activity times and floats directly from tabulated data is given first. This method is useful in making manual computations for those projects which have only a few activities, and also provides the basis for programing the digital computer to furnish the same information for both small and large projects.

A second method shows the computation of the major values by using the precedence network diagram as the work sheet. This has many applications, especially where the planner wishes to compute a moderate sized network and does not wish to employ the computer. It serves very well for quick preliminary solutions which are often needed when extensive revisions that will be made before deciding upon the final network are anticipated.

The third method uses a matrix for displaying the data and for making the calculations. It is beneficial where the project is to be adjusted for time-cost tradeoffs or resource levels and the computations are to be carried out manually.

Although each of these methods has its own particular uses, the serious student of critical path methods will find that an examination of the variation in these procedures offers a greater depth of insight than can be obtained by the study of one method alone.

7.2   THE FOUR ACTIVITY DATES

There are four values along the time scale that every activity in a network can have. They are:

ESD—Early start date

EFD—Early finish date

LSD—Late start date

LFD—Late finish date.

All of them are not equally important. In the precedence networking technique the early start and finish times are the most useful. There are many instances, however, in which it is helpful to know when an activity must finish and when it must start to avoid delaying the completion of the work. For this reason all four values will be computed routinely in the following sections. It is left to the user to exercise judgment as to whether the late values are beneficial.

The early start date, *ESD*, for an activity is the earliest point in time that the activity can begin. This value must be established by the finish of at least one other preceding activity or it must be assigned if the activity is the first in the network. The late finish date, *LFD*, for an activity is the latest point in time that the activity must be completed if the project is not to be extended in time. This value is controlled by the latest that at least one of the following activities can start, with the exception that the late finish date of the last activity in the network must be assigned in some way.

A single activity extracted from a precedence diagram is shown in Figure 7.1. The activity is illustrated in Figure 7.1(a) where the number of the activity is identified by the letter *I*, and the duration of the activity is designated T_I.

From the definitions of the activity times above, the total time available to perform activity *I* must be the time difference between the LFD_I and the ESD_I. The activity is shown as a time scaled bar in Figure 7.1*b* in two possible positions within this time range—one at the earliest and one at the latest time location. Note that there is no time relationship directly linking the LSD_I and the EFD_I. The schedule that results when all activities of the network are positioned in the early start location is termed an *early start schedule*. Similarly, when every activity is in the late position, the resulting schedule is a *late finish schedule*. It should be clear that other scheduling possibilities can be formulated for the benefit of the user. They are discussed in later chapters.

In precedence networks four dependency relationships may exist between pairs of the activity time values calculated for any two successive activities. The start of an activity may be set by the finish of the preceding activity, a finish-to-start relationship or, in some cases, by the start of the preceding activity, a start-to-start tie. Similarly, the activity may have its finish time set by the start of the preceding activity, a start-to-finish association, or by the completion of the preceding activity, a finish-to-finish link. The relationship

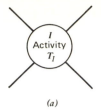

(a)

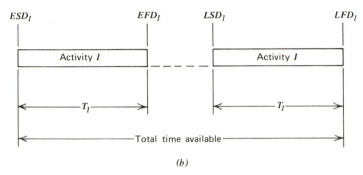

(b)

Figure 7.1   The four activity times—precedence diagram notation.

used in this chapter and most of the remainder of this text will be limited to the finish-to-start relationship. The basic principles to be developed will be applicable to the other three conditions with only minor modifications, and the reader is directed to references 7.1 and 7.4 and Chapter 13 for these extensions.

It was stated above that the initial activity must have its early start assigned. This value usually is zero but may be any other desired time if the schedule is to be coordinated with other projects in the organization or if the computations are being made for updating purposes. The early finish date of this beginning activity is found by adding its duration to the early start date. If the subscript 0 is used to denote the initial activity, these values may be put into equation form as follows:

$$ESD_0\text{—Assigned by the scheduler}$$
$$EFD_0 = ESD_0 + T_0 \tag{7.1}$$

The determination of the early start date for each of the other activities in the network depends upon the latest point in time that its preceding activities can finish. Figure 7.2a represents a portion of a network consisting of three activities —Activities 2, 4, and 6. In Figure 7.2b these same activities are shown in bar form. An examination of the figure will reveal that the ESD_6 is equal to the

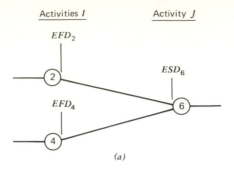

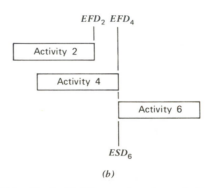

Figure 7.2   Early finish—early start relationships.

maximum of the EFD_2 and the EFD_4. As shown, EFD_4 is greater than EFD_2 and the ESD_6 is equal to the EFD_4. This choice of the maximum EFD value as the ESD of an activity may be expressed in a generalized equation as follows:

$$ESD_J = \underset{\forall I}{\text{Max}}\, EFD_I \qquad (7.2)$$

where the symbol $\underset{\forall I}{\text{Max}}$ implies that the maximization is to be over all links IJ terminating at activity J.

The early finish date for any activity, I, may be found by simply adding the activity duration, T_I, to the ESD_I or

$$EFD_I = ESD_I + T_I \qquad (7.3)$$

It also was stated earlier that the late finish date of the terminal activity in the network must have its value assigned. Usually this value is taken as the EFD, but in practice it may be given any desired assignment. This is often helpful when the network is assembled for a subproject that has a predetermined date set to assist in the coordination of other subprojects of the overall project. The late start date of the terminal activity is found by subtracting the activity's duration from the assigned LFD. When the subscript t denotes the terminal activity, the above values may be expressed as follows:

$$LFD_t\text{—Assigned, usually the } EFD_t$$
$$LSD_t = LFD_t - T_t \tag{7.4}$$

The late finish date for each of the other activities in the network is dependent upon the late start dates of its following activities. Figure 7.3a shows a part of a precedence diagram consisting of Activities 8, 10, and 12. In Figure 7.3b the same three activities are shown in time scaled bar form. It will be clear from the sketch that the LFD_8 is the minimum of the LSD values for Activities 10 and 12, and because the LSD_{12} is earlier in time than, or less than, the LSD_{10}, the LFD_8

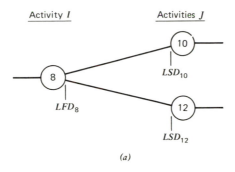

(a)

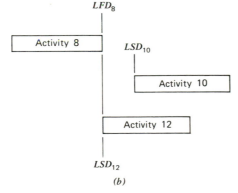

(b)

Figure 7.3   Late start—late finish relationships.

is equal to the LSD_{12}. The choice of the minimum value of the LSD to determine the LFD of any activity, I, may then be generalized by the following expression:

$$LFD_I = \operatorname*{Min}_{\forall J} LSD_J \tag{7.5}$$

where the symbol $\operatorname*{Min}_{\forall J}$ implies that the minimization is to be over all links IJ which begin at activity I.

The late start date for any activity, I, is taken as the difference between the LFD_I and the activity duration, T_I, or

$$LSD_I = LFD_I - T_I \tag{7.6}$$

7.3 LINK LAGS

It is traditional to perform scheduling computations for precedence networks by making forward and backward pass calculations as is done for arrow diagrams.[7.2,7.5] This procedure requires that schedulers have before them the diagram in order to determine the sequence of the activities. Furthermore, it was stated in the previous section that the late start and finish values frequently are not needed, especially for preliminary solutions. On the other hand, some of the floats may be desired to enable the planner to anticipate such things as probable delivery dates and labor and equipment demands. Traditionally, all the dates must be computed to provide these floats.

Procedures that can remove these restraints and are more efficient of computation time can be based upon the concept of lag associated with the "sequence line" as introduced by Fondahl.[7.2,7.3] All the methods to be presented in this chapter will be based upon these lags, and the sequence line will be referred to as a precedence link, or simply a link.

A link lag may be defined as the difference between the early start date of an activity and the early finish date of the preceding activity.

Figure 7.4 illustrates this concept for two activities, where the I and J refer to the activity numbers for any two successive activities in a precedence diagram.

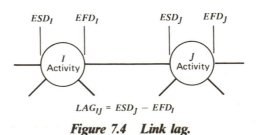

$$LAG_{IJ} = ESD_J - EFD_I$$

Figure 7.4   Link lag.

In equation form

$$LAG_{IJ} = ESD_J - EFD_I \tag{7.7}$$

There is a link lag, or as often stated, a lag, for every link in the network. As such, lag may be thought of as a property of the link and not the activity. The value of the lag may never be less than zero because under the finish-to-start assumption of the previous section the ESD_J may never be less than the EFD_I.

The values of these lags are the basic values to be computed and are used for the determination of the floats.

7.4   FREE FLOAT

It is customary to consider all the activities in the network as starting at their earliest possible time. This early start schedule will contain activities that may be completed at a time later than the early finish date and yet will not have any effect upon other activities in the network. This time period is the leeway that is called free float.

In a more formal definition,

free float is the time span in which the completion of an activity may occur and not delay the termination of the project nor delay the start of any following activity.

The boundaries of this time span are the earliest that any immediately following activity can start and the early finish date of the activity itself.

For any activity, I, that is linked to succeeding activities, J, the expression for free float, FF_I, may be written

$$FF_I = \operatorname*{Min}_{\forall J} ESD_J - EFD_I$$

where the symbol $\operatorname*{Min}_{\forall J}$ is interpreted to mean that the minimization is to be over all the links IJ that begin with activity I. For any activity, I, in an early start schedule, the EFD_I is a constant. This value may then be included in the minimization, thus

$$FF_I = \operatorname*{Min}_{\forall J} (ESD_J - EFD_I)$$

Substituting Equation 7.7 for the term in the brackets leads to

$$FF_I = \operatorname*{Min}_{\forall J} LAG_{IJ} \tag{7.8}$$

for all links IJ directly following activity I.

Because there are no links following the terminal activity, Equation 7.8 cannot apply and the free float for this activity must be treated as a special case.

The definition of free float above implies that one boundary of the free float time span is the early finish date of the activity. For the terminal activity the other boundary can be set as the latest that the project can finish, because by the same definition, the project must not be delayed. It may be recalled that in the discussion about the late finish times it was indicated that the late finish date for the terminal activity, LFD_t, was to be assigned by the scheduler. Therefore, the free float of the terminal activity may be taken as the difference between the two boundary values, the assigned LFD_t and the EFD_t.

Ordinarily, the value of the LFD_t is taken as being equal to the EFD_t, and the free float of the terminal activity, FF_t, becomes zero. As was the case with lag, the free float may never be less than zero in finish-to-start networks.

7.5 TOTAL FLOAT

The amount of leeway that an activity has after its duration is subtracted from the total time available for its performance is called the total float. More exactly,

the total float may be defined as the time span in which the completion of an activity may occur and not delay the termination of the project.

In Section 7.2 the late finish date was described as the latest point in time on which an activity can be completed without delaying the project. The early start date was similarly described as the earliest point in time that allows the activity to begin. Hence, the difference between these two values represents the total amount of time that is available to perform the activity. Figure 7.5 illustrates this difference for a generalized activity, I, shown as a time-scaled bar.

In Figure 7.5a the activity is shown in the early start position and it may be seen that when the activity duration, T_I, is taken from the total available time, the result is the total float, TF_I. It also may be seen that the activity may be terminated at any point between the EFD_I and the LFD_I. The following equation therefore can be written

$$TF_I = LFD_I - EFD_I \qquad (7.9)$$

Activity I is shown in the late finish position in Figure 7.5b. Again the activity duration, T_I, can be subtracted from the total time available and the remainder is the total float as before. In this case the expression for the total float may be written

$$TF_I = LSD_I - ESD_I \qquad (7.10)$$

It should also be evident that these two total float values are numerically equal, a fact that will become important when the late start and finish dates are to be computed.

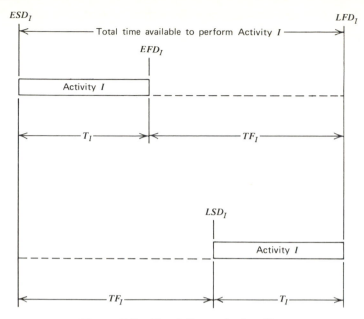

Figure 7.5   Total float relationships.

One of the advantages cited for the methods to be presented in this chapter is that the late start and finish dates are not needed for the computation of the total float. Instead, total float values may be calculated directly from the link lags found from the early start and finish dates. An expression for total float in terms of these lags must therefore be developed if this advantage is to be realized.

For any activity, I, the basic expression of Equation 7.9 may be used as the initial statement in such a derivation.

$$TF_I = LFD_I - EFD_I$$

Substituting the value of the LFD_I from Equation 7.5 gives

$$TF_I = \underset{\forall J}{\text{Min}} \, LSD_J - EFD_I$$

where the symbol $\underset{\forall J}{\text{Min}}$ is to be understood to imply that the minimization is to be over all links IJ which begin at activity I as before.

Equation 7.9 is written with the activity in the early start position; and for such early start schedules the value of the EFD_I is a constant for any activity, I, and it may be included in the minimization, thus

$$TF_I = \underset{\forall J}{\text{Min}} \, (LSD_J - EFD_I)$$

Now Equation 7.10 may be rearranged for activity J as

$$LSD_J = ESD_J + TF_J$$

Substituting this value gives

$$TF_I = \operatorname*{Min}_{\forall J}(ESD_J + TF_J - EFD_I)$$

Rearranging the expression and bracketing terms yields

$$TF_I = \operatorname*{Min}_{\forall J}((ESD_J - EFD_I) + TF_J)$$

Substituting from Equation 7.7 for the term in the inner brackets yields

$$TF_I = \operatorname*{Min}_{\forall J}(LAG_{IJ} + TF_J) \qquad\qquad (7.11)$$

for all links IJ directly following activity I. Note that the minimization is to be over the sum of the lag and the total float of the J activity, not merely the lag of the IJ link.

Equation 7.11 requires that there be a following activity having a total float, TF_J. Every activity in the network will have such a value except the terminal activity. The total float for this last activity must therefore be treated separately.

In the discussion concerning the late finish date it was stated that the LFD_t for the terminal activity was to be assigned by the scheduler. Hence, Equation 7.9 may be applied using the two values, the EFD_t and the assigned LFD_t, to obtain the total float of the terminal activity of the network.

Commonly, the LFD_t is taken to be equal to the EFD_t and the resulting total float becomes zero. Under this condition if the TF_I as computed from Equation 7.11 is zero, any slippage in completing activity I after it has been started at its earliest time would cause the project to have its terminal date delayed. Therefore, *when the total float of the last activity is zero, all other activities with total floats of zero are said to be critical activities.*

If the total float of the terminal activity is not zero, all activities in the network having total float values equal to that of the terminal activity are critical activities.

The chain, or chains, of critical activities that begin with the initial activity and end with the terminal activity is called the critical path. This path establishes the project duration.

7.6 INTERFERING FLOAT

Interfering float may be defined as the time span in which the completion of an activity may occur and not delay the termination of the project, but within which completion will delay the start of some following activity.

Its boundaries are the latest that the activity can be completed and the earliest that any following activity may start. An expression may then be written for the interfering float as follows:

$$INTF_I = LFD_I - \operatorname*{Min}_{\forall J} ESD_J$$

where the symbol $\operatorname*{Min}_{\forall J}$ is to be interpreted to imply that the minimization is to be over all links IJ which begin at activity I.

The value of the LFD_I from Equation 7.9 may be substituted to give

$$INTF_I = EFD_I + TF_I - \operatorname*{Min}_{\forall J} ESD_J$$

As with free float, in early start schedules the EFD_I is a constant for any activity, I, and may be included within the minimization. Thus,

$$INTF_I = TF_I - \operatorname*{Min}_{\forall J} (ESD_J - EFD_I)$$

The second term will be recognized as the free float from Equation 7.8; hence

$$INTF_I = TF_I - EF_I \tag{7.12}$$

Equation 7.12 allows for a simple and rapid determination of interfering float and will be used throughout the rest of this chapter.

7.7 INDEPENDENT FLOAT

The amount of leeway an activity can have and not be affected by the early or late starts and finishes of any of the other activities is termed *independent float*. For an activity to have this independent float, every task that follows it must be able to start as soon as possible and every activity that precedes it must be permitted to end as late as possible. These limits establish the boundaries of the minimum time span available to perform the activity.

Figure 7.6a represents a portion of a precedence diagram consisting of five activities. Activities 14 and 16 are to be considered the I activities and Activities 20 and 22 are to be the K activities. The independent float is to be derived for Activity 18, which is the J activity.

These same activities are drawn as time-scaled bars in Figure 7.6b, where the labels for the early starts of the K activities and the late finishes of the I activities are added. The figure shows the minimum time available for activity J established by the above boundaries. It should be clear that after the duration has been deducted the amount of time remaining in this time span will be the independent float.

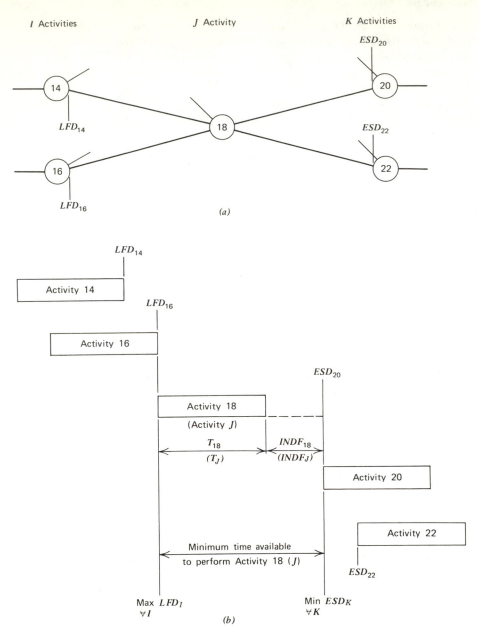

I Activities J Activity K Activities

Figure 7.6   Independent float relationships.

The definition of

   **independent float may be formalized as the time span in which the comple-
   tion of an activity may occur and not delay the termination of the project,
   not delay the start of any following activity, and not be delayed by any
   preceding activity.**

The mathematical expression summarizing the statements from the paragraphs above is

$$INDF_J = \operatorname*{Min}_{\forall K} ESD_K - \operatorname*{Max}_{\forall I} LFD_I - T_J$$

where I and K are subscripts relating to the activities preceding and following
activity J, respectively. The symbol $\operatorname*{Max}_{\forall I}$ implies that the maximization is to be
over all preceding activities I that form links with activity J, and the symbol
$\operatorname*{Min}_{\forall K}$ is understood to imply that the minimization is to be over all the activities
K that form links with activity J.

For the methods to be developed in this chapter, the late finish dates are not
obtained until after the floats are computed. The basic expression must therefore
be adjusted to allow for the direct computation of independent float from the
lag and float values previously obtained.

Equation 7.9 may be solved for the LFD_I and the result substituted into the
basic expression to obtain

$$INDF_J = \operatorname*{Min}_{\forall K} ESD_K - \operatorname*{Max}_{\forall I} (EFD_I + TF_I) - T_J$$

The EFD_J may be added to and subtracted from the first term and the ESD_J
may be added to and subtracted from the second term to obtain

$$INDF_J = \operatorname*{Min}_{\forall K} ESD_K + EFD_J - EFD_J - \operatorname*{Max}_{\forall I} (EFD_I + TF_I)$$
$$+ ESD_J - ESD_J - T_J$$

The value of the EFD_J and the ESD_J may be considered constant for any
activity, J, in early start schedules and therefore may be included within the
minimization or maximization. Hence, the above terms may be rearranged as
follows:

$$INDF_J = \operatorname*{Min}_{\forall K} (ESD_K - EFD_J) - \operatorname*{Max}_{\forall I} (TF_I - (ESD_J - EFD_I))$$
$$+ (EFD_J - ESD_J) - T_J$$

The terms $(ESD_K - EFD_J)$ and $(ESD_J - EFD_I)$ are LAG_{JK} and LAG_{IJ}, respectively, from Equation 7.7; also the term $(EFD_J - ESD_J)$ is equal to T_J from

Equation 7.3. Making these substitutions results in

$$INDF_J = \min_{\forall K} LAG_{JK} - \max_{\forall I} (TF_I - LAG_{IJ})$$

The application of Equation 7.8 to the first term gives

$$INDF_J = FF_J - \max_{\forall I} (TF_I - LAG_{IJ}) \qquad (7.13)$$

where the maximization is over all links IJ ending at activity J.

Because Equation 7.13 is based implicitly upon both early start and late finish dates it is possible that the minimum time span is insufficient for the performance of the activity. In this instance the value of the calculated independent float will become negative and because time may not be less than zero, the value is recorded as a zero.

It also should be clear from Equation 7.13 that if the free float for an activity is zero, the independent float will become negative. In this instance, independent float does not exist.

7.8   COMPUTATIONS FROM TABULAR DATA

Computations for activity times and floats in precedence networks may be carried out with satisfactory results in tabular form without reference to a diagram. When preliminary values are needed, this procedure may be superior because the time required to construct the diagram is eliminated. This method also has merit when the digital computer is to be employed. It has limitations, however, because projects with many activities may require a number of calculation sheets, and accuracy may be sacrificed when such extensive computations are necessary.

The method begins with a listing of the activities and their dependencies as presented in Chapter 4. Activity time durations are then added and the early start and finish dates are computed. From these values the lag for each network link is calculated. Float values are then determined from the lags, and finally, the late start and finish dates are obtained if needed.

Table 7.1 is an activity list for a sample project consisting of seven activities. This project will be used to demonstrate the steps in the application of the method and has been chosen because of its small size. The solution to the project of Chapter 4 will also be given for the reader's reference.

The data from Table 7.1 are arranged in a slightly different order in Table 7.2, where the activity's durations have been added. Note that the dependencies, or preactivities, have been listed on separate lines. Thus, the table shows every link in the network as well as the activities themselves. For example, the line under Activity B contains Activity 5 in the "Pre" column signifying the link between

TABLE 7.1

Activity List—Sample Precedence Network

No.	Activity	Depends upon
5	A	—
10	B	5
15	C	5
20	D	5
25	E	10, 15, 20
30	F	15, 20
35	G	25, 30

TABLE 7.2

Computation Input — Sample Precedence Network

Activity	T	Act (J)	Pre (I)	ESD	EFD	LAG	FF	TF	INTF	INDF	LSD	LFD
A	4	5										
B	8	10	5									
C	3	15	5									
D	2	20	5									
E	7	25	10 15 20									
F	5	30	15 20									
G	1	35	25 30									

Activities 10 and 5. Observe that the table has 17 lines, which is the sum of the number of activities in the network and the number of links between them. It also may be observed that the activities in the table are listed in sequence step order. This is done so that the computations to follow may be completed with ease and in the proper succession.

Determining the Early Start and Finish Dates

The computation of the early start and finish dates begins with the assignment of the initial time, or "time zero," to the first activity. For the example this has been chosen as the common value of zero which has been entered in Table 7.3 in the *ESD* column opposite Activity 5.

The *EFD* for Activity 5 has been computed by adding the duration time of 4 to the initial *ESD* of 0 in accord with Equation 7.1, and a 4 has been entered in the table in the *EFD* column opposite Activity 5.

TABLE7.3

Lag Determination—Sample Precedence Network

Activity	T	Assigned value Act (J)	Pre (I)	ESD	EFD	LAG	FF	TF	INTF	INDF	LSD	LFD
A	4	5		(0)	4							
B	8	10	5	4	12	0						
C	3	15	5	4	7	0						
D	2	20	5	4	6	0						
E	7	25	10 15 20	12	19	0 5 6						
F	5	30	15 20	7	12	0 1						
G	1	35	25 30	19	(20)	0 7						

Project duration

The second tabulated activity is considered next. Activity B, or Activity 10, is preceded by Activity 5 as shown. The value of the *ESD* for Activity 10 can be found by applying Equation 7.2. Because there is only one preceding activity, there is no choice for the maximization and the *EFD* of Activity 5 becomes the *ESD* of Activity 10, or 4 time units. An application of Equation 7.3 to Activity 10 results in the EFD_{10} being equal to 12 time units. Activities 15 and 20 have their *ESD* and *EFD* values calculated in the same manner.

Activity 25 will be seen to have three preceding activities. Equation 7.2 therefore requires that a choice be made of the maximum of the values for the EFD_{10}, EFD_{15}, and EFD_{20} (12, 7, and 6, respectively), and the *ESD* for Activity 25 becomes 12 time units. The remaining *ESD* and *EFD* values have been determined in the same fashion.

The early finish date of the last activity, calculated as 20 time units, is the project duration. This is because this value represents the greatest accumulated time along any continuous chain of activities beginning at the initial activity and ending at the terminal activity, and results from the repeated application of Equation 7.2. The project duration has been circled in Table 7.3.

Determining the Link Lags

The lag value for each network link is determined from the early start and finish dates just found. Lag values are computed from Equation 7.7 and are entered in Table 7.3 opposite the number of the Pre, or *I*, activity. Thus, the lag for link 5–10 has been computed as follows:

$$LAG_{5-10} = ESD_{10} - EFD_5$$
$$LAG_{5-10} = 4 - 4 = 0$$

and 0 has been entered opposite Activity 5 shown as the precedence to Activity 10. All other lag values have been calculated and entered in the table in a similar manner.

It should be clear that there must be a lag for every network link. In this case there are ten such values. Note that in every group of precedences related to each activity there is at least one zero lag. This is a necessary condition because every activity in the network must have its early start dependent upon the early finish of some preceding activity.

Determining the Free Floats

It was pointed out in the derivation of Equation 7.8 that the free float is the minimum lag of the links that follow an activity. To find the free float for any selected activity in the table, the Pre column is searched for that activity's number. The minimum of the lags opposite these numbers is then chosen and recorded opposite the activity.

In Table 7.4, Activity 5 was the first to be selected. In the Pre column there are three Activity 5 entries; that is, there are three links to which Activity 5 is the preactivity. For all three the lag is zero, hence, the free float for Activity 5 is zero and this value has been entered in the *FF* column opposite Activity 5. The free float of every other activity except the terminal activity has been calculated in a similar manner and the values have been recorded as shown. Note especially the determination of free float for Activity 20. There are two entries in the Pre column with lags of 6 and 1. The minimum value is 1, and thus, this has been listed as the free float opposite Activity 20.

The free float for Activity 35 cannot be found by Equation 7.8 because there are no links that follow this last activity. As was indicated in Section 7.4, the free float for the terminal activity may be determined from the difference between its late finish date and early finish date; also this procedure requires that the value

TABLE 7.4

Float Determination—Sample Precedence Network

Activity	Act T (K)	Pre (I)	ESD	EFD	LAG	FF	TF	INTF	INDF	LSD	LFD
* A	4 5		0	4		0	0	0	—		*
* B	8 10	5	4	12	0	0	0	0	—		*
C	3 15	5	4	7	0	0	5	5	—		
D	2 20	5	4	6	0	1	6	5	1		
* E	7 25	10 / 15 / 20	12	19	0 / 5 / 6	0	0	0	—		*
F	5 30	15 / 20	7	12	0 / 1	7	7	0	2		
* G	1 35	25 / 30	19	20	0 / 7	0	0	0	—		⃝20 *

Assigned value

of the *LFD*, be assigned even though the late start and finish dates are not to be computed.

As shown in Table 7.4, the value of the late finish date for Activity 35 has been chosen to be the value of the early finish date, or 20 time units. The free float was then computed as follows:

$$FF_{35} = LFD_{35} - EFD_{35}$$
$$FF_{35} = 20 - 20 = 0$$

and this value has been entered opposite Activity 35 in the table.

Determining the Total Floats

Total float is expressed by Equation 7.11 as the minimum of the sum of the lag and the total float at the *J* end of the link for all the links that follow an activity. These values may be obtained form the table with relative ease; however, because of this emphasis on the *J* end of the link, the terminal activity of the network must be the first activity considered in determining total float. The total float of this last activity must be established separately, as was discussed in Section 7.5. Whether or not the late start and finish dates are to be computed depends upon the assignment of the *LFD* of the terminal activity.

In the sample project, the late finish date of the terminal activity—Activity 35 —has been chosen as the same as the early finish date of that activity, as indicated on Table 7.4. The total float for Activity 35 was then computed from Equation 7.9 as follows:

$$TF_{35} = LFD_{35} - EFD_{35}$$
$$TF_{35} = 20 - 20 = 0$$

and 0 has been entered in Table 7.4 in the TF column opposite Activity 35.

The next activity to be considered was Activity 30. This number is found in the Pre column opposite Activity 35, indicating that a link exists between these two activities. Applying Equation 7.11, the total float for Activity 30 is the lag for link 30–35 plus the total float for Activity 35, thus,

$$TF_{30} = \text{Min}(LAG_{30-35} + TF_{35})$$
$$TF_{30} = \text{Min}(7 + 0) = 7$$

Of course, because there is only one link following Activity 30, there is no choice to be made for the minimization. This computed value of 7 time units has been entered in the table in the *TF* column opposite Activity 30.

The calculation of the total float for all the other activities was carried out in the same manner. Attention should be given to the computation of the value for

Activity 20, where there was a minimum choice, because there is more than one link following the activity. In this instance, the application of Equation 7.11 gave

$$TF_{20} = \text{Min} \left\{ \begin{array}{c} LAG_{20-25} + TF_{25} \\ LAG_{20-30} + TF_{30} \end{array} \right\}$$

$$TF_{20} = \text{Min} \left\{ \begin{array}{c} 6+0 \\ 1+7 \end{array} \right\} = 6$$

which is the recorded value. The numbers used in the above calculations have been indicated in Table 7.4.

Because the total float of the terminal activity—Activity 35—is zero, all the activities with total float values of zero are critical. Activities 5, 10, 25, and 35 meet this requirement and have been starred in Table 7.4. Note that these activities are the ones that determine the project duration of 20 time units and must therefore comprise the critical path for the network.

Determining the Interfering Floats

Equation 7.12 states that the interfering float is the difference between the total float and the free float. This equation has been applied to every activity to obtain the interfering float values tabulated.

Determining the Independent Floats

It was pointed out in the derivation of Equation 7.13 for independent float that if the free float is zero, there cannot be an independent float value. In the example in Table 7.4 there are only two activities that can have independent float under this stipulation, Activities 20 and 30.

Applying Equation 7.13 to Activity 20 gave the following:

$$INDF_{20} = FF_{20} - \text{Max}(TF_5 - LAG_{5-20})$$
$$INDF_{20} = 1 - (0 - 0) = 1$$

which has been entered in the table in the *INDF* column opposite Activity 20. The application of the equation to Activity 30 resulted in

$$INDF_{30} = FF_{30} - \text{Max} \left\{ \begin{array}{c} TF_{15} - LAG_{15-30} \\ TF_{20} - LAG_{20-30} \end{array} \right\}$$

$$INDF_{30} = 7 - \text{Max} \left\{ \begin{array}{c} 5-0 \\ 6-1 \end{array} \right\} = 2$$

Therefore this value of 2 time units has been entered in Table 7.4 opposite Activity 30.

Determining the Late Start and Finish Dates

After the float values have been computed, the late start and finish dates may be calculated by the application of Equations 7.9 and 7.10. Solving Equation 7.9 for the late finish date yields

$$LFD_I = EFD_I + TF_I$$

Similarly, solving Equation 7.10 for the late start date yields

$$LSD_I = ESD_I + TF_I$$

These two expressions have been applied to every activity in Table 7.5 and the values are tabulated under their respective columns and opposite the activity numbers.

TABLE 7.5

Late Date Determination—Sample Precedence Network

	Activity	T	Act Pre (J)	(I)	ESD	EFD	LAG	FF	TF	INTF	INDF	LSD	LFD	
*	A	4	5		0	4		0	0	0	—	0	4	*
*	B	8	10		4	12		0	0	0	—	4	12	*
				5			0							
	C	3	15		4	7		0	5	5	—	9	12	
				5			0							
	D	2	20		4	6		1	6	5	1	10	12	
				5			0							
*	E	7	25		12	19		0	0	0	—	12	19	*
				10			0							
				15			5							
				20			6							
	F	5	30		7	12		7	7	0	2	14	19	
				15			0							
				20			1							
*	G	1	35		19	20		0	0	0	—	19	20	*
				25			0							
				30			7							

TABLE 7.6

Schedule Computations — Remodeling Chemical Laboratory

	Activity Description	T	Act (J)	Pre (I)	ESD	EFD	LAG	FF	TF	INTF	INDF	LSD	LFD	
*	Contract award	0	5		0	0		0	0	0	—	0	0	*
	Obtain vinyl floor covering	5	10	5	0	5	0	21	21	0	21	21	26	
	Obtain cabinets	10	15	5	0	10	0	2	3	1	2	3	13	
	Strip room	3	20	5	0	3	0	0	1	1	—	1	4	
	Obtain fume hood	10	25	5	0	10	0	2	4	2	2	4	14	
	Obtain chemical sink	10	30	5	0	10	0	4	7	3	4	7	17	
*	Painter availability	20	35	5	0	20	0	0	0	0	—	0	20	*
	Replace existing fume duct	3	40	20	3	6	0	2	3	1	1	6	9	
	Rough-in plumbing and electrical	5	45	20	3	8	0	0	1	1	—	4	9	
	Repair walls and ceiling	4	50	40 45	8	12	2 0	0	1	1	—	9	13	
	Repair floor	1	55	45	8	9	0	3	4	1	2	12	13	

Activity							
(row above, cut off)			15, 50, 55		2, 0, 3	0, 2, 2	15
Install new fume hood	1	65	15, 50, 55	12, 13	2, 0, 3	0, 2, 2, —	14, 15
Install 1/3 base cabinets	1	70	15, 65	13, 14	2, 0, 3	0, 2, 2, —	15, 16
Install 2/3 base cabinets	2	75	70	14, 16	0	1, 2, 1, 0	16, 18
Install chemical sink	1	80	30, 70	14, 15	4, 0	2, 3, 1, 0	17, 18
Finish plumbing and electrical	2	85	60, 75, 80	17, 19	0, 1, 2	1, 1, 0, 0	18, 20
* Paint cabinets	6	90	35, 85	20, 26	0, 1	0, 0, 0, —	20, 26 *
Paint walls and ceiling	3	95	35, 85	20, 23	0, 1	3, 3, 0, 3	23, 26
* Lay vinyl floor	1	100	10, 90, 95	26, 27	21, 0, 3	0, 0, 0, —	26, 27 *

Summary

Table 7.5 represents the entire set of calculations for the sample project. This information would allow the planner either to schedule the project with early and late dates as shown or to use the float values to make other desired adjustments in order to smooth the flow of the work, to meet labor and equipment demands, and to control the progress of the work.

The above method of calculation does not depend upon the drawing of the precedence diagram when the sequence steps are determined in advance by the technique discussed in Chapter 4; yet it is complete. It is an easy and rapid procedure for manual computation and it can form the basis for computer programs for solving the precedence network.

Table 7.6 is a complete set of values for the project described in Chapter 4 which has been calculated by the above method. Readers may follow through this example to recall and reinforce the steps outlined in the previous paragraphs.

7.9 COMPUTATIONS ON THE DIAGRAM

The solution of precedence networks can be accomplished by making the computations directly on the network diagram. In those instances where the planner wishes to find the values of the project duration and the activity float but does not wish to make use of the computer this may be a superior procedure. It is economical of time, and with a small amount of instruction, almost any of the office staff may make the computations thus allowing the planner to concentrate on making decisions founded upon the results. It has a great deal of merit for the solution of preliminary networks where there may be some question about the best arrangement of the activities. If there are a number of these preliminary solutions to be computed, however, the tabular method should be used to avoid the repeated drawing of the diagram.

The method begins with the creation of the precedence network as was described in Chapter 4. Figure 7.7 shows such a network for the sample project used in this chapter. Note that the activity names are represented by the letters and the activity numbers have been entered above these letters. Below each activity name is found the duration of the activity.

The first step in the computations is the calculation of the early start and finish dates. This is accomplished by searching for the longest path through the network from the initial node to the terminal node with the imposed condition that every activity is to begin at its earliest possible time.

Figure 7.8 shows the calculations for the early dates. For every activity the early start date, *ESD*, is shown above and to the left of the circle containing the activity information. The early finish date, *EFD*, is similarly shown above and to the right of the circle.

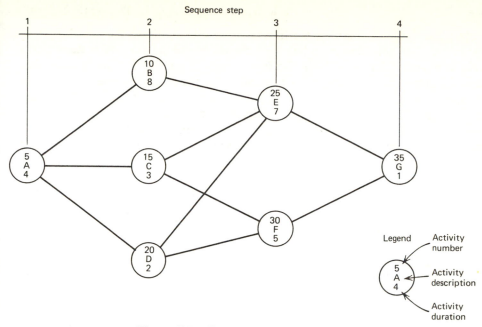

Figure 7.7   Sample precedence network.

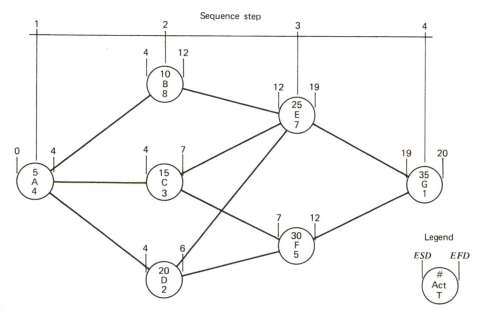

Figure 7.8   Early date determination—sample precedence network.

117

In making the calculations the first decision must concern the initial time, or "time zero." In this example it has been chosen as the most common value and a zero is recorded for the *ESD* of the first activity. Equation 7.1 has been applied and the duration of Activity 5 has been added to the ESD_5 to obtain an EFD_5 of 4 time units. The *ESD* of each of the following activities—Activities 10, 15, and 20—is the *EFD* of Activity 5 or 4. Again the activity durations are added to get the representative *EFD*'s. The reader will recognize that these values have resulted from the application of Equations 7.2 and 7.3. The maximization in Equation 7.2, of course, was not active because there was but one relationship to consider in each case.

When Equation 7.2 was applied for the determination of the *ESD* for Activity 25 the value was found to be 12 time units having been chosen from the maximum of the three preceding *EFD*'s, 6, 7, and 12. In a similar manner the *ESD* of Activity 30 was found to be 7 time units.

The calculations continue activity by activity through the network, and when the terminal activity is reached, its *EFD* marks the project duration. In this project it is 20 time units.

In this method, the second major step in the computations is the calculation of the link lags. This may be done readily by examining the *ESD* and *EFD* values at each end of every link. Equation 7.7 states that the difference in these values is the lag for that link. Figure 7.9 contains the values of the lags for the links of the sample network. Note that when the lag has a value of zero, the link line has been doubled to provide visual emphasis.

Because every activity in the network must be preceded by some other activity that sets its early start date, there must be at least one zero-lag link entering every activity. The only exception to this is the first activity where the *ESD* was assigned. The collection of such zero-lag links is termed the *early start tree* because these lags have been determined from the early start values. The longest path through the network therefore must be the path, or paths, having a zero-lag link entering the terminal node. The critical path may then be easily determined by tracing the zero-lag links backward from the terminal node to the initial node. This has been done in Figure 7.9 and is shown there as a triple line.

The third step in the solution of the network, using only the diagram, is to find the float values from the lags. These values represent the freedom of each activity for the operation of the project. They are shown in Figure 7.10.

The first float to be found is the free float. Equation 7.8 states that this is the minimum value of the lags on the links which exit from the activity. Thus, the free float for Activity 5 is zero because all the links immediately following this activity have zero lags. Activity 10 likewise has a zero free float. Activity 15 has two links to following activities, one with a lag of five and the other with a lag of zero. The smaller of the two became the free float for Activity 15. In a similar manner, Activity 20 has a free float of one. The free float for each of the activities in the network has been found in the same way with the exception of

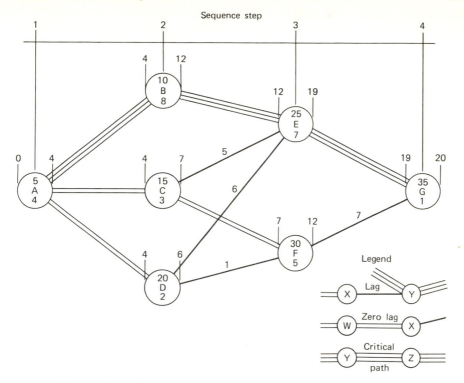

Figure 7.9   Lag determination—sample precedence network.

the free float of the terminal activity. In this instance, there is no following link and the free float is taken to be the difference between the *EFD* of the terminal activity and some assigned value of its late finish date, *LFD*, as was explained in Section 7.4. In most cases this late finish value is the same as the early finish and the free float is zero.

As with the free float of the terminal activity, the total float for the same activity depends upon the same assignment or the difference between the late finish date and the early finish date. In the sample project of Figure 7.10 this is zero.

Total float values for each activity are calculated by starting at the terminal node and stepping backward through the network until the initial node is reached. Because the total float of the terminal node has been assigned as above, the next activity for consideration is Activity 30. Equation 7.11 indicates that this total float may be found by taking the lag for link 30–35 and adding the value of the total float at the *J* end of the link. Thus the total float for Activity 30 is 7 time units.

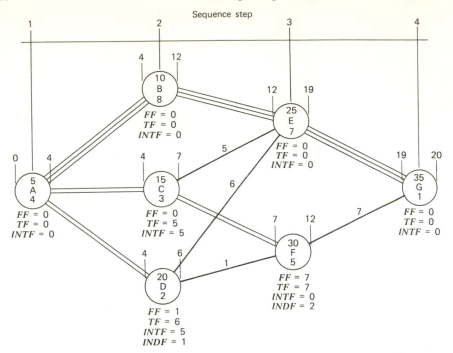

Figure 7.10   Float determination—sample precedence network.

Once the free float and the total float for each activity have been determined the intefering float values may be found by the application of Equation 7.12. It may be noted that in the example only two activities have interfering floats greater than zero; these are Activities 15 and 20. In each case the value is 5 time units.

It will be recalled that in the determination of Equation 7.13 for the independent float it was stated that if the free float is zero, there cannot be an independent float value. In the example in Figure 7.10 there are only two activities that can have independent float values; these are Activities 20 and 30. When Equation 7.13 was solved for the independent float for these two activities the results were 1 and 2, respectively.

The last step in this method is to determine the late start and finish dates for every activity. A rearrangement of Equation 7.9 yields

$$LFD_I = EFD_I + TF_I$$

and a similar rearrangement of Equation 7.10 gives

$$LSD_I = ESD_I + TF_I$$

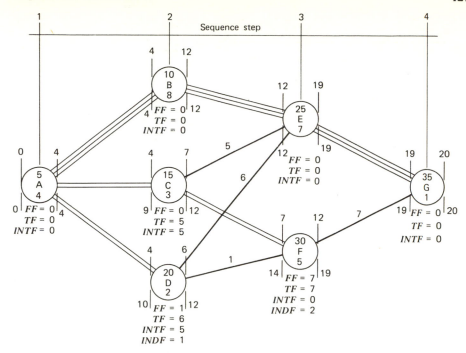

Figure 7.11   Late date determination—sample precedence network.

These two modified equations have been used to calculate the late start and finish dates and the values are shown on Figure 7.11. Note that the *LSD* value is shown below and to the left of the activity circle and the *LFD* value is shown below and to the right of the circle. Figure 7.11 represents the entire set of computations for the sample project and contains the same information as that given in Table 7.5.

Figure 7.12 represents the values for the project described in Chapter 4 calculated by the above method. The values of the interfering and independent floats and the late start and finish dates are not shown on this figure. The reader is encouraged to follow the steps outlined above to verify the given values and to compute the missing ones.

7.10   COMPUTATIONS ON A MATRIX

In using precedence networking techniques there are instances where the planner wishes to exceed the level of mere scheduling and expects to make adjustments for time-cost trade-offs, resource allocation, and leveling. These subsequent adjustments are facilitated if the initial computations are arranged in

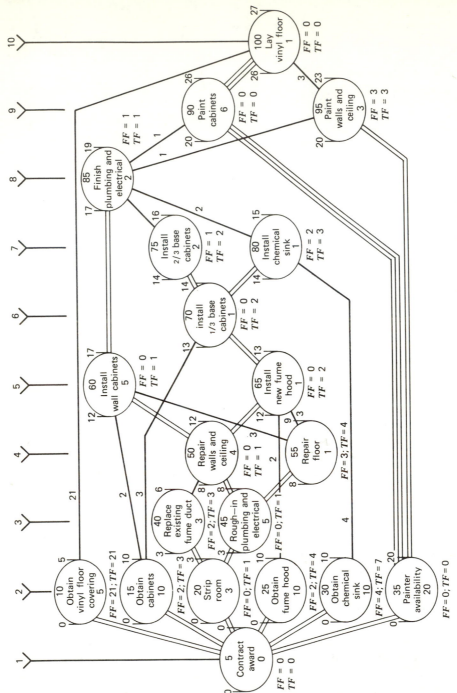

122

Figure 7.12 Precedence diagram—remodeling chemical laboratory.

such a way that the values of the activity dates and the link lags are readily observed and can be easily changed. These requirements can be met by creating a link matrix and making the computations directly upon it.

The method begins in the same manner as before: that is, an activity list must be created as is discussed in Chapter 2. This activity list for the sample project used in this chapter is shown in Table 7.1.

The construction of the link matrix, the second step, is illustrated in Figure 7.13 where each row in the matrix corresponds to an activity at the *I* end of the link and each column corresponds to an activity at the *J* end. By listing all activities in both the rows and columns all possible linkages between them are represented at the intersections of the rows and columns. Because the networks being considered are directional in nature as discussed in Chapter 4, only half of the total matrix is needed. To ensure that all possible entries may be expressed,

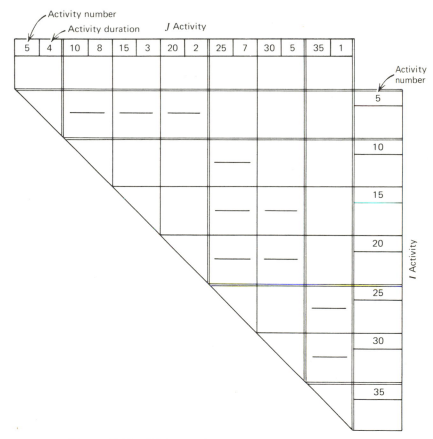

Figure 7.13   Link matrix—sample precedence network.

the activities in the rows and columns must be entered on the matrix in their sequence step order, but they may be listed in any order within the sequence step. Activity 15 may be interchanged with Activity 20 without difficulty, for example, but Activities 20 and 25 may not because they are on different steps. In addition to the individual activity numbers, the duration of each activity also is entered at the head of its J column.

Although each square in the matrix represents a possible linkage only certain ones are actually indicative of the links expressing the particular logic of the diagram. To identify these actual links a bar is placed across the link square. In Figure 7.13, for example, Activity 5 precedes Activities 10, 15, and 20, and bars are shown in the squares at the intersections in the Activity 5 row with the columns of Activities 10, 15, and 20

As with the other methods presented in Sections 7.8 and 7.9 for the calculations of the activity times and float values, the next step is to compute the early start and finish dates for each activity. The first activity, Activity 5, must have its early start date, ESD, assigned. In the sample problem this has been chosen as zero, and this value has been entered on the matrix below the activity number in the first column in Figure 7.14. In accord with Equation 7.1 the value of the early finish date, EFD, for Activity 5 has been found by adding the duration to the ESD just decided upon. The resulting 4 has been placed beneath the activity number at the right of the row.

In general, the ESD of an activity is determined by going down the column beneath the activity number until a bar is found in a square, thus signifying an actual link to the row activity. The ESD sought is then the EFD of that row activity. The column activity duration is then added to the ESD and the resulting EFD is entered at the right of the row and beneath the activity with the same number as the column activity.

For the sample project the ESD of Activity 10 has been determined by going down its column to the square with the bar and then going across to the right of the row where Activity 5 is shown as having an EFD of 4. The EFD_5 is therefore the ESD_{10} and this value has been entered beneath Activity 10 at the head of the column. The EFD for Activity 10 was calculated by applying Equation 7.3 and the result has been placed beneath the activity's number at the right of the row. The process was continued in a similar manner for the other activities. Note that when the ESD of Activity 25 was found the EFD values of Activities 10, 15, and 20 all were considered and the maximum value selected.

Once the ESD and EFD values for each activity have been computed, the lags of the links can be determined with ease by using Equation 7.7. The lag for each actual link, represented by a square with a bar through it, is computed by taking the difference between the ESD at the head of the square's column and the EFD at the right end of the square's row. Thus, in Figure 7.15 the lag for link 5–10 is zero and is 5 for link 15–25, and these values have been placed above the bar in their respective link squares.

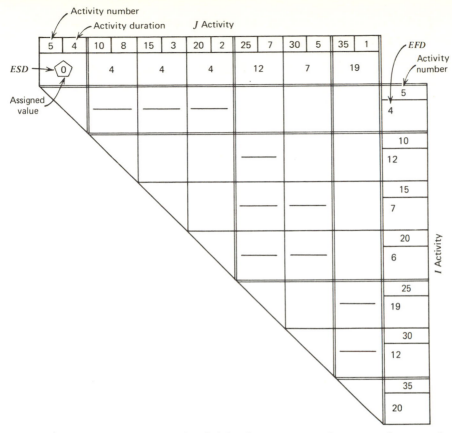

Figure 7.14 Early start, early finish date computation—sample precedence network.

Equation 7.8 states that the free float is the minimum of the lags following an activity. The free float of any activity, *I*, is found by entering the matrix at the right side and selecting the smallest link lag in the *I* row. These values have been identified and are shown to the left near the diagonal in the matrix of Figure 7.15. Note that the free float of Activity 35, the terminal activity, has been computed as the difference between the computed *EFD* of the activity and the assigned *LFD*, as was discussed in Section 7.4.

In Section 7.5 the total float for the last activity was shown to be determined by subtracting its computed *EFD* from the assigned *LFD*. It may be assumed that the assignment for the *LFD* of the last activity, Activity 35, was the same as its *EFD*, and that the computation resulted in a total float of zero for Activity 35. In Figure 7.16 this value has been entered on the matrix at the foot of the column headed by Activity 35.

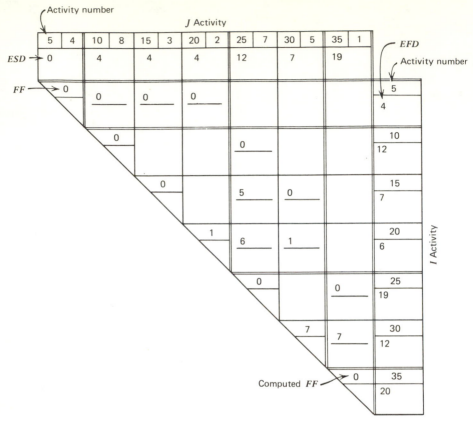

Figure 7.15   Free float computation—sample precedence network.

The total float of the other activities may be found by the application of Equation 7.11. In that equation the total float of the *J* activity is to be added to the lag of the link between the *I* and the *J* activities. The minimum value of this sum is then selected if there is more than one link following activity *I*. On the matrix, if the total float that is found at the foot of an activity's column is added to the lags in that column, the summation portion of the equation is satisfied. The minimization can then be found by selecting the smallest value in the row opposite the *I* activity.

In Figure 7.16 the previously computed total float for Activity 35 has been added to the lags in the link squares with the bars located in the Activity 35 column, and the result has been recorded in the lower part of the same squares. The total float of Activity 30 is then the value in the lower part of the square representing link 30–35. Because this is the only value to be considered, it is the true value of the total float for Activity 30 and has been recorded at the foot of

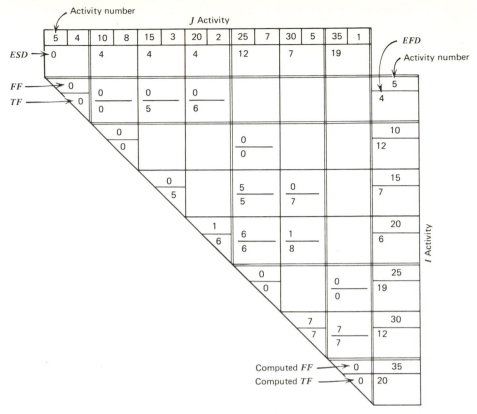

Figure 7.16   Total float computation—sample precedence network.

the Activity 30 column. Again, this float of 7 has been added to the lags in the Activity 30 column and the total float for Activity 25 was found. The process was continued up the rows of the matrix, activity by activity, until all the float values were calculated. Note that when the total float of Activity 20 was determined, it was the minimum of the values found in the lower parts of the link squares in the Activity 25 and 30 columns, or the value 6.

Interfering float may be found if desired by the application of Equation 7.12, and is the difference between the total float and the free float.

The above method is rapid and simple to use when manual computations are being made and provides the three most commonly needed floats as well as the early start and finish dates for every activity. There is a minimum of computation needed and the possibility of error is greatly reduced over the other procedures presented in this chapter. The method does not require the construction of the network diagram if the sequence steps are determined before the matrix is prepared by the technique discussed in Chapter 4.

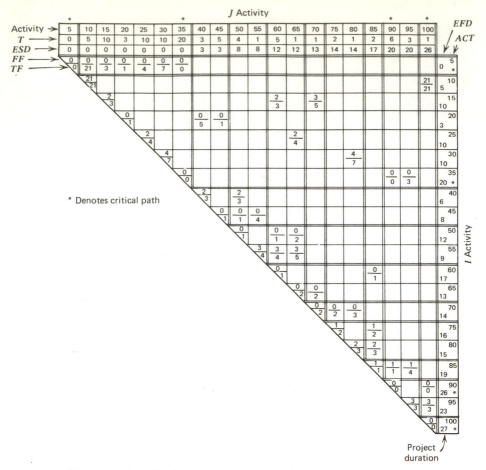

Figure 7.17   Matrix solution—remodeling chemical laboratory.

Figure 7.17 illustrates the solution to the network for the project presented in Chapter 4 when computed by the above method. The reader is encouraged to follow these computations through to verify the values shown.

REFERENCES

7.1   Anonymous, *Project Control System/360 (360A-CP-06X) Program Description and Operations Manual No. H20-0376-0*, IBM Corporation, White Plains, N.Y., 1967.

7.2   Fondahl, John W., *A Non-Computer Approach to the Critical Path Method for the Construction Industry*, Technical Report No. 9, The Construction Institute—Department of Civil Engineering, Stanford University, Stanford, Calif., 1961 (Second Edition, 1962).

7.3 Fondahl, John W., *Methods for Extending the Range of Non-Computer Critical Path Applications*, Technical Report No. 47, The Construction Institute—Department of Civil Engineering, Stanford University, Stanford, Calif., 1964.

7.4 Ponce-Campos, Guillermo, "Extensions to the Solutions of Deterministic and Probabilistic Project Network Models," Ph.D. Dissertation, The University of Michigan, Ann Arbor, 1972.

7.5 Priluck, Herbert M. and Peter M. Hourihan, *Practical CPM for Construction*, Robert Snow Means Co., Inc., Duxbury, Mass., 1968.

EXERCISES

7.1 Set up a table and compute the early start and early finish dates, the link lags, the four activity floats and the late start and late finish dates for the project whose relationships are given below. Do not draw the diagram. Identify the critical activities.

Activity	T	Depends Upon
A	4	—
B	2	A
C	2	A, B, F
D	6	C, L
E	6	D, G, H
F	1	A
G	1	F
H	2	G, L
K	5	A
L	3	F, K

7.2 Set up a table and compute the early start and early finish dates, the link lags, the four activity floats, and the late start and late finish dates for the project whose relationships are given below. Do not draw the diagram. Identify the critical activities.

Activity	T	Depends Upon	Activity	T	Depends Upon
A	3	B, D	L	5	—
B	8	F	M	3	P, W
C	4	A, D	N	6	L
D	4	F	P	2	S, U
E	5	A, D, R,	R	6	N
F	4	—	S	3	R, L
G	3	B, C, E	T	2	L
H	4	G, K	U	7	N, R, T
K	1	D, E	W	5	U

7.3   The activities of the bus stop project of Exercise 1.3 and their dependencies are
      given below. Set up a table and compute the early start and early finish dates, the
      link lags, the four activity floats, and the late start and late finish dates for the
      project. Do not draw the diagram. Identify the critical activities.

No.	Activity	T (Days)	Depends Upon
1.	Shelter slab	2	6
2.	Shelter walls	3	1
3.	Shelter roof	2	2, 4
4.	Roof beam	1/2	2
5.	Cut curb	1	—
6.	Excavation	2	5
7.	Curb and gutter	2	6
8.	Sidewalk	2	1, 6, 7
9.	Shelter seat	1	2, 3
10.	Lights	1	2
11.	Paint	1	2, 3, 9
12.	Paving	1	7

7.4   The activities of the small building project and their dependencies of Exercise 1.4
      are given below. Set up a table and compute the early start and early finish dates,
      the link lags, the four activity floats, and the late start and late finish dates for the
      project. Do not draw the diagram. Identify the critical activities.

No.	Activity	T (days)	Depends Upon
1.	Demolition	2	—
2.	Foundations	3	1
3.	Underground services	1	1
4.	Exterior walls	6	2
5.	Interior walls	3	4, 8
6.	Roof steel	2	4
7.	Roof finish	2	6
8.	Floor slab	3	2
9.	Floor finish	2	8
10.	Rough plumbing and heating	3	3
11.	Finish plumbing and heating	4	4, 5, 10
12.	Rough electrical	3	4, 5, 7
13.	Finish electrical	3	4, 5, 7, 12
14.	Rough carpentry	2	2, 8
15.	Finish carpentry	4	14
16.	Ceiling	3	6, 10, 12
17.	Display windows	1	14, 15
18.	Paint	3	4, 5, 9, 11 13, 15, 16, 17

7.5   From the data given in Exercise 7.1 draw the precedence diagram. On the diagram
       compute the early start and early finish dates, determine the link lags. Compute the
       four float values and the late start and late finish dates. Show all results on the
       diagram and indicate the critical path(s).
7.6   Solve Exercise 7.5 using the data from Exercise 7.2.
7.7   Solve Exercise 7.5 using the data from Exercise 7.3.
7.8   Solve Exercise 7.5 using the data from Exercise 7.4.
7.9   Use the precedence network data from Exercise 7.1 and compute on a link matrix
       the total and free floats for each activity.
7.10   Figure Ex. 7.1 represents a portion of a precedence diagram. From the data given
       compute the four float values for Activity E.
7.11   Figure Ex. 7.2 shows a precedence network of ten activities. Compute all the link
       lags and the total and free floats for the activities. Indicate the critical path.

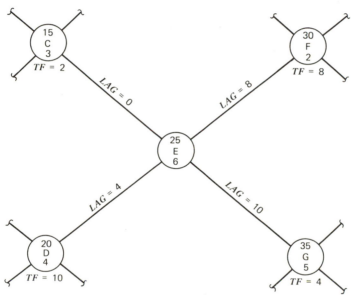

Figure Ex. 7.1

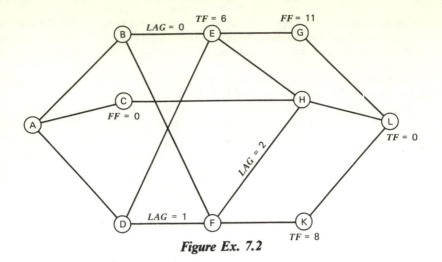

Figure Ex. 7.2

COMMUNICATING THE SCHEDULE

8.1 INTRODUCTION

In previous chapters it has been shown that a project can be planned and analyzed using either the arrow diagraming or precedence diagraming technique. Whichever is chosen, the computed start and finish dates and the activity floats must be communicated to the user before the technique can become a practical tool for performing and controlling the work.

The anticipated user plays a major role in determining the manner in which these results are transmitted. If the prospective recipient is to be upper-level management, there is no need for great detail and the presentation can be greatly simplified without any loss of effectiveness. An owner, architect, or engineer is primarily concerned with the total project and the progress of major groupings of activities. Middle management, on the other hand, is likely to be looking for detailed breakdowns covering a relatively long time span so that control of the work can be maintained at a satisfactory level. Superintendents and project engineers must plan for day-to-day utilization of human resources and equipment and should know what effects their decisions will have on the project. Detailed presentations are required by the foremen for their work, but they seldom will be required to know the extent of the schedule beyond a few weeks' duration.

Although those to whom the schedule is addressed set the level at which the results are presented, there are a number of communicating techniques and formats that may have distinct advantages. In some instances it may be sufficient to express the results verbally, whereas report or tabular forms may be called for in other cases. The basic CPM diagram and the modified bar chart are becoming widely accepted, whereas time-scaled diagrams are preferred by a few planners. Mechanical devices may be helpful in presenting the results under special conditions. These various procedures are discussed in the following sections of this chapter.

8.2 VERBAL AND WRITTEN INSTRUCTIONS AND RE-PORTS

Where a networking technique is used by a contractor with one or two employees or is applied to very small projects, the transmittal of the CPM results may be accomplished by giving verbal instructions. The scheduler may simply tell the employee which activities are to be done, together with the pertinent dates for each. This is the most direct manner for transmitting information, but is open to much misinterpretation on the part of the receiver. Verbal instructions must be repeated if they are to be understood. Furthermore, no record of them is available for future reference.

For most projects, large or small, foremen use verbal instructions when instructing their crews, and these are accepted as a sufficient technique for communication. Nevertheless, some form of written direction is usually desirable, and a list of activities and their scheduled dates should accompany these verbal directions. This procedure tends to decrease misunderstanding and provides a minimal record, but is not satisfactory if the instructions are complicated. When practical, written lists or diagrams provide an added advantage for improving the employees' rate of production.

It should be clear to the reader that the written report is closely associated with verbal communication. Reports have particular application and value for making preliminary information available to upper and middle levels of management because detail may be minimized. Reports that are accompanied by CPM diagrams or computer outputs which provide greater detail also benefit middle management.

Many report users agree that there is an advantage to there being a written record, but point out that some persons tend to discount the value of a report or ignore its results. One frequently cited disadvantage is the need to read extensively to obtain desired information. Another is that users must make their own interpretation of the contents. Many find difficulty in making correct interpretations because they may not be entirely familiar with the particular networking technique which governs the presented results.

8.3 TABULAR FORMATS

Tabular formats are among the most popular communications techniques used by CPM schedulers. They may take a wide variety of forms but they probably will differ little in content from Tables 6.3 and 7.6. Where the number of activities in the project is not great, these tables can be assembled manually. For more extensive projects the use of the digital computer will have a distinct advantage in both time and cost.

Probably the greatest advantage to using tabular formats is that the results can be easily displayed in a variety of orderings. One table may show the results with the activities arranged in sequence step order, another may show them in activity early start order, another in late finish order, another by total float, and so forth. When the application of resources in the project is a major concern, the tables may be arranged by craft divisions or by physical divisions of the project. Within these groupings the order may be presented in any or all of the ways suggested above.

There are many network-based scheduling systems that provide planners and schedulers with the above displays. Construction firms often rely on scheduling systems that are made available by computer manufacturers and that are readily recognized by their acronyms. For example, the Burroughs Corporation offers the PROMIS System for use with its computers; Honeywell, Inc. markets the PMCS/66 System; International Business Machines Corporation (IBM) makes available PMS/IV, PROJACS, JAS/3, and JAS/32; and the Sperry-Univac Division of Sperry Rand Corporation offers a system called MCS.

In addition to the software offered by computer vendors, some notable independent network systems are being used by construction companies. K&H Systems, an English firm, markets the PREMIS System. McDonnell Douglas Automatic Company (McAUTO), a subsidiary of McDonnell Douglas Corporation, is promoting the MSCS System, which was developed from IBM's PMS/I. Project Software and Development, Inc., offers PROJECT/2. Another example is the TRACE System of Project Management Associates, Inc., [8.1] which evolved from IBM's PCS System. In the rest of this chapter, the TRACE System is used as an introduction to the kind of output format available to schedulers.

Table 8.1 is a computer printed table produced by the TRACE System of Project Management Associates, Inc.[8.1] It presents the schedule data for the remodeling of the chemical laboratory used in Chapters 6 and 7. It is ordered by activity number and is intended for those interested in the total project. The main difference between this table and Table 7.6, which was computed by hand, is that the start and finish times are given by calendar date. Conversion from workdays to calendar days has been made automatically in the computer.

This same information is displayed in Table 8.2 but with the activities sorted according to groupings of procurement activities, architectural work, furnishings and equipment, and permanent mechanical and electrical work.

For field forces, Table 8.3 shows the data only by early start and finish date. The allowable delay corresponds to the free float and the maximum delay corresponds to the total float. The late start and finish dates are not given because their field use is minimal and their elimination reduces confusion for the field personnel. Table 8.4 again presents the data by groups for the field forces.

The TRACE System also produces a table of the activities with their immediate predecessor and successor activities. This report aids in evaluating the effect of changes on the network. It probably has its greatest utility for the scheduling office. One page of this network analysis report is reproduced as Table 8.5.

TABLE 8.1

SCHEDULE   220   REMODELING CHEMICAL LABORATORY

P M A'S **TRACE** SYSTEM FOR PROJECT MANAGEMENT

SCHEDULE REPORT   BY ACTIVITY CODE

		BASE DATE	27 SEP 76	DATA DATE	27 SEP 76
		FNSH DATE	2 NOV 76	CUTF DATE	30 JUL 76
				RUN DATE	4 JAN 77
		LOWR SPAN	27 SEP 76		
		UPPR SPAN	2 NOV 76	PERM	1

ID CODE ACTIVITY DESCRIPTION	DAYS LEFT	WORK WEEK	% COMP	START EARLY ( ) MEANS ACTUAL	START LATE ( ) MEANS ACTUAL	FINISH EARLY ( ) MEANS ACTUAL	FINISH LATE ( ) MEANS ACTUAL	TOTAL FLOAT	FREE FLOAT
5 CONTRACT AWARD	0.0	71	0	27SEP76	27SEP76	27SEP76	27SEP76	0.0	0.0
10 OBTAIN VINYL FLOOR COVERING	5.0	51	0	27SEP76	26OCT76	1OCT76	1NOV76	21.0	21.0
15 OBTAIN CABINETS	10.0	51	0	27SEP76	30SEP76	8OCT76	13OCT76	3.0	2.0
20 STRIP ROOM	3.0	51	0	27SEP76	28SEP76	29SEP76	30SEP76	1.0	0.0
25 OBTAIN FUME HOOD	10.0	51	0	27SEP76	1OCT76	8OCT76	14OCT76	4.0	2.0
30 OBTAIN CHEMICAL SINK	10.0	51	0	27SEP76	6OCT76	8OCT76	19OCT76	7.0	4.0
35 PAINTER AVAILABILITY	20.0	51	0	27SEP76	27SEP76	22OCT76	22OCT76	0.0	0.0
40 REPLACE EXISTING FUME DUCT	3.0	51	0	30SEP76	5OCT76	4OCT76	7OCT76	3.0	2.0
45 ROUGH IN PLUMBING & ELECTRICAL	5.0	51	0	30SEP76	1OCT76	6OCT76	7OCT76	1.0	0.0
50 REPAIR WALLS & CEILING	4.0	51	0	7OCT76	8OCT76	12OCT76	13OCT76	1.0	0.0
55 REPAIR FLOOR	1.0	51	0	7OCT76	13OCT76	7OCT76	13OCT76	4.0	3.0
60 INSTALL WALL CABINETS	5.0	51	0	13OCT76	14OCT76	19OCT76	20OCT76	1.0	0.0
65 INSTALL NEW FUME HOOD	1.0	51	0	13OCT76	15OCT76	13OCT76	15OCT76	2.0	0.0
70 INSTALL 1/3 BASE CABINETS	1.0	51	0	14OCT76	18OCT76	14OCT76	18OCT76	2.0	0.0
75 INSTALL 2/3 BASE CABINETS	2.0	51	0	15OCT76	19OCT76	18OCT76	20OCT76	2.0	1.0
80 INSTALL CHEMICAL SINK	1.0	51	0	15OCT76	20OCT76	15OCT76	20OCT76	3.0	2.0
85 FINISH PLUMBING & ELECTRICAL	2.0	51	0	20OCT76	21OCT76	21OCT76	22OCT76	1.0	1.0
90 PAINT CABINETS	6.0	51	0	25OCT76	25OCT76	1NOV76	1NOV76	0.0	0.0
95 PAINT WALLS & CEILING	3.0	51	0	25OCT76	28OCT76	27OCT76	1NOV76	3.0	3.0
100 LAY VINYL FLOOR	1.0	51	0	2NOV76	2NOV76	2NOV76	2NOV76	0.0	0.0

WORK WEEK = DAYS-PER-WEEK, START DAY, CALENDAR   S2 = SCHEDULED DATE, TYPE II
TOTAL FLOAT = MAXIMUM DAY DELAY   FREE FLOAT = ALLOWABLE DAY DELAY
TOTAL DURATION (CALENDAR DAYS) =   37

TABLE 8.2

SCHEDULE   220   REMODELING CHEMICAL LABORATORY

P M A' S   **TRACE**   SYSTEM   FOR   PROJECT   MANAGEMENT

SCHEDULE REPORT   BY EARLY START

BASE DATE 27 SEP 76   DATA DATE 27 SEP 76
FNSH DATE   2 NOV 76   CUTF DATE 30 JUL 76

LOWR SPAN 27 SEP 76   RUN DATE   4 JAN 77
UPPR SPAN   2 NOV 76   PERM   1

PROCUREMENT ACTIVITIES

ID CODE	ACTIVITY DESCRIPTION	DAYS LEFT	WORK WEEK	% COMP	START EARLY ( ) MEANS	LATE ACTUAL	FINISH EARLY ( ) MEANS	LATE ACTUAL	TOTAL FLOAT	FREE FLOAT
5	CONTRACT AWARD	0.0	71	0	27SEP76	27SEP76	27SEP76	27SEP76	0.0	0.0
10	OBTAIN VINYL FLOOR COVERING	5.0	51	0	27SEP76	26OCT76	1OCT76	1NOV76	21.0	21.0
15	OBTAIN CABINETS	10.0	51	0	27SEP76	30SEP76	8OCT76	13OCT76	3.0	2.0
25	OBTAIN FUME HOOD	10.0	51	0	27SEP76	1OCT76	8OCT76	14OCT76	4.0	2.0
30	OBTAIN CHEMICAL SINK	10.0	51	0	27SEP76	6OCT76	8OCT76	19OCT76	7.0	4.0
35	PAINTER AVAILABILITY	20.0	51	0	27SEP76	27SEP76	22OCT76	22OCT76	0.0	0.0

ARCHITECTURAL WORK

ID CODE	ACTIVITY DESCRIPTION	DAYS LEFT	WORK WEEK	% COMP	START EARLY ( ) MEANS	LATE ACTUAL	FINISH EARLY ( ) MEANS	LATE ACTUAL	TOTAL FLOAT	FREE FLOAT
20	STRIP ROOM	3.0	51	0	27SEP76	28SEP76	29SEP76	30SEP76	1.0	0.0
50	REPAIR WALLS & CEILING	4.0	51	0	7OCT76	8OCT76	12OCT76	13OCT76	1.0	0.0
55	REPAIR FLOOR	1.0	51	0	7OCT76	13OCT76	7OCT76	13OCT76	4.0	3.0
90	PAINT CABINETS	6.0	51	0	25OCT76	25OCT76	1NOV76	1NOV76	0.0	0.0
95	PAINT WALLS & CEILING	3.0	51	0	25OCT76	28OCT76	27OCT76	1NOV76	3.0	3.0
100	LAY VINYL FLOOR	1.0	51	0	2NOV76	2NOV76	2NOV76	2NOV76	0.0	0.0

TABLE 8.2 (Continued)

FURNISHINGS/EQUIPMENT

ID CODE	ACTIVITY DESCRIPTION	DAYS LEFT	WORK WEEK	% COMP	START EARLY ( ) MEANS ACTUAL	START LATE	START ACTUAL	FINISH EARLY ( ) MEANS ACTUAL	FINISH LATE	FINISH ACTUAL	TOTAL FLOAT	FREE FLOAT
60	INSTALL WALL CABINETS	5.0	51	0	13OCT76	14OCT76		19OCT76	20OCT76		1.0	0.0
65	INSTALL NEW FUME HOOD	1.0	51	0	13OCT76	15OCT76		13OCT76	15OCT76		2.0	0.0
70	INSTALL 1/3 BASE CABINETS	1.0	51	0	14OCT76	18OCT76		14OCT76	18OCT76		2.0	0.0
75	INSTALL 2/3 BASE CABINETS	2.0	51	0	15OCT76	19OCT76		18OCT76	20OCT76		2.0	1.0
80	INSTALL CHEMICAL SINK	1.0	51	0	15OCT76	20OCT76		15OCT76	20OCT76		3.0	2.0

PERMANENT MECH & ELEC

ID CODE	ACTIVITY DESCRIPTION	DAYS LEFT	WORK WEEK	% COMP	START EARLY ( ) MEANS ACTUAL	START LATE	START ACTUAL	FINISH EARLY ( ) MEANS ACTUAL	FINISH LATE	FINISH ACTUAL	TOTAL FLOAT	FREE FLOAT
40	REPLACE EXISTING FUME DUCT	3.0	51	0	30SEP76	5OCT76		4OCT76	7OCT76		3.0	2.0
45	ROUGH IN PLUMBING & ELECTRICAL	5.0	51	0	30SEP76	1OCT76		6OCT76	7OCT76		1.0	0.0
85	FINISH PLUMBING & ELECTRICAL	2.0	51	0	20OCT76	21OCT76		21OCT76	22OCT76		1.0	1.0

WORK WEEK = DAYS-PER-WEEK, START DAY, CALENDAR   S2 = SCHEDULED DATE, TYPE II
TOTAL FLOAT = MAXIMUM DAY DELAY   FREE FLOAT = ALLOWABLE DAY DELAY
TOTAL DURATION (CALENDAR DAYS) = 37

TABLE 8.3

SCHEDULE 220 REMODELING CHEMICAL LABORATORY

P M A'S **TRACE** SYSTEM FOR PROJECT MANAGEMENT

WORKPLAN REPORT   BY EARLY START

				BASE DATE	27 SEP 76			
				FNSH DATE	2 NOV 76			
				LOWR SPAN	27 SEP 76			
				UPPR SPAN	2 NOV 76			
				DATA DATE	27 SEP 76			
				CUTF DATE	30 JUL 76			
				RUN DATE	4 JAN 77			

ACTIVITY	DESCRIPTION	DAYS LEFT	% COMP	EARLY START	EARLY FINISH	ALLOWABLE DAY-DELAY	MAXIMUM DAY-DELAY	REMARKS
5	CONTRACT AWARD	0	0	27SEP76	27SEP76	0	0	
10	OBTAIN VINYL FLOOR COVERING	5	0	27SEP76	1OCT76	21	21	
15	OBTAIN CABINETS	10	0	27SEP76	8OCT76	2	3	
20	STRIP ROOM	3	0	27SEP76	29SEP76	0	1	
25	OBTAIN FUME HOOD	10	0	27SEP76	8OCT76	2	4	
30	OBTAIN CHEMICAL SINK	10	0	27SEP76	8OCT76	4	7	
35	PAINTER AVAILABILITY	20	0	27SEP76	22OCT76	0	0	
40	REPLACE EXISTING FUME DUCT	3	0	30SEP76	4OCT76	2	3	
45	ROUGH IN PLUMBING & ELECTRICAL	5	0	30SEP76	6OCT76	0	1	
50	REPAIR WALLS & CEILING	4	0	7OCT76	12OCT76	0	1	
55	REPAIR FLOOR	1	0	7OCT76	7OCT76	3	4	
60	INSTALL WALL CABINETS	5	0	13OCT76	19OCT76	0	1	
65	INSTALL NEW FUME HOOD	1	0	13OCT76	13OCT76	0	2	
70	INSTALL 1/3 BASE CABINETS	1	0	14OCT76	14OCT76	0	2	
75	INSTALL 2/3 BASE CABINETS	2	0	15OCT76	18OCT76	1	2	
80	INSTALL CHEMICAL SINK	1	0	15OCT76	15OCT76	2	3	
85	FINISH PLUMBING & ELECTRICAL	2	0	20OCT76	21OCT76	1	1	
90	PAINT CABINETS	6	0	25OCT76	1NOV76	0	0	
95	PAINT WALLS & CEILING	3	0	25OCT76	27OCT76	3	3	
100	LAY VINYL FLOOR	1	0	2NOV76	2NOV76	0	0	

ACTIVITY	DESCRIPTION	WORK DAYS	% CUMP	START ( ) MEANS ACTUAL	FINISH ( ) MEANS ACTUAL	FREE FLOAT	TOTAL FLOAT	REMARKS

TABLE 8.4

SCHEDULE   220   REMODELING CHEMICAL LABORATORY

P M A'S   **TRACE** SYSTEM FOR PROJECT MANAGEMENT

WORKPLAN REPORT   BY EARLY START

BASE DATE 27 SEP 76	DATA DATE 27 SEP 76
FNSH DATE 2 NOV 76	CUTF DATE 30 JUL 76
LOWR SPAN 27 SEP 76	RUN DATE 4 JAN 77
UPPR SPAN 2 NOV 76	PERM 1

PROCUREMENT ACTIVITIES

ACTIVITY	DESCRIPTION	DAYS LEFT	% COMP	EARLY START	EARLY FINISH	ALLOWABLE DAY-DELAY	MAXIMUM DAY-DELAY	REMARKS
5	CONTRACT AWARD	0	0	27SEP76	27SEP76	0	0	
10	OBTAIN VINYL FLOOR COVERING	5	0	27SEP76	1OCT76	21	21	
15	OBTAIN CABINETS	10	0	27SEP76	8OCT76	2	3	
25	OBTAIN FUME HOOD	10	0	27SEP76	8OCT76	2	4	
30	OBTAIN CHEMICAL SINK	10	0	27SEP76	8OCT76	4	7	
35	PAINTER AVAILABILITY	20	0	27SEP76	22OCT76	0	0	

ARCHITECTURAL WORK

LAST PROGRESS REPORT: 27SEP76

ACTIVITY	DESCRIPTION	WORK DAYS	% COMP	START ( ) MEANS ACTUAL	FINISH	FREE FLOAT	TOTAL FLOAT	REMARKS
20	STRIP ROOM	3	0	27SEP76	29SEP76	0	1	
50	REPAIR WALLS & CEILING	4	0	7OCT76	12OCT76	0	1	
55	REPAIR FLOOR	1	0	7OCT76	7OCT76	3	4	
90	PAINT CABINETS	6	0	25OCT76	1NOV76	0	0	
95	PAINT WALLS & CEILING	3	0	25OCT76	27OCT76	3	3	
100	LAY VINYL FLOOR	1	0	2NOV76	2NOV76	0	0	

TABLE 8.4 (Continued)

FURNISHINGS/EQUIPMENT

ACTIVITY	DESCRIPTION	DAYS LEFT	% COMP	EARLY START	EARLY FINISH	ALLOWABLE DAY-DELAY	MAXIMUM DAY-DELAY	REMARKS
60	INSTALL WALL CABINETS	5	0	13OCT76	19OCT76	0	1	
65	INSTALL NEW FUME HOOD	1	0	13OCT76	13OCT76	0	2	
70	INSTALL 1/3 BASE CABINETS	1	0	14OCT76	14OCT76	0	2	
75	INSTALL 2/3 BASE CABINETS	2	0	15OCT76	18OCT76	1	2	
80	INSTALL CHEMICAL SINK	1	0	15OCT76	15OCT76	2	3	

PERMANENT MECH & ELEC

ACTIVITY	DESCRIPTION	WORK DAYS	% COMP	START ( ) MEANS ACTUAL	FINISH ACTUAL	FREE FLOAT	TOTAL FLOAT	REMARKS
40	REPLACE EXISTING FUME DUCT	3	0	30SEP76	4OCT76	2	3	
45	ROUGH IN PLUMBING & ELECTRICAL	5	0	30SEP76	6OCT76	0	1	
85	FINISH PLUMBING & ELECTRICAL	2	0	20OCT76	21OCT76	1	1	

ACTIVITY	DESCRIPTION	DAYS LEFT	% COMP	EARLY START	EARLY FINISH	ALLOWABLE DAY-DELAY	MAXIMUM DAY-DELAY	REMARKS

141

TABLE 8.5

	BASE DATE	27 SEP 76	DATA DATE	27 SEP 76
	FNSH DATE	2 NOV 76	CUTF DATE	30 JUL 76
	LOWR SPAN	27 SEP 76	RUN DATE	31 DEC 76
	UPPR SPAN	2 NOV 76	PERM	1
			PAGE	1

PREDECESSOR ID CODE & DESCRIPTION / **ACTIVITY ID CODE & DESCRIPTION** / SUCCESSOR ID CODE & DESCRIPTION	LEAD TIME	LAG DAY	LAG DAYS LEFT	% COMP	START EARLY	START LATE	FINISH EARLY	FINISH LATE	TOTAL FLOAT	ORG LEVL 1	LEVL 2	LEVL 3	LEVL 4
5 CONTRACT AWARD	0	0	0	0	27SEP76	27SEP76	27SEP76	27SEP76	0	100			
10 OBTAIN VINYL FLOOR COVERING	0	0	5		27SEP76	26OCT76	27SEP76	26OCT76	21				
15 OBTAIN CABINETS	0	0	10		27SEP76	30SEP76	27SEP76	30SEP76	1				
20 STRIP ROOM	0	0	3		27SEP76	28SEP76	27SEP76	28SEP76	1				
25 OBTAIN FUME HOOD	0	0	10		27SEP76	1OCT76	27SEP76	1OCT76	4				
30 OBTAIN CHEMICAL SINK	0	0	10		27SEP76	6OCT76	27SEP76	6OCT76	7				
35 PAINTER AVAILABILITY	0	0	20		27SEP76	27SEP76	27SEP76	27SEP76	0				
10 OBTAIN VINYL FLOOR COVERING	0	0	5	0	27SEP76	26OCT76	27SEP76	1NOV76	0	100			
100 LAY VINYL FLOOR	0	21	1		2NOV76	2NOV76			21				
15 OBTAIN CABINETS	0	0	10	0	27SEP76	30SEP76	27SEP76	13OCT76	0	100			
60 INSTALL WALL CABINETS	0	2	5		13OCT76	14OCT76	8OCT76	13OCT76	3				
70 INSTALL 1/3 BASE CABINETS	0	3	1		14OCT76	18OCT76			1				
20 STRIP ROOM	0	0	0	0	27SEP76	28SEP76	27SEP76	29SEP76	0	900			
40 REPLACE EXISTING FUME DUCT	0	0	3		30SEP76	5OCT76	29SEP76	30SEP76	1				
45 ROUGH IN PLUMBING & ELECTRICAL	0	0	5		30SEP76	1OCT76			1				
25 OBTAIN FUME HOOD	0	0	0	0	27SEP76	27SEP76	27SEP76	8OCT76	0	100			
65 INSTALL NEW FUME HOOD	0	2	10		13OCT76	15OCT76	8OCT76	14OCT76	4				
			1						2				
30 OBTAIN CHEMICAL SINK	0	0	0	0	27SEP76	27SEP76	27SEP76	8OCT76	0	100			
80 INSTALL CHEMICAL SINK	0	4	10		15OCT76	20OCT76	8OCT76	19OCT76	7				
			1						3				
35 PAINTER AVAILABILITY	0	0	0	0	27SEP76	27SEP76	27SEP76	22OCT76	0	100			
90 PAINT CABINETS	0	0	20		25OCT76	25OCT76	22OCT76	22OCT76	0				
95 PAINT WALLS & CEILING	0	0	6		25OCT76	28OCT76			3				
			3										
40 REPLACE EXISTING FUME DUCT	0	0	3	0	30SEP76	5OCT76	29SEP76	4OCT76	1	1500			
50 REPAIR WALLS & CEILING	0	2	3		7OCT76	8OCT76	30SEP76	7OCT76	3				
			4						1				
45 ROUGH IN PLUMBING & ELECTRICAL	0	0	3	0	30SEP76	1OCT76	29SEP76	6OCT76	1	1500			
50 REPAIR WALLS & CEILING	0	0	5		7OCT76	8OCT76	30SEP76	7OCT76	1				
55 REPAIR FLOOR	0	0	4		7OCT76	13OCT76			4				
			1										

For the upper levels of management and those in the middle-management range who are completely familiar with the CPM technique, the use of tables may be quite satisfactory. This is not a successful way to acquaint most personnel at working levels with the project schedule, however. A foreman confronted with a stack of computer printout may often put it aside and proceed to do the work in any manner considered best. This action could lead to a costly mistake, the cause of which the foreman may assign to the demands of the "new system" rather than to the true cause.

8.4   GRAPHICAL PRESENTATIONS

There are three graphical schemes which are widely accepted and often used for the presentation of the CPM schedule, the annotated diagram, the bar chart, and the time-scaled diagram. Each has its characteristic role in transmitting the computed information to the various levels of management.

The Diagram

The CPM diagram, similar to Figures 6.4 or 7.12, may be employed to acquaint the user with the scheduled dates and floats. This procedure is quite satisfactory for office use because it allows the planner and his or her staff to see the scheduled values for the total project and the effect of any changes in the plan.

Diagrams do not provide the user with a sense of the time span in which the activity is to take place. Reliance must be placed in the computed values noted beside the activities. This may lead to an inaccuracy in interpretation, particularly when one chain of activities has considerably more items than another. The risk is that an activity which appears toward the right in the diagram may actually have earlier starting and finishing dates than an activity which appears to the left in the same diagram.

As with tabular formats, diagrams find the greatest utility for upper and middle levels of management where the technique is better understood. Diagrams are not as satisfactory where supervisors and the employees under their direction are involved. These persons find that the diagrams appear exceptionally complex and confusing and they may refuse to pay attention to the details found there.

The Bar Chart

Probably the bar chart type of presentation has the most universal communicating value for transmitting CPM results. To the upper levels of management, the bars can be overlapped to represent the various groupings of activities assembled from the basic diagram. A detailed activity-by-activity bar chart serves very well as the transmitting agent to the middle management group. It provides a foundation for the preparation and analysis of human resources, equipment, and financial schedules. At the lower levels in the organization the bar chart is readily accepted because it looks familiar even though it may show additional information that has not appeared on previously used bar charts for other projects. Because of this common acceptability, the bar chart can provide for the maximum use of the CPM technique without risk of committing serious errors in interpretation.

A typical bar chart is shown in Figure 8.1. It has been drawn from the results of the arrow network computations made in Chapter 6 for the remodeling of the chemical laboratory. Note that the activities which comprise the critical path are shown at the top of the chart and the activities that have float, including the dummy activities, are placed beneath. In Figure 8.2 the results derived from the precedence method network computations are similarly shown. In the most easily read charts these activities are arranged in the early start date order or in sequence step order, depending upon whether the arrow or precedence technique is being used.

In both Figures 8.1 and 8.2 the activities are shown as shaded bars beginning at their early start date and ending at their early finish date. For each noncritical activity a dashed line extends from the early finish date to the late finish date and represents the total float of the activity. The free float is indicated by doubling the dashed line in the proper range and the independent float is shown by the crossed bars of the free float. The dashed line between the free float and the late finish date indicates the interfering float of the activity.

Figure 8.3 is a computer produced bar chart for the above project derived from the TRACE System. The letters C and I substitute for the activity durations and the letters F and T define the termination of the free and total float, respectively.

The same information is presented in the computer drawn bar chart of Figure 8.4. This plot has the look of a hand-drawn chart and also includes reference marks which relate one activity to another.

A major disadvantage in the bar chart representation of CPM results is that the relationship between the activities is not as apparent as it is on the original diagram. Even so, the advantages of acceptability and simplicity offset this lack in the majority of instances.

Time-Scaled Diagrams

Closely associated with the bar chart presentation is the time-scaled diagram. Many planners prefer this representation because it permits the inclusion of the interrelationships between the activities as well as their time values.

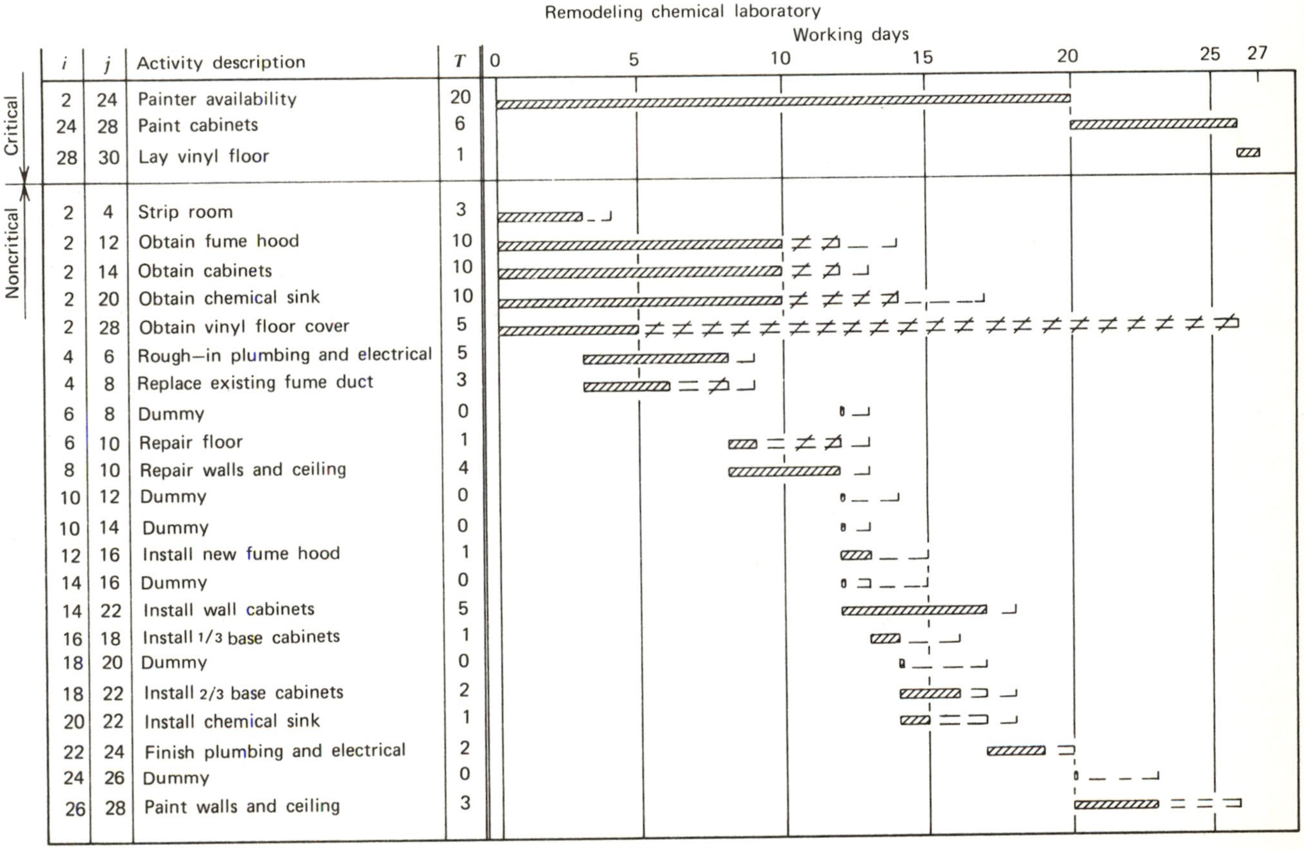

Remodeling chemical laboratory

Working days

i	j	Activity description	T
2	24	Painter availability	20
24	28	Paint cabinets	6
28	30	Lay vinyl floor	1
2	4	Strip room	3
2	12	Obtain fume hood	10
2	14	Obtain cabinets	10
2	20	Obtain chemical sink	10
2	28	Obtain vinyl floor cover	5
4	6	Rough–in plumbing and electrical	5
4	8	Replace existing fume duct	3
6	8	Dummy	0
6	10	Repair floor	1
8	10	Repair walls and ceiling	4
10	12	Dummy	0
10	14	Dummy	0
12	16	Install new fume hood	1
14	16	Dummy	0
14	22	Install wall cabinets	5
16	18	Install 1/3 base cabinets	1
18	20	Dummy	0
18	22	Install 2/3 base cabinets	2
20	22	Install chemical sink	1
22	24	Finish plumbing and electrical	2
24	26	Dummy	0
26	28	Paint walls and ceiling	3

Critical / Noncritical

Figure 8.1 Bar chart from arrow network computations.

145

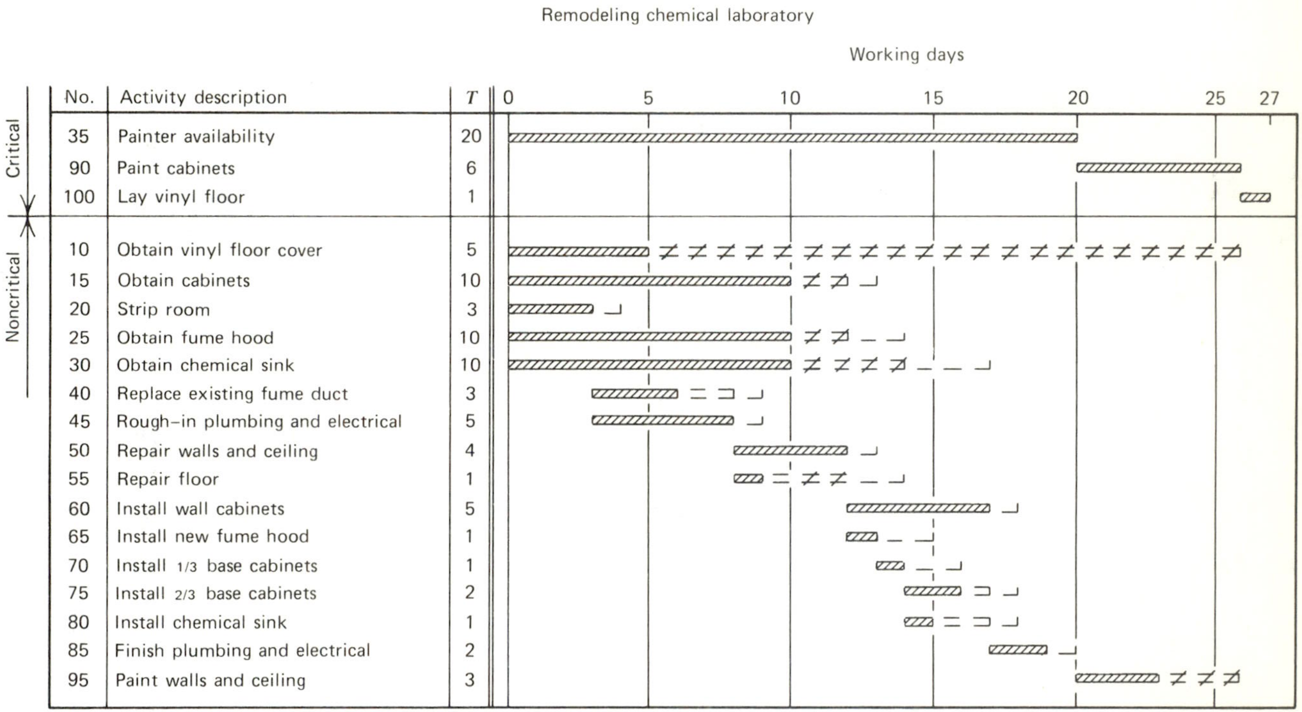

Remodeling chemical laboratory

Working days

	No.	Activity description	T
Critical	35	Painter availability	20
	90	Paint cabinets	6
	100	Lay vinyl floor	1
Noncritical	10	Obtain vinyl floor cover	5
	15	Obtain cabinets	10
	20	Strip room	3
	25	Obtain fume hood	10
	30	Obtain chemical sink	10
	40	Replace existing fume duct	3
	45	Rough-in plumbing and electrical	5
	50	Repair walls and ceiling	4
	55	Repair floor	1
	60	Install wall cabinets	5
	65	Install new fume hood	1
	70	Install 1/3 base cabinets	1
	75	Install 2/3 base cabinets	2
	80	Install chemical sink	1
	85	Finish plumbing and electrical	2
	95	Paint walls and ceiling	3

Figure 8.2 Bar chart from precedence network computations.

SCHEDULE   220   REMODELING CHEMICAL LABORATORY

P M A'S   TRACE   SYSTEM FOR PROJECT MANAGEMENT

DAILYBAR   BY EARLY START

	BASE DATE 27 SEP 76	DATA DATE 27 SEP 76
	FNSH DATE 2 NOV 76	CUTF DATE 30 JUL 76
	LOWR SPAN 27 SEP 76	RUN DATE 4 JAN 77
	UPPR SPAN 2 NOV 76	PERM 1

ACTIVITY	DESCRIPTION	DAYS LEFT	% COMP	MAX DELAY	MTWTFS 27SEP76	MTWTFS	MTWTFS 11OCT76	MTWTFS	MTWTFS 25OCT76	MTWTFS	MTWTFS 8NOV76
5	CONTRACT AWARD	0	0	0	D.						
10	OBTAIN VINYL FLOOR COVERING	5	0	21	DIIIII						
15	OBTAIN CABINETS	10	0	3	DIIIII	IIIII	.FT				
20	STRIP ROOM	3	0	1	DIIIT						
25	OBTAIN FUME HOOD	10	0	4	DIIIII	IIIII	. T				
30	OBTAIN CHEMICAL SINK	10	0	7	DIIIII	IIIII	. .T				
35	PAINTER AVAILABILITY	20	0	0	DCCCCC	CCCCC	CCCCC	CCCCC			
40	REPLACE EXISTING FUME DUCT	3	0	3	D. II	I T					
45	ROUGH IN PLUMBING & ELECTRICAL	5	0	1	D. II	IIIT					
50	REPAIR WALLS & CEILING	4	0	1	D.	II	III				
55	REPAIR FLOOR	1	0	4	D.	. I	.FT				
60	INSTALL WALL CABINETS	5	0	1	D.		. III	IIT			
65	INSTALL NEW FUME HOOD	1	0	2	D.		. II T				
70	INSTALL 1/3 BASE CABINETS	1	0	2	D.		. I T				
75	INSTALL 2/3 BASE CABINETS	2	0	2	D.		. I	IFT			
80	INSTALL CHEMICAL SINK	1	0	3	D.		. I	.FT			
85	FINISH PLUMBING & ELECTRICAL	2	0	1	D.		. IIF				
90	PAINT CABINETS	6	0	0	D.				CCCCC C		
95	PAINT WALLS & CEILING	3	0	3	D.				III F		
100	LAY VINYL FLOOR	1	0	0	D.				.C		

ACTIVITY	DESCRIPTION	DAYS LEFT	% COMP	TOTAL FLOAT	MTWTFS 27SEP76	MTWTFS	MTWTFS 11OCT76	MTWTFS	MTWTFS 25OCT76	MTWTFS	MTWTFS 8NOV76

X = COMPLETED DAYS OF WORK; I = REMAINING DAYS, NON-CRITICAL; C = REMAINING DAYS, CRITICAL; F = END OF FREE FLOAT (ALLOWABLE DELAY)

T = END OF TOTAL FLOAT (MAXIMUM DELAY); L = LATE START DATE (INDICATES SCHEDULE OVERRUN); D = DATA DATE (I.E. LAST PROGRESS REPORT)

Figure 8.3 TRACE daily bar chart.

147

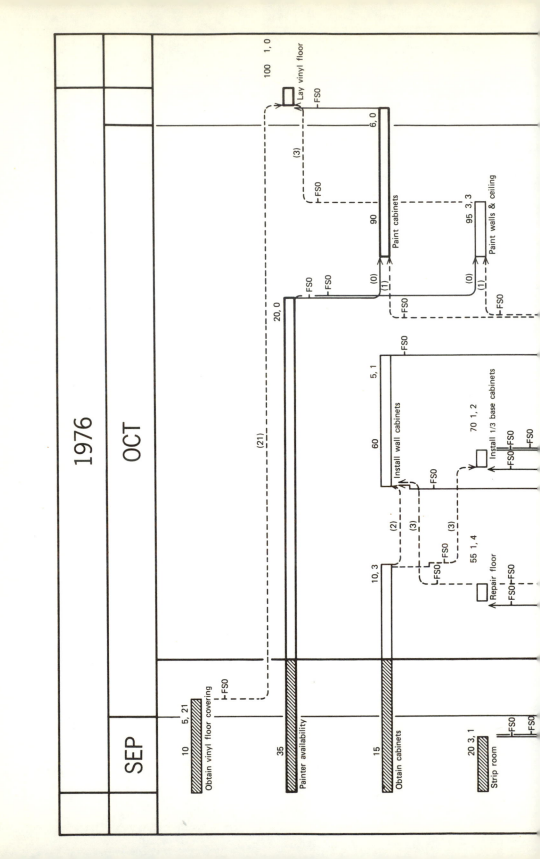

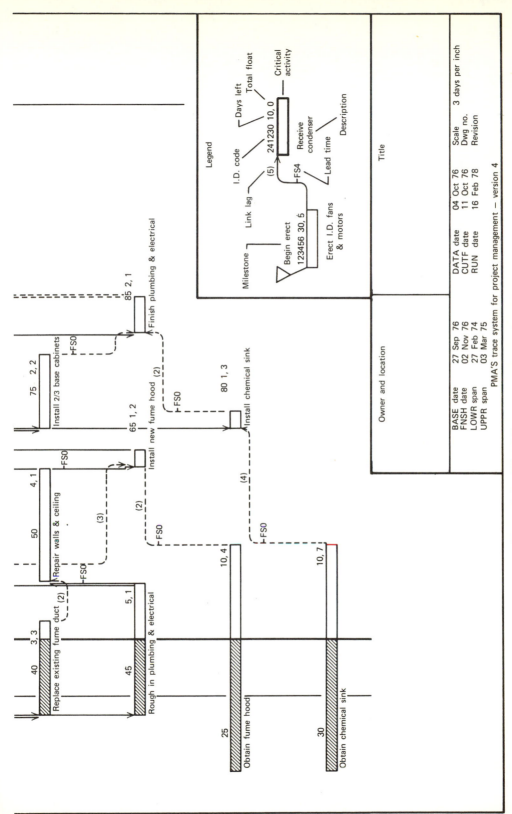

Figure 8.4 TRACE computer drawn bar chart.

149

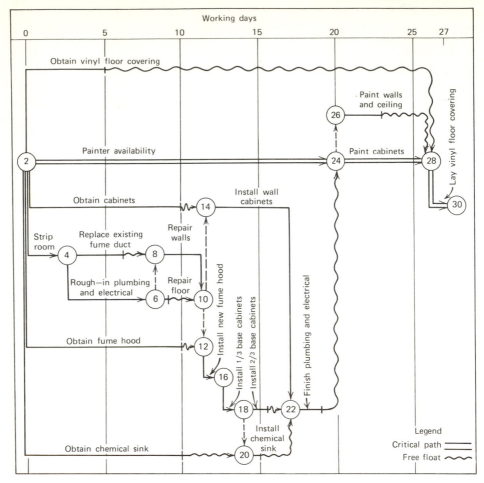

Figure 8.5   Time-scaled arrow diagram—remodeling chemical laboratory.

Figure 8.5 is a time-scaled arrow diagram for the remodeling of the chemical laboratory project used as the example. When the arrow diagraming technique is used, the arrows representing the activities can be placed along the time scale and the floats can be shown by the wavy lines as illustrated. The result is not much different than the bar chart shown in Figure 8.1.

When the precedence diagram is used, the time scaling can be accomplished by imagining that the balloons surrounding the activity descriptions are flattened until they take on the configuration of the bar. The connecting links can then be added and the floats indicated; this is shown in Figure 8.6.

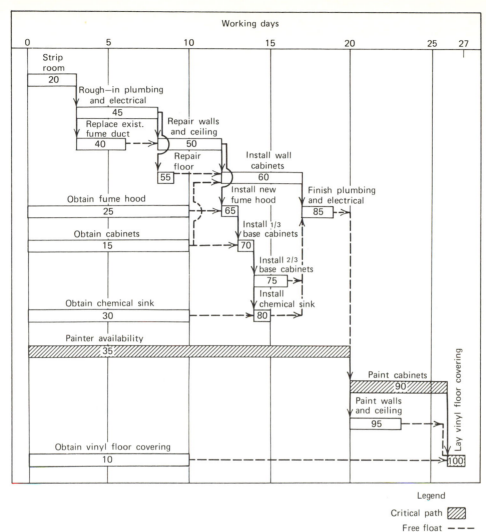

Figure 8.6   Time-scaled precedence diagram—remodeling chemical laboratory.

8.5   MECHANICAL DEVICES

There are a number of mechanical devices on the market that can be used to present the information derived from the CPM network computations. Most of these devices consist of a board upon which indicators of some kind can be inserted or attached. Some have large rolling sheets of Mylar or similar material upon which the information can be displayed. O'Brien[8.2] gives more complete descriptions of several of these devices.

Generally these devices are limited to a presentation function because it is often difficult, or at least slow, to prepare an initial schedule for them. Because they also are limited in size, only smaller projects or summary schedules can be displayed. Reproduction and distribution of the information is not easy except where photographic means may be employed. Because most of these devices are not portable, the range of communication to persons that need the information is restricted.

For the above reasons these devices have found little use in the construction industry. Their applicability seems to be in the office, where upper and middle management are involved with the schedule, and where they have access to the device.

REFERENCES

8.1 Anonymous, *TRACE User's Manual*, Project Management Associates, Inc., Ann Arbor, Michigan, 1975.

8.2 O'Brien, James J. (ed.), *Scheduling Handbook*, McGraw-Hill Book Co., New York, 1969.

EXERCISES

8.1 Construct a bar chart for the arrow network developed in Exercise 6.1. Use the following symbols for the floats: Total Float $---$; FreeFloat $===$; Independent Float $\neq\neq\neq$.

8.2 Construct a bar chart for the arrow network developed in Exercise 6.2. Use the following symbols for the floats: Total Float $---$; Free Float $===$; Independent Float $\neq\neq\neq$.

8.3 Construct a time-scaled arrow diagram to communicate the network of Exercise 6.2. Show only free floats.

8.4 Construct a time-scaled arrow diagram to communicate the network of Exercise 6.3. Show only free floats.

8.5 Construct a bar chart for the precedence network developed in Exercise 7.1. Use the following symbols for the floats: Total Float $---$; Free Float $===$; Independent Float $\neq\neq\neq$.

8.6 Construct a bar chart for the precedence network developed in Exercise 7.2. Use the following symbols for the floats: Total Float $---$; Free Float $===$; Independent Float $\neq\neq\neq$.

8.7 Construct a time-scaled precedence diagram to communicate the network of Exercise 7.2. Show only free floats.

8.8 Construct a time-scaled precedence diagram to communicate the network of Exercise 7.4. Show only free floats.

PROJECT CONTROL

9.1 INTRODUCTION

No project planned by the critical path method can be completed satisfactorily if only the planning and scheduling phases are performed. One additional phase needs to be carried out if there is to be a recognition of the dynamic nature of the construction process. Control, in a word, provides for this dynamic quality.

No system can reach its highest potential if it is allowed to proceed in an uninhibited manner; it must be controlled. Everyone is familiar with break-downs in control of a traffic system and the resulting chaos and delays. Uncontrolled water systems or electrical systems can bring destruction and a loss of the utility. A well-planned and scheduled construction system allowed to proceed without controls can lead to chaos, delays, and even to total abandonment of the system.

Essential control therefore demands a continuing application of critical path concepts and principles applied to a project to guide its execution. The control plan must insure that the project is performed economically, recognizing the limits of the schedule's deadlines and with attention paid to the resources available.

There are three major objectives that a good control plan should seek to accomplish. First and foremost, the plan should accurately represent the work and allow it to be carried out in a manner compatible with the designated construction plans and specifications. Second, the plan should permit deviations from the schedule to be detected, evaluated, and forecasted. And third, the plan should also make provision for periodic corrective actions to economically bring any remaining schedule into alignment with the proposed schedule.

In Section 1.7 it was pointed out that control includes both the monitoring and updating functions. Monitoring implies quality feedback from the project to identify what is happening, where the project is now, how it got there, and the prognosis for the future. Updating implies that there are to be revisions of a major consequence and that adjustments in the network will be necessary.

As with any system, control must be based upon some original concept or plan. There must be a "norm" against which changes can be measured. In this discussion the norm is designated as the target schedule.

9.2 LEVELS OF CONTROL

Project control plans have many variations. The particular scheme to be adopted will be influenced by factors such as the size and structure of the construction company, the past experience of the organization, the urgency of meeting the project duration, the demands of the owner or regulatory agency, and the size of the project. The most important of these for the contractor is the project size. Large projects naturally require greater control than do small ones. It seems desirable, therefore, to examine the levels of control demanded by various sized jobs.

For the small, low-cost, short duration project the minimum control plan needed is a detailed network and some kind of reporting mechanism, a two-level scheme. In these projects the duration can be considered a milestone date and the contractor develops the network and schedule to meet this milestone. The scheme is then used to prepare a day-by-day budget for the costs to be incurred during construction.

The reporting mechanism for small projects can be kept quite simple. The work can be evaluated for completion by the direct observation of the superintendent or the contractor. New cost information can be added or subtracted from the original costs and compared with the budget. Reports may be merely a bar chart with the completed work marked on it and a chart showing the cumulative costs of both the actual and budgeted expenditures.

Although this minimum may be satisfactory for the small project, additional networks and schedules may need to be prepared for the middle-sized one. A middle-sized project may be considered to have a few, probably not more than six, major milestones to be met. It will most likely be in the middle cost range for the contractor, and it may have up to 300 activities. The milestone dates are usually set at the time of contract signing and are determined by the contractor or by negotiation between the contractor and owner.

For such projects it frequently happens that, in addition to the usual detailed network, a summary network is prepared for advising the upper levels of the management team. This diagram is prepared by the project planning engineer with input from all responsible parties. The diagram's dates usually cannot be changed without the approval of the owner or his agent.

Occasionally a network must be drawn for a particular area of the project or for a single craft, such as carpenters or masons. These diagrams are semidetailed and are used by the project engineer and the construction manager to provide overall information to the lead engineers and construction craft supervisors.

The reporting function for both summary and craft networks for middle-sized projects requires a more formal feedback procedure than that for small networks. In addition to the overall graphical bar chart and the cumulative chart of costs, bar charts for each area and charts showing the targeted and actual utilization of the crafts may be required.

In large projects—those that have many milestones, take a long time to complete, and cost great sums of money—the levels of control become even more extensive. In most of these cases the contract is a negotiated one and may, in all probability, be of the cost plus a fee variety.

The first network to be drawn for these large projects is the milestone network. It is developed during the earliest stages of project development and is based upon the general scope of the work and on the constructor's experience on similar projects. The milestone network is finalized when the authorized date to proceed and the completion date are established. This network is usually incorporated into the project summary network at a later time. The milestone network and schedule are used by the project's construction manager when reporting the project status to the owner. The dates are fixed and are not altered except at the specific request of the owner.

The next level of control is the summary network and schedule described earlier for the middle-sized project. The third level almost always consists of area and craft networks and schedules. A fourth level consists of detailed networks and schedules prepared for engineering personnel and craft supervision. These detailed networks are created within the area or craft subdivisions and not for the project as a whole. They are typically prepared as the work progresses.

In the large project the reporting is very complete and is designed to reflect the conduct of each of the summary and detailed types of schedules. In addition, there will be reports produced for all the four types of resources being used: labor, equipment, material, and cost. Such reports will probably be in the form of computer printouts, but frequently graphical displays will also be created as was discussed in Chapter 8.

It would be impossible in this work to delineate all the networks, schedules, and reports that may be desired and used. Instead, some basic ideas will be presented which can be amplified and extended to cover almost all projects whether small, middle sized, or large.

9.3 TARGET ACTIVITY PROPERTIES

Before considering target schedules in detail it is proper to examine two properties of network activities. One of these is the way in which the resources are applied to the activity. Another is the manner in which the activity is to be measured for completion.

In the previous chapters a tacit assumption was made that each activity has had a constant rate of utilization of the required resources. In actuality, an activity may not have such a utilization. In most cases the activity's resources will be applied in a gradual manner and increased until a full resource utilization rate has been achieved, and then the resource rate is diminished until the

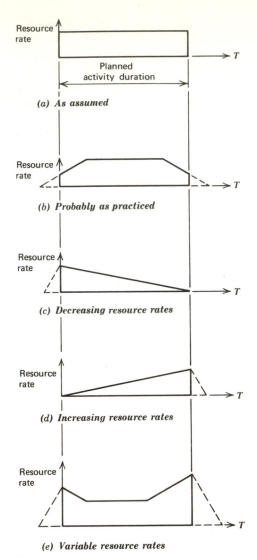

(a) *As assumed*

(b) *Probably as practiced*

(c) *Decreasing resource rates*

(d) *Increasing resource rates*

(e) *Variable resource rates*

Figure 9.1   Target activity durations.

activity is completed. Figure 9.1*a* represents this uniform assumption and Figure
9.1*b* shows the more probable variation in resource rate.

Some activities may have large resource demands at the outset which then
taper off over the entire duration. Other activities may have a pattern of
resource rates beginning at a very low level and increasing throughout the
duration, or they may have some other pattern of resource utilization. Some of
these variations are shown in Figure 9.1*c, d,* and *e.*

Although such variations can be recognized in the construction process, there is no way of determining which activities will have a particular variation in the field. The result is that the planner is forced to adopt some consistent assumption with regard to the utilization of the resources, and the uniform resource rate of Figure 9.1a generally has been used. All of the above variations would therefore have the same time duration expressed in the network.

Targeted activity durations are subject to the planner's decision as to starting and finishing dates and the value of any schedule reflects these decisions. The better the decisions made for activity durations, the better the resulting target schedule will be.

In most projects the measure of the resources used to determine the completion of an activity is assumed to be represented by the cost of the resources. Because of the uniform resource rate assumption, the cost of the activity is also considered to be uniform. Again, this may not be so, but there is no real way that this assumption can be validated, and the planner is forced to adopt it as a practical measure. Thus, if an activity has expended a third of its cost, the activity is said to be one-third finished.

There are instances where the measure of the utilization of resources on the activity is measured by some other means. There are activities in which the number of personnel required or the amount of material installed can be used. All such measures have their difficulties in application and may not be satisfactory.

Probably the most important consideration in measuring the completion of activities is that the measure be consistent throughout the project schedule. Mixing measures leads to confusion and a subsequent diminishing of the schedule's value, especially if it is to be used for project control.

9.4   SETTING THE TARGET SCHEDULE

Probably no single factor governs the quality of a project control plan more than the care taken in selecting the target schedule. Casual, off the cuff, choices lead to chaotic control conditions and undue expense in the process. Well-conceived target schedules, on the other hand, lead to smooth construction operations and true cost savings to both the owner and contractor.

The dynamics of the construction procedure force field supervisors to make decisions about the order for performing the activities of the project. Even with well-drawn networks, parallel activities will compete for labor, equipment, and material. On any given day some activities must continue to be performed, some will terminate, and some should be started. The questions that supervisors must answer are which are to be continued, terminated, or started.

In an ill-conceived control plan, activity timing decisions made one day generate the need for even more decisions later. The targeted dates begin to slip and costs begin to increase. In fact, the decisions become so numerous that all control is lost and the schedule itself is placed in jeopardy.

Many contractors have chosen the early start schedule as their target for control and have found themselves bogged down by the amount of effort required to keep the plan working. When they have lost control, they tend to blame the scheduling system rather than their own lack of understanding. Some, having had such a disastrous experience, shy away from using any critical path method unless it is forced upon them by the client. Even then their use of CPM is likely to be prefunctory and distasteful.

In order to overcome the inadequacies of the early start schedule, some planners and contractors have recommended that the late start schedule be used as the target one. This plan may be somewhat better because the amount of parallelism in the activities is reduced, but it still contains many of the same decision-making problems. Slippages still occur, and because every activity is timed to start at its latest, project overruns are sure to follow.

Properly developed target schedules will position activities in time so that each may be started at the early or late start date or somewhere between the two. Noncritical activities have varying amounts of float available which allow for these intermediate starts. The critical activities, of course, have common early and late start dates and must be performed accordingly.

In developing a target schedule the planner begins with the early start network and critically analyzes and evaluates each activity. Interactions among the individual activities and parallel chains of activities are carefully examined and consideration is given to a wide variety of factors before finally settling upon the activity starting dates.

Duration times for the activities from the early start schedule must be reevaluated and logic sequences must be verified. Contingency times should be added where necessary following the principles set forth in the discussion in Chapter 5. Project control can be truly effective only if potential problems and activity overruns are anticipated before the target schedule is established.

Activity overruns may be caused by many factors operating singly or in combination. Among the most frequently encountered factors are unexpected weather conditions, unexpected foundation conditions, approval delays, extended time estimates, deficient resource availability, inadequate work performance, and deficient management control.

The most severe weather aspect affecting construction is excess water. Rain is a greater problem than snow because snow may be removed before it melts. Rain water destroys exposed concrete, makes structural steel slippery and hazardous, warps wooden forms, and creates havoc with finishing and electrical materials. Rain turns construction sites into mud seas and slows the movement of materials and personnel.

High winds topple unfinished walls, blow away material that is not fastened securely and make it impossible to erect such things as siding and precast units. Work must be delayed until winds diminish and lost items must be replaced. Wind is a weather aspect that definitely must be anticipated.

The third most severe weather factor to be considered is temperature. Extremely cold weather requires that personnel wear protective clothing and slows the work. Heavy clothing may even cause some erection procedures to become hazardous. High temperature also slows work by reducing the effectiveness of construction personnel. It also tends to reduce the quality of concrete and causes deterioration of many construction materials. Anticipation of unusual temperature conditions is an essential part of a good problem analysis for a quality project control schedule.

The start-up of almost any project is dependent upon conditions at the site which affect foundation construction. Project delays arise when unexpected excavation conditions are met. High water tables or excessive water inflow will require pumping and other protective work in order to properly place footings and piers. Poor soil strata may require deeper excavation or may demand longer piles, which means that it will take longer to complete the foundation support. Any activity involving foundations should surely be investigated as to its sensitivity to these conditions.

Approvals by owners, architects, engineers, and governmental control agencies often take more time than initially planned. Detailed evaluation of the likelihood of these delays, especially on activities where approval of shop drawings is needed, should be a part of a good problem analysis. Have these approvals been given ample time? Is the expected supplier prompt in preparing shop drawings? Are there conditions attached to the expected approval that may require extra time for resolution? These and many more such questions must be answered. Then, is there float available in the schedule to accommodate these possible overruns or must times be altered or logic be adjusted?

It frequently happens that the initial activity durations may be inadequate. Methods may be changed, errors in judgment may be disclosed, or subcontractors may be different than those first selected. A complete review of activity durations should be made to insure their accuracy.

One dominant set of factors that has the potential of project delay involves the conditions surrounding the employment of personnel. The effect of labor agreements on the activities must be completely understood, especially the permissible interactions between crafts. Jurisdictional conditions, expressed in the labor agreement or implied, must be recognized and the activities must be scheduled to avoid the possibility of jurisdictional disputes.

The general and detailed concepts of labor utilization for the project should be examined. Some projects will require a uniform level of the labor force, whereas others will require a labor force that increases with time to a peak and then diminishes. Still other projects will permit a variable labor force, perhaps with a concern for a uniform utilization of each of the several crafts on the job.

Because major equipment is costly to acquire and is often difficult to move from place to place, target schedules generally are constructed to maximize equipment use. Projects such as large dams, for example, may have cableways to be built or they may have tressels with cranes running on them. The construction sequence is certainly controlled by these items and their influence on target dates for the milestone network must be considered early in the planning of the project.

Equipment that is to be permanently installed as a part of the structure frequently determines the scheduling of activities that may not be directly related. For example, it may be necessary to leave a part of the building open or unfinished so that air conditioning chillers, fans, boilers, and the like, are easy to install. This is particularly true when the equipment item requires a long time for delivery.

The arrival on the site of special material is also a factor that causes the schedule to be altered from the early start dates which the initial schedule predicts. Cut stone, glazed brick facings, or special wood paneling are typical materials that cause delays.

Most contractors are concerned about the flow of cash needed during the actual construction of the work. Cash flow is affected by the availability of money in the form of loans to the contractor and the resulting interest payments. The planner must keep in mind the payment plan set forth in the contract. Actual payment for work in place may not be made for several months after the work has been completed. High-cost items may be scheduled at times other than the earliest possible one so that the amount of borrowed funds is reduced. By scheduling the activities so that these loans and their interest charges are kept to a minimum, the contractor can gain added profit from the operation while still meeting the projected completion date.

Activities in which there is potential for low-quality work should be carefully evaluated; items such as welding and concrete walls are typical examples of such activities. The time needed to cut out and remake deficient welds must be determined and added to the activity's duration, or float time must be made available. Similarly, the probability that a concrete wall form might move out, resulting in concrete removal, reforming, and recasting should be considered and times and floats adjusted.

Although all activities do not require the same amount of control, those that may have potential problems must be strongly controlled. Project delays frequently arise because insufficient control has been applied to them. Critical activities are especially vulnerable and the review should attempt to measure their sensitivity to the anticipated control plan. It may be necessary to add contingency time to the network or to change the network logic if they are highly sensitive.

From the brief review above it should be clear that a complete analysis of the project after the early start schedule has been established is the prime requisite. The target schedule then accurately reflects the probable construction sequence and leads to high-quality control through the monitoring process.

9.5 MONITORING THE PROJECT

In the discussion of networks in Chapter 1 an analogy was drawn between a highway map and a CPM network. Let us return to this analogy and assume that a traveler has selected a particular destination, a route to follow, and a time of arrival. The driver starts out on this route and keeps track of two main instruments to regulate the progress of the journey, the odometer and the watch. The odometer reading tells how much distance has been covered and the watch tells how much time has elapsed. By monitoring these instruments the driver can judge whether or not the trip is proceeding according to the plan first conceived.

Similarly, the construction manager must monitor the various "instruments" measuring work progress to determine whether the project is meeting the planned schedule. The "odometers" and "watches" of the construction project are such items as delivery slips, time slips, written reports, and so forth.

Monitoring requires that provisions be made to get feedback about the progress of the project from the field forces and from other sources such as the accountant, equipment manager, or labor manager. In small organizations this may be a relatively simple task, whereas in others it may involve a rather complex set of internal reports, checkoff lists, or charts.

Feedback from Direct Contact

The project manager may get feedback from the field by direct contact and observation. This procedure can be very efficient both in time and effort, but it requires close cooperation between the manager and the field personnel. It is feasible only when there is a short span of control as is usually found in small organizations. Material delivery slips are forwarded to the manager by the field superintendent and time slips and costs are obtained from the timekeeper and accountant. The manager takes notes during visits to the work site and assembles all the information into some kind of report which can later be evaluated against the target which was expected.

Feedback from Photography

Feedback may also be obtained by photographic means. Contractors, large and small, have used photography for many years to record progress and to provide permanent documentation of the work. Still pictures taken for these purposes can be used to determine approximate project completion by a comparison of sequential photographs.

In simple projects this technique may have definite advantages. Interpretation of field reports is enhanced and procedural errors are quickly discovered. In complex work and large projects still photographs are not as effective in providing feedback from the field because many of the activities may not be evident from the pictures.

A major feedback disadvantage to still photographs for all projects is that a still picture tells nothing about the time taken to perform the work activities. Even though the pictures are taken at regular intervals, some of the activities may finish early in the interval between photos and some may start in the interval.

Time-lapse photography can be used to measure work progress and may overcome some of the timing disadvantages of still pictures. Time-lapse films do not serve well for overall work progress because of their expense, yet they can be very effective in depicting particular operations.

It is doubtful if photographic methods can ever be used as the only feedback for control purposes. However, their use as supplemental information to other techniques is certainly desirable and should be encouraged.

Feedback from Checkoff Lists

Many construction managers have adopted checkoff techniques to increase the exactness and accuracy in the feedback information. At the beginning of the reporting period the planner prepares a list of the activities that are to be started, to continue, or to be finished during the next time interval. The superintendent or foreman needs only to check the appropriate column next to the listed activity to indicate what work was accomplished. The list is then returned to the manager for evaluation.

Checkoff lists are very effective in obtaining field information. This is especially true if the reporting periods are kept short, say, daily or weekly. They are also effective when a small number of items is listed.

Because of the number of decisions and assignments the superintendent must make each day there is a tendency to put off checking the feedback list until just before it is to be returned. Long reporting periods lead to considerable inaccuracy in the information because of this tendency and should be avoided.

Lengthy lists of activities also lead to poor reporting. When many activities are shown, the superintendent may be unable to obtain sufficient information about each activity and then guesses are made about the status of those on which there is question. Long checkoff lists can usually be avoided if only the activities in a particular area or a particular craft are given.

One disadvantage of checkoff lists is that the superintendent may check off items as being completed when, in fact, they are not. This bias appears when the field supervision may not wish to appear deficient in performance. Hard-line management invites this kind of deception and tends to negate the value of the report.

Another frequently expressed disadvantage of the checkoff procedure is that the field supervision is unable to determine which activity to choose when only one can be started. The CPM float values for the activities are unknown and poor choices may be made which, in turn, may cause schedule overruns.

Feedback from Bar Charts

Closely related to the checkoff list is a procedure used by some contractors which utilizes the bar chart. A copy of the bar chart, which has been marked to show the status of the project at the beginning of the period, is sent to the field. The supervisory personnel mark directly on the copy the work completed during the reporting period. The marked bar chart is then returned to the project manager.

As with the checkoff list, this procedure is effective for short reporting intervals. The bar chart may contain too many activities, however, and this may be a serious disadvantage. It does have the advantage of allowing the superintendent to decide on activities to be started because the bar chart prepared from the CPM schedule will probably have activity floats given.

The unwieldiness of the overall bar chart may be corrected by constructing charts covering areas and crafts. Some planners also avoid the display of currently unneeded activities by reproducing only a segment of the bar chart covering one or two reporting periods before and after the period of the report.

Feedback from Networks

Another technique for obtaining feedback from the field is to use the target network itself. A copy of the overall network diagram is provided the field supervision. This copy is then marked to show what has taken place during the control period. Notations of unusual events or special conditions are added on the copy beside the affected activities before returning the diagram to the construction manager. The planner then adds this information to the original network and copies are made for the following period.

The overall network is too big and cumbersome for many projects, and only portions of the network that involve the affected activities are used. On large projects where subnetworks are prepared for areas and crafts they most likely will be the ones that are reproduced.

The major advantage of using networks as a reporting mechanism is that the superintendent has complete information about the status of the project and sound field decisions can be made. Probably the greatest disadvantage in using the network for feedback is that the diagram may appear confusing to field personnel. The procedure demands that field supervision be completely aware of the project's objectives and needs and that they have a good understanding of the networking and control methods being used by the company.

Field Personnel Needed

In all the methods for obtaining feedback from the field discussed above there is an implied need to have people in the field who are responsible for collecting and recording the required information. On small projects these duties will probably be combined with the timekeeping function and the timekeeper or the superintendent will do this. As projects get larger there may be a field engineer through which several superintendents report the data. On large projects scheduling offices may be set up with a staff of scheduling engineers and technicians.

Whatever organizational structure is adopted for a particular project, the emphasis should always be on obtaining complete and accurate information about the project's progress. Good evaluation, forecasting, and adjustment by the planner or project manager must be based upon good field feedback.

9.6   EVALUATING AND FORECASTING

Once the feedback from the field and office forces is received the scheduler must evaluate the data and decide what should be done to maintain the target duration. It is at this point that the skill of the scheduler is paramount, for the success of the work hinges on the decisions to be made. Many of these decisions may be handled by the scheduling employees themselves, but it is likely that some of the information should be brought to the attention of the upper levels of management. A good sense of team interaction is essential.

The evaluation process usually begins by producing the usual schedule tables with the information obtained from the feedback. Probably the first things that the scheduler looks at are the output tables from the computer, if that is being used, or from the tables prepared in the office. The scheduler examines these outputs for delaying sequences and compares the new start and finish dates with the ones that were targeted. It then becomes clear where the difficulties may lie.

Skillful planners can examine these schedules and quickly make the proper corrections. Some of the feedback information will suggest remedies, and the field superintendent may have thought of ways to recover lost time. This is valuable information and should be given considerable weight in the decision-making process. Other feedback items may not be as easily evaluated, especially if the delay will effect a whole series of activities. In these cases it may be necessary to develop additional displays to make effective adjustments.

Bar Chart Displays

One of the most widely used displays for evaluation is the bar chart. The feedback information may be added to a copy of the chart and a visual comparison is readily apparent. The effect of several possible decisions can then be seen. Adjustments are finalized and a new bar chart is produced for field use.

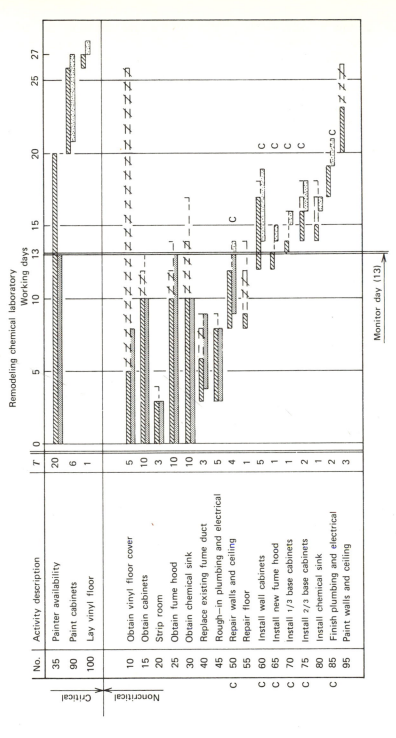

Figure 9.2 Bar chart from precedence network computations at monitoring day 13.

165

To illustrate this process the bar chart for the remodeling of the chemical laboratory as given in Chapter 8 will be used. Figure 9.2 shows this bar chart with solid bars added beneath the planned ones to represent the completed activities. The date at which the monitoring took place is day 13 and this is indicated by the vertical line.

It can be seen that Activity 10 has been finished later than was planned, but that since the delay used only free float, no other activities were affected. Activity 25 was also delayed in finishing by three days. Only two of these days were recovered from the free float and the third used up interfering float. As a consequence, other activities may be delayed at least one day. A further examination reveals that Activity 40 was also delayed, causing the start of Activity 50 to be delayed. Furthermore, feedback reports say that Activity 50 still has one more day to completion. In both cases the total float was completely used up and Activity 50 has now become critical with a one-day overrun. A letter C has been added to the diagram to indicate this new condition.

The result of these delays on Activities 40 and 50 is that the chain of activities following them has also been made critical. Dotted bars have been added below the affected activities to clearly define their predicted overruns. Activities 60, 65, 70, 75, 85, 90, and 100 have such indications. The predicted project overrun at this time is therefore one day.

With this information displayed, some decision must be made to bring the schedule back into agreement with the target. One decision that may be considered is to add more painters to Activity 90, Paint Cabinets, and to speed up the work by one day. This may not be feasible if the cabinets are close together and additional painters would interfere with each other. Another possibility would be to plan for the painters to work overtime and complete the painting of the cabinets on time. If this is not feasible, it might be possible to split Activities 60 and 75 into two parts and begin to finish the plumbing and electrical work, Activity 85, together with Activities 60 and 75. This would, of course, change the logic of the diagram.

S-Curve Displays

One of the most frequently prepared graphical displays used for project control is an S-curve. A plot of targeted costs versus time has the appearance of a letter S that has been somewhat flattened. Hence, the name given to this figure.

In many small projects the targeted S-curve can be anticipated by a technique given by Miller.[9.3] He proposes two control points, one at one third of the time and one quarter of the cost and the other at two thirds of the time and three quarters of the cost. Between these points it is assumed that the expenditures of funds will vary linearly. Between the start of the project and the first point the curve is assumed parabolic. The same assumption is made for the curve between the second point and project completion. Figure 9.3 represents these assumptions.

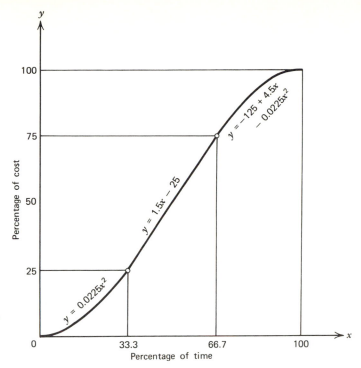

Figure 9.3   Anticipated target S-curve.

   This procedure may be used to establish S-curves for larger projects too, especially those with limited control budgets. It may also be adequate if the contract consists of many activities utilizing the same resources, such as an earth moving project or one comprised mainly of concreting activities.

   Miller's anticipated S-curve probably does not represent reality for most general contractor's projects or for the very large ones. In these instances the cost of each activity in the target schedule should be evaluated, and the curve should be constructed from these costs.

   It was stated in Section 9.4 that target schedules could be chosen with all activities starting as soon as possible, with all activities starting as late as possible, or with the activities starting at intermediate times. In each case an S-curve can be constructed, and Figure 9.4 shows these three possibilities.

   For a project with given activity durations and network logic, the S-curve derived from the early start schedule may be considered as one boundary of a field of S-curves. The curve derived from the late start schedule serves as the other boundary of the field, and all other schedules will produce S-curves that lie between the two. As stated previously, the most satisfactory schedule for control purposes will probably be represented by one of these intermediate curves.

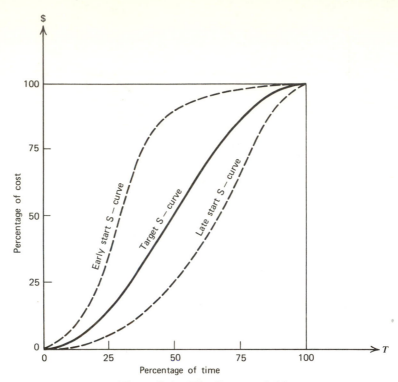

Figure 9.4   The S-curve field.

TABLE 9.1

Sample Project Cost Data

Activity	Duration (Days)	Cost Rate ($/Day)	Total Cost ($)
A	2	500	1,000
B	17	200	3,400
C	3	3,000	9,000
D	5	1,000	5,000
E	6	2,000	12,000
F	2	500	1,000
G	1	1,000	1,000

To illustrate these concepts consider a small network of seven activities having a total cost of $32,400. Table 9.1 provides the activity durations, cost rates, and total costs.

Figure 9.5 is a precedence diagram of this project and shows the early start and finish dates for each activity. Free floats and total floats are shown beneath the activities. Link lags are indicated by the double lines when the lag is zero and by a figure above the link otherwise. A diagram constructed in this way is often called the early start tree because the doubled zero lag links appear as branches of a tree rooted at the initial activity.

Another diagram for the same project is shown in Figure 9.6. This time the activities have been assumed to start as late as possible and the late start and finish dates for each activity are given together with the link lags. This diagram is the late start tree because the doubled zero lag links form the branches of the tree rooted at the terminal activity.

The target network for the project is represented by Figure 9.7. It has been developed from a series of decisions made by the planner so that the daily costs have been made as uniform as possible. Note that Activities C, D, and F have been scheduled to start later than the *ESD* but not as late as the *LSD*. Activity E has been scheduled to start as late as it can. Activities A, B, and G are critical and have not had their schedule adjusted because the project duration was maintained at 20 days.

The cumulative costs for each of the above networks are plotted against time to produce the S-curves of Figure 9.8. Assumed costs for each day have been

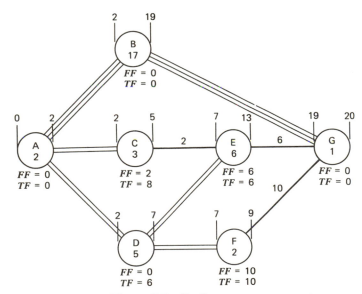

Figure 9.5 Early start tree.

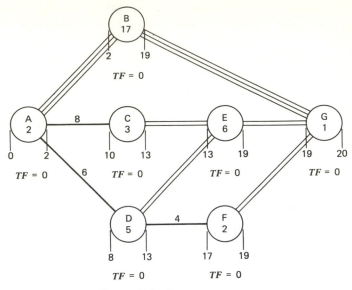

Figure 9.6   Late start tree.

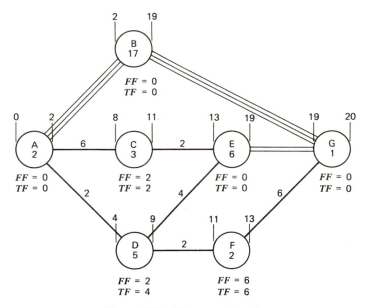

Figure 9.7   Target network.

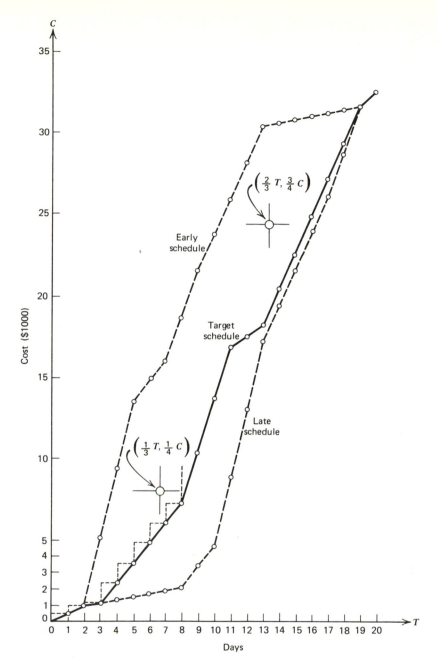

Figure 9.8 *Project S-curves.*

171

recorded at the end of the day. Also, costs have been linearized during each day so that the curves are not smooth but appear as broken lines.

Some planners may prefer to show the costs plotted as a step function because most financial transactions are assumed to occur at the close of the time period. If this convention were adopted, the target curve would be plotted as a series of steps instead of the broken line shown. A few of these steps have been dotted in for illustration.

Miller's two control points also have been plotted for comparison. It can be seen that the earlier one is closer to the target curve than the upper one. It may be inferred that if the Miller technique had been adopted for control, the daily costs would be required to be higher in the early part of the project than was desired by the planner.

No matter what technique is used to develop the target S-curve, control can be achieved only if a comparison is made between the actual and targeted costs. As work on the project proceeds, the actual cumulative costs may be plotted using the same axes as the target curve. In this way a visual concept of the progress of the work may be obtained.

Curves A and B of Figure 9.9 represent two possible ways that the actual costs

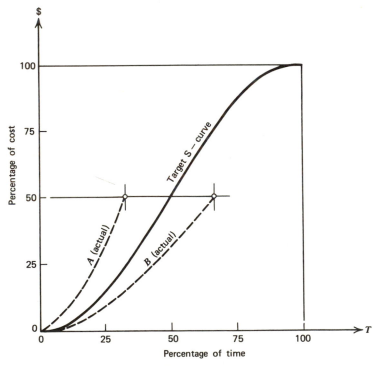

Figure 9.9   Actual versus target S-curves.

of a project could have been running. Each shows the status when 50 percent of the expense has occurred. It may be inferred from curve *A* that the project is ahead of the target schedule and that if performance continues in the same manner, completion will occur earlier than anticipated. Similarly, curve *B* would indicate that the project is behind schedule and a late completion would be forecasted. These inferences are based upon the constant utilization of the resources as stated previously and, hence, that the actual cost reflects the true rate of progress toward completion.

There is another interpretation of these plots that should not be overlooked. Curve *A* might indicate that the costs of the work have been exceeding those anticipated and that the percent of completion is correct. Continued performance would then predict a cost overrun and a smaller profit, or even a loss. Curve *B*, on the other hand, might indicate that costs have been less than anticipated, the percent of completion is correct, and the final cost will be lower than previously judged. The contractor would stand to have a profit gain under these circumstances.

Because these two interpretation possibilities always exist, an S-curve should not be used as the only measure for project control. Additional comparisons of material or craft costs should be available to evaluate any discrepancy between the actual and targeted S-curve.

Summary

Although effective project control is dependent upon good feedback from field and office on the status of the project, evaluation is one of the most important functions of the project scheduler. Data from many sources must be assembled and compared. Schedule networks, tables, bar charts, and S-curves must be combined with human resources, equipment, and cost summaries if excellence in evaluation is to be achieved. The quality of these reports and comparisons reflects in the decisions to be made.

No matter what techniques are used for evaluation, the resulting decisions are crucial to the outcome of the project. The scheduler's skill in deciding which activities to expedite, how to readjust the network logic, or what new method to select can mean either a loss or profit to the contractor.

9.7 CONTROL PERIODS

In preceding discussions on monitoring construction projects for control purposes, frequent references are made to control periods. These intervals between one report and another may be either long or short as the needs of the project dictate. In very tightly controlled projects they must be short, perhaps even daily. In projects with less demanding controls they may be lengthened to monthly or bimonthly intervals.

Economic considerations enter into the setting of these intervals in addition to the desired amount of control. It is costly to prepare reports, comparative charts, and the like, and the benefits to be gained in control must be offset by this expense. Projects similar to those previously experienced do not require as much control as do those that are new to the contractor or that have many unique features.

Control periods should be established very early in the life of the project contract. There is no reason, however, to insist that the original plan for these periods be maintained at all costs if changes in the project would dictate otherwise. The construction manager should retain a degree of flexibility in setting the period if effective control is to be achieved.

There is a tendency for a contractor using CPM for project control for the first time to set the control interval too short. The resulting expense may absorb a good share of profit without providing any real influence on the conduct of the work. For the great bulk of construction projects the usual control periods will be one or two weeks in length.

Control periods normally are set to coincide with other natural decision-making periods of the contractor's organization. They are influenced by the need to make status reports to the owner or the architect/engineer, by the need to expedite material and installed equipment deliveries, and by the conditions surrounding the financial commitments. They also may be influenced by the availability of craftsmen or construction equipment.

Monitoring Codes

Most commercial project control systems based on CPM make use of short, three- or four-letter codes to define the status of the network activities on their reports. Figure 9.10 is a page taken from the TRACE Users Manual[9.1] prepared by Project Management Associates, Inc. The codes given are typical of those used in other systems. The interval between the data date, DD, and the cutoff date, COD, is the control period being used. The bars represent typical activity conditions determined on the data date.
The explanations for each of the schedule item conditions are given below:

1. FNS   Activity is finished on or before the data date.

2. PIF   *Progress, Imminent Finish.* Applied to any activity in progress with a current late finish date earlier than the cutoff date. The activity must finish within the control period.

3. PPF   *Progress, Possible Finish.* Applied to any activity in progress with a current early finish date earlier than the cutoff date but with a current late finish date later than the cutoff date. The activity may finish within the control period.

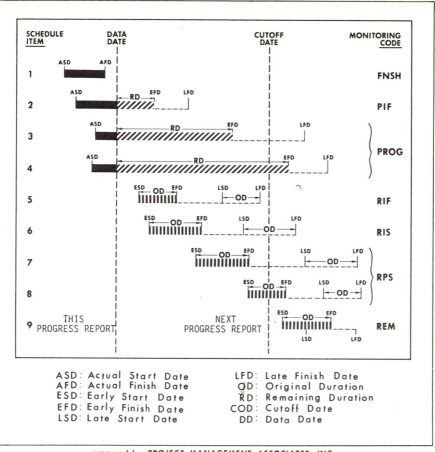

prepared by **PROJECT MANAGEMENT ASSOCIATES, INC.**

Figure 9.10   Monitoring codes.

4. PROG *Progress.* Applied to any activity in progress with both the current early finish date and the late finish date later than the cutoff date. The activity will not finish within the control period.

5. RIF *Remaining, Imminent Finish.* Applied to any activity not yet started but with a current late finish date earlier than the cutoff date. The activity must start and finish within the control period.

6. RIS *Remaining, Imminent Start.* Applied to any activity not yet started but with a current late start date earlier than the cutoff date and a current late finish date later than the cutoff date. The activity must start during the control period and may be finished within the period.

7. RPF *Remaining, Possible Finish.* Applied to any activity not yet started but with a current early finish date earlier than the cutoff date and a late start date later than the cutoff date. The activity may finish within the control period.

8. RPS *Remaining, Possible Start.* Applied to any activity with a current early start date earlier than the cutoff date and with both the current early finish and late finish dates later than the cutoff date. The activity may start within the control period.

9. REM *Remaining.* Applied to any activity that has its current early start date later than the cutoff date. The activity is not scheduled to start within the control period.

It may be observed that codes 3 and 4 in the explanations are grouped under the PROG, Progress, code shown in Figure 9.10. Also, codes 7 and 8 may be represented by the RPS, Remaining, Possible Start designation.

9.8 UPDATING

The third phase of good project control is updating. This process involves the correction of the target plan to economically meet the project's overall objectives, which are completion within the budgets of both time and cost. It consists of planning and scheduling the remaining work after some time interval has elapsed.

Updating is an expensive and time-consuming process that may take as long as the preparation of the original plan, and the benefits to the company from an updating action must be weighed against the costs to be incurred. The decision to update the project is a top management decision and should not be made in an arbitrary manner. In fact, dates for making updating decisions should be established while the original target schedule is being prepared. Maximum use of the critical path method as a management tool cannot be realized unless updating is not only anticipated but is actually carried out.

As discussed earlier, priorities given to starting times and adjustments in activity durations are constantly made to keep the actual schedule in agreement with the target. Nevertheless, slippages in the schedule can be expected to increase in most projects, and there will be times when actions from monitoring alone will not suffice. It is then that a complete revision of the target schedule becomes a necessity and updating must be undertaken.

As monitoring proceeds, period after period, unforeseen events that lie outside the responsibility of the contractor create delays in the project schedule which must be overcome. A few of these problems may be solved quickly but many others may permanently affect the target plan. Resolutions to these accumulating problems must be found, and the usual solution is to make major changes in the target network and schedule.

During the monitoring phase, errors in activity durations and network logic may be recognized. Correction of these errors may forecast a significant project duration overrun and changes in network logic will have to be made to keep on schedule.

Changes in project design or in project scope may be imposed by the owner and the design team. The updating process accounts for these changes, but the revised target plan may force project durations to be extended.

Procurement delays accumulate as the project progresses. As they begin to affect the critical path, the probability for a project duration overrun becomes more certain. Expediting may resolve some of these delays but others may be resolved only by changes in the network logic.

Procurement delays are among the most difficult construction problems to overcome. Some contractors have cited these problems as a reason for not using a critical path method for project control. This is a shortsighted attitude because it is precisely because of these problems that contractors benefit most from CPM through the updating phase.

Impending strikes, jurisdictional disputes, and sudden changes in the availability of craftsmen are problems that usually can be resolved only by rescheduling the work. When a project is first targeted, assumptions about labor conditions play a major role, and any changes in these assumed conditions tend to have a negative influence on the project duration. Updating may never regain such losses but it can minimize their impact.

Another major problem often met in construction is the effect of an accident. Very few construction projects can be completed without some kind of accident, either to equipment or to employees. Accidents to personnel, being dramatic, receive much publicity, but accidents involving the work and equipment, without injury to employees, may be more devastating to the project schedule. Delays mount because of the need to remove debris and rebuild portions of the job, because equipment is unusable while being repaired, or because new equipment must be obtained. Again, the updating process allows the construction manager to minimize these overruns in time and cost.

Although changes in design, procurement delays, labor difficulties, and accidents account for the bulk of accumulating problems requiring updating, there are others that occur less frequently which also must be solved. Weather allowances disappear and severe storms cause walls to be destroyed, flood excavations, impair newly cast concrete, and the like. Sudden illness of key personnel causes delays because of gaps in information about the work and because of the time necessary to train new people. Furthermore, owners and outside agencies with an interest in the work may be slow in giving approvals. Updating is necessary if such conditions exist for more than a short time interval.

An Example

To illustrate the updating process consider the example of remodeling the chemical laboratory used in Chapters 6 and 7 and diagramed in Figure 7.12. Assume that the work has been underway for 15 days and that the accumulated problems from monitoring are as follows:

1. The cabinet supplier has stated that it is impossible to deliver all the cabinets within 10 days. The base cabinets can be delivered on the tenth day but the wall cabinets take longer to build and the expected delivery will be delayed two weeks. Thus, the wall cabinets are now expected on the twentieth day.

2. The fume hood manufacturer needs 17 days to deliver the hood instead of the 15 days projected.

3. The replacement of the fume duct actually took 4 days to complete but it is now finished.

The planner begins the analysis by marking off the completed activities on the network and making the time changes required by the procurement delays. Computations are then made to determine new schedule times for the remaining activities.

Sometimes it may be necessary to make a new network drawing to avoid confusion. Figure 9.11 is such a drawing. Note that only the remaining activities have been shown and logic links from completed activities have been eliminated. The data date of 15 days has been introduced as Event Activity 6 with a zero duration. The duration of Activities 15, 25, and 35 have been changed to show only the time remaining.

The calculations are shown on the diagram and it can be seen that the project completion is now 34 days, or 7 days longer than the original project duration. The critical path has also shifted so that it now passes through the activities involving the wall cabinets instead of being dependent upon the availability of the painters.

After reviewing the situation with the superintendent it is agreed that the installation of the wall cabinets can be speeded up if one additional carpenter is assigned to this task. This will change the duration of Activity 60 to four days and shorten the project by one day.

Further discussion results in the decision to start painting the walls and ceiling before the cabinets are in place and before the plumbers and electricians have completed their work. This will require that the painters have one day to touch up around the cabinets and the plumbing and electrical fixtures after their

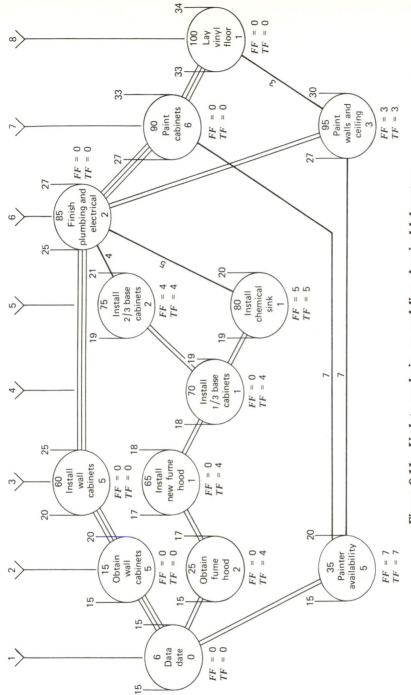

Figure 9.11 Update analysis—remodeling chemical laboratory.

179

180

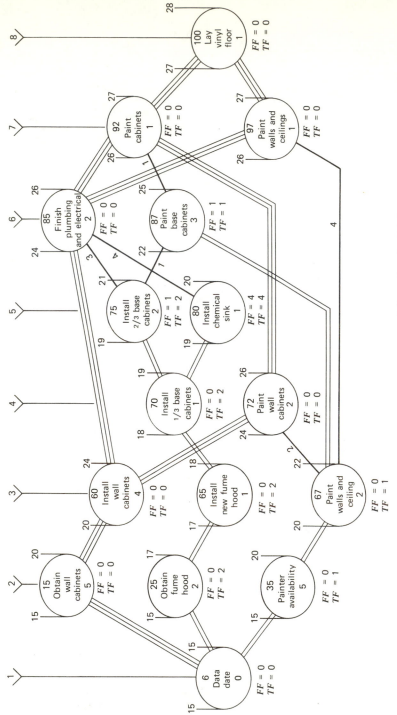

Figure 9.12 Updated network—remodeling chemical laboratory.

installation. The plumbers and electricians will still need two days to finish their work.

Figure 9.12 is the updated network showing the above adjustments. The revised schedule is calculated, and the project duration is now 28 days or one day longer than was originally targeted. The management agrees that this one day will pose no serious problems and approves this schedule as the new target.

Note that the painters and mechanical trades will be working in the same room at the same time, which is less than desirable, but it appears that this is the best solution. The superintendent will need to work with these persons to insure that no further delays occur and that the new target can be met.

9.9 UPDATING INTERVALS

It was stated earlier that the dates to be considered for updating actions should be planned at the time the target schedule is prepared. If this is to be done, some base should be laid upon which to judge the frequency of such actions.

Many contractors are reluctant to establish updating dates in advance, reasoning that updating may never be needed and that such plans are a waste of effort. It is assumed by them that if the project's needs demand updating, then it will be done. The fallacy in this approach is that when the needs for updating arise the contractor and his team are preoccupied with efforts to get the project back on schedule and have no time for updating.

There is, of course, no requirement to update a project at some previously assigned date if the project is proceeding well. On the other hand, well-chosen assigned dates incorporate the process into the routine of project control and when updating is required, it can be accomplished with a minimum of disruption to the conduct of the work.

Three plans for setting updating intervals, each with advantages and disadvantages, may be considered. Updating may take place at uniform intervals, at intervals of decreasing length, or at intervals of a random nature determined by the milestones of the project.

Probably the greatest advantage to setting uniform updating intervals is that they fit in easily with routine business reporting periods. Labor payment schedules, accounting reports, loan payment schedules, and other fiscal reports are due weekly, monthly, or quarterly. Project status reports to owners, engineers, and architects as well as internal monitoring reports are also periodic. All these reporting documents provide decision-making information for the construction manager, and when updating is needed these uniform intervals minimize the time required to complete the revised target plan.

Uniform updating intervals are also advantageous for two particular types of projects, those with a small scope and those with a linear network. Small-scale projects can be expected to require only a few updates because they usually are of rather short duration. It is therefore natural and economical to space the updating dates to coincide with reports as required by the owner or the architect/engineer.

Some kinds of projects have most of their activities performed in a sequential manner resulting in very few parallel activity chains, and there is a decided linear appearance to these networks. Figure 9.13 illustrates this linear kind of project. It can be seen that the percentage of critical activities tends to be high.

An overall objective of project control is to complete the work within the targeted duration and critical activities must always be monitored carefully to meet this objective. As work on the project is completed, activity-by-activity, the percentage of critical activities naturally increases until only one activity remains. The project then is 100 percent critical.

Criticality of linear networks, beginning at a high level, increases slowly toward the project's end. This is qualitatively shown by curve A of Figure 9.14. Uniform updating periods continuously match these high criticality levels and provide for the necessary control throughout the life of the work.

Middle-and large-sized projects tend to have networks with many parallel activities and many interacting links. These may be classed as fan-shaped networks, an example of which is shown in Figure 9.15. At the start of these projects a relatively low number of the activities are critical. As work progresses the criticality of the schedule increases slowly and then rises abruptly during the last quarter of the duration. This characteristic is depicted in curve B of Figure 9.14.

Because of the sudden increase in criticality in fan-shaped networks and the corresponding increase in the necessity for control of the critical activities, an updating interval that decreases in length toward the end of the project may be preferred. For instance, a project of four years duration may have updating periods set at six months for the first year, at three months for the second year, at two months for the third year, and at monthly intervals during the final year.

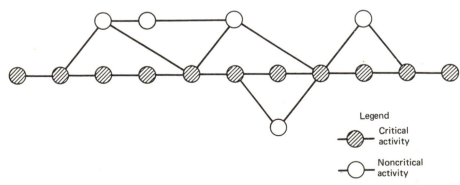

Figure 9.13   A linear precedence network.

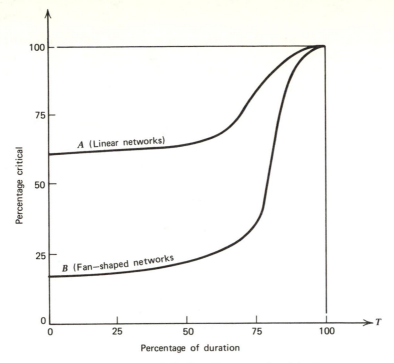

Figure 9.14   Variations in network criticality.

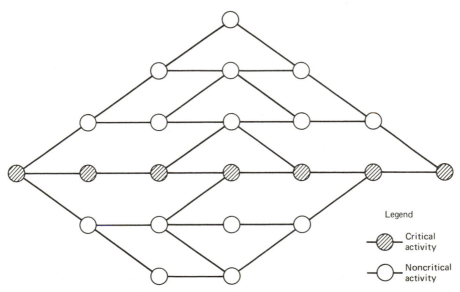

Figure 9.15   A fan-shaped precedence network.

183

Projects of all sizes, large and small, frequently have well-defined milestones that are set by the work. In such instances these milestone dates are excellent times for reevaluation. Milestone dates do not usually arise at any particular interval, and the updating interval becomes random in length.

An example will help to clarify this randomness. Assume that a contractor is building a small commercial structure. Reporting and financial considerations may dictate an evaluation at the time the foundations and basement walls have reached the ground surface. Assume that the second milestone is reached when the building is closed-in from weather and that the third milestone is reached when the major equipment has been installed and before finishing takes place. The first interval may then be two months long, the second interval four months, and the third, one month. The updating intervals can be clearly defined before work starts, but they are random in length.

There are other times in the lifespan of some projects when updating is required. If there is a prolonged interruption in the work because of changes in the project scope by the owner, target dates must be reestablished and a new construction plan must be developed. Lengthy interruptions because of accidents, strikes, severe weather, fire, or other calamities also demand a new start, and updating cannot be avoided. If one of the above updating plans had been adopted, it too must be revised to meet the project's future expectations.

Frequency of Updating

In the discussions above nothing has been said about the number of updating periods required. Very little definite evaluation of the frequency for updating periods is available but, as stated before, updating must involve economic considerations surrounding the work. It would appear that during the life of an average project of one to two years duration, probably not more than six updates are economically feasible. Naturally, some projects may need updating more frequently and some less.

Elvers[9.2] has examined updating frequency in some detail on a limited scale. His work has been based on the probability of completion of critical activities and the PERT concepts of critical path analysis which will be discussed in Chapter 12.

REFERENCES

9.1 Anonymous, *TRACE User's Manual*, Project Management Associates, Inc., Ann Arbor, Michigan, 1975.

9.2 Elvers, Douglas A., "Planning Monitoring Frequencies for CPM Projects," *J. Construction Division*, Proceedings ASCE, Vol. 97, No. C02, November 1971.

9.3 Miller, Lawrence C., *Successful Management for Contractors*, McGraw-Hill Book Co., New York, 1962.

EXERCISES

9.1 Data for a small project is tabulated below.
   (a) Plot the S-curve of costs for this project derived from the early schedule tree.
   (b) Plot the S-curve of costs for this project derived from the late schedule tree. Plot this curve on the same sheet used for part (a).
   (c) The project scheduler has decided that the target schedule will be an early start schedule except for Activities E and G which will be scheduled at their latest times. Plot the S-curve of costs for this project derived from the target schedule.

Activity	Duration (Days)	Depends on	Cost rate ($/Day)	Total Cost ($)
A	2	—	200	400
B	10	A	300	3000
C	7	A	400	2800
D	15	B	400	6000
E	5	B	600	3000
F	6	C	500	3000
G	3	E, F	800	2400
H	6	F	700	4200
K	3	D, G, H	200	600

9.2 The project of Exercise 9.1 has been worked on for ten days. During this time $4800 has been charged against the costs. Using the target S-curve developed in Exercise 9.1(c), what would you infer as to the status of the project at this time? Predict the level of expense expected at the end of day 20.

9.3 Data for a small project are given below. The initial starting date, or base date, is zero and the data date is 20. All activities except F, G, H, K, and L have been completed. Activity F has four days left. Activity G has five days left. Activity L has been reduced by one day and Activities H and K remain unchanged.
   (a) Construct the reduced network.
   (b) Update the project and determine the new total and free floats, the project duration, and the new critical path.

Activity	Duration	Depends Upon
A	9	—
B	5	A
C	2	A
D	7	A
E	1	B, C
F	8	B, C, D
G	6	C, D
H	1	E, F, G
K	3	E, F, G
L	8	H, K

9.4 (a) Data for a small project is tabulated below. Construct a precedence network for this project and compute early start and finish dates, total floats, and free floats for each activity. Show these values on the network and indicate the critical path.

Activity	Duration	Depends Upon
A	3	—
B	6	A
C	8	A
D	10	A
E	5	B, C
F	7	E
G	12	D, E
H	17	E
X	9	Y, Z
Y	3	H, D
Z	4	F, G

(b) On Day 12, the Field Scheduler gives you the following information and asks you to update the network and provide an accurate precedence diagram showing the updated schedule. The new diagram is to show early start and finish dates, total floats, and free floats for each activity. Indicate the critical path, or paths.

Information from field scheduler:

1. The project has been underway for 12 working days.

2. Some concrete forms broke during one pour, and Activity B was delayed in completion by two days.

3. Activity D is now in progress but five days were lost waiting for better weather.

4. Activity A was completed on schedule.

5. Activity C was completed one day early.

6. The precast concrete supplier has been delayed; he can have the concrete on the job so that Activity Y can begin on the morning of Day 36.

In addition to the items provided by the Field Scheduler, your own office personnal have brought the following to your attention:

Information from office personnel:

1. Activity H will not require 17 days, but 7 days; the Scheduling Engineer discovered a 10-day error in the computations.

2. Activity Z, originally planned to last 4 days, is projected to take an additional 2 days because of a decrease in the labor force in the local area due to a strike.

3. An error in logic in the precedence diagram was discovered by the recently hired Field Engineer. He quickly pointed out to the Project Engineer that Activity Z

must *precede* Activity F instead of following it. Activity Z is still dependent on Activity G, and Activity F is still dependent on Activity E. All other activity dependencies remain as originally planned.

9.5 Solve Exercise 9.4 using arrow diagraming techniques throughout instead of the given precedence requirement.

9.6 The activities and their dependencies for a precedence network are shown below. Their durations, targeted early start and finish dates, and the estimated total costs for each are given. All times are in weeks. Assume that the contract calls for billing finished work every four weeks with payment expected eight weeks after billing. There is a 10 percent retainage by the owner.

Plot an S-curve of expected costs. On the same plot show the expected income.

Activity	T (Weeks)	Targeted		Expected Total Cost
		ESD	EFD	
A	3	0	3	$ 600
B	4	5	9	2,400
C	1	6	7	800
D	10	3	13	10,000
E	8	12	20	12,000
F	6	13	19	6,000
G	2	15	17	1,800
H	1	22	23	500
K	6	19	25	4,200
L	5	25	30	1,500

10
TIME-COST ADJUSTMENTS

10.1 INTRODUCTION

In the previous chapters the mechanics for computing activity times and floats have been based upon the assumption that every activity in the network is to start at its earliest possible time. The resulting early start schedules usually are not satisfactory for conducting the work, and adjustments should be made to improve their utility.

Networking techniques can be used to predict project durations, but because of the expense involved in making and solving detailed networks, few contractors use CPM for this purpose. Hence, project durations usually are set by other means. For any given project, the contractor may use previous experience with similar work or may estimate the duration based on the dollar volume per unit of time to which his firm is accustomed. The owner may specify a time duration to suit his requirements, or the duration may be set by the demands of the weather, or some arbitrary estimate of duration may be made.

Whatever means are employed, the project duration is often made a condition of the construction contract. It is only after a contractor has signed a contract that the network is detailed and solved. The resulting project duration may then turn out to be greater than the time permitted by the contract documents. Adjustments must therefore be made to reduce the project duration to fall within the contractural time limit.

10.2 ACTIVITY TIME-RESOURCE CONCEPTS

It was pointed out in Chapter 5 that an activity's duration depends upon the method to be used for performance as well as upon the quantity of the work involved. Usually, the estimating office will be aware of the quantity, but field forces may have to be consulted to determine the method to be followed.

Once the method has been agreed to by everyone concerned, the resources for the activity can be established. Again, discussions among the field and office personnel will reveal several possibilities.

In the discussions among field and office there are two concepts that should be kept in mind. The first is that there is a relationship between the rate at which

188

the resource is applied to the activity and the cost rate. The second is that there also is a relationship between the total amount of resource applied and the duration time for the activity.

It is the usual assumption that if a given resource rate (resource units divided by the time interval) is doubled, its cost rate (dollars per time interval) will also double provided that the task and method used remain unchanged. This basic straight line relationship is not always true; for it may be commonly assumed that if there is a possibility to assign more than one unit of resource to an activity, the least costly unit will be assigned first. Under this assumption the cost per unit of time for doing the activity will increase more rapidly as the resource rate increases. This function is shown qualitatively by curve A in Figure 10.1. These increases are mainly a result of activity overhead costs.

When the resource is that of manpower the resource rate can be thought of as the crew size. The increase in cost may come about because of the increasing costs of supervision or because of requirements such as union rules, which call for additional personnel, or foremen, above a stated number of employees. When the rate is a measure of the equipment, the increase stems from the greater ownership and operating costs required by the added units. In the case

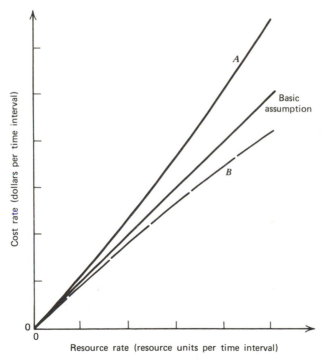

Figure 10.1   Resource rate-cost relationships for an activity.

of material as the resource, the increase can be attributed to the increase in handling costs for the larger amounts.

Curve *B* in Figure 10.1 illustrates the variation that might take place if the assignment of resources is made by using the most costly resource unit first. This may be the pattern in some instances, but it would be exceptional.

The second concept is qualitatively illustrated by Figure 10.2. The basic assumption which results in the curve shown is that the product of the total resources applied to the activity and the time required to do the work remain constant; that is, that the task contains a constant volume of work. For example, if a task takes 20 man-hours to complete, it is assumed that this can be done by one person working 20 hours, four persons working 5 hours, five persons working 4 hours, or 20 persons working 1 hour. Letting T represent the time, R equal the total resources, and W stand for the work volume, this relationship may be written mathematically as $TR = W$, which will be recognized as the equation of a hyperbola.

There are two implied assumptions being made in support of the basic hyperbola. The first is that the resources are not restrained in any way by the physical conditions of the activity. For example, it may not be possible to use only 1 person to do the job as the curve suggests; it may take a minimum of 2

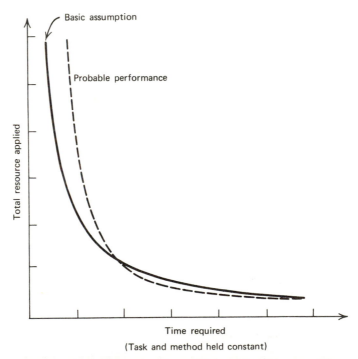

Figure 10.2   Resource-time relationships for an activity.

persons. Also there may not be room enough to work more than 5 persons at one time, rendering the 20-person crew meaningless. These restraints are ignored by the diagram, although they may be actual necessities for any given activity.

The second implied assumption is that resource units are mutually independent. That is, that all units are equally efficient and that when used in combination, the sum effort is the sum of the individual efforts of the units. To illustrate, if two bulldozers are used to move earth and can be worked side by side, their combined output will be more than the sum of the two bulldozer outputs considered separately. This gain in efficiency is not accounted for by the basic curve.

Efficiency factors alter the basic curve and may lead to a variation that might appear as the probable performance curve of Figure 10.2. The upper branch of this curve represents less efficient production and the lower branch results from more efficient outputs.

Variations in efficiency arise from two major sources, the physical characteristics surrounding the task and the limitations of the resource. Some typical physical situations leading to inefficiencies are; too many employees for the task at hand or the work space available, too many pieces of equipment on the job so that not all are able to work at capacity, and too many units of material stored on the site, causing cluttered working conditions. The quality of workmanship expected for the task, the overall size of the job, and the amount of detail needed, also exert strong influences on efficiency as do the environmental factors affecting humans, equipment, and material.

Probably the most important factors that determine efficiencies are caused by the limits inherent in the resource itself. Certain crew sizes are more efficient than others, for example, and the size of the equipment being used is most efficient if the machine is properly proportioned to the size and content of the work to be done. Material handling is most efficient if the quantity of material is balanced with respect to equipment and workers. Major intangible factors affecting efficiency relate to the human characteristics of the workers. These center about external motivational factors, job satisfaction, and psychological fulfillment. A detailed discussion of such human factors and their influences may be found in Parker.[10.6]

All of the above enumerated conditions must be considered in estimating time durations as well as in the estimation of costs.

In cases where the task to be performed is a repetitive one, an increase in efficiency may be expected with time because there is an experience factor, or learning curve effect. Parker[10.6] points out that such learning curves for construction work can be expected to fall within a range between the 70 and 90 percent curves. The functions shown in Figure 10.2 do not account for this type of increasing efficiency.

The following example illustrates the concepts discussed above. A contractor is to dig a service trench for the installation of water and sewer lines to a new

TABLE 10.1

Laborers	Hourly Rate	Remarks
1	$10	
2	20	
3	32	Third man has a longevity rate of $12 per hour
4	44	Second $12 per hour man added
5	59	Forman added at $14 per hour

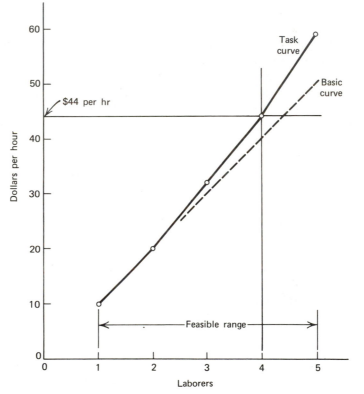

Figure 10.3   Resource-cost curve for a trenching activity.

house. The plans show that the trench is to be 50 feet long, 6 feet deep, and $2\frac{1}{2}$ feet wide. Field investigation has shown that the soil is an ordinary clay-loam that will stand by itself for a reasonable length of time. The contractor has elected to dig the trench with hand shovels, has laborers available, and would have to rent trenching equipment if a mechanical method is to be used. It is estimated that one laborer can dig one-half cubic yard per hour under the conditions on the job site. The hourly costs and the order in which the laborers are to be employed have been determined as given in Table 10.1. The contractor knows that one laborer can do this work and that no more than five should be assigned because the length of the trench will not permit more than this number without considerable interference. Figure 10.3 is a plot of the rates from Table 10.1 over the feasible human resource range. Note the similarity to curve A in Figure 10.1.

The contractor estimates that the efficiency of two laborers working together will increase production over that for one by as much as 25 percent. As additional laborers are added to the crew the efficiency will drop. Because the total amount of excavation is about 28 cubic yards, one laborer working at the assumed rate will complete the task in 56 hours. Table 10.2 gives the adjusted estimate for times of completion by crew size. Figure 10.4 shows a plot of these time durations together with the basic hyperbola drawn without efficiency considerations.

TABLE 10.2

Laborers	Estimated Time
1	56.0 hours
2	22.5
3	18.7
4	17.5
5	16.0

The contractor has decided to assign four laborers to the task. This assignment will result in a time duration of 17.5 hours as shown. The cost of this work is then computed as the product of the rate and the time ($44×17.5 hrs.), or $770. If the time constraints of the project will allow, a crew of three laborers can be used and the time will increase to almost 19 hours, but the cost will drop to about $600. Several other options are evident and the contractor must judge which of the crew sizes and times provide the greatest advantage.

When costs are computed for each of the five crew sizes and are plotted against the activity time the result is as shown in Figure 10.5. It is clear from this diagram that the most optimum time in which to perform the activity would be

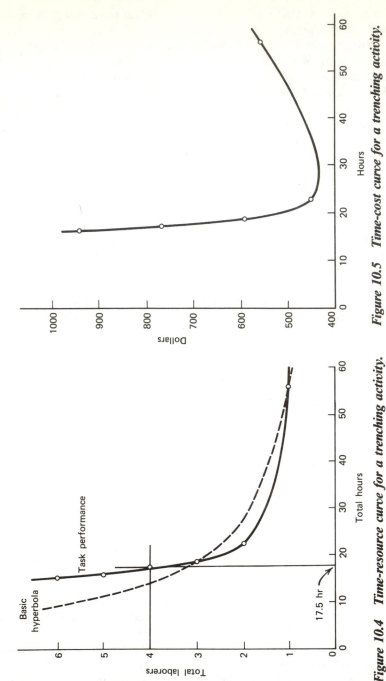

Figure 10.5   Time-cost curve for a trenching activity.

Figure 10.4   Time-resource curve for a trenching activity.

194

about 28 hours employing somewhat less than two laborers. Because there is no continuous function between the plotted points as might be inferred from the figure, the assignment for optimum cost is two laborers at a cost of $450 with an expected activity duration of 22.5 hours.

10.3   ACTIVITY TIME-COST RELATIONSHIPS

It was shown in the previous section that there is a relationship between the duration time for an activity and the cost of performing it. The example used was of a specific nature, and although serving to outline the basic concept, the example did not result in a form that will permit an analysis of the trade-off between time and cost occurring in a project. To accomplish this analysis objective, several assumptions must be made concerning the time-cost curve.

The first of these assumptions is that each activity has some kind of time-cost relationship. This is true for most activities in a network, but there may be some activities that seem to have only a fixed cost regardless of the time needed to perform them. These cannot enter into any adjustment process and are therefore treated as constant values.

The second assumption is that the variation in the times and costs is a linear one. In Figure 10.5 there is a slight curve between the minimum cost point represented by the crew size of two laborers and the upper point represented by the crew size of five. A straight line between these two points would approximate the true variation without much error. It can be assumed that this is a fairly typical case and this concept can then be extended to all the activities.

Figure 10.6 illustrates such a generalized activity. The point labeled N is the minimum cost point. Its coordinates are CN and TN on the cost axis and the duration time axis, respectively. The point labeled C is the point established by the minimum time and is indicated by coordinates TC and CC on the time axis and cost axis, respectively. The dashed curve suggests the true curve between the points C and N.

The minimum cost point, N, is called the *normal point*. Note that this is not the usual use for the word *normal*, which in ordinary usage means *common*. Here it has the connotation of being the minimum value, the commonly sought condition that every contractor would hope to achieve.

The minimum time point, C, is called the *crash point* because its achievement implies expending a great deal of effort to reduce the time to its minimum.

It will be noted that in Figure 10.6 there is another point, E, shown on the line between C and N. This represents the conventionally derived estimate of the activity duration and cost. Actually, the point should lie on the dashed curve, but the assumption of linearity places it on the solid line with an anticipated small error. The associated duration time, TE, and cost, CE, are shown on the respective axes.

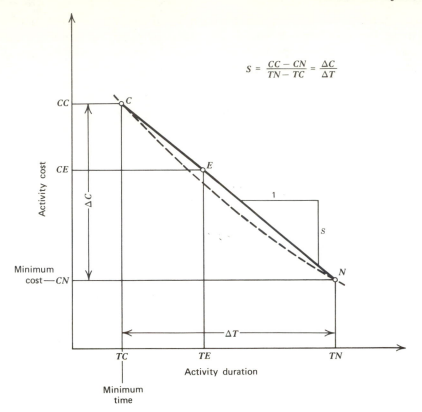

$$S = \frac{CC - CN}{TN - TC} = \frac{\Delta C}{\Delta T}$$

Figure 10.6   *Activity time-cost relationships.*

Although the determination of the conventional estimate point can be found from usual estimating procedures, the determination of the normal and crash points is not as easily obtained. In most cases a direct question approach to the person able to provide the data for these extreme points is not satisfactory because it induces a bias in the values. The tendency for any respondent is to shade the time and cost to reflect favorable performance should the estimate be incorrect; this tends to move the extreme points toward the center. A more satisfactory approach seems to be to establish the conventional estimate point first and then to ask the respondent to estimate the extremes based on the best and worst conceivable conditions that can be imagined.

In the derivation of these points it should be emphasized that the method for performing the work is to be held constant with only the quantities of the resources being allowed to vary. A common tendency is to try to substitute one resource for another. If this is done, the activity should be re-estimated because the original definition of the activity has been materially altered. In the example of the trenching operation in the previous section, only the crew size was varied. If a trenching machine had been added, the activity would have been entirely different with a different variation for the activity's times and costs.

The time-cost variations being considered here do not include the calamitous situation. Rather, the customary practice in the performance of the activity is assumed. Unusual conditions of weather, windstorms, strikes, and the like must be handled as exceptions, which they are, and not as variations of the activity's performance.

With the above restrictions on the activity's time-cost curve, it is necessary to give some direction as to how the resources can be augmented to cause these changes. For example, to shorten the duration and increase the cost, the human resource for the activity may be placed on overtime, more workers may be hired, crews may be doubled up, more equipment may be brought to the site, equipment may be worked at a faster rate or for longer hours, equipment with larger capacities may be employed, and so forth. Of course, to extend the duration of the activity and lower the cost the reverse actions may be taken.

The assumption that the costs vary linearly from the normal point to the crash point allows for the determination of the cost slope for the activity. This value is important to the adjustment process and can be taken as the difference in the costs divided by the difference in the duration times. It may be expressed mathematically as

$$S = \frac{CC - CN}{TN - TC} = \frac{\Delta C}{\Delta T} \tag{10.1}$$

where S is the cost slope, ΔC is the total change in costs, ΔT is the total change in time, and the other symbols are as defined earlier. It may be observed from Figure 10.6 that the mathematical slope is negative. This sign will be ignored and only the absolute value will be used in the following adjustment procedures.

Occasionally an activity will have a time-cost curve that varies between the normal and crash points so as to make the assumption of linearity inappropriate. In this case the activity may be replaced with pseudoactivities whose slopes may be considered linear without great error. Figure 10.7 shows such a case. The dashed line clearly should not be used as it departs too radically from the true curve. A point M is chosen to divide the curve into two parts and the slope is calculated for each piecewise linear segment. Meyer and Shaffer[10.5] present a technique that can be used as a model for this type of adjustment. Figure 10.8a represents the two piecewise linear segments of the curve of Figure 10.7. The conversion of Activity A into the two pseudoactivities $A1$ and $A2$ is illustrated in Figure 10.8b. Because this procedure is independent of the type of diagram that is being used, the replacement is shown for both the Precedence Diagram notation and the Arrow Diagram notation. The upper segment, $A1$, is shown in Figure 10.8c and the lower segment is shown in Figure 10.8d. The concept employed is that of shifting the origin so that one of the axes passes through the

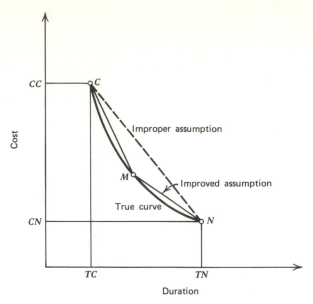

Figure 10.7   Creation of a piecewise linear time-cost curve.

auxiliary point M. The slopes are therefore computed as follows:

$$S_{A1} = \frac{CC - CM}{TM - TC}$$

and

$$S_{A2} = \frac{CM - CN}{TN - TM}$$

A similar situation occurs when an activity's true time-cost curve has a shape that is double curved as shown in Figure 10.9a. In this case three pseudo-activities are used to replace the single one. Again, the slopes can be calculated in a manner similar to that above.

Another condition frequently encountered in practice is where the time-cost curve is not continuous between points. Figure 10.9b represents such a situation. In reality this reduces to two separate activities, and the slopes can be calculated in the same way as for pseudoactivities.

Time-cost relationships are not always represented by continuous curves between the normal and crash points. Instead, there may be a series of discrete time-cost points with no real possibilities for times and costs at intermediate points. The techniques to be presented in this chapter depend upon cost slopes and, hence, an adjusting assumption must be made to fit the data to this requirement.

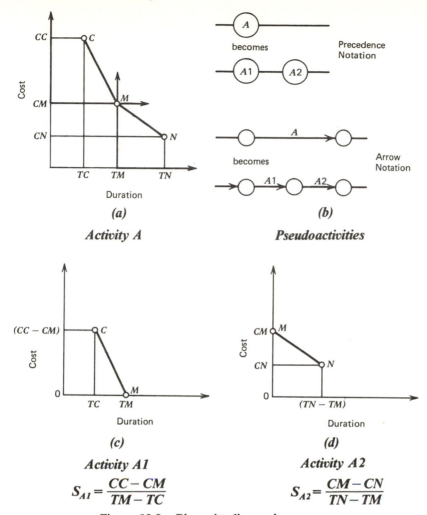

Figure 10.8   Piecewise linear time-cost curve.

$$S_{A1} = \frac{CC - CM}{TM - TC}$$

$$S_{A2} = \frac{CM - CN}{TN - TM}$$

Virtual slopes are assumed between any discrete point and all the other points in the system. These virtual slopes are then used in the computations with care being taken to avoid the intermediate positions. To illustrate, consider the following example.

Discrete times and costs for an activity are given in Table 10.3. These are plotted in Figure 10.10. The five points have been connected with dashed lines indicating the slopes that can be computed for any change from one of the points to another. This same information may be conveniently shown by the construction of a cost slope matrix as in Figure 10.11.

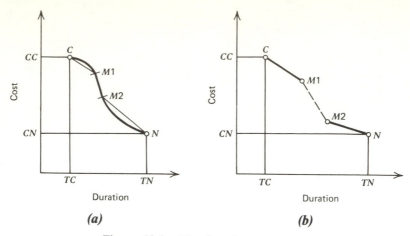

Figure 10.9   Varying time-cost curves.

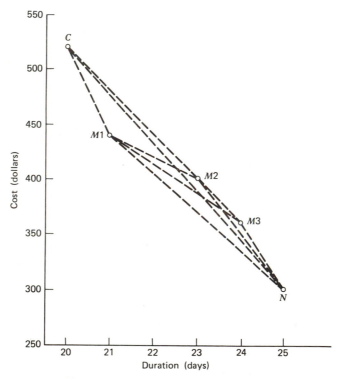

Figure 10.10   Activity with discrete time-cost values.

		To				
Points	Days	C	M1	M2	M3	N
		20	21	23	24	25
C	20	0	−80	−40	−40	−44
M1	21	80	0	−20	−26.7	−35
M2	23	40	20	0	−40	−50
M3	24	40	26.7	40	0	−60
N	25	44	35	50	60	0

Figure 10.11   Cost slope matrix—activity with discrete time-cost values.

TABLE 10.3

Duration Times and Costs for an
Activity with Discrete Time-Cost Values

Point	Duration Time	Cost
C	20 days	$520
M1	21	440
M2	23	400
M3	24	360
N	25	300

Assume that it is desired to add resources and change the time duration of the activity from 23 days to 21 days. The difference in cost between these two days is $40 as can be determined from Table 10.3. The difference in time duration is two days; hence, the slope is $20 per day. This is entered in the matrix in the row marked M2 23 at the intersection with the column marked M1 21. All the other values are found in a similar fashion. Note that all the values in the upper right portion of the matrix have negative signs, indicating that the values represent a decrease in the cost when changing from the point on the left of the row to the point at the top of the column.

10.4   PROJECT TIME-COST RELATIONSHIPS

Total construction project costs may be divided into two types, indirect costs and direct costs. Indirect costs are those that apply to the project as a whole. Direct costs are those that can be assigned to the individual activities.

Indirect Costs

The major indirect cost is the general overhead that the construction organization must carry. In short, it is the cost of doing business. The costs of secretarial assistance, telephone service, and heat and light for the central office are typical costs that fall into this category. Also, the managerial expenses of cost accounting, payroll, and purchasing are general burdens included in this category, as are the expenses of estimating, bid preparation, and scheduling. In some organiza-

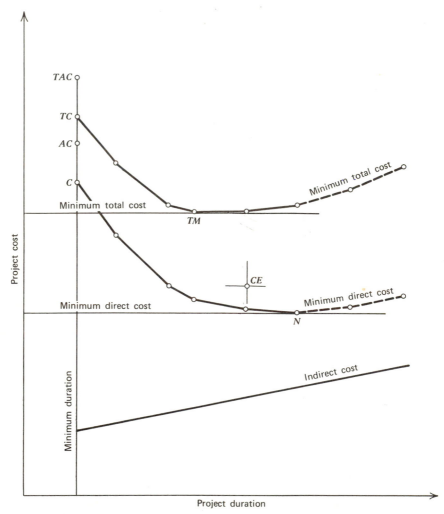

Figure 10.12 Project time-cost relationships.

tions the costs associated with equipment rental and interest on financial transactions are considered indirect costs.

The second main group of indirect costs are those that apply to a particular contract. Included in this group are the costs of operating the site office, applying safety programs, supervising the job, and so forth.

Occasionally there are costs that may be considered indirect yet are associated with a network activity incidental to the main activities of the project. In this category can be placed costs associated with incidental site fencing, winter heating of the work space, the preparation and maintenance of haul roads, and equipment to be used on a demand basis through the life of the project.

When the contract has a liquidated damages clause and/or a bonus clause, any charges arising therefrom are usually considered as indirect costs. Similarly, the costs associated with lost revenues incurred by both the owner and the contractor are indirect costs.

Indirect costs have two main characteristics: they increase with time and the rate of increase tends to vary linearly. Such costs can be expected to have different rates of increase depending upon any particular job organization and location. They are unlikely to have the same rate for all jobs being performed by the same company. A typical indirect cost curve without liquidated damages is shown as the lower curve in Figure 10.12. If liquidated damages or bonus clauses are included, the curve could have more than one cost slope over the duration of the project.

Direct Costs

Costs directly assignable to each network activity as discussed in the previous section can be added together to obtain the direct project cost. Also, it was previously pointed out that an individual activity cost tends to decrease with increasing activity duration. Because the project duration is found by summing activity durations along the critical path, it therefore follows that the direct project cost will also tend to decrease with an increase in project duration. This decrease will take place in a piecewise linear fashion.

Individual activities can be performed at any duration time between the normal and crash points. There is therefore a wide range of possible combinations of schedule times and costs for every possible project time duration. The combination of activity times and costs that gives the minimum value at every project duration results in the minimum direct project cost curve. The minimum direct cost curve is segmental between feasible project duration times because the individual activities have been assumed to have linear cost functions as discussed earlier. The middle curve in Figure 10.12 represents a typical minimum direct cost curve.

The minimum point on the minimum direct cost curve is called the "normal" point for the project. The use of the word "normal" has the same connotation as for an individual activity, that is, minimum cost. This point can be found easily because it represents the sum of all the normal costs of the activities in the network. Its corresponding project duration time is found by summing the durations of the activities determining the critical path when all activities are scheduled at their normal times; it is the point labeled N in Figure 10.12.

It will be observed that there is a portion of the minimum direct cost curve extending to the right of the normal point that is shown dashed in Figure 10.12. This represents the possibility that there can be schedules that are caused by the improper utilization of resources on some of the activities. This is referred to as the "drag-out" phase of the project. Its extent is unlimited and will be avoided if at all possible.

For every project there is a minimum project duration. It is established when all the critical activities along some critical path are scheduled to be performed at their crash times. As was the case with the individual activity, this point is called the "crash" point. It is shown in Figure 10.12 as the point labeled C.

At the project crash time there is the possibility that there will be activities in the network that are not being scheduled at their crash times. When these activities are crashed, the project cost is increased but the project duration time remains the same. On the minimum direct cost curve in Figure 10.12 this is represented by the vertical line extending upward from the crash point. When every activity in the network is being scheduled at its crash point, the resulting project direct cost point is called the "all crash" point. It is labeled AC in Figure 10.12.

The direct cost curve shown in Figure 10.12 has been defined as the minimum curve. If conventional estimating procedures are used to determine the costs and durations of the activities, it is likely that the subsequent project duration time and cost will not fall on the minimum curve. Instead, it will lie somewhere above the curve. This point, labeled CE, is indicated on Figure 10.12 and is called the conventional estimate point. In the following sections of this chapter this point assumes an increasingly important significance.

Total Cost

The sum of the indirect and direct costs at any duration time gives the total project cost at that duration. Plotting these values for all possible project duration times gives the project total cost curve. This total cost curve is shown as the upper curve in Figure 10.12.

As indirect costs increase with duration time and direct costs decrease with time, the minimum total cost will occur at the project duration where the slopes of the indirect and direct cost curves are equal. If equality cannot be obtained, the minimum point will occur where the slope of the total cost curve changes from negative to positive. This point is labeled TM in Figure 10.12. Note that it is found at a duration time less than the project direct cost normal point, N.

It is natural for a contractor to want to perform any project at the minimum total cost. Because the indirect cost rate can be reduced by only a relatively small amount in any given situation, most project cost savings must come from the direct costs.

To achieve the minimum total cost a contractor must therefore plan the project to achieve the schedule resulting in point *TM* while maintaining the utilization of resources on each activity at the lowest permitted levels and within the permitted constraints of the logic of the network.

10.5 THE EFFECT OF ACTIVITY DURATION CHANGES ON THE NETWORK

Before presenting a technique for the determination of the minimum direct cost curve for a project, it is desirable to examine the changes that can occur in the project network when an activity has its duration changed. It will be assumed that the resulting schedule is to be an early start schedule and that the activities will remain continuous. That is, each activity will be performed continuously once started and will not be divided into segments with time intervals between them.

Under the above conditions, as an activity duration is altered it will cause the critical path to be either lengthened or shortened if that activity is critical. Whether the changed activity is critical or not, there is always the possibility that the total and free floats of some of the network activities will be changed.

Figure 10.13*a* represents an activity, *I*, taken from a precedence network. Initially, it is represented by the circle and has a duration of two days and an early finish date, *EFD*, of two. If the duration is increased to three, the activity, now represented by the elipse, will have an *EFD* of three. Note that the early start date, *ESD*, of the activity has not been changed owing to the assumption of a desired early start schedule. The increase in the *EFD* value of Activity *I* is emphasized by the arrow pointing to the right. This concept of a change in the *EFD* can be extended to identify increases in the *ESD* and *EFD* values of other activities which are linked together in the network.

Figure 10.13*b* is a simple precedence network with the early start and finish dates shown. Assume that it is desired to lengthen the duration of Activity B. Assume also that Activity B can be lengthened by five days as determined from its activity time-cost curve. Activity B corresponds to the activity just discussed, Activity *I*, and any lengthening will alter its *EFD*. A mark, >, signifying the arrow placed above the same location in part *a* of Figure 10.13 has therefore been added. It may be thought of as the head of the arrow.

The *ESD* of Activity C must also be increased because the start of this activity depends upon the finish of Activity B as indicated by the zero lag in Link B–C. Another arrowhead has been placed above this *ESD* to designate this increase. Now, Activity C is not being altered and its duration of four days

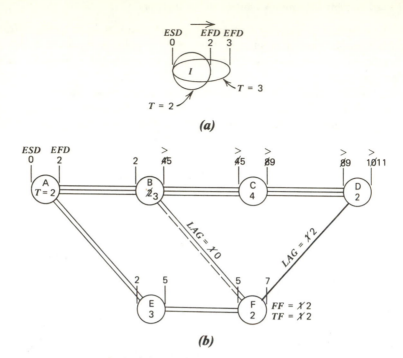

(a)

(b)

Activity B, lengthened one day

Links		I	J		I	J	Rev.
I Act	J Act	EFD	ESD	LAG	EFD	ESD	LAG
A	B	2	2	0			
A	E	2	2	0			
B	C	4	4	0	≫	>	
B	F	4	5	1	⊘		0
E	F	5	5	0			
C	D	8	8	0	>	>	
F	D	7	8	1		>	2

Network limit

(c)

Figure 10.13   Network limit concepts.

206

remains the same. Hence, the *EFD* of Activity C must also be shifted to a later time and another arrowhead has been inserted. The same procedure has been carried out with respect to the *ESD* and *EFD* of Activity D.

Link B–F has a lag value of one. The shift of the *EFD* of Activity B does not affect Activity F because the *ESD* of Activity F depends upon the completion of Activity E. Nevertheless, this lag in Link B–F does impose a restriction on the possible increase in the *EFD* of Activity B, for if Activity B's *EFD* is increased more than the one day permitted by the lag, it would become the determining precedent for Activity F. It should be clear that this lag is the limit imposed by the network for changing the duration of Activity B even though Activity B could be changed by the total five days.

Link F–D also has a lag of one day. The increase in the *ESD* of Activity D increases the lag in this link by the same amount. Because Activity B was limited in its increase in duration by the network limit from Link B–F to one day, the increase in the lag in Link F–D will also be increased by one day. Beneath Activity F is shown the free float and the total float. These values are derived from the lag in the F–D link so they are each increased by one day.

The network has been updated to show the changes in all the *ESD* and *EFD* values and the lags in the two affected links. Link B–F has had a dashed line added to show its new zero lag condition.

Figure 10.13*c* shows the same network limit determination in a tabular format. Each of the links of the network are listed in the first two columns. The next two columns show the *EFD* and *ESD* values at each end of the links. In the fifth column is shown the lag value for each link. The last three columns are reserved for the calculation. The sixth column is to contain the arrowheads for those *EFD*'s that are being changed, and the seventh column is to contain the arrowheads for those *ESD*'s that are affected. The eighth column will be used for the revised lag values.

Activity B is the activity whose duration is being lengthened and the *EFD* of this activity is shifted to a later time. The arrowhead is placed in the sixth column opposite the Links B–C and B–F to show that the *EFD* at the *I* end of these links is being increased. These arrowheads have been doubled to show that they are the initial entries in the table. The lag in Link B–C is zero as shown so an arrowhead is added to the seventh column opposite the one in the sixth column, indicating that the *ESD* at the *J* end of this link is being increased.

Because the duration of Activity C is not changed the *EFD* of Activity C must have its value increased, as was the case in the diagram. This is indicated by the insertion of the arrowhead in the sixth column opposite the *I* end of the Link C–D. Again, the *ESD* of the *J* end of Link C–D is marked in the seventh column. Note also that there is an arrowhead in the seventh column opposite the Link F–D because the *ESD* of the *J* end of the link has already been marked.

It can now be seen that there is only one arrowhead opposite the Link B–F, indicating that this link lag is being reduced. The single arrowhead opposite

Link F–D is in the seventh column and indicates that this link lag is being increased. The network limit is determined by the link that is being reduced, or closed, and is equal to the lag in that link. Should there be more than one closing link, the one with the smallest value of lag would be the network limit.

Assuming that the duration of Activity B is increased to the limit just determined, the revised lags are shown in the eighth column. These agree with the values found on the network of Figure 10.13b and the reader should compare the diagram with the table for a clear understanding.

10.6 THE FONDAHL TECHNIQUE FOR TIME-COST ADJUSTMENTS

There have been techniques proposed for the determination of the project direct cost curve since early in the development of critical path methods. In 1961 Kelley[10.4] published a method for finding an optimal feasible schedule using the primal-dual algorithm for solving linear programs. Fulkerson[10.3] approached the solution by means of network flow computations, and Meyer and Shaffer[10.5] adapted integer programming to the problem. All these methods involve considerable calculation and the use of the digital computer.

Fondahl, in his publications of 1961[10.1] and 1964,[10.2] approached the solution for these direct cost curves from the standpoint of the practicing construction manager. His solution is a close approximation to the more exact methods, is more direct in its application, and can be performed easily by hand calculations. These computations are facilitated by a systematic ordering of steps and the maintenance of various tables of information about the network. His scheme is cyclical and is comprised of eight main steps to be carried out in each cycle. They are enumerated below.

> **Step 1**   Each cycle begins with the selection of a proper combination of activities to be changed from an Activity Selection and Tally Table and a Critical Path Tally.
>
> **Step 2**   Data from the Activity Selection and Tally Table is entered in the Summary Table.
>
> **Step 3**   The network limit is determined in a Network Limit Determination Table.
>
> **Step 4**   The network limit is entered in the Summary Table and a new point on the Time-Cost Curve is established.
>
> **Step 5**   The Network Limit Determination Table is Updated.
>
> **Step 6**   The Network is updated.
>
> **Step 7**   The Activity Selection and Tally Table is updated.
>
> **Step 8**   The Critical Path Tally is updated.

At the end of Step 8 the process repeats. The number of cycles needed to complete the curve will depend upon the constraints in the network, the amount of possible change available on each of the activities, and the total number of activities in the network. As can be seen from the scheme's steps, there are four tables to be set up and maintained in addition to the network and the direct cost curve being plotted.

Fondahl's scheme is a general one and may be used to obtain the minimum time-cost curve or the maximum time-cost curve and either the arrow or precedence network may be used. The precedence network facilitates the understanding of the method and will be used in the remainder of this chapter.

To start the solution the scheme requires that a known point in the time-cost field be available. Ordinarily, this point is the normal project cost point, but it may be the project's all crash cost point or the project's conventional estimate point. In the following sections of this chapter each of these points will be used as a starting point, and the direct minimum cost curve will be developed for a small remodeling project.

10.7   MINIMUM COST CURVE FROM NORMAL START

It was shown in Section 10.4 that the minimum total cost for a project is achieved when the slope of the indirect cost curve is equal to that of the minimum direct cost curve. It is therefore necessary to determine this curve of minimum direct cost.

For any given project duration the direct cost can be found by adding the direct costs of the activities of the network. If it is assumed that each activity has its own minimum, or normal, cost, the minimum direct cost for the project occurs when these normal costs are added. This project normal point is therefore one known point on the project's minimum direct cost curve.

To find another point on the curve, certain critical activities are selected and their durations are reduced by some increment with a corresponding increase in their costs. By adding the activity costs of these reduced activities to the costs of the activities that were not reduced, a new project cost is found. A new project duration is determined by the time length of the reduced critical path. This new duration coupled with the new project cost establishes the new point on the curve. By successively reducing activity durations and computing the gain in cost occasioned thereby, the entire minimum curve may be developed.

To illustrate this compression in the network, the Fondahl Adjustment Technique will be applied to a small project. The computations for the curve will start at the normal point and proceed to the project's all crash point.

The project selected is to remodel two rooms into a general work area and offices for the purchasing department of a construction company. A sketch plan of the rooms is shown on Figure 10.14. The work consists of removing an existing partition between the two rooms, building partitions for two offices, and building two floor-to-ceiling bookcases along one wall in the work area. The

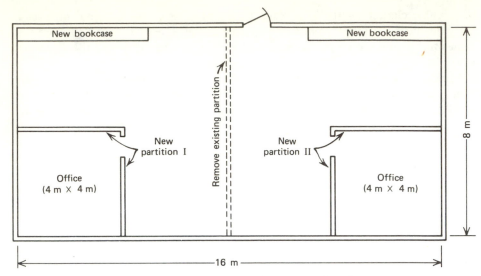

Figure 10.14   Plan for remodeling purchasing department.

activities that have been decided upon are described below. They have been numbered to correspond with their positions in the precedence diagram prepared for the work. This diagram is shown in Figure 10.15.

Activities for Remodeling Purchasing Department

10. *Clear Room.* This activity is to be accomplished by the present occupants of the rooms. It is estimated that financial support in the amount of $500 will be assigned for this work and that one week is to be allowed for the move.

20. *Remove Partition.* This activity includes the demolition of the present partition and the removal of debris from the site.

30. *Rough Mechanical and Electrical.* This activity includes the necessary alterations to the heating, air conditioning, and ventilation systems in the area so that the new office spaces can be controlled separately from the general work area. It also includes the installation of conduit for telephone and computer service.

32. *Sand Floor.* This activity includes the removal of vinyl tile presently on the wood floor, sanding the floor, and making all needed repairs so that the floor will be ready for the carpet.

40. *Partition I.* This activity includes the erection of metal studding and the application of drywall to both sides, taping, and necessary preparation for painting. No doors are required, but a door casing needs to be provided as a part of this activity.

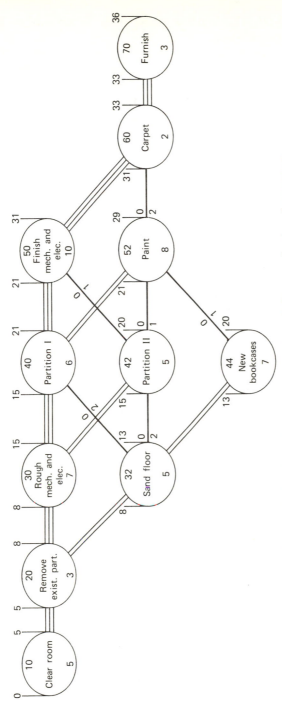

Figure 10.15   Precedence diagram—remodeling purchasing department.

42. *Partition II*. This activity is the same as Activity 40 but is for the second office space.

44. *New Bookcases*. This activity includes the building on the site of the two new bookcases and their preparation for finishing.

50. *Finish Mechanical and Electrical*. This activity includes the installation of the heating grills, lighting fixtures, thermostats, and all other heating and electrical controls. It also includes the installation of new wire for telephone and computer terminal service.

52. *Paint*. This activity includes the application of two coats of paint to all wall and ceiling surfaces and the finishing of the bookcases with three coats. It has been bid and let to a subcontractor. The subcontractor quoted a price of $800 and a time of eight days for the work. The subcontractor also quoted alternate prices of $1000 and $1500 for six days and four days, respectively.

60. *Carpet*. This activity includes the installation of new carpeting over the entire area.

70. *Furnish*. This activity includes the moving in of the new furnishings and equipment including desks, files, telephones, computing terminals, and so forth. Its cost includes the cost of these furnishings and equipment.

Table 10.4 contains the times and costs for each of the above activities. These are arranged into three groups, one for the normal times and costs, one for the crash times and costs, and the third for the conventional estimate of time and cost. The cost slope for each activity and the difference between the normal and crash durations, ΔT, are shown in the two right-hand columns. The conventional estimate values in the table will not be used in this section but will be needed later in this chapter.

It will be noted that there is no cost slope shown for the Paint activity, Activity 52, because it has only three feasible time and cost points. A cost slope matrix has been developed for this activity and it is shown in Figure 10.16.

Figure 10.15 is a precedence network prepared for the project. The early start and finish dates have been computed and are shown above the activities. The links having zero lags are shown by double lines and the critical path is indicated by the triple lines. The values of lag in the remaining links have been written below the link lines. Immediately above each of these lag values is a zero, which indicates that this is the initial value of the lag in that link.

The Fondahl Technique requires frequent reference to the network. It also requires that the network be updated in each cycle. The updating typically includes changes in activity durations, link lags, and paths. Figure 10.17 is the network of Figure 10.15, which has been updated during the computations. These changes are discussed below.

Tables 10.5 to 10.8 are the tables that will be needed in the computations that follow. Table 10.5, the Summary Table, will be used to record the activities that

TABLE 10.4

Times and Costs—Remodeling Purchasing Department

Activity	Act. No.	Normal		Conventional		Crash		ΔT (TN-TC)	Cost Slope
		TN	CN	TCE	CCE	TC	CC		
Clear rooms	10	5	$ 500	5	$ 500	5	$ 500	—	—
Remove partition	20	3	900	2	1050	1	1200	2	$150
Rough mechanical and electrical	30	7	3250	5	3850	4	4150	3	300
Sand floors	32	5	1000	3	1300	3	1300	2	150
Partition I	40	6	1400	5	1850	3	2750	3	450
Partition II	42	5	1100	4	1500	3	1900	2	400
New bookcases	44	7	1500	4	2400	4	2400	3	300
Finish mechanical and electrical	50	10	4200	8	5400	5	7200	5	600
Paint	52	8	800	6	1000	4	1500	4	Variable (See Matrix)
Carpet	60	2	1100	2	1100	1	1300	1	200
Furnish	70	3	1300	3	1300	2	1500	1	200
		36*	$17,050	30*	$21,250	21*	$25,700		

*From CPM diagram.

213

		To Days	
	4	6	8
	4	0	−250	−175
From Days	6	250	0	−100
	8	175	100	0

Figure 10.16 $ slope matrix—activity 52—paint.

TABLE 10.5

Summary Table

	Combination			ΔT				Days	$	$	Project	Project
CY	1	2	3	1	2	3	NL	Changed	Slope	Changed	Cost	Days
0											(N) $17,050	36
1	20			2			None	2	150	300	17,350	34
2	60			1			None	1	200	200	17,550	33
3	70			1			None	1	200	200	17,750	32
4	30			3			1	1	300	300	18,050	31
5	30			2			1	1	300	300	18,350	30
6	30	32		1	2		None	1	450	450	18,800	29
7	40			3			1	1	450	450	19,250	28
8	50	52		5	2		None	2	700	1400	20,650	26
9	50	52		3	2		None	2	850	1700	22,350	24
10	50	44		1	3		2	1	900	900	23,250	23
11	40	42	44	2	2	2	None	2	1150	2300	(C)25,550	21
12	32			1			1	1	150	150	(AC)25,750	21

are being changed in each cycle together with their current possible change in duration, ΔT. The column headed NL is used to record the network limit. The five columns to the right are to record the decision as to the amount of activity shortening occurring in each cycle and the coordinates of the new points on the time-cost curve.

Table 10.6, the Activity Selection and Tally Table, is used in conjunction with Table 10.7 to determine the activities subject to change. Those entries in the Combination Selection area assist in deciding the particular activity or combination of activities to be changed cycle by cycle. The table is also used to keep a running tally of the activities that become critical in the column headed CP CY.

The column headed FIN CY records the cycle in which an activity has been changed in duration by the maximum amount. The columns to the right of the table record the revisions in the duration times and the current amount of change that an activity possesses.

Table 10.7, the Critical Path Tally, lists the critical paths that exist in the network at the end of each cycle. It is arranged by sequence step and all the activities on a single sequence step are listed in the second column for easy reference.

Table 10.8, the Network Limit Determination Table, is used to compute the network limit for each cycle. The first two columns list the links in the network. The next two columns record the *EFD* and *ESD* values at the ends of the links, and the fifth column gives the lags on the links at the normal starting point.

Initial Entries

To start the adjustment process a zero is placed in the first column of Table 10.5 to identify the initial condition. Opposite this the project cost and project duration are entered. In this instance the values are for the normal time-cost point and are taken from Table 10.4.

Each activity in the network is listed in the column headed ACT in Table 10.6 in increasing order of the cost slope. Note that Activity 10 is listed first because it has a fixed cost and no slope. The second activity, Activity 52, is listed next because it is the one that has a variable set of cost slopes. In the CP CY column activities that are initially critical have been indicated by the insertion of a zero. In the FIN CY column a zero has also been inserted to show that Activity 10 cannot be changed. The zero will always be understood to indicate the initial condition.

In Table 10.7 the initial critical path is shown. The slash across Activity 10 is to indicate that this activity cannot be changed and will not be a candidate for the selection decision.

In Table 10.8 the initial values of the *EFD* and *ESD* at the ends of the links are entered. The lags are also shown. This information is taken from the network of Figure 10.15.

Figure 10.17 repeats the initial values from Figure 10.15. In practice, it is usually unnecessary to construct two diagrams. It has been done here only for the sake of clarity.

Criteria for Normal Start

The main object to be met in developing the project's minimum direct cost curve from the normal time-cost point is to shorten the project duration at the least

TABLE 10.6

Activity Selection and Tally Table

12	11	10	9	8	7	6	5	4	3	2	1	ACT	$ Slo
												10	—
			⊗ ×	× ⊗								52	VA
											⊗	20	150
⊗						⊗						32	150
										⊗		60	200
									⊗			70	200
						⊗	⊗	⊗				30	300
	⊗	⊗ ×	×	×								44	300
	⊗	×	× ×	× ×								42	400
	⊗	×	× ×	×	⊗	×						40	450
	⊗	× ⊗	× ⊗	×	×	×						50	600

Column totals: 150 · 1150 · 900 · 1150 · 900 · 850 · 1100 · 1150 · 950 · 900 · 700 · 1150 · 600 · 450 · 600 · 450 · 450 · 300 · 300 · 200 · 200 · 150

TABLE 10.7

Tally of Critical Paths at End of Cycle

Step	ACT.	0	1	2	3	4	5		6		7.8				
1	10	~~10~~	~~10~~	~~10~~	~~10~~	~~10~~	~~10~~	~~10~~	~~10~~	~~10~~	~~10~~	~~10~~	~~10~~	~~10~~	~~10~~
2	20	20	~~20~~	~~20~~	~~20~~	~~20~~	~~20~~	~~20~~	~~20~~	~~20~~	~~20~~	~~20~~	~~20~~	~~20~~	~~20~~
3	30, 32	30	30	30	30	30	30	32	~~30~~	32	~~30~~	32	32	~~30~~	32
4	40, 42, 44	40	40	40	40	40	40	40	40	40	40	40	42	42	44
5	50, 52	50	50	50	50	50	50	50	50	50	50	50	50	50	~~52~~
6	60	60	60	~~60~~	~~60~~	~~60~~	~~60~~	~~60~~	~~60~~	~~60~~	~~60~~	~~60~~	~~60~~	~~60~~	~~60~~
7	70	70	70	70	~~70~~	~~70~~	~~70~~	~~70~~	~~70~~	~~70~~	~~70~~	~~70~~	~~70~~	~~70~~	~~70~~

216

TABLE 10.6 (Continued)

CP CY	FIN CY	T	ΔT	\multicolumn{12}{c}{Revised $T/\Delta T$}											
				1	2	3	4	5	6	7	8	9	10	11	12
0	0	5	—												
7	9	8	4								6/2	4/0			
0	1	3	2	1/0											
5	12	5	2						4/1						3/0
0	2	2	1		1/0										
0	3	3	1			2/0									
0	6	7	3				6/2	5/1	4/0						
7	11	7	3										6/2	4/0	
7	11	5	2											3/0	
0	11	6	3							5/2				3/0	
0	10	10	5								8/3	6/1	5/0		

TABLE 10.7(Continued)

\multicolumn{5}{c}{9}					\multicolumn{5}{c}{10}					\multicolumn{5}{c}{11}					\multicolumn{2}{c}{12}	
~~10~~	~~10~~	~~10~~	~~10~~	~~10~~	~~10~~	~~10~~	~~10~~	~~10~~	~~10~~	~~10~~	~~10~~	~~10~~	~~10~~	~~10~~	~~10~~	~~10~~
~~20~~	~~20~~	~~20~~	~~20~~	~~20~~	~~20~~	~~20~~	~~20~~	~~20~~	~~20~~	~~20~~	~~20~~	~~20~~	~~20~~	~~20~~	~~20~~	~~20~~
~~30~~	32	32	~~30~~	32	~~30~~	32	32	~~30~~	32	~~30~~	32	32	~~30~~	32	~~30~~	~~30~~
40	40	42	42	44	40	40	42	42	44	~~40~~	~~40~~	~~42~~	~~42~~	~~44~~	~~40~~	~~42~~
50	50	50	50	~~52~~	~~50~~	~~50~~	~~50~~	~~50~~	~~52~~	~~50~~	~~50~~	~~50~~	~~50~~	~~52~~	~~50~~	~~50~~
~~60~~	~~60~~	~~60~~	~~60~~	~~60~~	~~60~~	~~60~~	~~60~~	~~60~~	~~60~~	~~60~~	~~60~~	~~60~~	~~60~~	~~60~~	~~60~~	~~60~~
~~70~~	~~70~~	~~70~~	~~70~~	~~70~~	~~70~~	~~70~~	~~70~~	~~70~~	~~70~~	~~70~~	~~70~~	~~70~~	~~70~~	~~70~~	~~70~~	~~70~~

TABLE 10.8

Network Limit Determination Table

Link I	Link J	I (EFD)	J (ESD)	LAG	C1 I	C1 J	C1 LAG	C2 I	C2 J	C2 LAG	C3 I	C3 J	C3 LAG	C4 I	C4 J	C4 LAG	C5 I	C5 J	C5 LAG
Cycle					1			2			3			4			5		
Activity Changed					20			60			70			30			30		
Network Limit					None			None			None			1			1		
Days Changed					2			1			1			1			1		
10	20	5	5	0															
20	30	8	8	0	≪	<													
20	32	8	8	0	≪	<													
30	40	15	15	0	<	<								≪	<		≪	<	
30	42	15	15	0	<	<								≪	<		≪	<	
32	40	13	15	2	<	<						None Affected			<	1		Ⓒ<	0
32	42	13	15	2	<	<									<	1		Ⓒ<	0
32	44	13	13	0	<	<													
40	50	21	21	0	<	<								<	<		<	<	
40	52	21	21	0	<	<								<	<		<	✗	1
42	50	20	21	1	<	<								<	<		<	<	
42	52	20	21	1	<	<								<	<		<	✗	2
44	52	20	21	1	<	<								Ⓒ<		0		✗	
50	60	31	31	0	<	<								<	Ⓒ<		<	<	
52	60	29	31	2	<	<								<	<		✗	<	1
60	70	33	33	0	<	<		≪	<					<	<		<	<	

TABLE 10.8 (Continued)

6			7			8			9			10			11			12		
30,32			40			50,52			50,52			44,50			40,42, 44			32		
None			1			None			None			2			None			1		
1			1			2			2			1			2			1		
I	J	L A G	I	J	L A G	I	J	L A G	I	J	L A G	I	J	L A G	I	J	L A G	I	J	L A G
«	<																			
«	<																			
«	<																	«		1
«	<																	«		1
«	<																	«	<	
<	<		«	<											«	<				
<	<		«	(<)	2 0							(<)		1	«	<		(<)		0
<	<											(<)		1	«	<		(<)		0
<	<					«	<		«	<		«	<		«	<		<	<	
<	<		<	(<)	0	«	<<		«	<<		«	<		<	<<		<		1
<	<		<			<	<<		<	<<		<	<		<	<<				
<	<											<	<		<	<<				

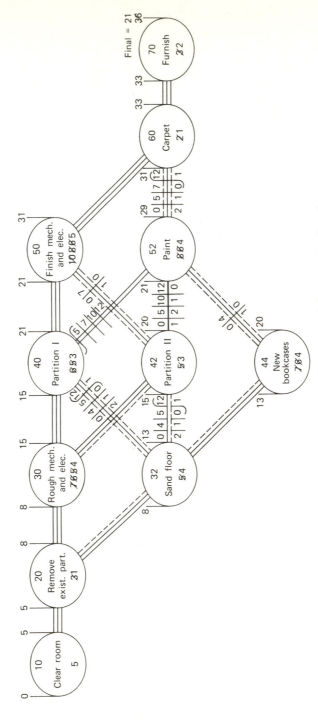

Figure 10.17 *Normal start solution—remodeling purchasing department.*

220

possible increase in cost. In the selection of activities to achieve this objective there are three conditions to be satisfied.

1. The activity or activities must be critical and, if shortened, must shorten all existing critical paths.
2. The activity or activities must have the smallest current cost slope.
3. The activity or activities must be currently available for shortening. That is, they must have some remaining ΔT value.

SOLUTION

The solution of the minimum direct cost curve will now be carried out. Detailed cycle-by-cycle and step-by-step entries in the tables will be discussed to assist the reader in gaining a complete understanding of the technique.

Cycle 1

From an examination of Table 10.7 there is one critical path. Of the activities on this path Activity 20 is found to have the minimum slope in Table 10.6. An X is entered in the Combination Selection portion of this table under the number 1, standing for the cycle. It is circled to indicate that this is the chosen activity. At the foot of this column is entered the value of the slope of $150.

In the second step of the process Activity 20 is entered in Table 10.5 in the Combination area and its ΔT from Table 10.6 is entered in the ΔT portion. The cost slope is also entered in the slope column.

The third step is to compute the network limit in Table 10.8. The cycle number and the activity being considered are entered here at the top of the column. Arrowheads are placed opposite the links listed in accordance with the procedure given in Section 10.5. However, these arrowheads point to the left to signify that the activity is being shortened. The initial entries for this cycle are opposite Links 20–30 and 20–32 and are doubled. Both these links have zero lags so the *ESD* at the 30 and 32 ends are also marked with an arrowhead. The links beginning with Activities 30 and 32 are also marked. These links again have zero lags and the process is repeated for them. This procedure continues on down the table until no further markings can take place. In this instance, all the links below Link 20–30 are marked in both their *I* and *J* ends. There is therefore no network limit when the reduction in duration of Activity 20 takes place.

In Step 4 the result from the network determination is added in the NL column of the Summary Table. Because the activity can be changed only by the minimum amount from either the ΔT or NL columns, the number of days to be changed is 2. The product of this change and the cost slope results in a total cost change of $300 and raises the project cost to $17,350. The project duration is reduced to 34 days.

The fifth step requires that the number of days changed be added to the

Network Limit Determination Table. Because no links have had their lags increased or decreased, this is all that is needed at this time.

The sixth step of the technique is to update the network, but because there was no change in lag in Table 10.8, there is no change to be made in the network except to show that Activity 20's duration is now one day as shown by the slash through the 3 and the addition of 1.

The seventh step is to add the revised activity duration to Table 10.6 together with the revised ΔT of zero. These values have been entered in the column for Cycle 1 at the right of the table. Because Activity 20 can no longer be shortened, a 1, for Cycle 1, is added in the FIN CY column.

The eighth step is to add the existing critical path in the Critical Path Tally, Table 10.7. Note that Activity 20 has been slashed to indicate that it has been changed to its maximum and cannot be reduced further. The tables have now been updated and are ready for the start of the second cycle.

Cycle 2

Of the critical activities remaining at the end of Cycle 1, Activity 60 has the minimum slope and can be changed one day. This activity is marked with a circled X in Table 10.6 and the same series of steps is followed as in Cycle 1.

Cycle 3

The activity that meets the criteria for adjustment in this cycle is Activity 70. The only variation in the procedure occurs in the Network Limit Determination Table. There are no links beginning with this activity because it is the last one in the network. Clearly, a change in this activity's duration will be unrestrained by the network, and this has been indicated by the notation "None Affected."

Cycle 4

The activity that meets the criteria for this cycle is Activity 30. It will be seen that after the ends of the links have been marked in Table 10.8, there are three links having arrowheads in the J column indicating that these links have the ESDs at their right ends reduced. Links 32–40 and 32–42 each have lags of two days, whereas Link 44–52 has a lag of one day. It is this link that will control the network limit. It has been circled and the limit of 1 has been entered at the top of the column.

In the Summary Table the network limit is smaller than the possible ΔT for Activity 30. The number of days changed is therefore the smaller of these two values or one day.

In the updating step for Table 10.8 the lags in Links 32–40 and 32–42 have been reduced to one day and the lag in Link 44–52 has been reduced to zero.

The network, Figure 10.17, shows the changes made in Table 10.8 on each of the affected links. A small 4, the cycle number, is added above the link line and the correct lag is shown below the line. Also a dashed line has been added to the link to further emphasize this condition.

The revision in Table 10.6 shows that Activity 30 now has a duration of six days and that it can still be changed by two days.

In the Critical Path Tally there is no change in the paths and no further slashes because Activity 30 did not reach its maximum reduction.

Cycle 5

Even though Activity 30 was changed in the fourth cycle, it is still the activity that meets the criteria for change in this cycle. It is entered in the Summary Table as before with the new ΔT of 2.

In Table 10.8 the arrowhead marks are first entered opposite Links 30–40 and 30–42. Each of these activities has zero lags so that the 40 and 42 ends of links are also marked. In fact, all the markings are the same as in Cycle 4. The network limit would then appear to be zero as determined by Link 44–52 and would apparently indicate that no change in Activity 30 can take place. When this situation arises it indicates that the control for the start of the activity at the right end of the link is being shifted to another activity. In this instance, Activity 52 originally had its zero lag link from Activity 40 but in the fourth cycle it also acquired a zero lag link from Activity 44. Because any activity needs only one zero lag link to satisfy the early start schedule, Activity 52 can therefore be supported by Activity 44 and the link from Activity 40 can be allowed to acquire a lag. To correct Table 10.8 the arrowheads for Activity 52 are crossed out with an X. Note that this is the activity creating the apparent zero network limit and not the activity being changed. Care should be exercised in this operation to insure that all the arrowheads at either end of the links involving Activity 52 are crossed out. After these corrections have been made the network limit is seen to be 1 as determined by Links 32–40 and 32–42.

In the step for updating the network the break in the link between Activities 40 and 52 is shown by a curved line across the link in Figure 10.17. The new zero lag links between Activity 32 and Activities 40 and 42 have had dashed lines added. Further, because Activity 40 is a critical activity, the closure of Link 32–40 placed Activity 32 on a new critical path. This is indicated by the addition of a third dashed line on Links 20–32 and 32–40.

The updating of Table 10.6 includes the addition of a 5 in the CP CY column opposite Activity 32 to indicate that this activity is now critical.

In Table 10.7 the new critical path is added beside the original one.

Cycle 6

To reduce the project duration, all the critical paths must be changed. In an examination of the Critical Path Tally, Table 10.7, it will be seen that Activities

40 and 50 occur on both paths. Thus, either of these activities could be changed and reduce the project duration. The other possibility would be to change both Activities 30 and 32 in combination. *Combinations cannot be considered if the activities in them are in series with each other*; hence, no other possible combinations are available.

These three possibilities have been entered in the Combination Selection portion of Table 10.6. The combination that satisfies the criteria for change is comprised of Activities 30 and 32 and they have been circled to identify this choice. Their combined cost slope, the sum of the slopes of each, is $450.

In the Summary Table both activities have been entered and their respective ΔT's of 1 and 2 appear in the ΔT area.

In the Network Limit Determination Table both Activities 30 and 32 are initially marked with arrowheads. In this instance, as in the first cycle, there are no closing links and the network limit is none.

Cycle 7

At the end of Cycle 6 there are still two critical paths in the network. Activity 30 was reduced to its minimum duration in Cycle 6 and Activity 32 by itself would not change both paths. There are therefore only two possible choices of activities for change, Activities 40 and 50.

In Table 10.6 the choices have been entered in the Combination Selection area and Activity 40 has been circled to signify that it is the one which satisfies the criteria.

The remainder of the computation for this cycle follows the procedures already discussed.

Cycle 8

In considering the combinations for this cycle Activity 52 is permitted to change by only two days. As can be seen in the Cost Slope Matrix of Figure 10.16, Activity 52 could be changed from eight days to four days at a cost of $175 per day. The two-day change from eight days to six days costs only $100 per day, and this has been selected in keeping with the criterion to maintain the minimum possible cost slope.

Once this decision has been made, the remaining steps of the process in this cycle are as previously discussed.

Cycles 9 through 11

In these cycles of this solution to the minimum cost curve there are no additional points to be discussed. The reader is encouraged to follow each of these cycles through to gain facility in the compression process.

Cycle 12

At the end of Cycle 11 all the critical activities have been shortened to their ΔT limits with the exception of Activity 32. If this activity is shortened by its remaining one day, there would be no change in the project duration but there would be an increase in the project cost amounting to $150.

In the Network Limit Determination Table it will be observed that Links 30–40 and 30–42 would give an apparent network limit of zero. As in Cycle 5, both Activities 40 and 42 are supported by zero lag links from Activities 30 and

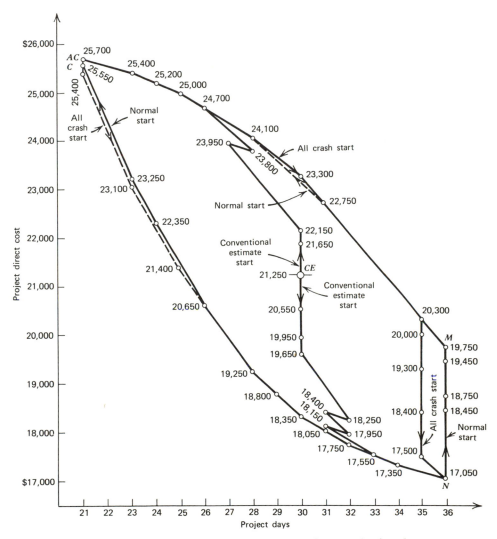

Figure 10.18 *Project time-cost curves—remodeling purchasing department.*

32 so the 30–40 and 30–42 links may be allowed to acquire lags. All the arrowhead marks for Activities 40 and 42 are therefore removed.

The remainder of the adjustments in this cycle are as discussed earlier.

At the end of Cycle 12 the project cost is $25,700. This amount is the total cost of the activities when they have all been shortened by the maximum value, and agrees with the crash value in Table 10.4.

The total cost at the end of Cycle 11 is called the project minimum crash cost because it lies on the minimum cost curve at the crash duration of the project.

The project costs taken from the Summary Table are plotted against the project durations in Figure 10.18 as one of the curves shown there. It should be emphasized that each point on this curve represents a project schedule of the early start variety. If the activity durations and the link lags in the network corresponding to a particular point are identified, free and total floats can readily be calculated following the procedures of Chapter 7.

10.8   MINIMUM COST CURVE FROM ALL CRASH START

The minimum direct cost curve for remodeling the purchasing department of a construction company will now be developed beginning at the all crash point. This is the same project that was used in Section 10.7. The solution will begin at the point in the time-cost field established by the project cost when all the activities are being performed at their maximum cost, or crash, value and by the project duration when each activity is being performed at its minimum, or crash, duration. The Fondahl Adjustment Technique will be used and the minimum curve will be developed in steps until the normal point is reached.

Criteria

The major difference between the all crash solution and the normal solution lies in the criteria for the selection of the activities to be changed. These criteria can be divided into two sets, one for extending the cost curve downward to the minimum curve and the other for the successive lengthening of the project duration until the normal point is found.

To extend the costs downward the criteria are as follows.
1.   The activity or activities must be noncritical.
2.   The activity or combination of activities must have the current maximum cost slope.
3.   The activity or activities must be able to be lengthened.

To extend the project duration the criteria are:
1.   The activity or activities must be critical.
2.   The activity or combination of activities must have the current maximum cost slope.
3.   The activity or activities must be able to be lengthened.

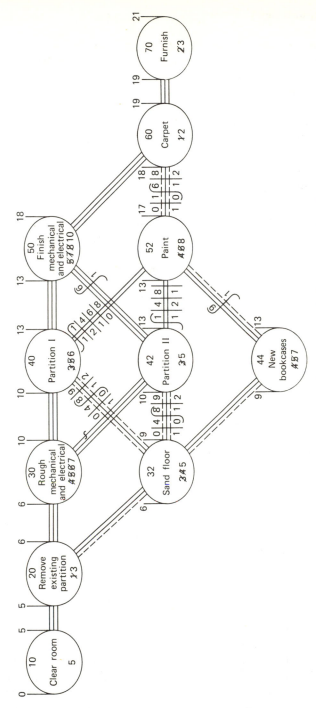

Figure 10.19 All crash start solution—remodeling purchasing department.

227

Network, Tables, and Initial Entries

The crash durations for each activity are taken from Table 10.4 and a precedence network is prepared. This network is shown in Figure 10.19. The network
is computed for the early and late start times and the link lags. The critical path
is identified and the zero lag links are doubled. The links with lags have these
lags entered below the link line with the cycle number above the line. Initially,
these cycle numbers are zero as was the case in the normal start solution.

Tables 10.9 to 10.12 are the four recording and tally tables to be used in the
process. They are the same tables that are used in the normal start solution. The
initial entries in Table 10.9, the Summary Table, are a zero in the first column
standing for the initial cycle, and the project cost and project time from Table
10.4 and Figure 10.19, respectively.

The entries in Table 10.10 are the activities and their cost slopes plus the crash
duration of each activity and the amount of lengthening that each has. Again,
Activity 10 is listed first and a zero is placed in the CP CY and FIN CY
columns. The other critical activities are indicated with a zero in the CP CY
column.

Table 10.11 lists both paths that are initially critical. As before, the slash
across Activity 10 signifies that this activity cannot be changed.

Table 10.12 records the initial EFD and ESD for each end of the links in the
network. The initial lags are also entered in the LAG column.

TABLE 10.9

Summary Table

CY	Combination 1	2	3	ΔT 1	2	3	NL	Days Chg'd	$ Slope	$ Chg'd	Project Cost	Proj Days
0											(AC) $25,700	21
1	44			3			1	1	300	300	(C) 25,400	21
2	40	42	44	3	2	2	None	2	1150	2300	23,100	23
3	50	52		5	2		None	2	850	1700	21,400	25
4	32	50		2	3		1	1	750	750	20,650	26
5	50	52		2	2		None	2	700	1400	19,250	28
6	40			1			2	1	450	450	18,800	29
7	30	32		3	1		None	1	450	450	18,350	30
8	30			2			1	1	300	300	18,050	31
9	30			1			None	1	300	300	17,750	32
10	70			1			None	1	200	200	17,550	33
11	60			1			None	1	200	200	17,350	34
12	20			2			None	2	150	300	(N) 17,050	36

SOLUTION

The solution of the minimum cost curve follows the same pattern as was followed in the normal start case. The first cycle will be detailed and the other cycles will have their special considerations discussed.

Cycle 1

Initially there are two critical paths in the network as listed in Table 10.11. The first objective is to extend the cost curve from the all crash point downward to the crash point which lies on the minimum cost curve. To do this, the first set of criteria given above will be employed. Of the activities in the network only three are noncritical—Activities 32, 44, and 52, which are in series with each other. Only one can be changed, and it is the one with the maximum cost slope, Activity 44. This is indicated by the circled X in the column headed 1 in the Combination Selection portion of Table 10.10.

Activity 44 also has been entered in Table 10.9 together with its ΔT of three days.

In Table 10.12 the 44 end of Link 44–52 is initially marked with a double arrowhead. Note that this arrowhead points to the right to signify that the *EFD* of Activity 44 is being increased in value. Because Link 44–52 has a zero lag, the *ESD* of Activity 52 will also be increased and an arrowhead is placed in each of the right-hand columns opposite the links ending with Activity 52. Because Activity 52 is not being changed an arrowhead is placed also in the *EFD* column opposite Link 52–60. This completes the marking, and it will be observed that Link 52–60 is the only one that will have its lag reduced. The amount of this reduction can be one day as determined by the lag in this link. The network limit of 1 is therefore entered at the top of the column.

The network limit just found is entered in the NL column of Table 10.9. It is the smaller of the ΔT and NL values so the days to be changed becomes one. The slope of Activity 44, $300 per day, is then the cost increase in the project due to this change. The project duration is still 21 days because Activity 44 was a noncritical activity.

The one day change is added to Table 10.12 and the lags in Links 40–52 and 42–52 are increased to 1. The lag in Link 52–60 is decreased by one and is now zero.

The changes from Table 10.12 are now added to the network of Figure 10.19. The closing of Link 52–60 creates another critical path through Activities 32, 44, and 52.

In the revision of Table 10.10, Activity 44 is now shown to have a duration of five days and a possible change of two days. Activities 32, 44, and 52 have the cycle number 1 added in the CP CY column to show their critical nature.

The three critical paths at the end of Cycle 1 are entered in Table 10.11, and the cycle comes to an end.

TABLE 10.10

Activity Selection and Tally Table

						Combination Selection							Cost
12	11	10	9	8	7	6	5	4	3	2	1	ACT	Slope
												10	—
							⊗	× × ×	⊗	×		52	VAR
⊗												20	150
						⊗ ×	×	⊗ ×	× ×	× ×		32	150
	⊗											60	200
			⊗									70	200
		⊗		⊗	⊗	× ×	×			× ×		30	300
										× × ⊗	⊗	44	300
										⊗		42	400
						⊗		× ×	× ×	⊗		40	450
							× ⊗	⊗ ×	× ⊗ ×	× ×		50	600

Cost: 150 200 200 300 300 450 450 450 300 600 700 450 450 750 550 600 700 700 600 750 850 750 600 900 450 1150 850 300

Cycle 2

At the end of Cycle 1 all the activities in the network have become critical. Therefore, it is no longer possible to satisfy the first set of criteria and the project crash point has been found. Any further reduction in project cost will require the lengthening of some critical activity or activities in combination and results in lengthening the project. The choice of activities to be lengthened in Cycle 2 and subsequent cycles must follow the second set of criteria given above.

Any single critical activity may be lengthened and will lengthen the project's critical path. Furthermore, any combination of activities on parallel critical paths may be lengthened and will also lengthen the critical path. There are 11 single critical activities and six combinations that would satisfy these possibilities. Clearly, combinations will give larger cost slopes than single activities so only the six combinations have been entered in the Combination Selection portion of Table 10.10. The combination that completely meets the criteria is comprised of Activities 40, 42, and 44. These have their X marks circled for identification.

All three activities selected have been entered in Table 10.9 together with their respective ΔT values. The network limit is found from Table 10.12 to be "none" and the project has been lengthened by two days at a reduction in cost of $2300. The network and the tables have been updated in the usual manner.

TABLE 10.10 (Continued)

CP CY	FIN CY	T	ΔT	1	2	3	4	5	6	7	8	9	10	11	12
															Revised T/ΔT
0	0	5	—												
1	5	4	4			6/2		8/0							
0	12	1	2												3/0
~~16~~	7	3	2				4/1			5/0					
0	11	1	1											2/0	
0	10	2	1										3/0		
0	9	4	3							5/2	6/1	7/0			
~~16~~	2	4	3	5/2	7/0										
~~06~~	2	3	2		5/0										
0	6	3	3		5/1				6/0						
0	5	5	5			7/3	8/2	10/0							

Cycle 3

The point of significance in Cycle 3 is that when Activity 52 is used in combination, it is permitted to be lengthened only by two days. This is done to satisfy the criterion that the maximum cost slope always be used.

The remainder of Cycle 3 follows the usual pattern and results in a lengthening of the project to 25 days at a decrease in cost to $21,400.

Cycles 4 through 12

No new points of significance are to be examined in these cycles. The process proceeds as in Cycle 1 until Cycle 12 has been completed. At that time the curve has reached the project normal point where the project cost is $17,050 and the project duration is 36 days.

The project costs from Table 10.9 and their related project days have been plotted in Figure 10.18. The curve through these points does not exactly follow the time-cost curve developed by starting at the normal time-cost point. As can be seen for the shorter durations, the all crash curve falls below the normal start one by a small amount. The reason for this discrepancy is that the Fondahl Technique allows only one activity or combination to be altered in any cycle. The technique does not permit the possibility of changing activities in series,

TABLE 10.11

Tally of Critical Paths at End of Cycle

Step	ACT	0		1			2,3			4				
1	10	1̶0̶	1̶0̶	1̶0̶	1̶0̶	1̶0̶	1̶0̶	1̶0̶	1̶0̶	1̶0̶	1̶0̶	1̶0̶	1̶0̶	1̶0̶
2	20	20	20	20	20	20	20	20	20	20	20	20	20	20
3	30,32	30	30	30	30	32	30	30	32	30	30	32	32	32
4	40,42,44	40	42	40	42	44	40	4̶2̶	4̶4̶	40	4̶2̶	4̶4̶	40	4̶2̶
5	50,52	50	50	50	50	52	50	50	52	50	50	52	50	50
6	60	60	60	60	60	60	60	60	60	60	60	60	60	60
7	70	70	70	70	70	70	70	70	70	70	70	70	70	70

TABLE 10.12

Network Limit Determination Table

Cycle					1	2	3	4	5	6
Activity Changed					44	40,42,44	50,52	32,50	50,52	40
Network Limit					1	None	None	1	None	2
Days Changed					1	2	2	1	2	1

Link I	J	EFD	ESD	LAG	I J	LAG	I J	LAG	I J	LAG	I J	LAG	I J	LAG	I J	LAG
10	20	5	5	0												
20	30	6	6	0												
20	32	6	6	0												
30	40	10	10	0												
30	42	10	10	0												
32	40	9	10	1							⊗	0				
32	42	9	10	1							⊗	0				
32	44	9	9	0							≫ >					
40	50	13	13	0			≫ >								≫ >	
40	52	13	13	0	>	1	≫ >				>	2			⊗	1
42	50	13	13	0			≫ >								>	1
42	52	13	13	0	>	1	≫ >				>	2				
44	52	13	13	0	≫ >		≫ >				> >					
50	60	18	18	0			> >		≫ >		≫ >		≫ >		> >	
52	60	17	18	1	>	0	> >		≫ >		> >		≫ >		>	1
60	70	19	19	0			> >		> >		> >		> >		> >	

232

TABLE 10.11 (Continued)

5					6		7		8	9	10	11	12
10	10	10	10	10	10	10	10	10	10	10	10	10	10
20	20	20	20	20	20	20	20	20	20	20	20	20	20
30	30	32	32	32	30	32	30	32	30	30	30	30	30
40	42	44	40	42	40	40	40	40	40	40	40	40	40
50	50	52	50	50	50	50	50	50	50	50	50	50	50
60	60	60	60	60	60	60	60	60	60	60	60	60	60
70	70	70	70	70	70	70	70	70	70	70	70	70	70

TABLE 10.12 (Continued)

7		8		9		10		11		12	
30,32		**30**		**30**		**70**		**60**		**20**	
None		**1**		**None**		**None**		**None**		**None**	
1		**1**		**1**		**1**		**1**		**2**	
I J	L A G	I J	L A G	I J	L A G	I J	L A G	I J	L A G	I J	L A G
										≫ >	
										≫ >	
≫ >		≫ >		≫ >						> >	
≫ >		≫ >		≫ >						> >	
≫ >		>	1	>	2					> >	
≫ >		>	1	>	2	None Affected				> >	
≫ >										> >	
> >		> >		> >						> >	
> >		⊘ >	0	> >						> >	
> >		> >		> >						> >	
> >		>	1	> >						> >	
> >				>	1					> >	
> >		> >		> >						> >	
> >		> >	2	> >						> >	
> >		> >		> >				≫ >		> >	

233

shortening one and lengthening another to achieve a smaller or larger cost slope and a subsequent increase or decrease in the project duration. It is this condition that accounts for the approximate nature of the technique and the variation in the resulting time-cost curves.

10.9 MINIMUM COST CURVE FROM CONVENTIONAL ESTIMATE START

Having developed the minimum direct cost curve beginning at the normal and all crash time-cost points in the previous two sections it is now possible to extend the technique to develop the same curve by using a conventional estimate start point as proposed by Fondahl.[10.1] All three sets of criteria for making adjustments will be employed in the solution.

The conventional estimate of time and cost for a project provides the third of the known time-cost points in the time-cost field required to start the solution. The cost of the project is derived from an addition of the estimated costs of each of the project's activities. For most of the activities this conventionally estimated cost will lie on, or very close to, the linear representation of the activity's cost variation. In some instances it will be a particular value at considerable variance from the linear assumption and a cost slope matrix will have to be employed.

The conventional estimate of the project duration is derived from a network prepared using the individual activity estimates of time associated with the conventional estimate of cost.

The approach to be used in this solution is to first find a point on the minimum direct cost curve and then to proceed toward either the project's normal point or all crash point. By its nature, the conventional estimate point lies somewhere above the minimum curve so the first cycles will be the same type as used in the all crash start. That is, noncritical activities will be lengthened and the project cost reduced.

Because of the limitation of the technique to change only one activity or combination of activities in each cycle, the minimum curve will generally not be reached when all the noncritical activities have been lengthened as much as permitted either by their own ΔTs or the network limit. A critical activity or combination having a maximum cost slope must then be selected to decrease the project cost. This selection will increase the project duration.

Should additional critical activities or combinations be chosen as in the all crash solution, the time-cost curve would tend to follow a parallel course to the minimum curve. Because of this tendency, an approach to the curve should be made which minimizes the project duration. Of course, this shortening must not increase the cost any more than necessary, so a critical activity or combination which has a minimum cost slope must be chosen for the next cycle.

Again, if shortening the project duration as in the normal start solution were

continued, the time-cost curve would also parallel the minimum curve. Consequently, a critical activity or combination with a maximum slope must then be
selected.

This alternate lengthening and shortening of activities or combinations is
continued until no further such changes can take place. When this is accomplished, noncritical activities or combinations are again selected and the entire
process repeated.

When it is found that the cost slope of a lengthening, or shortening, activity or
combination is identical to the slope of the previously shortened, or lengthened,
activity or combination, the two time-cost points derived lie on the minimum
time-cost curve. Either of these points can then be chosen and the remainder of
the curve developed following the normal start or all crash start procedure.

To illustrate the process of finding the minimum time-cost curve, the same
example that was used in Section 10.7 and 10.8 will be chosen. Conventional
estimates of activity durations and costs are given in Table 10.4. In this example
all the conventional times and costs lie on the linear curve between normal and
crash except Activity 52 which has the cost slope matrix shown in Figure 10.16.

Network and Tables

The precedence network has been drawn in Figure 10.20 and the conventional
activity durations from Table 10.4 are given. This network is computed in the

TABLE 10.13

Summary Table

C or Y	L or S	Combination 1	2	3	ΔT 1	2	3	NL	Days Chg'd	$ Slope	$ Chg'd	Project Cost	Project Days
0												(CE) $21,250	30
1	L	42	44		1	3		1	1	700	700	20,550	30
2	L	44			2			2	2	300	600	19,950	30
3	L	32			2			2	2	150	300	19,650	30
4	L	50	52		2	2		None	2	700	1400	18,250	32
5	S	20			1			None	1	150	150	18,400	31
6	L	40			1			None	1	450	450	17,950	32
7	S	60			1			None	1	200	200	18,150	31
8	L	30			2			None	2	300	600	17,550	33
9	S	70			1			None	1	200	200	17,750	32
10	L	60			1			None	1	200	200	17,550	33

(Curve)

TABLE 10.14

Activity Selection and Tally Table

10	9	8	7	6	5	4	3	2	1	ACT	$ Slope	CP CY	Fin CY S	Fin CY L
										10	—	0	0	0
						⊗				52	VAR	3		4
					⊗	×				20	150	0	5	
							⊗			32	150	~~3~~	~~0~~	3
⊗		⊗	×							60	200	0	7	~~0~~
	⊗		×							70	200	0		~~0~~
		⊗				×				30	300	0		8
							⊗	⊗		44	300	~~3~~	~~0~~	2
								⊗		42	400	~~1~~		1
				⊗		×				40	450	0		6
					×	⊗				50	600	0		4

Tally: 200 200 300 200 450 200 200 150 600 450 300 150 700 150 300 700

the usual manner, and the early start and finish dates, the link lags, and the critical path are determined. These are shown in the figure (page 240) in the customary way.

Tables 10.13 to 10.16 have been set up to facilitate the computations. They are essentially the same tables as were used in the two previous solutions. Table 10.13, the Summary Table, has had one additional column added, headed L or S. This column is used to identify whether the cycle being worked on is a lengthening or shortening one.

Table 10.14, the Activity Selection and Tally Table, is the same as Tables 10.6 and 10.10 with modifications. The column headed FIN CY has been divided to permit identification of the cycle in which the activity has been shortened or lengthened to the maximum amount of its ΔT value in either direction. Instead of recording the activity duration and the possible change, it is more appropriate to keep track of the ΔT in either the shortening or lengthening aspects. Therefore, the T and ΔT columns are now headed ΔT_S and ΔT_L. The revision in these values is also tallied in the Revised $\Delta T_S / \Delta T_L$ area.

Table 10.15 is identical to Tables 10.7 and 10.11; Table 10.16 is also the same as Tables 10.8 and 10.12.

The initial entries in all these tables follow the same pattern as previously discussed. Note, however, that some of the activities are initially finished in either their shortening or lengthening modes.

TABLE 10.14 (Continued)

ΔT_S	ΔT_L		Revised $\Delta T_S/\Delta T_L$									
		1	2	3	4	5	6	7	8	9	10
0	0										
2	2				4/0						
1	1					0/2					
0	2			2/0							
1	0							0/1			1/0
1	0								0/1		
1	2									3/0	
0	3	1/2	3/0								
1	1	2/0									
2	1						3/0				
3	2				5/0						

SOLUTION

Cycle 1

The noncritical activities at the beginning of this cycle are Activities 32, 42, 44, and 52. The only combination suitable for lengthening is comprised of Activities 42 and 44. A combination of either of these with Activities 32 and 52 would not be permitted because of the series prohibition.

At the end of Cycle 1 Activity 42 can no longer be lengthened but it has become critical by the closing of Link 42–50.

Cycle 2

The greatest cost slope for this cycle leads to the choice of Activity 44 for lengthening. This is a typical lengthening cycle and no new paths are created even though Activity 44 has finished its lengthening.

Cycle 3

Activity 32 is the next noncritical activity eligible. At the end of the cycle this activity has finished its lengthening, Links 32–40, 32–44, and 52–60 all acquire

238

TABLE 10.15

Tally of Critical Paths at End of Cycle

0	1L, 2L		3L								4L								5S								6L				7S				8L		9S		10L	
10	10	10	10	10	10	10	10	10	10	10	10	10	10	10	10	10	10	10	10	10	10	10	10	10	10	10	10	10	10	10	10	10	10	10	10	10	10	10	10	10
20	20	20	20	20	20	20	20	20	20	20	20	20	20	20	20	20	20	20	20	20	20	20	20	20	20	20	20	20	20	20	20	20	20	20	20	20	20	20	20	20
30	30	30	30	30	32	32	32	32	32	30	30	30	32	32	32	32	32	30	30	30	32	32	32	32	32	30	30	30	32	32	30	30	32	32	30	30	30	30	30	30
40	40	42	40	42	40	42	44	40	42	42	40	42	40	42	44	40	42	42	40	42	40	42	44	40	42	42	40	40	40	40	40	40	40	40	40	40	40	40	40	40
50	50	50	50	50	50	50	52	52	52	52	50	50	50	50	52	52	52	52	50	50	50	50	52	52	52	52	50	52	50	52	50	52	50	52	50	52	50	52	50	52
60	60	60	60	60	60	60	60	60	60	60	60	60	60	60	60	60	60	60	60	60	60	60	60	60	60	60	60	60	60	60	60	60	60	60	60	60	60	60	60	60
70	70	70	70	70	70	70	70	70	70	70	70	70	70	70	70	70	70	70	70	70	70	70	70	70	70	70	70	70	70	70	70	70	70	70	70	70	70	70	70	70

TABLE 10.16

Network Limit Determination Table

Cycle (L or S)	1L					2L					3L					4L					5S					6L					7S					8L					9S					10L				
Activity Changed	42,44					44					32					50,52					20					40					60					30					70					60				
Network Limit	1					2					2					None					None					None					None					None					None					None				
Days Changed	1					2					2					2					1					1					1					2					1					1				

Sub-columns for each cycle: I J L A G

Link I J	EFD I	ESD J	LAG
10 20	5	5	0
20 30	7	7	0
20 32	7	7	0
30 40	12	12	0
30 42	12	12	0
32 40	10	12	2
32 42	10	12	2
32 44	10	10	0
40 50	17	17	0
40 52	17	17	1
42 50	16	17	1
42 52	16	17	1
44 52	14	17	3
50 60	25	25	0
52 60	23	25	2
60 70	27	27	0

(Cycle 9S column: None Affected)

239

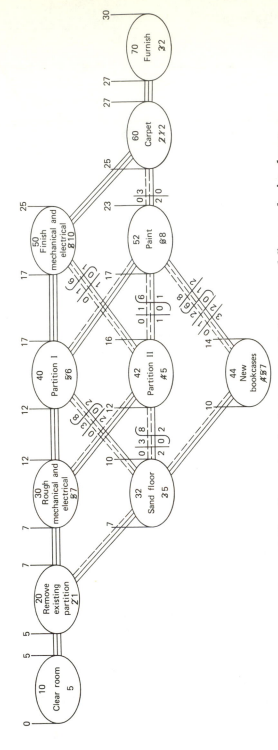

Figure 10.20 Conventional estimate start solution—remodeling purchasing department.

zero lags, and every activity in the network is now critical. There are now eight critical paths to be dealt with.

Cycle 4

Cycle 4 begins the second phase of the solution, changing critical activities alternately. There are five critical activities which can be lengthened. The only combination is with Activities 50 and 52 and they produce the maximum slope. Note that Activity 52, the variable one, can only be changed by two days at a cost of $100 per day.

In the revision of Table 10.15, the Tally of Critical Paths, the activities that have been crossed out are those that have finished *shortening* even though Cycle 4 was a lengthening cycle. This is done to aid in identifying the activities eligible for selection for the fifth cycle. The remainder of the cycles in this solution will also anticipate the succeeding cycle in this regard.

Cycle 5

Because Cycle 4 was a lengthening cycle, Cycle 5 must be a shortening one. The activity to be selected must have the minimum slope and must change all eight paths. Activity 20 is the activity satisfying all the criteria and is chosen. At the conclusion of this cycle Activity 20 has been shortened as much as possible but there is no change in link lags nor the critical path.

Cycle 6

This cycle is a lengthening one, and the critical activity meeting the lengthening criteria is Activity 40. At the end of the cycle, Links 42–50, 42–52, and 44–52 each acquire lags of one day, causing the number of critical paths to be reduced to four. Activity 40 has also reached the limit of its lengthening. Activities 42 and 44 are no longer critical, and this fact has been indicated in Table 10.14 by the slash across the cycle numbers previously entered in the CP CY column.

Cycle 7

Cycle 7 is a typical shortening cycle using Activity 60. The change in this cycle does not affect the network.

Cycle 8

The activity chosen for lengthening in Cycle 8 is Activity 30. At the end of this cycle Links 32–40 and 32–42 have acquired lags of two days each and the number of critical paths has been reduced to two. Link 44–52 has increased its lag from one day to three days.

The breaking of Links 32–40 and 32–42 has removed Activity 32 from the critical list, and its previously entered cycle number in the CP CY column of Table 10.14 has been crossed out.

Cycle 9

Activity 70 meets the criteria for shortening in Cycle 9. The resulting change does not affect the network relationships.

Cycle 10

Activity 60, which was shortened in Cycle 7, is now the only available activity that meets the lengthening criteria. It happens that the cost slope of this activity, $200 per day, is the same as the cost slope used in Cycle 9. Because of this identity the time-cost points derived in both Cycles 9 and 10 are points that lie on the minimum time-cost curve.

The point established by the project cost of $17,550 and the project duration of 33 days can be used to develop the minimum curve downward and to the right until the normal point is found. In this development the all crash, or lengthening, criteria are used and the present values in Table 10.14 are used for starting values. The details of the cycles needed can be observed if reference is made to Section 10.7.

The minimum curve can be developed upward and to the left to reach the all crash point by beginning at the project cost of $17,750 and the project duration of 32 days. In this process the normal start criteria are used and the present values in Table 10.14 are again used as starting values. The detail of the cycles needed to develop this segment of the minimum curve may be seen in Section 10.8.

The time-cost points found in Table 10.13 have been plotted in Figure 10.18 and the zig-zag nature of the process is clearly evident. It may be observed that whereas the conventional estimate of project duration was 30 days, the minimum curve was met at 33 days. The minimum project cost for the 30-day project duration is easily found by using the procedure of the immediately proceding paragraph.

10.10   MAXIMUM COST CURVES

It was pointed out at the end of Section 10.7 that each point in the time-cost field represents an early start schedule for the project. At any particular project duration there is a critical path or a set of critical paths which established that duration. The minimum cost at this particular duration is the sum of the costs of these critical activities plus the minimum costs of the noncritical activities.

It can be assumed that there is some other combination of critical and noncritical activities which will define the same particular project duration and will give a greater cost than minimum. Such a point in the time-cost field has already been shown to exist at the conventional estimate point. It may further be assumed that there can be found a combination of critical paths whose activity costs may be added to the maximum, or crash, costs of the noncritical activities to produce a maximum project cost at that particular duration.

The determination of the maximum costs for all possible project durations can be made using the Fondahl Adjustment Technique. The only difference in the determination of the maximum time-cost curve and the determination of the minimum curve lies in the criteria to be used for the selection of the activities to be lengthened or shortened. Any of the three known time-cost points may be used as the starting point.

Criteria for Maximum Curve from Normal Start

If it is assumed that the maximum time-cost curve is to be developed from the project normal point, the criteria must first allow the noncritical activities to be shortened, thereby increasing the project costs without a change in project duration. Second, the critical activities must be shortened in successive cycles to maintain the maximum possible project costs. These criteria are summarized below.

To extend the costs upward the criteria are:
1. The activity or activities must be noncritical.
2. The activity or combination of activities must have the current maximum cost slope.
3. The activity or activities must be able to be shortened.

To reduce the project duration the criteria are:
1. The activity or activities must be critical.
2. The activity or combination of activities must have the current maximum cost slope.
3. The activity or activities must be able to be shortened.

It sometimes happens that after the second set of these criteria has been applied, it is seen that there are current noncritical activities which can be shortened with an increase in project cost. If this should be the case, activities are changed according to the first set of criteria and then the second set is reused. When no changes can be made using either set of criteria, the project all crash point has been reached.

Other than these criteria, the details of the cycles of the technique follow the procedures already discussed. The tables to be used are the same as used in Section 10.7.

For the example of remodeling the purchasing department of a construction company this maximum cost curve beginning at the normal project point has been plotted in Figure 10.18.

Criteria for Maximum Curve from All Crash Start

To develop the maximum time-cost curve beginning at the project's all crash point the project duration is increased in successive cycles at the minimum decrease in project cost. When no further increase in project duration can take place, noncritical activities are lengthened and the project cost is reduced without changing the project duration. The criteria to be used for these changes is summarized below.

To extend the project duration the criteria are:
1. The activity or activities must be critical.
2. The activity or combination of activities must have the current minimum cost slope.
3. The activity or activities must be able to be lengthened.

To extend the project costs downward the criteria are:
1. The activity or activities must be noncritical.
2. The activity or combination of activities must have the current minimum cost slope.
3. The activity or activities must be able to be lengthened.

As in the normal start case, it sometimes happens that when the second set of criteria has been used there will be an activity or activities that are critical. At this time the first set of criteria must again be employed to ensure that the maximum project costs are maintained. When no further changes in the activities can be made under either set of criteria, the project normal point has been reached.

The tables to be used for these adjustments are the same as in Section 10.8 and the detailed cycles follow the same pattern previously discussed.

The remodeling of the purchasing department example has had its maximum time-cost curve derived and this curve is plotted in Figure 10.18. Note that because the Fondahl Technique permits only one combination of activities to be adjusted in each cycle, there is a difference in the maximum curve depending upon the the starting point. In this case, the normal start curve rises directly from the normal point, whereas the all crash start curve descends one day earlier and then another critical activity is changed. Also the normal start curve lies below the all crash start one in the region between project durations of 28 and 31 days.

Maximum Curve from Conventional Estimate Start

The conventional estimate point is the third of the known time-cost points and it also can be used to develop the maximum cost curve. The process is similar to the development of the minimum time-cost curve from this point.

Because the conventional project cost will never be more than the maximum cost at the conventional project duration, the first step is to shorten noncritical activities and thereby increase the project cost but maintain the conventional project duration. The criteria for these changes is the same as the first set used for the normal start approach.

When all the noncritical activities meeting the criteria have been changed, the maximum curve probably will not have been reached. This is because of the limitation in the technique to change only one activity or combination of activities in a single cycle. Critical activities or combinations having the greatest cost slope must therefore be shortened.

As discussed in Section 10.9, if the normal start process is continued, the resulting curve will be parallel to and below the maximum curve. Another activity or combination of activities having the current minimum cost slope is then selected to approach the curve by increasing the project duration at the minimum penalty in cost and the all crash criteria are employed.

Again, a continued selection of activities under the all crash criteria will cause the curve to be parallel to the maximum curve and the approach is reversed.

This alternate shortening and lengthening of activities or their combinations is repeated until the cost slopes for both the shortening and lengthening cycles are the same. At that time the points established in either the shortening or lengthening cycles are points on the maximum time-cost curve. The remainder of the curve may be developed using these points as starting locations and employing the normal start criteria and the all crash start criteria. These segments of the maximum curve are the same as previously found in the normal start and all crash start solutions. Figure 10.18 has the conventional estimate start adjustments plotted and the zig-zag nature of the process is evident.

The true minimum time-cost curve is defined by those segments of the minimum curve that are found from either of the start approaches and that produce the minimum cost at each project duration. Similarly, the true maximum time-cost curve is defined by those segments of the maximum curve that are derived from either approach and that produce the maximum cost at each project duration. The area between the true minimum time-cost curve and the true maximum time-cost curve represents all the possible time-cost schedules for the project, given the stated relationships among the activities and the time-cost variables assumed for them.

Any conventionally estimated time-cost point will lie within this envelope. This fact allows certain implications to be drawn concerning any conventional estimate of time and cost that a contractor may have.

10.11   TIME-COST IMPLICATIONS FOR THE CONTRACTOR

Every contractor is interested in the reduction of project costs because the lowering of costs increases profits and probabilities of contract awards. The development of time-cost curves greatly assists the contractor in meeting these objectives. But even though the curves are not derived, the concepts embodied in the derivation process can be used to achieve significant cost reductions for most projects.

After a critical path network has been drawn the contractor can examine the noncritical activities with respect to the projected use of resources. These resources can be reduced to their lowest levels consistent with the network constraints and the project will not be extended in time but costs will fall. This is tantamount to the changes made in the first cycles of the conventional estimate start solution of Section 10.9. In the example being used in this chapter such a reduction amounted to $1600, as is shown in Figure 10.18.

Another option open to the contractor is to identify high-cost slope and low-cost slope critical activities. The high-cost slope activities can be lengthened in duration by reducing the resource levels and the low-cost slope activities can be shortened in duration by increasing the resource levels. This trade-off will not change the project duration but will reduce the cost. This action is the same as finding another but lower time-cost point in the field than the initial conventional estimate point.

For most construction projects, conventional estimate points will tend to lie in the upper one third of the time-cost field. This is so because of the pressures on construction work from owners, their agents, and from contractors themselves to perform the work in the minimum amount of time. In many instances these desires are necessary, but there are many cases where a longer project duration may be acceptable if the costs to all can be lowered. Many owners agree that the exact project duration is of little consequence; but once a completion date is established, it is essential that the date be met. A contractor can therefore prepare a preliminary critical path network and examine critical activities to identify those having high-cost slopes. These activities can then be lengthened and the increased project duration submitted with the bid will most likely be accepted.

It is apparent from the above that the conventional estimate is the most important of the three time-cost points readily available for starting any time-cost adjustment. It is also evident that the cost slope of each activity is of considerable importance in making any reduction in costs. In this chapter it has been assumed that an activity's normal and crash points can be found so that cost slopes can be calculated.

It may not be possible nor practical to obtain true normal and crash times and costs for each activity. On the other hand, most contractors can determine with a fair degree of accuracy the increase or decrease in cost occasioned by decreasing or increasing an activity duration. The cost slope can therefore be estimated within reason. Naturally, the greater the time interval between the longest and shortest activity duration, the greater will be the accuracy of the cost slope.

The inexactness of the individual activity cost slopes implies an inexactness in the time-cost curves subsequently derived. But an inexact minimum cost curve is more informative to the contractor than no minimum curve at all. The decisions resulting from the use of an inexact curve will not be ideal but will be valid for most attempts at reducing project costs.

If an effort is made by a contractor to develop time-cost curves, the savings that can be gained will more than offset the costs incurred. The Fondahl Technique, although seemingly tedious and time consuming, can be applied by a skilled person in a relatively short time and at a relatively low cost.

The example of remodeling the purchasing department of a construction company has been shown to have a conventional direct project cost of $21,250. Figure 10.21 is a plot of the anticipated indirect costs for this project with a minimum of $500 and an increasing cost slope of $167 per day. For the 30-day conventional estimate of project duration these overhead charges amount to $2000. The total conventional estimate cost is then $23,250.

Figure 10.22 shows the total time-cost field for this project. The total costs are the direct costs from Figure 10.18 plus the indirect costs from Figure 10.21. The conventional estimate of total cost also has been shown.

It can be seen in Figure 10.22 that if the project network is adjusted, the minimum total cost at the 30-day conventional duration is $20,350 or $2900 less than the total conventional cost. This represents a significant saving of 12 percent on this rather small project. If it would be possible to extend the project duration by four days, the minimum total project cost of $20,017 could be achieved and the savings would amount to $3233 or 14 percent.

If time permits, maximum and minimum curves could be developed before

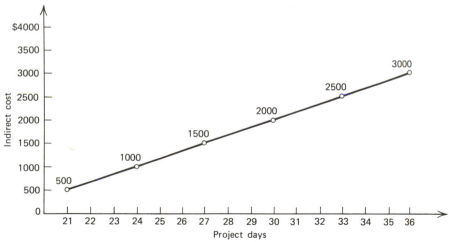

Figure 10.21   Project indirect costs—remodeling purchasing department.

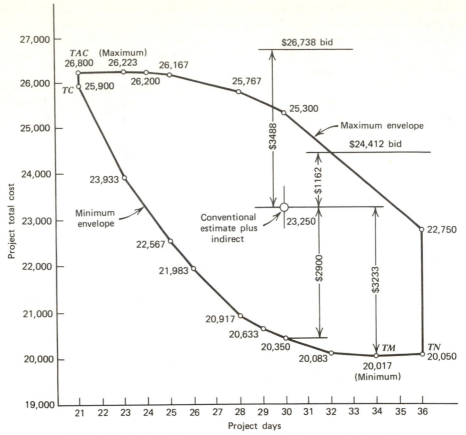

Figure 10.22 Project total cost curves—remodeling purchasing department.

bidding. Decisions could then be made that would not only increase profit but would enhance the possibility of winning the contract. Assume that the contractor has decided to add a profit of 15 percent of cost. The bid would then be $26,738 or $515 more than the maximum total cost which occurs at a project duration of 23 days. This value is $3488 more than the conventional estimate total cost. Should this bid be the accepted one, the contractor could adjust the schedule to the minimum total cost at the 30-day duration and save an additional $2900. The profit gain in this case would be $6388 or 27 percent of the conventional total cost.

Assume that another contracting company might bid on this job. It is anticipated that this company's total cost may be $25,000. This company would need only to add a profit of 7 percent to win the bid. In a tight construction market there is a high probability that this could happen. Therefore, to be more competitive, the contractor might decide to add only 5 percent for profit. The bid price would then be $24,412 or $1162 more than the conventional total cost. By making this choice, the chance of winning the bid is increased greatly. The contractor still has the possibility of adjusting the schedule and gaining a profit of 20 percent at a project duration of 30 days. If the duration can be extended to 34 days, the profit would rise to 22 percent.

Assume that the contractor wishes to make a minimum 15 percent profit at the 30-day duration. By adjusting the project, a bid of $23,403 can be given. This is only $153 over the conventional total cost and the chance of winning the bid is very good. The contractor still can negotiate for the additional four days in project duration and the profit would rise to 17 percent. Even bidding at the total conventional cost, profits would be 14 percent and 16 percent for the 30- and 32-day project durations.

It cannot be expected that all projects will produce as favorable a profit picture as this example. It can be expected that most projects are capable of substantial profit gains. In addition, a close analysis of the relationships among the activities in a network will permit a contractor to make decisions which can produce excellent cost savings with or without the benefit of formal time-cost curves.

REFERENCES

10.1   Fondahl, John W., *A Non-Computer Approach to the Critical Path Method for the Construction Industry*, Technical Report No. 9, The Construction Institute, Department of Civil Engineering, Stanford University, Stanford, CA, 1961, (Second Edition, 1962).

10.2   Fondahl, John W., *Methods for Extending the Range of Non-Computer Critical Path Applications*, Technical Report No. 47, The Construction Institute, Department of Civil Engineering, Stanford University, Stanford, CA, 1964.

10.3   Fulkerson, D. R., "A Network Flow Computation for Project Cost Curves," *Management Science*, Vol. 7, No. 2, January 1961, pp. 167–179.

10.4   Kelley, James E., Jr., "Critical Path Planning and Scheduling: Mathematical Basis," *Operations Research*, Vol. 9, No. 3, 1961, pp. 296–320.

10.5   Meyer, W. L. and L. R. Shaffer, *Extensions of the Critical Path Method Through the Application of Integer Programming*, Civil Engineering Construction Research Series, No. 2, University of Illinois, Urbana, Ill., July 1963.

10.6   Parker, Henry W. and Clarkson H. Oglesby, *Methods Improvement for Construction Managers*, McGraw-Hill Book Company, New York, 1972.

EXERCISES

10.1   One of the activities in your project is to form continuous wall footings and spread footings for columns. The estimate shows that there are 600 sq ft of this formwork. Select the minimum cost crew size for this activity and determine the time it will take to do the work. Five different crews have been suggested. Their composition, hourly rates and total estimated time are tabulated below.

Crew	Hourly Cost Rate for the Crew	Total Estimated Duration (Hours)
1. One carpenter One laborer	$20.00	30
2. Two carpenters One laborer	31.00	18
3. Four carpenters Two laborers One foreman	72.50	8
4. Three carpenters One laborer	45.50	12
5. Three carpenters Two laborers	55.50	10

10.2   It has been determined that one of the activities of your project can be done in 15 days at a cost of $1675. If you can take 16 days for the activity, it will only cost $1600, and if you can extend the time to 20 days, the cost will reduce to $800. On the other hand, if you must do the activity in 12 days, the cost will be $2800, and if 10 days is desired, the cost will rise to $4000. Construct a cost slope matrix to serve for a time-cost adjustment for this project.

10.3   A project has been adjusted using Fondahl's Technique and the following minimum direct costs have been obtained.

Project Duration (days)	Minimum Direct Cost
32	$79,300
34	78,200
36	77,300
38	76,500
41	75,450
42	75,200
44	74,850
47	74,550

At a 32-day duration the maximum direct cost has been found to be $80,000 and the indirect cost is $1500. Indirect costs increase linearly at a rate of $325 per day. The bid submitted for this project is $97,500.

(a)   What profit can the contractor realize if the project is scheduled for completion in 35 days?

(b)   What is the maximum profit obtainable and what is the project duration associated with it?

10.4 Five columns taken from a Network Limit Determination table are given below.

(a) Assume a total project duration of 18 days and construct the precedence network. Show the activity durations and the initial critical path.

(b) Activity C may be shortened two days from normal to crash. Determine the Network Limit and shorten C as much as permitted for this cycle.

(c) Assume that the next cycle required the continued shortening of C. Determine the Network Limit for this case and shorten the project as much as permitted in this cycle.

(d) On the network of part (a) indicate the critical path or paths as they exist after part (c).

I Act.	J Act.	I EFD	J ESD	LAG
A	B	2	2	0
A	C	2	2	0
B	D	8	8	0
C	D	6	8	2
C	E	6	6	0
D	F	11	12	1
E	F	12	12	0
E	G	12	12	0
F	H	15	16	1
G	H	16	16	0

10.5 Time and cost data for a small project are given below.

(a) Determine the minimum direct cost curve for this project using Fondahl's Adjustment Technique.

(b) Determine the maximum direct cost curve for this project using Fondahl's Adjustment Technique.

No.	Act.	Preceding Activities	Normal Time	Normal Cost	Crash Time	Crash Cost
5	A	—	2	$2400	2	$2400
10	B	5	10	5000	10	5000
15	C	5	15	3000	7	3800
20	D	10	5	5000	2	6500
25	E	15	3	1800	3	1800
30	F	10	9	4500	9	4500
35	G	20, 25	5	6000	5	6000
40	H	25	6	3600	4	4200
45	K	30, 35, 40	4	4800	4	4800

10.6 Use the normal time-cost data from Exercise 10.5 and construct the predecence diagram. On the diagram compute the early start and finish dates and determine the total and free floats for each activity. For each of the following situations analyze the effect that a change of the listed activity's duration will have on the total and free floats of the other activities in the network. Consider each change in reference to the normal schedule.

	Activity No.	Change in T	Effect on TF and FF of Activity?
(a)	10	4 day increase	20, 25, 30
(b)	15	1 day decrease	20, 25, 30
(c)	20	2 day decrease	20, 25, 35
(d)	30	4 day increase	10, 30, 35
(e)	40	1 day decrease	20, 30, 35

10.7 Time and cost data for a project are given below.

(a) Using Fondahl's Adjustment Technique determine the minimum direct cost curve for this project beginning at the project normal point.

(b) Prepare a bar chart for the normal schedule of 34 days. List the critical activities first. On the same plot show a bar chart for a 27-day schedule.

		Preceding	Normal		Crash	
No.	Activity	Activities	Time	Cost	Time	Cost
5	A	—	5	$ 5000	5	$ 5000
10	B	5	8	6000	3	18000
15	E	5	6	3000	5	4500
20	C	10	2	1000	2	1000
25	D	10	6	5000	2	9000
30	H	15	5	2000	4	3000
35	F	20, 25	7	18000	3	20000
40	G	15, 25	5	1000	3	4000
45	K	30, 35, 40	8	15000	8	15000

10.8 Time and cost data for a project are tabulated below. All activity time-cost functions are linear except Activity F whose discrete data are given below the table.

(a) Using Fondahl's Adjustment Technique determine the minimum direct cost curve for this project beginning at the project normal point.

(b) Determine the minimum direct cost curve beginning at the project all crash point.

(c) Determine the maximum direct cost curve beginning at the project normal point.

(d) Determine the maximum direct cost curve beginning at the project all crash point.

No.	Activity	Preceding Activities	Normal Time	Normal Cost	Crash Time	Crash Cost
5	A	—	4	$1200	2	$ 4800
10	B	5	4	3800	4	3800
15	C	5	3	4500	2	5400
20	D	5	6	3000	3	12000
25	E	10, 20	4	2100	3	2550
30	F	10, 20	7	4320	4	5070
35	G	25, 30	9	2500	4	8500
40	H	15, 25, 30	3	3500	1	8500
45	K	25, 30	5	2000	3	3500
50	L	35, 40	10	2250	5	5000
55	M	35, 40, 45	8	3750	4	4750
60	N	50, 55	6	1400	4	2400

Discrete Values for Activity F:

Time	7	6	5	4
Cost	$4320	4470	4720	5070

10.9 Conventional times and costs for the project of Exercise 10.5 are given below.

(a) Beginning at the conventional estimate time-cost point develop the minimum direct cost curve.

(b) Beginning at the conventional estimate time-cost point develop the maximum direct cost curve.

(c) Indirect costs are $2800 at a project duration of 25 days and increase at the rate of $200 per day. Determine the maximum and minimum profit a contractor can realize if the project duration is held to 26 days.

(d) Determine the range of the contractor's profit and the project durations associated with the maximum and minimum amounts.

Activity No.	Conventional Time	Conventional Cost
5	2	$2400
10	10	5000
15	12	3300
20	4	5500
25	3	1800
30	9	4500
35	5	6000
40	4	4200
45	4	4800

11
RESOURCE LEVELING

11.1 INTRODUCTION

In Chapter 10 adjustments to the basic schedule were discussed in light of the relationship between time and cost. In these discussions changes in the schedule were made by allocating resource rates to individual activities. Having established a preferred project duration and a certain resource utilization rate for each activity in the network, whether by using a time-cost trade-off process or by other means, the scheduler still has the opportunity to make adjustments in the project schedule by allocating the resources to the project as a whole.

It may be recalled that throughout the previous chapters all the schedules developed have been of the early start variety. That is, every activity was assumed to start as soon as it was possible to do so. Activities other than those on the critical path all had amounts of float that would permit them to be scheduled to start at later dates. By choosing to schedule these noncritical activities at other than their earliest possible times, the demand for the resources on the various project dates can be reduced. The process for making these adjustments is usually termed *resource leveling*.

Leveling procedures for construction work can be effective in the management of all kinds of resources. One of the most common resources to be considered is that of personnel where the need for leveling stems from the desire to maintain the lowest possible number of employees to perform the work. Equipment usage is also a frequent resource that requires study to keep demands to a minimum. Leveling can be used effectively in establishing plans for material delivery, particularly in urban areas where onsite storage space is severely limited. Applications of leveling can be of great value to the contractor faced with cash flow problems. By reducing the daily demand for dollars, interest and other financial costs are kept to their lowest levels.

Leveling applies to all types of projects and is independent of the type of network being used. However, the network does influence the results in many of the leveling procedures proposed.

In modern projects, particularly very large ones, the need for leveling is more pronounced than in smaller projects because there is a greater economic gain in making the adjustment. In these large projects the quantity of resource is often large. Furthermore, some of the resources themselves may be large in the sense

254

that they may be of considerable size and may be quite expensive to obtain and to operate. It is not surprising therefore that many attempts have been made to find a satisfactory method to level resources.

A study of modern operations research techniques suggests that linear programing can be applied to solve the problem. This procedure quickly becomes infeasible, however, because it exceeds the computational capacity of even the most modern relatively large storage computers when construction projects are considered. It is therefore unlikely that any truly exact solution will be developed in the near future. Instead, attention has turned to the development of heuristic processes designed to give good answers while recognizing that the results may not be optimal. A heuristic is a set of rules-of-thumb designed to progressively lead the user to a feasible solution.

There have been two approaches to these heurisitc solutions. One sets as its objective the minimization of the levels, and thereby the costs, of the resource while holding to the CPM project duration. The other takes as its objective the minimization of the duration time of the project while keeping the resource limits fixed. Moder[11.6] refers to the first as "Unlimited Resource Leveling" and to the second as "Limited Resource Allocation." In this chapter the limited resource allocation approach is termed the *traditional approach*.

The basic works aimed at minimizing project durations to meet fixed resource limits are those of Wiest[11.11, 11.12] and his subsequent extension.[11.13] He uses the arrow diagraming method and gives rules for choosing the order of scheduling the individual activities. Paulson[11.9] applies Wiest's ideas to the precedence diagram. In the book by Shaffer, Ritter, and Meyer,[11.10] similar choices are made but the network logic is altered at every step in the process. Shaffer uses the precedence diagram for his procedure. More recently Davies[11.4] has statistically analyzed the selection criteria and concludes that cost per unit of time is the main criterion. Davies used the arrow diagram for the test projects.

Commercial adaptations of limited resource allocation are discussed in the publications of O'Brien[11.7, 11.8] where he refers to RAMPS (Resource and Manpower Scheduling) by CEIR and to RPSM (Resource Planning and Scheduling Method) by Mauchly Associates.

Unlimited resource leveling is dealt with in the paper by Galbreath[11.5] wherein he discussed the application to a construction project of large size. Wiest[11.11, 11.12] and Burgess[11.3] have also concerned themselves with the constraint on the project duration. Burgess introduces the sum of the squares of the daily resource demands as a means to determine the quality of the leveling. Antill and Woodhead[11.2] present a heuristic involving chains of activities treated in increasing total float order. They also suggest that resources may be leveled in series fashion. In his book Adrian[11.1] favors the techniques of both Shaffer et al., and Antill and Woodhead. All of the works cited in this paragraph have used the arrow diagraming procedure and node numbers have been used for controlling the order of the activities being considered.

The Minimum Moment Algorithm presented in this chapter is an attempt to extend and refine the efforts of the above authors. It is an unlimited resource leveling procedure and as such does not extend the project length. From a construction point of view this is thought desirable because a contractor usually has a project terminal date established by the contract documents. It is only after contract award that the contractor's scheduler is faced with the need to do the detailed planning requiring the adoption of a leveling procedure.

As the name implies, the minimum moment algorithm approaches the problem by considering the resource histogram as an area in the time-resource field and sets its objective as the minimization of the moment of that area. The method has been termed an *algorithm* although the use of this term is not strictly true in the mathematical sense. This use is believed justified because the method's rules do not contain random decisions. Given a particular set of input values the results are reproducible with repeated applications. It is therefore a direct method of solution.

The minimum moment method is based upon the use of a precedence diagram, although it is shown that it may easily be used for an arrow diagram should this representation be desired. It assumes that the activities in the diagram may not be split. Thus, the resource rates are continuous throughout each activity's duration. No altering of the network logic is made.

The algorithm assumes an early start schedule derived from the CPM network computations, shifts the activities to the right, and then shifts those that are not necessary to maintain the resource constraints back to the left. In this way it avoids the resource buildup late in the project, which occurs when the Burgess procedure is used.

The method uses the concept of Burgess' sum of the squares of the daily resource sums and develops an "improvement factor" to select the activity to be shifted. Improvement as used here refers to the reduction of the histogram moment when an activity is shifted.

Logical sequence steps discussed in Chapter 4 together with the improvement factors are chosen to order the shifting of the activities. Shifting begins with activities on the latest sequence step and the improvement factor is used to select the particular one on the step to be shifted. When all activities on a step have been considered the next earlier step is examined. This process continues until the first step has been reached. Free float is used to set the range of possible shifting of the activities. The order is then reversed starting with the first sequence step and proceeding to the last step, using the back float to set the range of shifting.

The results obtained by using the minimum moment algorithm have proven to be equal to or greater than those from other procedures. The method appears tedious to perform manually but because it is a direct method, the total effort is less than when using more traditional techniques. For large projects, it is readily programmed for the computer.

The algorithm provides a great deal of flexibility for the scheduler. Resources may be leveled in series as suggested by Antill and Woodhead, or they may be combined before leveling in a single application. Predetermined weighting of the resources may be used to give results that favor resources in a chosen priority. Varied resource levels can also be handled in a single application because it is possible to level the resources to a preferred histogram. Thus, the minimum moment algorithm provides the scheduler with an excellent tool to answer the contractor's basic question about resources: How much of this resource do I need to get the project done within the time period?

11.2 RESOLVING RESOURCE CONFLICTS

It will be recalled that it was said near the end of Chapter 2 that the planner should make use of the unlimited resources assumption. This assumption states that if a resource is needed by any activity in the network, then that resource can be provided. Clearly, this is not feasible in the majority of situations. The planner must therefore make some corrections to the original schedule computations, and perhaps to the original network, to reflect reality.

If a bar chart of CPM results is examined, it may be seen that there are several groups of activities whose early start dates are alike. If the activities within a group are competing for the same resource, there will be an apparent buildup of demand for that resource on the days following the common *ESD*. In practice, these buildups, or resource conflicts, cannot be tolerated and the scheduler must again find a way to make the necessary adjustment.

Some of the adjusting may be done before any calculations are made. Extreme care must be exercised in doing so, however, because a poor decision at this point will worsen the resource demand or will unnecessarily prolong the project. Usually the calculations must at least reach the point where the early start and finish dates are known before a wise decision can be made.

The temptation to make a before calculation decision occurs when the scheduler knows in advance that there is an upper limit on the availability of one of the resources. Suppose, for example, that a network for a bridge project has two subpaths containing the activities for driving piles, capping piles, and casting concrete on the north and south abutments. These may be logically planned in parallel as illustrated by Figure 11.1a. If the contractor has but one pile driving rig available and does not wish to buy or rent another, one of the abutments must be chosen to work on first. It might be decided to drive the piles on the north abutment and then on the south abutment. In this case the path between activities 10 and 17 will be lengthened by five days, the time duration of the driving activity. The logic would be altered as shown in Figure 11.1b. As long as the times remain as shown in the figure, it does not matter which abutment is chosen first because the total time span between activities 10 and 17

258

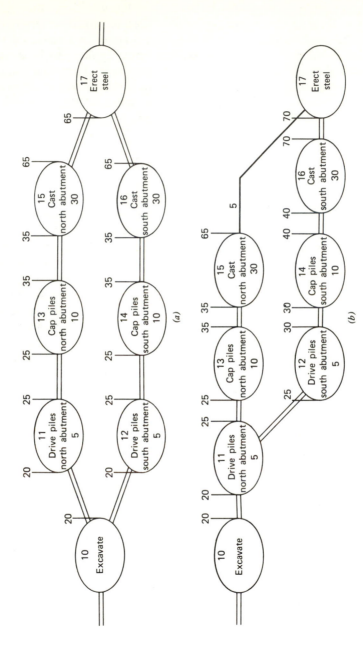

Figure 11.1 *Resolving resource conflicts on parallel paths.*

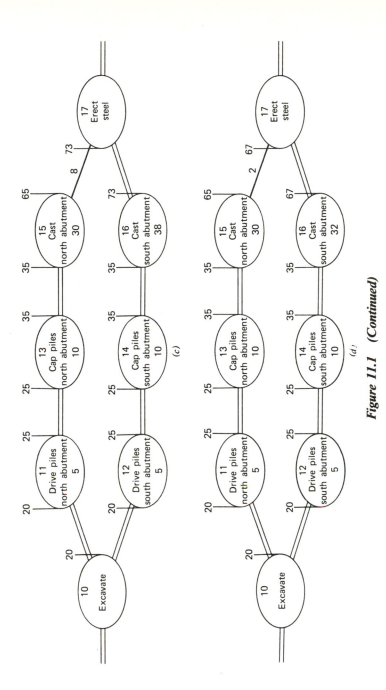

Figure 11.1 (Continued)

259

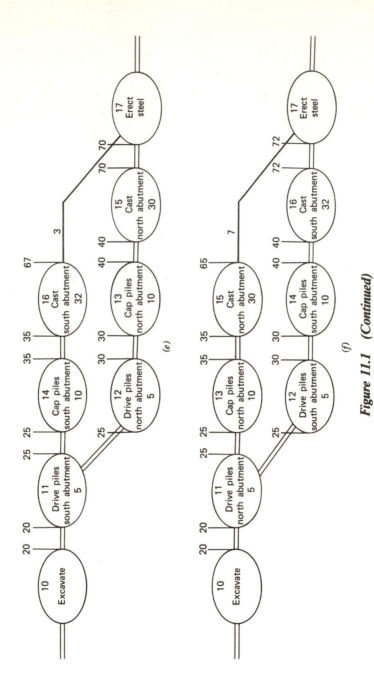

Figure 11.1 (*Continued*)

260

in Figure 11.1*b* will remain constant at 50 days. The most critical of the two paths will be the one containing the last employed sequence.

Now further suppose that the south abutment is somewhat taller and more complex than the north one so that the time duration for the south abutment casting activity is 38 days as shown in Figure 11.1*c*. The float in the north abutment chain between activities 10 and 17 in the original plan is then 8 days. In this case there is no real conflict for the pile driver because part of this float can be used and the driving of the north abutment piles need not be scheduled until after the south ones have been driven. The path will not be lengthened, but all the north abutment activities will be delayed from their early start positions by 5 days.

Again, assume that in the original plan the south abutment's casting activity duration is 32 days. The time span in Figure 11.1*d* between activities 10 and 17 is then 47 days and the float in the north abutment chain is 2 days. It would be expeditious to schedule the south abutment pile driving first as in Figure 11.1*e*, because to do so would only lengthen the path by 3 days over the 47-day time span. On the other hand, if it had been decided to schedule the north abutment pile driving first without the benefit of the computations as in Figure 11.1*f*, the path would be 5 days longer.

In summary, the decision to schedule an activity before any calculation is made must be done only if certain network conditions are met. These are:

1. There must be parallel chains of activities.

2. The parallel chains must have common beginning and ending nodes.

3. The chains must be identical with respect to both the activities and their duration times.

4. One activity in each chain must use the identical resource.

In some practical situations, these conditions cannot be met and the scheduling priority must wait until the early start schedule is available.

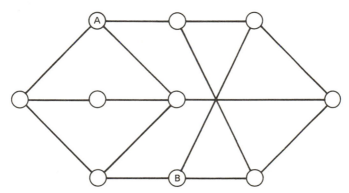

Figure 11.2   Possible resource conflicts.

The above examples dealt with the resolution of resource conflicts where there was reason to suspect their existence. There are cases where the conflict exists without being suspect and the only way to make the resolution is after the computations have been completed.

Figure 11.2 illustrates a network for a small project. If both Activity A and Activity B require the same resource, say a crane, then inspection alone cannot determine that a conflict exists. After the early start calculations have been made the early start and finish dates and the floats can be examined. If this analysis shows a possible conflict, the float in the system may be used to resolve it as suggested earlier. The network can also have its logic altered by scheduling one activity to come before another so that overall duration times are held to a minimum.

11.3   LEVELING OBJECTIVES

In Chapter 10 the trade-off between time and cost was discussed at length. It was stated there that an activity's cost is related to the amount of resource applied to it. The allocation of resources to each activity as represented by the cost was varied to produce feasible schedules, having the logic constraints given by the network.

Resource leveling, on the other hand, is a process wherein the activities in the network are positioned in time such that the project resources are minimized on a day-to-day basis. In a sense this is an allocation of resources to an entire project rather than to an individual activity. Leveling may be considered as a way to efficiently carry out the project once a basic schedule has been established.

There are a number of reasons why a planner feels the need to use resource leveling. These reasons can be grouped into three major categories. The first is the need to meet the physical limits of the resource. The second is the need to avoid the day-to-day fluctuations in resource demands, and the third is the need to maintain an even flow of application for the resource.

In the previous section it was stated that leveling can serve as a possible way to resolve resource conflicts. Basic early start schedules typically tend to create conflicts by demanding large numbers of workers on some days of the project. If it is known that only a limited number of workers are available in the area where the project is located, or if journeymen for a particular trade are in short supply, leveling will assist in reducing these daily demands so that they fall within the prescribed limits.

When all the daily demands for a resource in an early start schedule are examined, it will be seen that there is considerable daily fluctuation. The rise and fall in this demand level is very undesirable, especially when the resource is labor. The implied hiring and releasing of workers on a short-term basis is troublesome, inefficient, and costly. It is not conducive to attracting and keeping top-quality journeymen.

There are clerical costs incurred in processing the hiring or releasing papers for employees. Under many state laws there is an unemployment compensation cost that must be paid by the contractor when an employee is released. To continue the employment of persons so that they may be available at a later date is wasteful of their talents, and costs are incurred by the contractor for which little or no production is received. There are also costs that accrue owing to work inefficiencies because new employees need time to learn their tasks, and even previously employed persons need time to readjust to the working conditions of a particular job. In addition to the above costs there is also the possibility that employees who are furloughed may find other employment during the interim period and not be available upon recall. Any technique that will prevent worker fluctuations and reduce or eliminate these costs and difficulties is certainly worthy of consideration. This is the main objective of resource leveling.

The third need for resource leveling appears when the project employs high-cost resource units. Here the emphasis is placed upon the continuous application of the resource once it is assigned to the work. Cranes, pavers, and the like, should be able to work continuous days because considerable ownership costs are involved in having such equipment stand idle on the job site. Skilled trades required for the execution of the project represent another typical resource that requires continuous employment to provide for efficient project management.

Most contractors faced with the need for these kinds of adjustments in their schedules use a trial and error method. This may be a satisfactory solution when the project is small and the resource demands are light. On more complex work the cost for an employee's time to produce even a feasible solution by trial and error is greater than the cost involved in employing the higher early start resource levels. It is then that some systematic scheme is sought to reach an economical solution.

The traditional method assumes a resource level thought to be satisfactory, and then tests the resource demand against this assumption on a day-to-day basis. When the test shows that the demand cannot be met, a set of rules is applied to reduce the demand to the level that was assumed. A more recent scheme for making a leveling adjustment is to determine the moment of the daily resource demands, then to shift the activities in time so that this moment approaches a minimum. The next sections of this chapter will enlarge upon these two schemes and will discuss their advantages and disadvantages.

11.4   THE TRADITIONAL LEVELING APPROACH

The traditional approach to leveling resources begins with the addition on every project day of the resource rates for each activity scheduled in its early start schedule position. These sums are called the daily resource sums and represent the demands for the resource over the time duration of the project.

An examination of the activity resource rates reveals a possible minimum level that can be assumed as an upper limit on the daily resource sums. The resource demands are then tested day-by-day to determine if they are less than or greater than the assumed value. When the demand exceeds the assumed limit an activity is selected from a priority list and shifted one day. The daily resource sum is again examined and another activity shifted until the demand has been reduced below the limit. After this day's level has been fixed, the next successive day is examined in the same way and the procedure continues until the project duration is reached. If there are still demands greater than the assumed limit, the project is extended in time until all the daily resource sums are below the limit.

The process can be demonstrated by means of an example. Figure 11.3 is an arrow diagram for a sample project of six activities and Figure 11.4 is a precedence diagram for the same project. Leveling is independent of the type of diagram used and the results will be the same no matter which is chosen.

Table 11.1 contains the necessary information about the six activities as determined from the early start calculations. As can be seen, the early start and finish date of every activity is given together with the total and free float. The resource rate for each activity is shown in the seventh column of the table. This is the number of resource units required for each day of performance of the activity. If personnel is the resource, the number of employees working on the activity each day would be listed as the resource rate.

The product of the resource rate and the activity duration appears in the eighth column identified as "resource days." The total of these resource days represents the total resource load for the project. This figure, 49 resource days in the example, remains constant throughout the leveling process.

The upper part of Figure 11.5 is a bar chart of the project. Above each bar is the name of the activity, a letter in the example, together with the resource rate from Table 11.1. Note that the critical activities are plotted first. This has been done so that the noncritical activities with float can be quickly identified as they are the ones which will be shifted later. The noncritical activities are also plotted in sequence step order to avoid confusion in reading the chart.

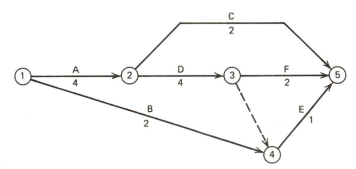

Figure 11.3   Arrow diagram for leveling example.

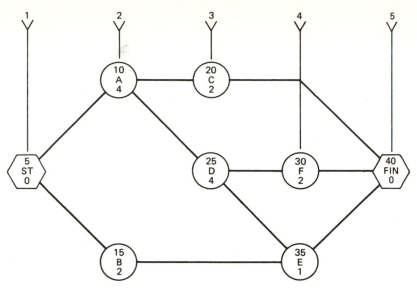

Figure 11.4   Precedence diagram for leveling example.

TABLE 11.1

Early Start Schedule Information

Activity	T	ESD	EFD	TF	FF	Res Rate	Res Days
A*	4	0	4	0		2	8
B	2	0	2	7	6	2	4
C	2	4	6	4	4	4	8
D*	4	4	8	0		6	24
E	1	8	9	1	1	1	1
F*	2	8	10	0		2	4
						Total	49

*Critical.

265

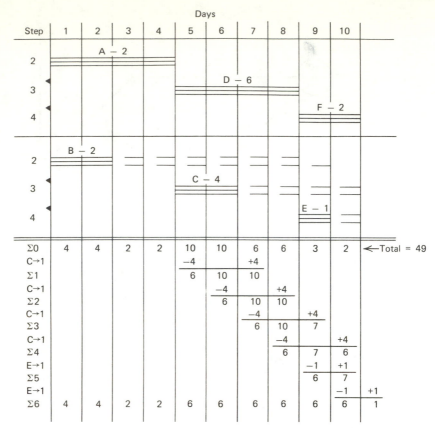

Figure 11.5   Leveling example—traditional approach.

Step	1	2	3	4	5	6	7	8	9	10	
Σ0	4	4	2	2	10	10	6	6	3	2	←Total = 49
C→1					−4		+4				
Σ1					6	10	10				
C→1						−4		+4			
Σ2						6	10	10			
C→1							−4		+4		
Σ3							6	10	7		
C→1								−4		+4	
Σ4								6	7	6	
E→1									−1	+1	
Σ5									6	7	
E→1										−1	+1
Σ6	4	4	2	2	6	6	6	6	6	6	1

Below the bar chart the sums of the resource rates for each day, the daily resource sums, appear in the line indicated by Σ0. The total of these daily resource sums is 49 resource days. This is the total resource load as shown before in Table 11.1. For an ideal uniform level the sums would average 4.9 units because the project duration is 10 days. This figure could have been used as the assumed resource limit. It will be observed, however, that there is one activity in the network that has a daily resource rate of 6 units. Clearly, the minimum level that can be assumed and still complete the project is then 6 units. This was therefore selected as the assumed limit to serve as the test value. Some other assumption might have been made but the maximum resource rate for any activity, critical or noncritical, would be the minimum possible value to use as a limit.

Figure 11.5 shows that the first day has a resource demand of 4 units. This is less than the assumed 6 and meets the test. The second day is also satisfactory, as are the third and fourth days. The fifth day has a 10 unit demand and some activity must then be shifted to reduce this value to a level equal to or below the assumption. Activities C and D are both scheduled to start on the fifth day, but Activity D is critical and cannot be shifted without prolonging the project duration. Activity C was therefore selected and shifted one day so as to be scheduled on days 6 and 7.

The shifting of Activity C is illustrated by the subtraction of the resource rate of 4 units from the sum for day 5 and adding this same rate to the sum for day 7. Note that there is no subtraction or addition on day 6 because Activity C will demand 4 units in either of its two positions. The revised daily resource sums for days 5, 6, and 7 are shown on line $\Sigma 1$. The fifth day is now within the assumed 6 unit limit.

The sixth day has been tested next and the same reasoning has led to an adjusted daily resource sum for that day. The process has been continued for days 7 and 8. On day 9 there were two noncritical activities to be examined. Activity C had used all the float available to it and the only activity that could be moved was Activity E. The revised sums are as shown on line $\Sigma 5$.

On day 10 both Activity C and Activity E had used all their float and were critical. Consequently, the only possibility for reducing the daily resource sum below the assumed limit of 6 was to lengthen the project duration. Of course, this extension was done keeping in mind that the choice for shifting must decrease the daily sum below the limit and at the same time must result in a minimum lengthening of the project. In the example, Activity E was selected and shifted. The final daily resource sums are given on line $\Sigma 6$.

Figure 11.6 is a diagram of the sample project's resource histogram showing the original values of the resource demands before and after leveling. It can be seen that should a contractor for this project not care to lengthen the project

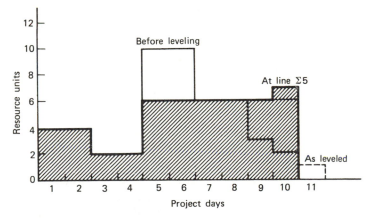

Figure 11.6   Resource histogram—leveling example—traditional approach.

duration, at least 7 units of the resource would have to be provided on the tenth day. That is, the contractor would have to meet the demand levels on line $\Sigma 5$ shown in Figure 11.5.

Some general observations may be drawn from the above example. Although satisfying the first objective stated in the previous section of this chapter, the procedure tends to cause a buildup of resources toward the end of the project. Such a buildup is a poor solution, as a contractor usually wishes the resources to taper off as the project draws to a close.

The testing procedure also permits fluctuations to remain in the resource histogram when the demand is below the assumed limit. This is illustrated in Figure 11.6 by the demand of 4 units on days 1 and 2 followed by the demand of 2 units on days 3 and 4. This does not completely satisfy the second objective stated above.

Furthermore, under this procedure there is a real possibility that the project duration may need to be extended to accommodate the assumed resource limit. For a contractor who has already established the project duration and has agreed to a completion date by contract, this is not acceptable. Of course, the process may be repeated with the test limit assumed at successively higher levels until no time extension is required. This trial-and-error process is also time-consuming for any real project, and the benefit to be derived may be greatly diminished or completely negated. It should be remembered that a contractor usually cannot afford to refine schedules in this way until certain that there is a valid contract for the work.

The major advantage to be obtained in using this technique applies to the case where there is truly a fixed set of resources available. This is the situation in many industrial plants where there is a predetermined type and amount of machinery at the planner's disposal. In the construction area such a procedure can also be of great help, especially for the highway and heavy contractor. For example, if such a contractor has a limited fleet of earthmoving equipment available, this method might be chosen to smooth the resource levels even with a penalty caused by exceeding his target date for project completion.

11.5   THE MINIMUM MOMENT APPROACH

The minimum moment approach to resource leveling begins in the same manner as the traditional approach began. The daily resource sums for a chosen resource are first determined assuming that the activities are in their early start positions. Instead of choosing a test limit, however, a resource improvement factor is computed for all activities on the last sequence step. From these computations the largest positive improvement factor is determined and the associated activity is shifted. These two processes are successively repeated for each sequence step until the first step is reached. The computations are again repeated, beginning at the first sequence step and ending at the last step. The resulting daily resource sums are the ones that provide the minimum moment and represent the leveled resource demands.

Before stating the detailed algorithm and discussing an example, it will be necessary in the following sections to establish the concept of the minimum histogram moment and to develop the mathematics of the improvement factor and other relationships. It will also be shown that the application of the algorithm provides the contractor with a direct answer to the question: How much of this resource will be needed to accomplish this project within the stated time interval?

The following sections will further show that the method has some advantages. It does not extend the project duration as does the traditional approach scheme. It does not tend to cause a resource buildup toward the end of the project, but does tend to give the largest resource demands during the central part of the duration. Also, the method can be used to adjust the resources to a predetermined resource demand histogram, allowing the contractor to closely match his resource availabilities.

The examples will demonstrate that there are some disadvantages. Not all the resource fluctuations can be removed, but the technique removes more of the variations than does the traditional approach. Manual solutions tend to be computationally slow and a computer is necessary if the project is very extensive. Because the scheme operates with an implied assumption that every activity is independent with respect to its position assignment, and this is not so, the scheme does not necessarily give a true minimum moment of the histogram.

In summary, the minimum moment method for leveling resources meets more of a contractor's needs for smoothing resource demands and has fewer disadvantages than the traditional approach. The reader should gain an in-depth appreciation of the technique from the remainder of this chapter.

11.6   DETERMINING THE MINIMUM MOMENT

As the name implies, the minimum moment method for resource leveling assumes that there is a histogram moment that is minimum. This assumption must be verified if the procedure is to have validity. That there is such moment can be demonstrated by the proof of the following theorem.

> **When a given set of elements is arranged into a histogram over a fixed set of intervals, the minimum moment of the elements exists when the histogram is a rectangle over the fixed set of intervals.**

There are a number of ways that this theorem can be proven. The procedure adopted here is an indirect approach, chosen because it bears a close relationship to the actual manual leveling process.

Figure 11.7 shows a given set, $\{A\}$, of elements $y_1, y_2, y_3, \ldots, y_n$ over the fixed set of intervals 1 to n. Set $\{A\}$ represents the area of a resource histogram and

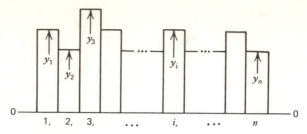

Figure 11.7 *Elements arranged into a histogram over fixed intervals 1 to n.*

the elements, y_i, represent the daily resource sums. Then

$$\sum_{i=1}^{n} y_i = \{A\}$$

The moment of an element is $\frac{1}{2}y_i^2$ about axis $0-0$. The total moment of the set is

$$M_0' = \frac{1}{2} \sum_{i=1}^{n} y_i^2$$

which is to be a minimum. Hence,

$$M_0 = \sum_{i=1}^{n} y_i^2$$

is to be minimum.

As a trial solution for y_i take

$$y_i^* = \frac{\{A\}}{n} \qquad \text{(for all } i=1,2,\ldots,n)$$

Thus, y_i^* represents the height of a rectangle distributed over the intervals 1 to n and the result is

$$M_0 = \sum_{i=1}^{n} y_i^{*2}$$

Any other solution may be obtained by adding a very small amount, Δy, to y_i^* at location k and subtracting Δy from y_i^* at location j for any pair of elements jk, such that $\{A\}$ is constant and $j \neq k$. Figure 11.8 shows this addition and subtraction to the rectangle. Let y_h stand for this alternate solution to M_0. Then

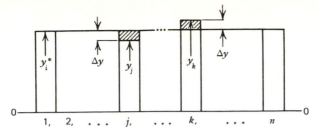

Figure 11.8 *Rectangular histogram with addition and subtraction of Δy.*

let

$$y_h^* = y_i^* \qquad\qquad (h=1,2,\ldots,n)(h\neq j,k)$$

and

$$y_j = y_i^* - \Delta y$$

and

$$y_k = y_i^* + \Delta y$$

Now

$$M_0 = \sum_{i=1}^{n} y_h^2$$

$$M_0 = y_j^2 + y_k^2 + \sum_{i=1}^{n} y_h^{*2} \qquad\qquad (h\neq j,k)$$

$$M_0 = y_i^{*2} - 2(\Delta y)y_i^{*2} + (\Delta y)^2 + y_i^{*2} + 2(\Delta y)y_i^{*2} + (\Delta y)^2 + \sum_{h=1}^{n} y_h^{*2}$$

$$M_0 = 2y_i^{*2} + 2(\Delta y)^2 + \sum_{h=1}^{n} y_h^{*2} \qquad\qquad (h\neq j,k)$$

Hence

$$M_0 = 2(\Delta y)^2 + \sum_{i=1}^{n} y_i^{*2} \qquad\qquad (\text{all } i)$$

This value of M_0 is larger than that obtained using the trial solution y_i^* by the quantity $2(\Delta y)^2$. The minimum moment is therefore given by a rectangular histogram distributed over the fixed set of intervals 1 to n as given by the solution

$$y_i^* = \frac{\{A\}}{n}$$

11.7 THE IMPROVEMENT FACTOR

In Section 11.5 it was stated that an improvement factor is used to determine which activity is to be chosen for shifting so as to reduce the histogram moment. This section will mathematically develop this factor.

Assume $x_1, x_2, \ldots, x_m$ is the set of daily resource sums,

$$\{X\} = \sum_1^m x_i$$

from which m daily resource rates, r, are to be deducted. Also assume that $w_1, w_2, \ldots, w_m$ is the set of daily resource sums,

$$\{W\} = \sum_1^m w_i$$

to which m daily resource rates, r, are to be added.

The moment of the histogram before shifting an activity can be defined as the sum of the squares of the x_i and w_i. Thus

$$M_1 = \sum_1^m x_i^2 + \sum_1^m w_i^2$$

Similarly, the moment of the histogram after shifting the same activity can be defined as the sum of the squares of $(x_i - r)$ and $(w_i + r)$. Thus

$$M_2 = \sum_1^m (x_i - r)^2 + \sum_1^m (w_i + r)^2$$

Improvement in the histogram, that is, a lowering of the value of the histogram moment, can be said to occur if $M_2 < M_1$. Hence,

$$\sum_1^m (x_1 - r)^2 + \sum_1^m (w_i + r)^2 < \sum_1^m x_i^2 + \sum_1^m w_i^2$$

Expanding the above expression gives

$$\sum_1^m x_i^2 - 2r\sum_1^m x_i + mr^2 + \sum_1^m w_i^2 + 2r\sum_1^m w_i + mr^2 < \sum_1^m x_i^2 + \sum_1^m w_i^2$$

Collecting terms

$$-2r\sum_1^m x_i + 2r\sum_1^m w_i + 2mr^2 < 0$$

Dividing by -2 and factoring results in

$$r\left(\sum_1^m x_i - \sum_1^m w_i - mr\right) > 0$$

The left side of the inequality is termed the *improvement factor*. Thus for any activity, ACT, and shift, S, the improvement factor, IF, is

$$\text{IF (ACT, } S) = r\left(\sum_1^m x_i - \sum_1^m w_i - mr\right) \qquad (11.1)$$

The value of m used as the limit in the above summations is defined as the minimum of either the days that the activity is to be shifted, S, or the activity duration, T. Thus,

$$m = \min(S, T) \qquad (11.2)$$

The variable, S, may assume any vlaue from 1 up to and including the value of the free float of the activity. No matter what particular value of S or T controls, the value of m will always be equal to the number of days on which the rate is subtracted from the daily resource sums.

An examination of Figure 11.9 will help to clarify the above relationships. Computations are shown below the diagram for the improvement factor for an activity with a duration of two days which is to be shifted three days. For comparison, the value of the moments of the resource histogram, M_1 and M_2 are given before and after the shift. Note that the improvement factor is equal to one-half the difference between M_1 and M_2. That this is so should be evident if it is recalled that in Section 11.6 the constant $1/2$ was dropped when determining M_0.

It should also be noted that because of the division by -2 in the derivation, the improvement factor must always have a positive value if improvement in the histogram moment is to be achieved.

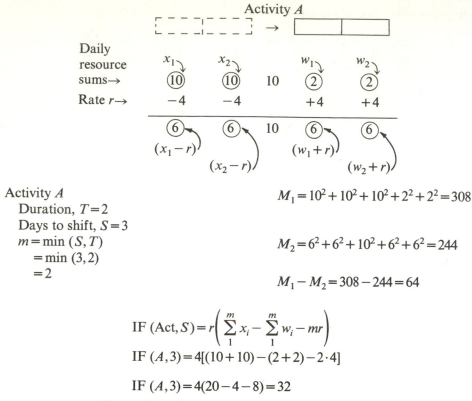

Activity A $M_1 = 10^2 + 10^2 + 10^2 + 2^2 + 2^2 = 308$

Duration, $T = 2$

Days to shift, $S = 3$

$m = \min(S, T)$ $M_2 = 6^2 + 6^2 + 10^2 + 6^2 + 6^2 = 244$

$\quad = \min(3, 2)$

$\quad = 2$ $M_1 - M_2 = 308 - 244 = 64$

$$\text{IF (Act, } S) = r\left(\sum_{1}^{m} x_i - \sum_{1}^{m} w_i - mr \right)$$

$$\text{IF }(A, 3) = 4[(10 + 10) - (2 + 2) - 2 \cdot 4]$$

$$\text{IF }(A, 3) = 4(20 - 4 - 8) = 32$$

Figure 11.9   Improvement factor relationships.

11.8   BACK FLOAT

It was shown in Section 11.7 that the variable, m, in the improvement factor computation could assume the minimum value of either the activity duration or the number of days that the activity could be shifted. This latter assumption leads to the need to reexamine the limits within which an activity can be performed.

    The start boundary for an activity is established by the latest of the early finish dates of the preceding activities as discussed in Chapters 6 and 7. Similarly, the finish boundary of an activity is set by the earliest of the early start dates of the following activities. Consequently, the activity can be performed during any time between these two limits.

    When an activity is scheduled to start at its earliest, the time period between its early finish and the finish boundary is the free float. The activity can be shifted to use any or all of this free float. When an activity is scheduled at its late finish position, the activity can be shifted back toward the earliest position by any part of an amount that will be called "back float."

In a formal definition,

> **the back float is the time span in which an activity can be started and not cause a preceding activity to be finished earlier than its early finish date.**

It is the difference between the early start date of the activity and the latest of the early finish dates for all the preceding activities.

For any activity, I, that is linked to preceding activities, H, the expression for back float, BF_I, may be written as

$$BF_I = ESD_I - \operatorname*{Max}_{\forall H} EFD_H$$

where the symbol, $\operatorname*{Max}_{\forall H}$, is to be interpreted to mean that the maximization is to be over all the links, HI, that end with activity I. For any given schedule the ESD of activity I is a constant. The expression may then be written to associate the ESD_I and the EFD_H by changing the maximization to minimization, thus

$$BF_I = \operatorname*{Min}_{\forall H}(ESD_I - EFD_H)$$

The term in the brackets may be evaluated by Equation 7.7 leading to

$$BF_I = \operatorname*{Min}_{\forall H} LAG_{HI} \qquad (11.3)$$

for all links directly preceding activity I.

Figure 11.10a illustrates an activity I extracted from a precedence diagram along with activities H and J. The lags are shown on each link. The same activities are diagramed in bar chart form in Figure 11.10b. Note that there are two links from preceding activities H to activity I, 14–18 and 16–18. The back float for activity 18 can be computed from Equation 11.3 as follows:

$$BF_{18} = \operatorname{Min}\begin{bmatrix} LAG_{14-18} \\ LAG_{16-18} \end{bmatrix}$$

$$BF_{18} = \operatorname{Min}\begin{bmatrix} 4 \\ 2 \end{bmatrix} = 2$$

It can be observed from 11.10b that if the activity is in its early start position, the back float will be zero and the free float will be at its maximum. Also, that if the activity is in its late finish position, the free float will be zero and the back float will be at its maximum.

In the shifting process the early start and finish dates of the activity are changed to reflect the scheduled position. The terms ESD and EFD are retained

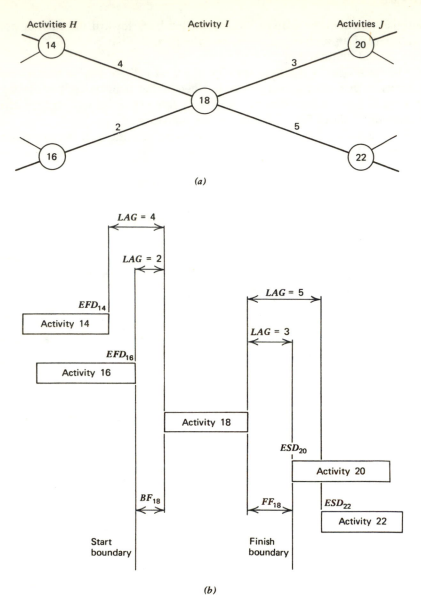

(b)

Figure 11.10   Free float and back float relationships.

to denote the start and finish of the activity even though they no longer have the same connotation as they did in the early start schedule.

The above concepts will be helpful in understanding the leveling algorithm that is described in the following section.

11.9 MINIMUM MOMENT ALGORITHM FOR RESOURCE LEVELING

The minimum moment approach to resource leveling was described briefly in Section 11.5. This section will present the minimum moment algorithm and present an example of its application. A commentary on the algorithm will also be given together with the example.

The algorithm is divided into two parts. The first part deals with the setup for manual computation and the second part deals with the actual procedure.

Setup

A. Prepare an arrow or precedence network of the project and determine the sequence step number for each activity.
B. Prepare a link matrix and compute the *ESD* and *EFD* for each activity. Compute the lags for each link. Determine the total float for each activity and identify the critical path.
C. Select a resource to be leveled.
D. Determine the amount of the selected resource which is required per day for each network activity. Call this required resource rate, "*r*."
E. Prepare a bar chart showing the early start time for each activity and its duration. Plot critical activities first, followed by noncritical activities.
F. For each day of the project, total the resource rates at the foot of the bar chart to obtain the daily resource sums.

Procedure

The procedure begins with the activities on the last sequence step.

1. Examine the activities on the sequence step.
    (a) Every activity on the sequence step having zero free float is passed over.
    (b) Every activity on the sequence step having a zero resource rate is shifted to the limit of the activity free float to allow preceding activities to be shifted.
    (c) For each activity on the sequence step having a positive resource rate, determine the extent of its free float and compute improvement factors

for all possible days that the activity can be shifted until the free float limit is reached.

2. Select the activity having the largest improvement factor determined in algorithm step 1(c).

   (a) If the largest improvement factor is negative, no shifting takes place. Go to the next sequence step and examine the activities as in algorithm step 1.

   (b) If there is a tie in the value of the largest improvement factor for several activities:

      (i) Select the activity with the greatest "r" value.
      (ii) If still tied, select the activity which creates the greatest free float for preceding activities.
      (iii) If still tied, select the activity with the latest start date.
      (iv) If still tied, select the first activity in the queue.

3. Shift the selected activity subject to the following:

   (a) If the largest improvement factor is zero or positive, shift the selected activity by subtracting the activity resource rate from each of the daily resource sums at the position being vacated and adding this same rate to each of the daily resource sums at the position being occupied.

   (b) If there is a tie in the value of the improvement factor at several of the possible activity positions, shift the activity the greatest number of time units.

4. If shifting has occurred in algorithm step 3, update the lags, *ESD* and *EFD*, in the link matrix.

5. Reexamine the activities on the sequence step and repeat algorithm steps 1 through 4 until all shifting is complete on this step.

6. Examine the next earlier sequence step and repeat algorithm steps 1 through 5. Continue in this manner until all activities have been considered and all possible shifting has taken place on every sequence step.

7. Repeat algorithm steps 1 through 6 until no further shifting takes place. This is the end of the forward cycle.

8. Beginning with the first sequence step, using back float instead of free float, and progressing to the next latest· sequence step instead of to the next earliest sequence step, repeat algorithm steps 1 through 7 until all activities have been considered and shifted, where possible, to an earlier time position. This is the end of the backward cycle and completes the leveling.

The example chosen for discussion is the same one that was used in Section 11.4. The diagram may be either the one shown in Figure 11.3 or Figure 11.4. The activity durations and the resource rates are taken from Table 11.1.

Algorithm Step A requires the determination of the sequence step number for each activity. In precedence networks, these numbers are computed in the manner discussed in Chapter 7. For arrow networks, they may be computed by assigning to each real acitivty a sequence step value of one and to each dummy activity a sequence step value of zero. A forward pass calculation is then performed as though early start and finish dates were being computed. The resulting start step numbers will be the sequence step numbers to be used.

Table 11.2 shows these calculations for the arrow diagram of Figure 11.3. Note that the initial start step number is assumed to be one.

The reader may observe that the sequence step numbers thus determined for the arrow network are one number less than those for the precedence network of Figure 11.4. The reason for this difference is that the precedence network needs an initial dummy activity to provide a single node at the beginning of the diagram. The leveling algorithm uses these numbers to order the progression of the calculations. Hence, either set of numbers is satisfactory.

Figure 11.11 is the link matrix for the example project. The techniques discussed in Chapter 7 have been used to obtain the values of *ESD*, *EFD*, lag, free float, and total float. The matrix not only meets the requirements of Algorithm Step B, but will be used to maintain the current value of these items as the leveling proceeds.

Step C in the algorithm requires that a single resource be selected. In most projects there is one resource that stands out as having the highest priority and this is usually chosen. Sometimes a combination of resources is chosen or a second priority resource to be leveled following the leveling of a first priority one is selected. Such choices are left to the planner and following sections in this chapter will examine the effects of some of them in detail.

The upper part of Figure 11.12 is a bar chart of the example project drawn according to Algorithm Step E. The plotting of the activities has been in

TABLE 11.2

Sequence Step Numbers Computed for an Arrow Network					
*I**	*J*	ACT	Seq. Step Value	Start Step No.	End Step No.
1	2	A	1	1[†]	2
1	4	B	1	1	2
2	5	C	1	2	3
2	3	D	1	2	3
3	4	Dummy	0	3	3
3	5	F	1	3	4
4	5	E	1	3	4

*Refer to Figure 11.3.
[†]Initial number assumed to be 1.

Sequence step numbers

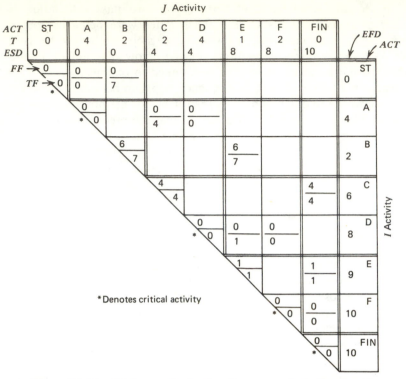

Figure 11.11   Link matrix for leveling example before leveling.

sequence step order in both the critical and noncritical list. By plotting the bars in this way, the chart is easy to construct and has clarity.

Immediately beneath the bar chart on line $\Sigma 0$ are found the daily resource sums. These summations mark the completion of the setup and satisfies Algorithm Step E.

The leveling process begins with Sequence Step 4, the last step with real activities. There are two activities on this step, Activities E and F. Activity F has no free float and is critical. Activity E has a free float of one day as shown in the link matrix. The improvement factor for E for this possible shift of one day is computed by Equation 11.1 to be

$$IF(E, 1) = 1(3 - 2 - 1 \cdot 1) = 0$$

The zero result signifies that there would be no improvement in the moment of the resource histogram if this shift were made. Because of the zero result however, Algorithm Step 3(a) requires the shifting of the activity.

This requirement is imposed to allow increases in the lags of the links between

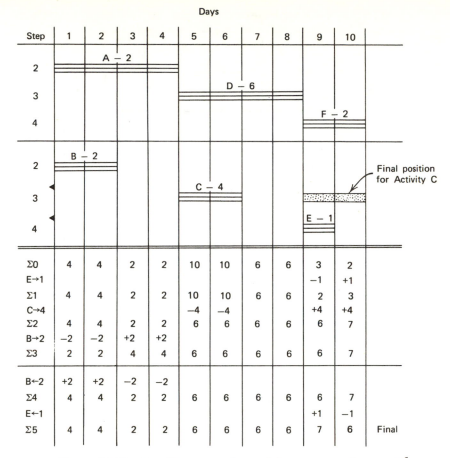

	1	2	3	4	5	6	7	8	9	10	
Σ0	4	4	2	2	10	10	6	6	3	2	
E→1									−1	+1	
Σ1	4	4	2	2	10	10	6	6	2	3	
C→4					−4	−4			+4	+4	
Σ2	4	4	2	2	6	6	6	6	6	7	
B→2	−2	−2	+2	+2							
Σ3	2	2	4	4	6	6	6	6	6	7	
B←2	+2	+2	−2	−2							
Σ4	4	4	2	2	6	6	6	6	6	7	
E←1									+1	−1	
Σ5	4	4	2	2	6	6	6	6	7	6	Final

Figure 11.12   Leveling example—minimum moment approach.

the activity and its immediately preceding activities. These increases, in turn, become the free floats for the preceding activities and may allow them to be shifted in later steps of the algorithm. In this instance, the shifting of Activity E allows the lags in links D-E and B-E to be increased by one. Thus, the free float of Activity B became seven instead of six. The free float of Activity D was unchanged because it was determined by the lag in the link between Activities D and F.

The shifting of Activity E by one day is shown in Figure 11.12 by the subtraction of the resource rate, 1, from the daily resource sum on day 9 and the addition of the rate, 1, to the daily resource sum on day 10. The augmented daily resource sums are shown in Row Σ1.

The updating of the link matrix in Figure 11.13 has been made in the following manner. In the row opposite Activity E the lag in link E–FIN,

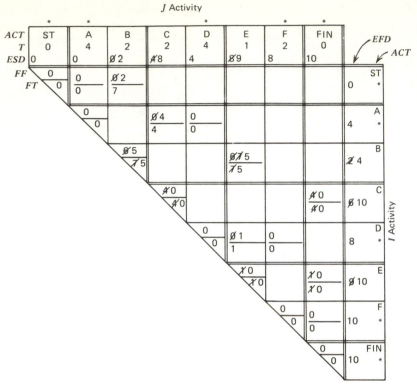

Figure 11.13   Link matrix for leveling example of end of forward pass.

representing the free float for Activity E, has been reduced to zero and the *EFD* of E has been increased by one. Moving to the diagonal of the matrix and up the column headed by Activity E, the lags in links D–E and B–E have each been increased by one and the *ESD* of Activity E has been increased by one.

   Sequence Step 4 was reexamined and it was found that there were no activities with free float. Hence, Sequence Step 3 was next examined. Here, Activity C was seen to be the one with a free float amounting to four days. The improvement factors for Activity C for the four possible days of shifting are as follows:

$$IF(C,1)=4(10-6-1\cdot4)=0$$
$$IF(C,2)=4(20-12-2\cdot4)=0$$
$$IF(C,3)=4(20-8-2\cdot4)=16$$
$$IF(C,4)=4(20-5-2\cdot4)=28$$

The largest of these factors is 28, indicating that Activity C should be shifted 4 days.

The actual shift is indicated in Figure 11.12 by the subtraction of the rate, 4, and the addition of the same rate as before. The resulting resource sums are shown on line $\Sigma 2$.

The matrix has been updated as shown in Figure 11.13. The lag in link C-FIN has been decreased to zero and the *EFD* for Activity C has been increased by four to 10. In the column headed by Activity C the lag in link A-C and the *ESD* of C have each been increased by four.

A reexamination of the sequence step showed that there was no activity remaining with a free float. Sequence Step 2 was therefore examined and it was found that Activity B had a free float of seven.

The improvement factors for the seven possible days of shift for Activity B are:

$$IF(B, 1) = 2(4 - 2 - 1 \cdot 2) = 0$$
$$IF(B, 2) = 2(8 - 4 - 2 \cdot 2) = 0$$
$$IF(B, 3) = 2(8 - 8 - 2 \cdot 2) = -8$$
$$IF(B, 4) = 2(8 - 12 - 2 \cdot 2) = -16$$
$$IF(B, 5) = 2(8 - 12 - 2 \cdot 2) = -16$$
$$IF(B, 6) = 2(8 - 12 - 2 \cdot 2) = -16$$
$$IF(B, 7) = 2(8 - 12 - 2 \cdot 2) = -16$$

For this situation the largest improvement factor is zero. Note that there is a tie for this factor on shift days 1 and 2. The algorithm indicates that the later one should be selected. The activity has therefore been shifted two days.

The changes have been made in Figures 11.12 and 11.13, and the daily resource sums are now as shown on line $\Sigma 3$ in Figure 11.12.

Because there were no more activities with free float on any of the sequence steps, the forward pass was ended.

For the backward pass, the algorithm requires the use of the back float instead of the free float. Back float, as defined by Equation 11.3, is the minimum lag of the links preceding the activity. In Figure 11.13 it can be found by searching the column under the activity for the minimum lag.

The examination of the sequence steps for the backward pass begins with Sequence Step 1. On this step Activity ST was found to be critical and was passed over.

Sequence Step 2 was next considered and was found to contain two activities, A and B. In Figure 11.12, it can be seen that the back float for Activity A is zero and that for Activity B is two. Activity A was therefore passed over.

The improvement factors for Activity B for the two possible days of shift are:

$$IF(B, 1) = 2(4 - 2 - 1 \cdot 2) = 0$$
$$IF(B, 2) = 2(8 - 4 - 2 \cdot 2) = 0$$

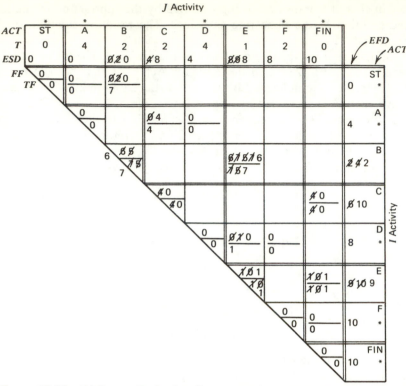

Figure 11.14   Link matrix for leveling example at end of backward pass.

Because the largest improvement factor is zero and there is a tie, the activity should be shifted backward two days. The shifting and the resulting daily resource sums are shown in Figure 11.12.

The matrix has been updated in Figure 11.14. In the column under Activity B the lag in link ST–B has been reduced by two days and the *ESD* of B has been made zero. In the row opposite Activity B the lag in link B–E has been increased to 7 and the *EFD* has been reduced to 2.

A reexamination of Sequence Step 2 showed that there were no more activities with back float and the activities in Sequence Step 3 have been examined next. Activity C has a back float of 4 days; hence, improvement factors were computed as follows:

$$IF(C,1) = 4(\ 7 - 6 - 1 \cdot 4) = -12$$
$$IF(C,2) = 4(13 - 12 - 2 \cdot 4) = -28$$
$$IF(C,3) = 4(13 - 12 - 2 \cdot 4) = -28$$
$$IF(C,4) = 4(13 - 12 - 2 \cdot 4) = -28$$

In this case there were no improvement factors that were zero or positive and no shifting of Activity C took place.

Activity E on Sequence Step 4 has a back float of 1. The improvement factor for this possible shift is:

$$IF(E, 1) = 1(7 - 6 - 1 \cdot 1) = 0$$

Activity E has therefore been shifted back one day.

The shift is shown in Figure 11.12 and the resulting daily resource sums are shown on line $\Sigma 5$.

The matrix of Figure 11.14 has been updated to show this new position for the activity. The lag in links B-E and D-E both have been reduced by one and the *ESD* and *EFD* have also been reduced by one, whereas the lag in the row opposite E has been increased by one.

Because there were no more activities with back float that could be shifted, the algorithm came to an end and the last daily resource sums in Figure 11.12 became the leveled resources. The corrected free and total floats for all activities at the end of the leveling are shown in Figure 11.14.

The setup detailed in the above algorithm is for manual computation, but the method can be programed for the digital computer. In addition to the usual input of activity number, activity name, and time duration, the values of the resource rates will need to be provided. Output formats can be programed to suit the user and may be either in the form of tables or charts.

Although the example above demonstrates the application of the algorithm, it cannot illustrate all the different conditions that arise in its use for more extensive project networks. The following sections will expand the reader's understanding of the method and some of its implications.

11.10 RESOURCE IMPROVEMENT COEFFICIENT

In the minimum moment procedure the improvement in the histogram moment is measured by the reduction in the squares in the daily resource sums. The magnitude of the improvement may be misleading when it is desired to compare more than one resource. The total demand for the first resource will usually be quite different than that for the second resource and the magnitudes of the Σy^2 values after leveling will reflect this variation. It is therefore necessary to have another measure that is independent of the total resource demand. Such a measure is the resource improvement coefficient, RIC.

It was shown in Section 11.6 that when a given set of elements is arranged into a histogram over a fixed set of intervals, the minimum moment of the elements exists when the histogram is a rectangle over the fixed set of intervals.

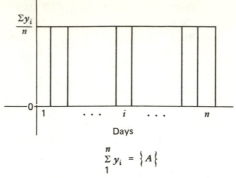

$$\sum_{1}^{n} y_i = \{A\}$$

Figure 11.15   Ideal histogram.

If $\{A\}$ is the set of resources being considered, then

$$\sum_{1}^{n} y_i = \{A\}$$

and Figure 11.15 is a representation of this ideal histogram. The ordinate for all the elements is

$$y_i^* = \frac{\sum_{1}^{n} y_i}{n} = \frac{\{A\}}{n}$$

and the moment of the ideal histogram can be written as

$$M_0' = \frac{1}{2} \cdot \frac{\left(\sum_{1}^{n} y_i\right)^2}{n}$$

Omitting the $1/2$

$$M_0 = \frac{\left(\sum_{1}^{n} y_i\right)^2}{n}$$

This moment is the minimum possible for any resource histogram regardless of the total amount of the resource.

At any stage in the leveling process the moment of the current histogram can be divided by the above minimum moment, and the result is the resource improvement coefficient, RIC.

$$RIC = \frac{n \sum y_i^2}{\left(\sum y_i\right)^2} \qquad (11.4)$$

where it is understood that the summation is over the n intervals covered by the histogram. Ideally, the value of this coefficient would be one; hence, the nearer the value of the RIC is to one, the more closely the resource histogram is to a rectangle.

11.11 LEVELING RESOURCES IN SERIES

It was pointed out in Section 11.9 that the Minimum Moment Algorithm allows only a single resource to be leveled at one time. It might seem that this restriction is a most serious one for a contractor who is required to manage several resources simultaneously. However, one characteristic of construction projects that greatly modifies this restriction is the dependence among the resources. Thus, *when one resource is leveled, other resources tend to be leveled as well.*

The network of Figure 11.16 represents a construction project of 14 activities. The accompanying table lists every activity and its resource rate for each of two resources. It may be assumed that Resource 1 has been chosen to have first priority and Resource 2 to have second priority.

A bar chart for the early start schedule of the project is shown in the upper part of Figure 11.17. The resource rates for Resource 1 are given alongside the activity names. The final position for each activity after the leveling of Resource 1 has been accomplished is shown by the crosshatched bars, and the initial position is shown by the open bars.

In the lower part of the figure the several adjusting steps taken during the leveling process are shown. It may be seen immediately following line $\Sigma 3$ that Activity H has been shifted to its current limit of free float. In the backward pass Activity H was shifted back to its original position as permitted by its then current value of back float. Such shifts are treated as special cases by Algorithm Step 1(b) because the activity resource rate is zero. The same sequence of shifts may also be seen with regard to Activity A.

Immediately following line $\Sigma 4$ it may be observed that either Activity E or Activity G could have been shifted because the improvement factor for each would have been zero. Algorithm Step 2(b)(i) requires that the activity with the maximum r value be selected, and Activity E was shifted. The improvement factor for Activity G remained zero and it was selected for shifting next. In the backward pass there was also a tie in the improvement factor for Activities D

Act	T	Resource 1		Resource 2	
		Rate	Res Day	Rate	Res Day
ST	0	—	—	—	—
A	2	0	0	2	4
B	5	2	10	3	15
C	3	2	6	0	0
D	2	1	2	4	8
E	6	2	12	5	30
F	6	3	18	2	12
G	6	1	6	0	0
H	4	0	0	5	20
K	2	4	8	5	10
L	7	2	14	0	0
M	3	2	6	8	24
N	2	4	8	3	6
P	2	0	0	0	0
			$\Sigma y = 90$		$\Sigma y = 129$

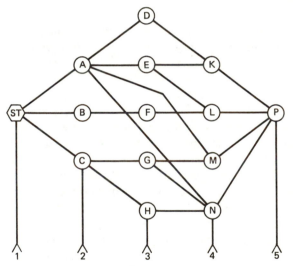

Figure 11.16   Leveling network with two resources.

288

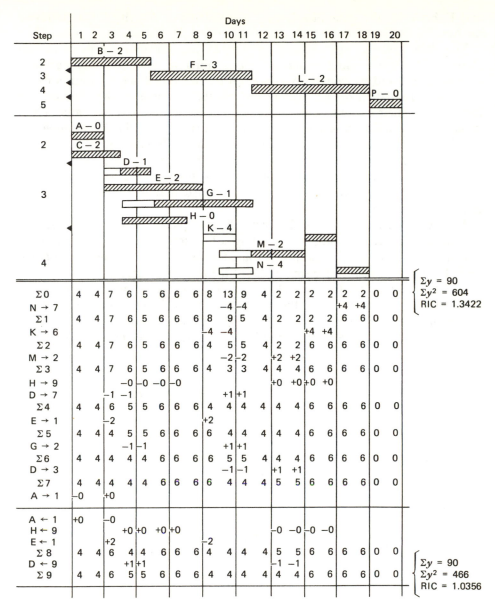

	1	2	3	4	5	6	7	8	9	10	11	12	13	14	15	16	17	18	19	20	
$\Sigma 0$	4	4	7	6	5	6	6	6	8	13	9	4	2	2	2	2	2	2	0	0	$\Sigma y = 90$
N → 7										−4	−4						+4	+4			$\Sigma y^2 = 604$
$\Sigma 1$	4	4	7	6	5	6	6	6	8	9	5	4	2	2	2	2	6	6	0	0	RIC = 1.3422
K → 6										−4	−4				+4	+4					
$\Sigma 2$	4	4	7	6	5	6	6	6	4	5	5	4	2	2	6	6	6	6	0	0	
M → 2										−2	−2		+2	+2							
$\Sigma 3$	4	4	7	6	5	6	6	6	4	3	3	4	4	4	6	6	6	6	0	0	
H → 9			−0	−0	−0	−0							+0	+0	+0	+0					
D → 7			−1	−1						+1	+1										
$\Sigma 4$	4	4	6	5	5	6	6	6	4	4	4	4	4	4	6	6	6	6	0	0	
E → 1			−2						+2												
$\Sigma 5$	4	4	4	5	5	6	6	6	6	4	4	4	4	4	6	6	6	6	0	0	
G → 2				−1	−1					+1	+1										
$\Sigma 6$	4	4	4	4	4	6	6	6	6	5	5	4	4	4	6	6	6	6	0	0	
D → 3										−1	−1		+1	+1							
$\Sigma 7$	4	4	4	4	4	6	6	6	6	4	4	4	5	5	6	6	6	6	0	0	
A → 1	−0	+0																			
A ← 1	+0	−0																			
H ← 9			+0	+0	+0	+0							−0	−0	−0	−0					
E ← 1			+2						−2												
$\Sigma 8$	4	4	6	4	4	6	6	6	4	4	4	4	5	5	6	6	6	6	0	0	$\Sigma y = 90$
D ← 9				+1	+1								−1	−1							$\Sigma y^2 = 466$
$\Sigma 9$	4	4	6	5	5	6	6	6	4	4	4	4	4	4	6	6	6	6	0	0	RIC = 1.0356

Figure 11.17   Leveling Resource 1.

and E, however, the value of r favored the shifting of Activity E first followed by Activity D.

The daily resource sums shown in line $\Sigma 9$ are the resource demands for Resource 1 after leveling within the constraints of total network duration, network logic, and the continuity condition for individual activity durations.

At the termination of the leveling process the positions of the activities are indicated by their current values of the early start and early finish dates. These values may be taken from the link matrix used (not shown in this example). It should be remembered that these early start and finish dates are now modified from the original early start schedule. As such they are not truly the early start and finish for any given activity, but they do represent the earliest start and finish dates that will produce the daily resource demands of the leveled histogram for the priority resource.

The resource histogram for Resource 1 is depicted in Figure 11.18. The maximum resource demand before leveling is 13 resource units and after leveling the maximum has been reduced 6 resource units. It is also visually clear that there has been a considerable smoothing of the resource demand.

It was stated earlier that one of the main measures of improvement in the histogram was the reduction of the moment, Σy^2. As shown in Figure 11.18, the Σy^2 value has been reduced from 604 to 466. Also the RIC has been reduced from 1.3422 to 1.0356. Note that the histogram extends over 18 days before and

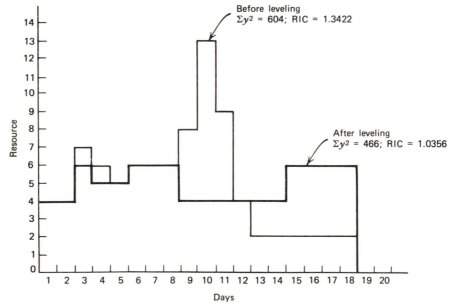

Figure 11.18 Histogram for leveling Resource 1.

after leveling, and this quantity was used as n in the computations instead of the 20-day project duration.

Leveling the Second Resource

A bar chart of the project is shown in Figure 11.19 with the activities positioned as they were after the leveling of the first priority resource. Values of the second priority resource rates have been added to the identification of each activity. The crosshatched bars show the final positions of the activities after all leveling has taken place.

One line $\Sigma 2$–0 the resource sums for the second resource are given with the activities positioned as above. The steps taken in leveling the second resource follow. It may be observed that only three activities were shifted in the forward pass, which indicates the already rectangular nature of the histogram due to the leveling of Resource 1.

In the backward pass three activities were shifted, only one of which had been shifted in the forward pass. The shifting of Activities D and G caused the first priority resource to be upset, or unleveled, in favor of the second resource, of course. This change represents a compromise to accommodate both resources. Line $\Sigma 2$–3 gives the final demands for Resource 2 leveled after leveling Resource 1.

The diagram of Figure 11.20 illustrates the changes in the histogram for Resource 2. The fine line is the histogram for Resource 2 before the leveling of either resource took place. The RIC is 1.1502, a fairly low value, indicating that the initial histogram approached a rectangle with a narrow base of 12 days. The corresponding Σy^2 value of 1595 is a relatively high value. The dotted line in the figure represents the histogram obtained after leveling Resource 1. Its Σy^2 has been reduced to 1301, but the RIC has been increased to 1.4072. These figures reflect that the histogram has been extended to 18 days and that the daily resource demand for Resource 2 has become more varied. The heavy line depicts the final resource demand for Resource 2 from Figure 11.19 where the Σy^2 has been reduced to 1035 and the RIC to 1.1195. Such variations are typical of the process.

Any number of resources can be leveled in series as above and the process may be terminated arbitrarily at any intermediate summation.

Leveling resources one priority at a time will cause some activities to be shifted from a previous position established by the leveling of a higher priority resource, as with Activities D and G above. Hence, when leveling resources in series it should not be expected that the resource requirements for any one of the resources would be minimal.

It can be shown that if Resource 2 is leveled first followed by Resource 1 the Σy^2 for Resource 2 is 1211 and for Resource 1 is 466. Similarly, the RIC for Resource 2 becomes 1.0399 and for Resource 1 becomes 1.0356. It may be

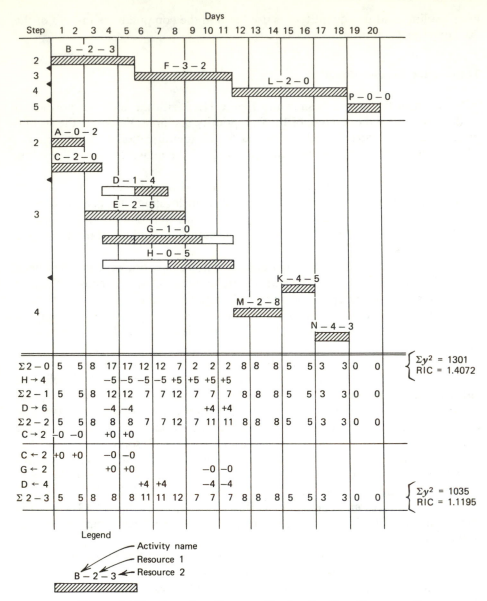

Figure 11.19   Leveling Resource 2 after leveling Resource 1.

292

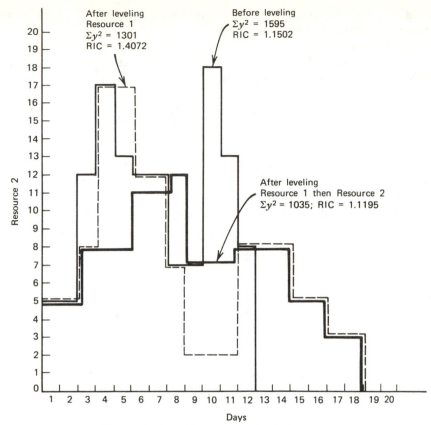

Figure 11.20   Histograms for Resource 2.

concluded that the resource which is leveled last will have the controlling values for both the Σy^2 and the RIC. The computations for this case are not given but the reader is encouraged to perform them and verify these results.

11.12   ADDING A CONSTANT TO THE RESOURCE HISTO-GRAM

Before attempting to make further extensions to leveling the resource histogram using the Minimum Moment Algorithm, it will be necessary to consider some adjustments to the histogram that have not yet been discussed. One of these is the addition of a constant to each daily resource sum.

It has been shown that each histogram has values which might be affected by such an addition, the improvement factor, the area of the histogram, the moment of histogram, and the resource improvement coefficient. These possible changes will now be discussed.

Assume a resource histogram whose elements are y_i distributed over n intervals. The improvement factor for an activity, ACT, with a possible shift, S, is given by Equation 11.1 found in Section 11.7.

$$\text{IF(ACT}, S) = r\left(\sum_1^m x_i - \sum_1^m w_i - mr \right)$$

Now assume further that each y_i has a constant, C, added to it so that $y_j = y_i + C$. Then because x_i and w_i are particular values of y_i, $x_j = x_i + C$ and $w_j = w_i + C$. The improvement factor for the same activity, ACT, and shift, S, over the same locations in the augmented histogram can be written as

$$\text{IF(ACT}, S) = r\left(\sum_1^m x_j - \sum_1^m w_j - mr \right)$$

$$= r\left(\sum_1^m (x_i + C) - \sum_1^m (w_i + C) - mr \right)$$

expanding gives

$$\text{IF(ACT}, S) = r\left(\sum_1^m x_i + mC - \sum_1^m w_i - mC - mr \right)$$

$$\text{IF(ACT}, S) = r\left(\sum_1^m x_i - \sum_1^m w_i - mr \right)$$

This is the same as for the unaugmented histogram. Therefore, the addition of the constant does not change the value of the improvement factor, and it can be seen that the factor varies with the difference in the daily resource sums employed and not with the magnitude of them.

The area of the assumed histogram above is

$$\sum_1^n y_i$$

The area of the augmented histogram,

$$\sum_1^n y_j,$$

will then be found by substitution to be

$$\sum_{1}^{n} y_j = \sum_{1}^{n} (y_i + C)$$

$$\sum_{1}^{n} y_j = \sum_{1}^{n} y_i + nC \tag{11.5}$$

Thus, the area of the assumed histogram has been changed by the addition of the quantity nC to obtain the area of the augmented histogram.

The moment of the assumed histogram is

$$\sum_{1}^{n} y_i^2$$

When the y_i values have the constant, C, added, the moment of the augmented histogram,

$$\sum_{1}^{n} y_j^2,$$

is found to be

$$\sum_{1}^{n} y_j^2 = \sum_{1}^{n} (y_i + C)^2$$

$$= \sum_{1}^{n} (y_i^2 + 2Cy_i + C^2)$$

$$= \sum_{1}^{n} y_i^2 + 2C \sum_{1}^{n} y_i + nC^2 \tag{11.6}$$

In this case, the moment of the assumed histogram has been changed by the addition of the quantity

$$2C \sum_{1}^{n} y_i + nC^2$$

to get the moment of the augmented one.

The effect on the resource improvement coefficient caused by adding a constant to the y_i values can be determined in a manner similar to that above.

The RIC for the assumed histogram is given by Equation 11.4 as

$$RIC = \frac{n \sum_1^n y_i^2}{\left(\sum_1^n y_i\right)^2}$$

Identifying the RIC for the augmented histogram by $(RIC)_j$, it may be stated that

$$(RIC)_j = \frac{n \sum_1^n y_j^2}{\left(\sum_1^n y_j\right)^2}$$

Substituting $(y_i + C)$ for y_j and expanding the terms results in

$$(RIC)_j = \frac{n \sum_1^n y_i^2 + 2nC \sum_1^n y_i + n^2C^2}{\left(\sum_1^n y_i\right)^2 + 2nC \sum_1^n y_i + (n^2C^2)} \qquad (11.7)$$

It is clear therefore that the augmentation of the y_i values changes the assumed RIC by the addition of the quantity

$$2nC \sum_1^n y_i + n^2C^2$$

to the numerator and the denominator.

Figure 11.21 represents the sample project presented in Figure 11.12 and will serve to illustrate the above effects. It was shown by Equation 11.5 that the area of the histogram, Σy, was altered by the quantity nC. This value may be considered to be a rectangle having a width of n and a height of C added to the base of the histogram. These additions to the base may be either positive or negative. When a positive constant is added the histogram will be termed *addbased* and when a negative constant is added it will be termed *debased*.

In Figure 11.21 the original daily resource sums are given on line $\Sigma 0$. The debasing constant has been chosen as -2 and the debased histogram is represented by the sums on line $\Sigma 0'$. The leveling procedure follows with the various improvement factors being computed in the usual manner. Note that after the leveling was completed, the histogram was addbased to obtain the true leveled daily resource sums as determined in Figure 11.12.

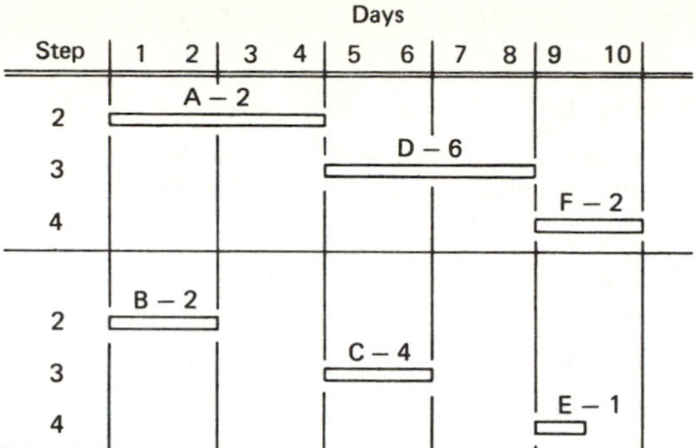

Days

Step	1	2	3	4	5	6	7	8	9	10
2		A − 2								
3						D − 6				
4									F − 2	
2	B − 2									
3						C − 4				
4									E − 1	
Σ0	4	4	2	2	10	10	6	6	3	2
Debasing constant −2										
Σ0′	2	2	0	0	8	8	4	4	1	0
E → 1									−1	+1
Σ1	2	2	0	0	8	8	4	4	0	1
C → 4					−4	−4			+4	+4
Σ2	2	2	0	0	4	4	4	4	4	5
B → 2	−2	−2	+2	+2						
Σ3	0	0	2	2	4	4	4	4	4	5
B ← 2	+2	+2	−2	−2						
Σ4	2	2	0	0	4	4	4	4	4	5
E ← 1									+1	−1
Σ5	2	2	0	0	4	4	4	4	5	4
Addbasing constant +2										
Σ6	4	4	2	2	6	6	6	6	7	6	Final

$\Sigma y = 49$
$\Sigma y^2 = 325$
RIC = 1.3536

$\Sigma y = 29$
$\Sigma y^2 = 169$
RIC = 2.0095

Figure 11.21   Leveling example illustrating debasement.

One benefit to be derived from the debasing-addbasing procedure is that it permits a reduction in the magnitude of the numbers being manipulated. If the computations are to be carried out manually, such changes can greatly increase the speed of the calculation. Another benefit permits the adjustment of the virtual histogram when leveling to a predetermined curve, as will be discussed in a later section.

The values for $\Sigma y, \Sigma y^2$, and RIC are shown on the figure for both the Σ0 and Σ0′ lines. The reader is encouraged to use Equations 11.5, 11.6, and 11.7 to verify that these values are correct.

11.13   WEIGHTING RESOURCE HISTOGRAMS

Resource histograms may be added together, element by element, to obtain a combined histogram. Before using such combinations in the leveling process, the effect of each histogram in relation to the total should be determined. These effects, or weights, can be derived as follows.

Assume a project to have a duration of n days and to consist of k activities. Assume also that each activity in the project will employ resources of two kinds. Designate one of the resources as Resource 1 and the other as Resource 2. Assign the symbol a to the resource rates for Resource 1 and b to the rates for Resource 2.

For each activity it may be assumed that it is possible to have a resource rate assigned for each project day. Because the activity is constrained by the network logic, there will be a demand for the resource only on particular days in the project duration, and only on those days will the rate have a value. On all other days the rate will be zero. By making these assumptions, a matrix of the resource rates may be established.

In Figure 11.22a the resource rate matrix for Resource 1 is shown and in Figure 11.22b the matrix for Resource 2 is given. When the resource rates are added on each project day it may be observed that the result is the daily resource sum for that day. Expressed mathematically,

$$\sum_1^k a_{ji} = (y_i)_1$$

and

$$\sum_1^k b_{ji} = (y_i)_2$$

In the above expressions, the subscripts 1 and 2 refer to the resources. Note also that in the matrix and the above equations the subscripts i and j are interchanged from the usual notation.

Let the resource rates for Resource 1 be related to those of Resource 2 by a weighting factor, f, applied to each element such that

$$a_{ji} = (fb)_{ji}$$

Then for any day, i, the ratio of the daily resource sums is

$$\frac{(y_i)_1}{(y_i)_2} = \frac{\sum_1^k a_{ji}}{\sum_1^k b_{ji}} = \frac{\sum_1^k (fb)_{ji}}{\sum_1^k b_{ji}} = K_i$$

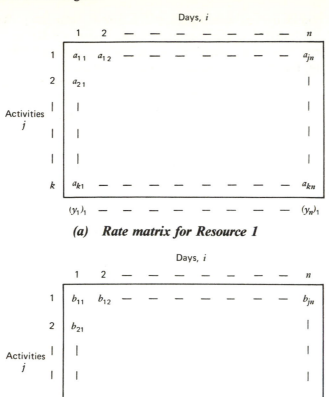

(a)   *Rate matrix for Resource 1*

(b)   *Rate matrix for Resource 2*

Figure 11.22   Resource rate matrices.

Hence,

$$(y_i)_1 = K_i (y_i)_2 \qquad (11.8)$$

Observe that the weighting factor does not need to be the same for every activity, although it is frequently made so. When it is equal, the value of K_i will also have the value of f.

It has been shown that changes in the moment of the resource histogram are accomplished by the successive application of the improvement factor. In Section 11.12 it was demonstrated that the improvement factor varies with the difference in the daily resource sums and not with their magnitude. It may therefore be concluded that the amount of adjustment needed to produce the leveled histogram must be dependent upon the number and size of the differences used by the improvement factors during the process.

All the differences in the daily resource sums which will be used during the leveling cannot be known in advance, but some measure of them can be realized if the absolute difference between successive daily resource sums is totaled over the histogram length, n.

For the project above, the histogram length and the project duration are the same. It should be clear to the reader that this does not need to be a restriction because any part of the project may be considered a subproject having a duration that is a part of the total.

In the project as defined let the absolute difference between two successive daily resource sums for Resource 1 be defined by Δ_1. Then

$$\Delta_1 = |y_{i+1} - y_i|_1$$

Summing all the differences in the histogram gives

$$\sum \Delta_1 = \sum_1^{n-1} |y_{i+1} - y_i|_1 \tag{11.9}$$

Similarly, for Resource 2 the differences are

$$\sum \Delta_2 = \sum_1^{n-1} |y_{i+1} - y_i|_2$$

The ratio of these $\sum\Delta$'s can be written as

$$\frac{\sum \Delta_1}{\sum \Delta_2} = \frac{\sum_1^{n-1} |y_{i+1} - y_i|_1}{\sum_1^{n-1} |y_{i+1} - y_i|_2}$$

$$= \frac{\sum_1^{n-1} |K_i(y_{i+1})_2 - K_i(y_i)_2|}{\sum_1^{n-1} |y_{i+1} - y_i|_2}$$

$$\frac{\sum \Delta_1}{\sum \Delta_2} = \frac{\sum_1^{n-1} (K_i|y_{i+1} - y_i|_2)}{\sum_1^{n-1} |y_{i+1} - y_i|_2} = K_D$$

Hence,

$$\Sigma \Delta_1 = K_D \Sigma \Delta_2 \qquad (11.10)$$

The weight of the sum of the differences for Resource 1 to the total found when Resource 1 and Resource 2 are added together is as follows.

$$WD_1 = \frac{\Sigma \Delta_1}{\Sigma \Delta_1 + \Sigma \Delta_2} = \frac{K_D \Sigma \Delta_2}{K_D \Sigma \Delta_2 + \Sigma \Delta_2}$$

$$WD_1 = \frac{K_D}{K_D + 1} \qquad (11.11)$$

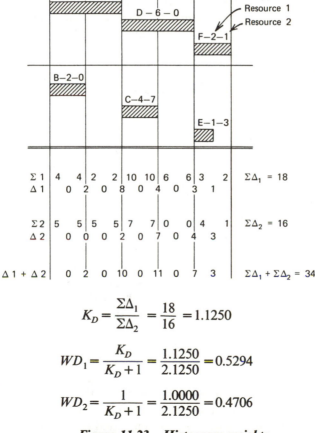

$$K_D = \frac{\Sigma \Delta_1}{\Sigma \Delta_2} = \frac{18}{16} = 1.1250$$

$$WD_1 = \frac{K_D}{K_D + 1} = \frac{1.1250}{2.1250} = 0.5294$$

$$WD_2 = \frac{1}{K_D + 1} = \frac{1.0000}{2.1250} = 0.4706$$

Figure 11.23   Histogram weights.

For Resource 2 to the total the weight is

$$WD_2 = \frac{\sum \Delta_2}{\sum \Delta_1 + \sum \Delta_2} = \frac{\sum \Delta_2}{K_D \sum \Delta_2 + \sum \Delta_2}$$

$$WD_2 = \frac{1}{K_D + 1} \tag{11.12}$$

Figure 11.23 will serve to illustrate the application of the above equations. The figure shows the sample project used previously with the resource rates for two resources shown following each activity name. The daily resource sums for Resource 1 are given on line $\Sigma 1$ immediately below the bar chart. On line $\Delta 1$ the differences are given for these daily resource sums. Similar values are given for Resource 2 on lines $\Sigma 2$ and $\Delta 2$. The values for the sum of the $\Sigma \Delta$s is shown on the line identified as $\Delta 1 + \Delta 2$.

The computations result in a K_D of 1.1250 and weights WD_1 and WD_2 of 0.5294 and 0.4706, respectively. These values imply that if the two resources are added before leveling, Resource 1 will dominate the leveling process by a ratio of about 53 to 47 or 1.13 to 1.0.

11.14 LEVELING COMBINED RESOURCES

It was pointed out in the beginning of Section 11.10 that when one resource on a construction project is leveled, other resources tend to be leveled as well. There are obviously cases to which this trend does not apply. In such situations the scheduler may wish to consider several resources simultaneously. Leveling combinations of resources can be done by adding the resource rates together, leveling the resulting daily resource sums, and separating the daily resource sums into their respective histogram values at the conclusion of the progress.

The main advantage to this approach is that the algorithm is applied only once. A great saving in time and expense is realized because the number of series leveling runs increases factorially with the number of resources being leveled. For example, if three resources are leveled in series, six applications of the leveling algorithm, six runs, will have to be made. If the number of resources is increased to five, it will take 120 runs and a choice of the lowest value combination of Σy^2 and RIC will have to be made from an examination of over 240 computed numbers. If seven resources are in series, the number of runs is over 5000 and the choice must be made from more than 10,000 items, an almost impossible task.

Figure 11.24 shows the leveling tableau for the combination of the two resources for the project introduced in Section 11.11. As before, the resource rates for Resource 1 and Resource 2 are indicated above the activity bars in the

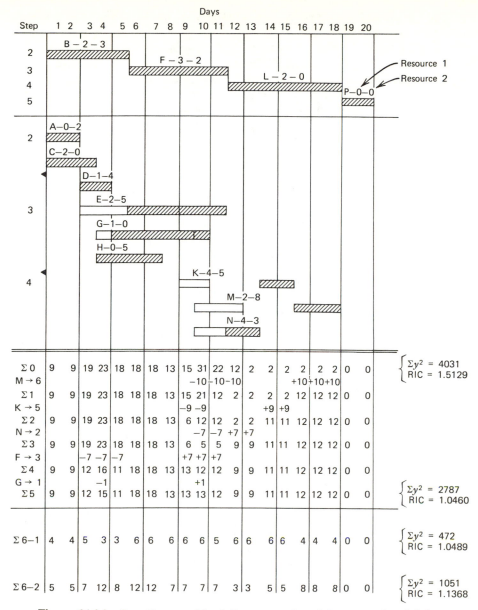

Step	Days																				
	1	2	3	4	5	6	7	8	9	10	11	12	13	14	15	16	17	18	19	20	

Resource 1
Resource 2

Σ0	9	9	19	23	18	18	18	13	15	31	22	12	2	2	2	2	2	2	0	0		Σy² = 4031
M → 6										−10	−10	−10				+10	+10	+10				RIC = 1.5129
Σ1	9	9	19	23	18	18	18	13	15	21	12	2	2	2	2	12	12	12	0	0		
K → 5									−9	−9				+9	+9							
Σ2	9	9	19	23	18	18	18	13	6	12	12	2	2	11	11	12	12	12	0	0		
N → 2										−7	−7	+7	+7									
Σ3	9	9	19	23	18	18	18	13	6	5	5	9	9	11	11	12	12	12	0	0		
F → 3			−7	−7	−7				+7	+7	+7											
Σ4	9	9	12	16	11	18	18	13	13	12	12	9	9	11	11	12	12	12	0	0		
G → 1			−1						+1													Σy² = 2787
Σ5	9	9	12	15	11	18	18	13	13	13	12	9	9	11	11	12	12	12	0	0		RIC = 1.0460

Σ6−1	4	4	5	3	3	6	6	6	6	6	5	6	6	6	6	4	4	4	0	0		Σy² = 472 RIC = 1.0489

Σ6−2	5	5	7	12	8	12	12	7	7	7	7	3	3	5	5	8	8	8	0	0		Σy² = 1051 RIC = 1.1368

Figure 11.24   Leveling combined Resources 1 and 2—natural weighting.

303

bar chart portion of the diagram. The crosshatched bars give the final positions of the activities after leveling.

On line $\Sigma 0$ the daily resource sums for the combined rates are shown together with the values of the Σy^2 and RIC. Notice that the combined rates are used in the additions and subtractions to the daily resource sums throughout the leveling.

Lines $\Sigma 6$–1 and $\Sigma 6$–2 show the separation of the final leveled combination into the daily resource sums for Resource 1 and Resource 2, respectively. These sums were determined by adding the separate resource rates on each day with the activities in their final leveled positions.

The combination of resources may lead the scheduler to believe mistakenly that each resource is equally influencing the outcome. It was shown in Section 11.13 that this is not so, but that the resource with the greater weight in the differences of the daily resource sums will be favored.

The histogram daily resource sums for Resource 1 before leveling are shown below together with their successive absolute differences.

Day	1	2	3	4	5	6	7	8	9	10	11	12	13	14	15	16	17	18	19	20	
$(y_i)_1$	4	4	7	6	5	6	6	6	6	8	13	9	4	2	2	2	2	2	0	0	$(\Sigma y)_1 = 90$
Δ_1		0	3	1	1	1	0	0	0	2	5	4	5	2	0	0	0	0			$\Sigma\Delta_1 = 24$

Similarly, the histogram for Resource 2 before leveling with its daily resource sums and differences is depicted below.

Day	1	2	3	4	5	6	7	8	9	10	11	12	13	14	15	16	17	18	19	20	
$(y_i)_2$	5	5	12	17	13	12	12	7	7	18	13	8	0	0	0	0	0	0	0	0	$(\Sigma y)_2 = 129$
Δ_1		0	7	5	4	1	0	5	0	11	5	5									$\Sigma\Delta_2 = 43$

The histogram for Resource 1 extends over 18 days so an n of 18 is used or the computation of $\Sigma\Delta_1$ by Equation 11.9. Resource 2 extends over 12 days and n is taken as 12 when computing $\Sigma\Delta_2$. The value of K_D from Equation 11.10 is

$$K_D = \frac{24}{43} = 0.5581$$

and the weights for each resource to the total from Equations 11.11 and 11.12 are

$$WD_1 = \frac{0.5589}{1.5589} = 0.3580$$

$$WD_2 = \frac{1.0000}{1.5589} = 0.6420$$

Resource 2 is therefore weighted over Resource 1 by a ratio of 0.6420/0.3580 or 1.79 to 1.00.

The above computation does not take into account the variation in the extent of the two histograms, and even though it is indicative of the fact that Resource 2 dominates the leveling, it cannot serve without further adjustment to properly weight the histograms if they are to share equally. Equations 11.11 and 11.12 were based on a histogram that had the same value of n. To correct for the variation in n the average $\Sigma\Delta$ may be used.

If the histograms are to be equally weighted, then the value of K_D must equal 1.00 as can be observed from Equations 11.11 and 11.12. Therefore

$$\frac{\dfrac{\Sigma\Delta_1}{n_1}}{\dfrac{\Sigma\Delta_2}{n_2}} = K_D = 1.00$$

$$\Sigma\Delta_1 = \frac{n_1}{n_2}\Sigma\Delta_2 \qquad\qquad (11.13)$$

In the example $\Sigma\Delta_2$ is 43. To make each histogram equal the value of $\Sigma\Delta_1$ must be

$$\Sigma\Delta_1 = \frac{18}{12}(43) = 64.5$$

Now because $\Sigma\Delta_1$ is actually 24, all the resource rates for Resource 1 must be increased by 64.5/24 or 2.69 rather than 1.79 as computed above. Table 11.3 gives the original and adjusted rates for each activity for Resource 1. Resource 2 rates are also given and the combination of the two is shown.

Figure 11.25 is the leveling tableau for leveling the combined resources, assuming that it is desired to weight each resource to share equally in the process. Line $\Sigma0$–1 shows the original resource sums for Resource 1. As with the rates, the y_i values must be increased by 2.69 and these are shown on line 2.69 $\Sigma0$–1.

Note that the new y_i values are no longer equal to the daily sums of the rates. This is due to round-off error. All rates and y_i quantities are rounded to the nearest integer number for simplicity. Such rounding tends to provide a slightly greater weighting and is more pronounced in small histograms than in larger ones.

Line $\Sigma0$–2 shows the y_i values for Resource 2 and beneath it is shown the combined y_is, which are the ones to be leveled. The leveling proceeds in the usual manner using the combined rates from Table 11.3. The example ends with line $\Sigma5$.

TABLE 11.3

Combining Resource Rates

| Activity | Resource 1 | | Resource 2 | Combined |
	Original	Adjusted		Res. 1 + Res. 2
A	0	0	2	2
B	2	5	3	8
C	2	5	0	5
D	1	3	4	7
E	2	5	5	10
F	3	8	2	10
G	1	3	0	3
H	0	0	5	5
K	4	11	5	16
L	2	5	0	5
M	2	5	8	13
N	4	11	3	14
P	0	0	0	0

With the activities in the leveled positions the original rates are used to obtain the final resource sums for each resource. Line $\Sigma R1$ and $\Sigma R2$ give these daily resource sums for Resource 1 and Resource 2, respectively. The Σy^2 for Resource 1 has been reduced from the combination with the natural weighting, whereas that for Resource 2 has been increased, which indicates the greater influence of Resource 1 in the procedure as was desired.

Combining Resources with a Common Base

Multiple resources may be leveled concurrently if each resource is expressed in terms of a common base and the resource rate is considered as the sum of these proportionate values for each activity. It often happens in construction projects that considerations of cash flow will dictate that the daily cost of the project is the prime concern. Each resource can then be expressed in dollars to be expended day by day and the sum of these dollars becomes the resource rate. In other situations, the total work force may be limited by work space requirements and the resource rates can be translated into the number of persons required each day. Other common denominators can be used to meet the demands of the particular project. After leveling on the common basis the individual resource rates can be added to give the resource demand histograms for the use of management. Of course, the individual resources are weighted according to their share in the common denominator when this procedure is adopted.

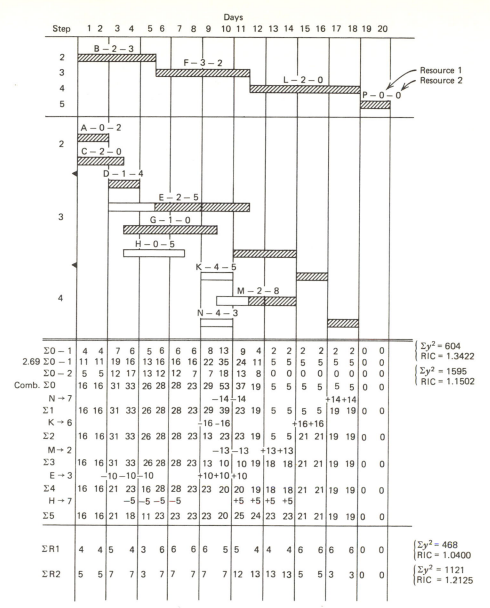

Figure 11.25 Leveling combined Resources 1 and 2—weighted to share equally.

11.15   LEVELING TO A PREFERRED HISTOGRAM

There are many instances in construction where the amount of a particular resource on a project must not exceed certain daily limits because of expected employee availability, expected equipment usage, expected space limitations, and so forth. These daily resource limits constrain the time positions of the activities and must be taken into account if effective management is to be obtained.

A histogram made up of the preferred limits may be used to adjust the constraints of the original histogram. It was shown in Section 11.14 that histograms may be combined before leveling. The negative of the preferred, or virtual, histogram may be added to the original histogram and then removed after the procedure has been completed. In effect, this addition adjusts the base of the original histogram to the assumed shape and the Minimum Moment Algorithm can then be used.

Any arbitrary shape may be selected, but to control the leveling it must be equal to or greater than the original in its weighting. Suppose that for the example project a preferred histogram has the following daily resource sums.

Day	1	2	3	4	5	6	7	8	9	10	11	12	13	14	15	16	17	18	19	20	
y_i	0	2	2	4	4	6	8	8	10	13	13	15	12	10	8	8	4	0	0	0	$\Sigma y = 126$
Δ		0	2	0	2	2	0	2	3	0	1	2	2	2	0	4					$\Sigma\Delta = 22$

The Σy for this virtual histogram is 126, its n is 16, and its $\Sigma\Delta$ is 22. In order to give it equal weight both the n and $\Sigma\Delta$ must be made equal to that of the original histogram.

Suppose further, that the original histogram is that for Resource 1 whose $\Sigma y = 90$, $\Sigma\Delta = 24$, and $n = 18$. Then the virtual histogram may be changed as below to match n and $\Sigma\Delta$.

Day	1	2	3	4	5	6	7	8	9	10	11	12	13	14	15	16	17	18	19	20	
y_i	1	3	3	3	3	6	8	8	10	13	13	13	10	10	9	8	4	1	0	0	$\Sigma y = 126$
Δ		2	0	0	0	3	2	0	2	3	0	0	3	0	1	1	4	4			$\Sigma\Delta = 24$

The above histogram meets the requirements of shape and weighting and could be used. If a direct comparison is to be made between the original and virtual histograms, however, the latter must be debased to make Σy for both equal. If the virtual histogram is debased by -2, this desire may be met and the resulting daily resource sums become the ones to be combined with Resource 1.

This adjustment is shown below.

Day	1 2 3 4 5 6 7 8 9 10 11 12 13 14 15 16 17 18 19 20	
y_i	−1 1 1 1 1 4 6 6 8 11 11 11 8 8 7 6 2 −1 0 0	$\Sigma y = 90$
Δ	2 0 0 0 3 2 0 2 3 0 0 3 0 1 1 4 3	$\Sigma\Delta = 24$

Figure 11.26 shows the leveling tableau for the project of Section 11.11 with the rates for Resource 1 given beside the activity names above the bars. Again the crosshatched bars show the final positions of the activities after leveling. Line $\Sigma 0$ represents the daily resource sums for the original histogram for Resource 1. Beneath it the values of the virtual histogram just discussed are given. On the line designated New $\Sigma 0$ the combination of the original and the virtual histograms is shown.

The leveling procedure takes place in the usual manner but it should be noticed that the resource rates are the original ones. These are used because the virtual histogram is effectively changing the base of the histogram and not the rates themselves. In the computation of the improvement factors for the various shifts some of the daily resource sums are negative, and when they are substituted in Equation 11.1 their sign becomes positive. This may be seen in the sample improvement factors for Activity K shown below.

$$\text{Act. K; } r=4; \text{ FF}=8$$

$$\text{IF }(K,1)=4(0+ 2-4)= -8$$

$$\text{IF }(K,2)=4(2+ 9-8)= 12$$

$$\text{IF }(K,3)=4(2+13-8)= \boxed{28}$$

$$\text{IF }(K,4)=4(2+12-8)= 24$$

$$\text{IF }(K,5)=4(2+11-8)= 20$$

$$\text{IF }(K,6)=4(2+ 9-8)= 12$$

$$\text{IF }(K,7)=4(2+ 4-8)= -8$$

$$\text{IF }(K,8)=4(2- 3-8)= -36$$

The greatest improvement factor still controls the shifting and that value has been circled.

The leveled values are given on line $\Sigma 8$ and the final daily resource sums for Resource 1 are shown on line $\Sigma 9$ after reversing the virtual histogram.

Figure 11.27 graphically shows the final result. The thin line represents the preferred limits and the heavy line shows the final histogram. The dotted line is the virtual histogram. The final daily sums stay within the preferred limits except for days 1, 2, 3, and 18. On these days it was not possible to accommodate the preference because of the logic constraints in the network.

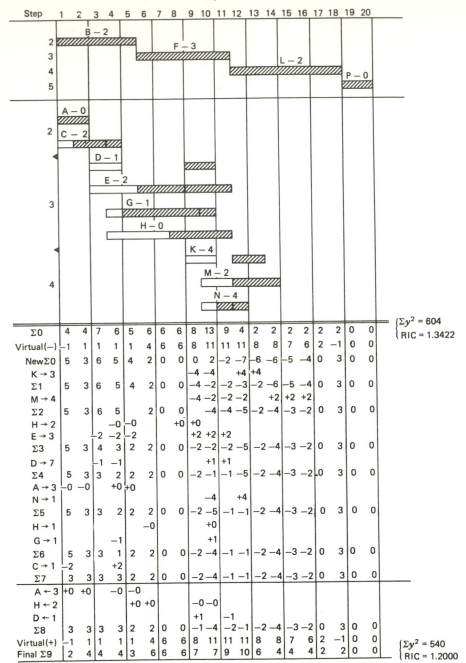

Figure 11.26 Leveling to a preferred histogram.

310

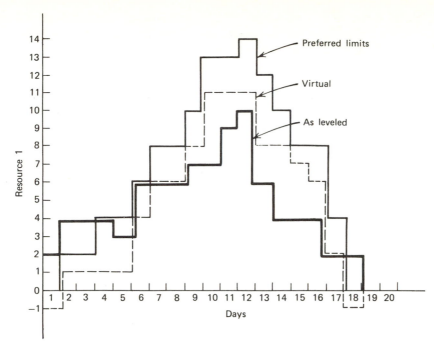

Figure 11.27   Histograms after leveling to preferred limits.

TABLE 11.4

Leveling Summary

	Resource 1		Resource 2	
Leveling Case	Σy^2	**RIC**	Σy^2	**RIC**
1. No leveling	604	1.3422	1595	1.1502
Res. 1: $\Sigma y = 90$; $\Sigma\Delta = 24$				
Res. 2: $\Sigma y = 129$; $\Sigma\Delta = 43$				
2. Resource 1 alone	466	1.0356	—	—
3. Resource 2 alone	—	—	971	1.0503
4. Resource 1 then 2	478	1.0622	1035	1.1195
5. Resource 2 then 1	466	1.0356	1211	1.0399
6. Resource 1 and 2 (Natural weighting)	472	1.0489	1051	1.1368
7. Resource 1 and 2 (Res. 1 WTD 2.69x)	468	1.0400	1121	1.2125

311

Table 11.4 lists the final values of Σy^2 and RIC of both Resource 1 and Resource 2 after leveling for the several cases described in Sections 11.11, 11.14, and 11.15. The greatest change in the moment and the improvement coefficient occurs when a single resource is leveled, as can be seen by comparing Cases 2 and 3 with the original values given in Case 1.

Cases 4 and 5 give the results of series leveling and the greatest improvement in both Σy^2 and RIC is obtained for the resource last leveled. Series leveling does not, in general, match the improvement obtained when the resource is leveled alone, even though that is the situation in Case 5.

Cases 6 and 7 give the results when the resources are combined. It was pointed out in Section 11.15 that with only natural weighting Resource 2 was favored, as can be seen in Case 6. When the resources shared equally in the leveling, as in Case 7, the Σy^2 and RIC values for Resource 1 were reduced and the same values for Resource 2 were increased, thereby reflecting the change in the weighting of one resource over the other.

REFERENCES

11.1   Adrian, James J., *Quantitative Methods in Construction Management*, American Elsevier Publishing Co., New York, 1973.

11.2   Antill, James M. and Ronald W. Woodhead, *Critical Path Methods in Construction Practice*, Second Edition, Wiley-Interscience, New York, 1970.

11.3   Burgess, A. R. and J. B. Killebrew, "Variation in Activity Level on a Cyclical Arrow Diagram," *J. Industrial Engineering*, Vol. 13, No. 2, March–April, 1962.

11.4   Davies, E. Mary, "New Criterion For Resource Scheduling," *J. Transportation Engineering*, Proceedings ASCE, Vol. 99, No. TE4, November 1973, pp. 741–756.

11.5   Galbreath, Robert V., "Computer Program for Leveling Resource Usage," *J. Const. Div.*, Proceedings ASCE, Vol. 91, No. CO1, May 1965.

11.6   Moder, Joseph J. and Cecil R. Phillips, *Project Management with CPM and PERT*, Reinhold Publishing Corp., 1964. Second Edition, Van Nostrand Reinhold Co., New York, 1970.

11.7   O'Brien, James J., *CPM in Construction Management*, McGraw-Hill Book Co., New York, 1965.

11.8   O'Brien, James J. (ed.), *Scheduling Handbook*, McGraw-Hill Book Co., New York, 1969.

11.9   Paulson, Boyd C., Jr., "Project Planning and Scheduling: Unified Approach," *J. Construction Div.*, Proceedings ASCE, Vol. 99, No. CO1, July 1973, pp. 45–58.

11.10 Shaffer, L. R., J. B. Ritter, and W. L. Meyer, *The Critical Path Method*, McGraw-Hill Book Co., New York, 1965.

11.11 Wiest, Jerome D., "The Scheduling of Large Projects with Limited Resources," Ph.D. Dissertation, Carnegie Institute of Technology, May 1963.

11.12 Wiest, Jerome D., "Some Properties of Schedules for Large Projects with Limited Resources," *Operations Research*, Vol. 12, No. 3, May–June, 1964, pp. 395–418.

11.13 Wiest, Jerome D., "A Heuristic Model for Scheduling Large Projects with Limited Resources," *Management Science*, Vol. 13, No. 6, February 1967, pp. B359–B377.

EXERCISES

11.1   A certain small project is ten days long. The daily resource sums for masons are:

6 9 6 6 9 6 6 6 8 9 0

Determine the values of Σy^2 and RIC.

11.2   A certain activity has a duration of three days. It has a free float of six days and a total float of nine days. It starts on day 2 and requires three resource units per day. Four different sets of daily resource sums are given below. Compute the improvement factors and indicate the shifting of this activity needed to level the resource sums for each of the four sets. Treat each set as a separate problem.

Set	Day 1 2 3 4 5 6 7 8 9 10 11 12 13 14
(a)	5 5 5 5 8 8 8 6 4 2 0 0 0 0
(b)	5 6 6 6 8 8 4 2 0 0 4 4 4 0
(c)	5 6 5 5 3 2 3 3 3 3 4 4 4 3
(d)	9 6 6 6 9 6 3 2 3 6 6 6 0 0

11.3   For the small project whose data are given below determine the schedule after leveling the resource. Use the traditional approach with a maximum daily resource sum limited to ten units. Shift the highest resource rate first when a choice between two or more rates is needed. At the conclusion show the free floats and total floats. Identify the critical path and any other critical activities.

Activity	Duration	Depends Upon	Resource Rate
A	2	—	0
B	11	A	3
C	3	A	4
D	6	A	5
E	4	C,D	6
F	5	D	3
G	3	E,F,H	1
H	4	B,C	0

11.4   Data for a small precedence network are given below together with the resource rate for each activity. Use the minimum moment algorithm and level the resources. Show the final position of each activity on a bar chart.

Activity	Duration	Depends Upon	Resource Rate
A	2	—	1
B	6	A	5
C	4	A	4
D	9	B, C	4
E	3	C	0
F	5	C	3
G	3	D, E	1
H	6	E, F	1
K	4	E, F	3
L	2	G, H, K	0

11.5 Data for a small precedence network are given below together with the resource rate for each activity. Making use of the minimum moment leveling algorithm, determine the early start and finish dates and the free and total floats for each activity after leveling. Compute the Σy^2 and RIC before and after leveling.

Activity	Duration	Depends Upon	Resource Rate
A	8	—	3
B	3	—	6
C	1	—	6
D	4	A	0
E	4	B, C	5
F	8	B	4
G	3	C, N	0
H	1	D, E	4
K	6	A, E	4
L	3	H, K, M	0
M	5	F, G	2
N	2	—	4

11.6 Data for an arrow network are given below together with the activity resource rates for each of two resources.
(a) Using the minimum moment algorithm level Resource I.
(b) Level Resource II after having leveled Resource I. Begin this leveling with the activities in the positions occupied at the end of part (a).
(c) Draw histograms for each resource after the leveling accomplished in part (b).

i	j	Activity	Duration	Resource Rate Resource I	Resource II
1	3	A	2	3	0
1	5	B	4	5	2
1	7	C	5	1	6
1	9	D	3	9	7
3	11	E	11	5	7
5	7	Dummy	0	0	0
5	13	F	5	6	3
7	17	G	8	0	8
9	15	H	7	4	0
9	19	K	6	1	6
11	13	L	7	3	6
11	15	M	8	2	3
13	17	N	2	5	0
15	21	P	7	4	0
17	21	Dummy	0	0	0
17	23	Q	4	7	4
19	21	Dummy	0	0	0
19	23	R	10	5	8
21	23	S	7	2	2

11.7 Data for a simple precedence network are given below along with the activity resource rates for each of two resources.

(a) Using the minimum moment algorithm level Resource I.

(b) Level Resource II after leveling Resource I. Begin this leveling with the activities in the positions occupied at the end of part (a).

(c) Draw three resource histograms for Resource I; before leveling, after leveling Resource I, and after leveling Resources I and II in series.

(d) Draw three resource histograms for Resource II; before leveling, after leveling Resource I, and after leveling Resources I and II in series.

Activity	Duration	Depends Upon	Resource Rate Resource I	Resource II
A	4	—	3	4
B	9	A, C	2	6
C	8	—	6	4
D	4	A, E	2	6
E	3	—	4	2
F	5	A	1	8

11.8 Data for a precedence network are given below.
   (a) Determine the natural weight of the histogram for Resource 2 over that for Resource 1.
   (b) Compute the revised resource sums for Resource 1 such that the histogram for Resource 1 is weighted twice the weight for Resource 2.

Activity	Duration	Depends Upon	Resource Rate	
			Resource 1	Resource 2
A	1	—	0	1
B	19	A	2	3
C	8	A	4	3
D	6	A	6	9
E	3	B	0	4
F	5	C, D	2	5
G	3	D	8	11
H	7	F	0	7
K	4	F, G	0	13
L	2	E, H, K	0	1

11.9 A precedence network for a project has the logic shown below. The resource rates for each activity are given for each of two resources.
   (a) Level Resource I using the minimum moment algorithm and draw the histogram for this resource before and after the leveling. Use the same axes for plotting both histograms.
   (b) Level Resource II using the minimum moment algorithm and draw the histogram for this resource before and after the leveling. Use the same axes for plotting both histograms.

Activity	Duration	Depends Upon	Resource Rate	
			Resource I	Resource II
A	2	—	3	1
B	8	A	4	6
C	6	A	8	6
D	4	A	6	5
E	3	A	4	1
F	12	B	2	0
G	4	C, D	7	9
H	6	C, D, E	9	5
K	3	F, G, H	2	0

11.10 For the network and resource rates given in Exercise 11.9 combine Resource I and Resource II without weighting and level the combination using the minimum moment algorithm. Draw the final histograms for each resource and compare them with the results obtained in Exercise 11.9.

11.11   For the network and resource rates given in Exercise 11.9 level the combination of Resource I and Resource II. In combining the resources adjust the histogram for Resource I so that it has three times the weight of the histogram for Resource II. Draw the final histograms for each resource and compare them with the results obtained in Exercise 11.9.

11.12   Data for a precedence network and the resource rate for each of its activities are tabulated below. Level these resources to conform as closely as possible to the preferred resource histogram indicated.

Activity	Duration	Depends Upon	Resource Rate
A	2	—	0
B	3	A	1
C	6	A	8
D	7	A	1
E	4	A	3
F	6	A	5
G	6	B, D	6
H	8	D, E	3
K	2	D, F	2
L	5	C, H	2
M	2	G, K, L	0

Preferred histogram

Day	Daily Resource Sum	Day	Daily Resource Sum
1	0	13	22
2	0	14	17
3	2	15	17
4	2	16	9
5	2	17	9
6	4	18	4
7	4	19	4
8	9	20	2
9	9	21	2
10	16	22	2
11	16	23	0
12	22	24	0

12

PROGRAM EVALUATION AND REVIEW TECHNIQUE (PERT)

12.1 AN OVERVIEW

As was stated in Chapter 1 a critical path system now known as Program Evaluation and Review Technique, PERT, was developed by the U.S. Navy Special Projects Office in conjunction with Booz, Allen, and Hamilton and the Lockheed Missile and Space Division. The Special Projects Office published their report on Phase I in July 1958,[12.1] based largely upon the work of Malcolm, Roseboom, Clark, and Fazar, which was later published in *Operations Research*.[12.6]

Being a critical path technique, PERT has similarities to CPM. It uses an arrow diagram to graphically model a project and allows the planner to determine a project duration and the amount of time available to perform noncritical tasks. Its computations follow closely those made for a CPM arrow network and planners familiar with one system have little difficulty in adapting to the other.

There are likewise some significant differences between the two systems. The emphasis in CPM is placed upon the activities to be accomplished, whereas in the PERT system the completion data for these activities is stressed. As a result, the events of a PERT diagram, representing starting and finishing dates of the activities, are labeled with both an identifying number and description. In this sense, PERT can be said to be event oriented.

Another major difference is that the activities in PERT are assumed to be distributions of time with relatively large variances. In contrast, CPM assumes activity durations to have such small variances that they may be considered deterministic. This probabilistic character of PERT activities naturally grew out of the early applications of the system to the research and development aspects of the POLARIS project.

Because no reliable data is available to evaluate particular PERT distributions, it is necessary to assume a characteristic mean and variance for each activity based upon an optimistic, most likely, and pessimistic estimate of an activity's duration. Clark[12.4] presented a defense of his assumptions concerning an activity's duration following the controversy which arose after the earlier work.[12.1] These assumptions will be more fully discussed in Section 12.3.

Even though the activity durations are assumed to be probabilistic in character, the computations leading to the expected project duration and the critical path are made deterministically once the means of the activities have been found. As in a CPM arrow network early and late event times are obtained from the addition and subtraction of activity means. Float values, generally termed *slack* in PERT, are also calculated in essentially the same manner as in CPM.

An advantage of PERT's probabilistic character is that it allows for the determination of an estimate of the probability of meeting a schedule date for the project duration or any other milestone event. The PERT system recognizes that event times are essentially means of distributions. By applying probability theory to these distributions and expressing the computed values in standardized form, the probability that a particular date for an event will be equal to or less than a specific value may be ascertained.

PERT's probabilistic character also allows for a ranking of the criticality of the events, and hence the activities, of a project network. This ranking can be made by computing the probability that the slack at any event will be equal to or less than zero.

Throughout the rest of this chapter the discussions follow the approaches made in the basic, or classical, PERT. No attempt is made to examine any of the many variations of this system because of their seemingly limited application to the construction industry. It is only an occasional construction project that will have large variances in activity durations. There are instances, however, where the construction manager may wish to estimate the probability of completion of a project, and the principles given here can be applied with satisfactory results.

12.2 PROBABILITY CONCEPTS IN PERT

It has been said that PERT is probabilistic in nature so a brief review of some probability concepts used in the technique is appropriate. To make clear these principles a simple example is formulated for discussion.

Assume that you are a sidewalk contractor and that your typical installation is 5 feet wide, 4 inches thick, and 60 to 90 feet in length. (In SI units these values would be about 1.5 meters wide, 10 centimeters thick, and 18 to 27 meters in length). Your jobs usually have a curb cut and driveway apron to install together with the sidewalk. You have been keeping records of the time it takes your crews to make an installation. The time, in hours, and the number of occasions that a job has been completed in this time are given in Table 12.1.

Measures of Central Tendency

When the data from Table 12.1 are plotted, a histogram is formed as shown in Figure 12.1. It can be observed that the data is concentrated in the 15 to 19 hour

TABLE 12.1

Sidewalk Jobs and Times

Hours to Complete	12	13	14	15	16	17	18	19	20	21	22	23	24	25	26	27	28	29
Number of Jobs	1	1	3	5	8	7	5	4	3	3	2	2	1	1	1	1	1	1

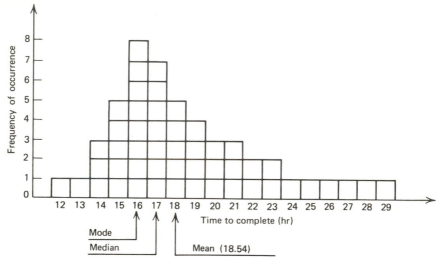

Figure 12.1   Sidewalk job histogram.

range. To identify this centralizing tendency of the data, three measures are commonly used. They are the mode, median, and mean, each of which may be defined as follows:

The *mode* is the value at which the greatest frequency occurs. The time of 16 hours is the mode in the histogram of Figure 12.1.

The *median* is the value that divides the total number of cases in half. In Figure 12.1, 50 cases are represented. Twenty-five occur at 17 hours or less and 25 occur at more than 17 hours. The median in the example may then be said to be 17 hours. The median is most applicable to large amounts of data.

The *mean* is the value that is the arithmetic average of the data and is computed from the following formula:

$$\text{Mean} = \bar{m} = \frac{1}{n} \sum_{1}^{n} a_i y_i$$

where $n = \sum\limits_{1}^{n} y_i$, or the total number of cases y_i, and a_i is the value associated with each y_i. In the example n is 50, a_i is the time of occurrence for each job, and y_i is an individual job. When computed by this formula the example value for the mean is found to be 18.54 days.

When the histogram is symmetrical about the mean value the mode, median, and mean assume identical values.

Continuous Distributions

In Table 12.1 the time of completion for each job is given to the nearest hour. However, this arbitrary interval could be reduced, say to a half hour or smaller. If completion times were recorded to the nearest minute, it would be probable that each time would have only one, or maybe two, occurrences. Yet if a large number of jobs were in the sample with these very small intervals, the histogram would again approach the same shape as in Figure 12.1, but at any reasonable scale the steps would become so small as to approach a smooth curve. Such smoothing of the sidewalk job data is shown in Figure 12.2. The resulting curve would be termed a continuous distribution, implying that any time interval could be selected and its anticipated frequency would be given by the curve.

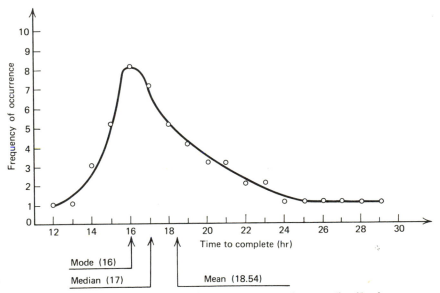

Figure 12.2   Sidewalk job times as a continuous distribution.

It may be observed in Figure 12.2 that the mean value is to the right of the modal value. This distribution is said to be skewed to the right. Should the mean fall to the left of the mode, the curve would be skewed to the left. When the continuous data is symmetrical, the mode, median, and mean all fall at the same value.

Probability Functions

Frequency distributions can be made into probability distributions by dividing by the total size of the sample, thus making the total number of occurrences equal to one. Each ordinate to the frequency curve is divided by the sample size, and the ordinate becomes the probability of occurrence for that value of the variable. The summation of these ordinates results in a cumulative probability distribution. Under a continuous curve this amounts to the integration of the function, $f(x)$, with the result equal to one. This integration can be expressed mathematically as

$$\int f(x)\,dx = 1 \qquad (12.1)$$

$$f(x) \geqq 0$$

Many variables distribute themselves in a symmetrical pattern about the mean value resulting in the familiar bell-shaped distribution curve. Such is the case when the probabilities of occurrence for particular values of a natural variable are plotted. In the eighteenth-century, mathematicians De Moivre, Gauss, and Laplace derived the expression for this curve which is now known as the Guassian or Normal Probability Density Function.[12.10] Allowing y to be the ordinate representing the probability and x to be the variable, the expression is

$$f(x) = y = \frac{1}{\sigma(2\pi)^{1/2}} e^{-(2\sigma)^{-2}(x-\bar{x})^2} \qquad (12.2)$$

The symbol e is the base of the Napierian logarithms (2.7183); π is the familiar ratio of circumference to diameter of a circle (3.1415); $\bar{x}$ is the true mean of the data; and σ is the standard deviation that is a measure of the dispersion in the data. This curve is asymptotic to the abcissa and includes all possible values from minus infinity to plus infinity. The constant $1/(2\pi)^{1/2}$ is especially chosen to ensure that the area under the curve is one.

Although the Gaussian equation serves to represent a probability density function, it does not permit direct comparisons among different sets of probability data. The two parameters, the mean and standard deviation, must be standardized if such comparisons are to be completely satisfactory. In other words, not only must the area beneath the curve be equal to one, but the mean and standard deviation of each compared set of data must be the same. The standard adopted is to make the mean equal to zero and the deviation equal to one. The result is the Standard Normal Probability Density Function whose expression is

$$f(x) = y = \frac{1}{(2\pi)^{1/2}} e^{-2x^2} \tag{12.3}$$

The value, x, is now measured from the new origin, or mean, in standard deviation units.

By integrating the standard probability function up to a particular value of the variable x_i expressed in standard deviation units, the cumulative probability that any value will be equal to or less than x_i can be determined. Figure 12.3 shows a cumulative normal probability distribution with the value x_i located at 0.52σ units less than the mean value $\bar{x}$. The area of the shaded portion from minus infinity up to x_i is 0.3, indicating that in this instance there is a probability of 30 percent that a random value of x will be equal to or less than x_i. There are tables widely published that give the cumulative probabilities for the standard normal distribution function for various values of x_i in terms of standard deviation units. One such set of tables is given in Moder and Phillips.[12.9]

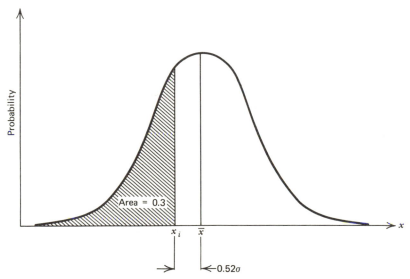

Figure 12.3   Cumulative normal probability distribution.

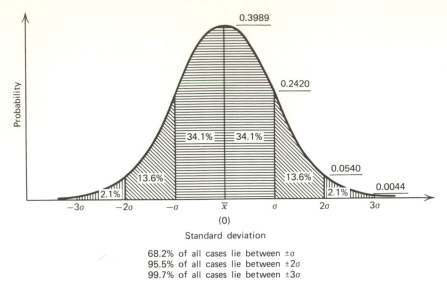

Figure 12.4 Approximate areas beneath the standard normal probability function.

The area under the standard probability function up to the value of $\bar{x}$ is 0.5. Thus, the area under the curve between x_i and $\bar{x}$ is the difference between the two integrations, or 0.2. In other words there is a 20 percent probability that a random value of x will lie between the values of x_i and $\bar{x}$.

It frequently happens that tables of the standard function are not readily available. Approximate probabilities can be ascertained if the areas under the curve between standard deviation values are known. Figure 12.4 illustrates the approximate areas between the mean and one standard deviation, one and two standard deviations, and two and three standard deviations. These are, respectively, 34.1 percent, 13.6 percent, and 2.1 percent. The reader may note that these percentages do not exactly add to give the values listed below the diagram. This is because of roundoff error. Values of the ordinates to the standard curve are also shown for reference.

Measures of Dispersion

The most important measure of dispersion in either a frequency or probability distribution is the standard deviation, σ. It can be expressed mathematically as

$$\sigma = (n-1)^{-1/2}\left(\sum_{1}^{n}(x_i-\bar{x})^2\right)^{1/2} \tag{12.4}$$

In dealing with the discrete data of a given sample, the true mean is approximated by $\bar{m}$. Also, if the sample size is relatively large, $(n-1)$ will differ little from n. Hence, for most practical samples the standard deviation may be found from the following expression:

$$\sigma = n^{-1/2}\left(\sum_{1}^{n}(x_i - \bar{m})^2\right)^{1/2}$$ (12.5)

The term $(x_i - \bar{m})$ is the deviation of any value, x_i, from the arithmetic mean, $\bar{m}$.

It can be demonstrated by taking the second derivative of the normal distribution function that the points of inflection of the curve lie at plus and minus one standard deviation. This fact is especially helpful in sketching an approximate normal curve.

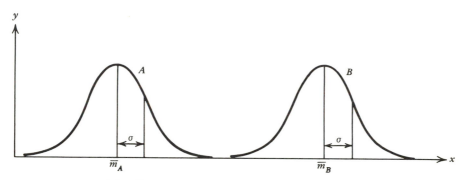

(a)   *Same standard deviation, different means*

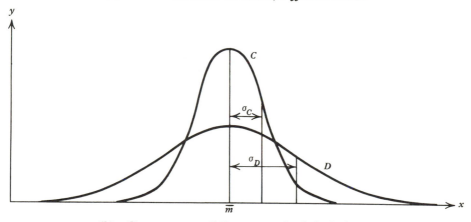

(b)   *Same means, different standard deviations*

Figure 12.5   Relationships between normal distributions.

Examples of two normal distribution functions having the same standard deviations but different means are given in Figure 12.5a. Both curves A and B have the same appearance but are displaced along the abcissa by the difference in their mean values.

In Figure 12.5b two normal distributions having the same means but different standard deviations are shown. Curve C has the smaller standard Deviation and is necessarily taller than curve D because the area under each is unity.

Because of the square root in the expression for standard deviation it is not possible to add the standard deviation from one distribution to another. Nevertheless, it will become necessary to find the dispersion of a resulting distribution when two or more are added together. The variance, which is the square of the standard deviation, may also be considered a measure of dispersion and variances may be added.

Another measure of dispersion of a distribution is the range. This is defined as the difference between the largest value of the variable and the smallest value. In a standard probability density function the range is from minus infinity to plus infinity. In a given sample for either frequency or probability the range is the difference between the highest measured value and the lowest measured value.

In naturally occurring distributions, 99.7 percent of the total cases lie between minus 3σ and plus 3σ. Hence, the standard deviation may be approximated as one-sixth the range. Range is a weak measure of dispersion because it is not related to the other characteristics of the distribution.

Central Limit Theorem

As was implied above, it will be necessary in the PERT computations to find certain values of a distribution resulting from the addition of two or more distributions. A widely used statistical theorem known as the Central Limit Theorem allows for these values. The theorem may be stated as follows:

> **If independent probability distributions are to be summed, then the mean of the sum is the sum of the individual means, the variance of the sum is the sum of the individual variances, and the distribution of the sum tends to the shape of the normal curve regardless of the shape of the individual distributions.**

12.3   ACTIVITY ASSUMPTIONS

Before discussing details of the PERT calculations several assumptions made with regard to the activities of the network must be considered. The first of these is that every activity is assumed to have duration times that are randomly distributed. The shape of this distribution may be uniform, triangular, exponential, or of any other type.

Activity durations are assumed to occur naturally in the course of carrying out the activity function. They should not include allowances for infrequent or unusual happenings. Almost every activity in a construction project could be influenced by accidents, strikes, or similar events. But should these occur, the duration must be reevaluated and corrected by an updating procedure.

The variation in an activity duration should be the natural result of a fixed method of performance. Construction activities are particularly susceptible to changes in method that alter completion times. Suppose that an activity involves placing a large pipe under water and the distribution of durations has been estimated assuming that the pipe will be placed from barges during midsummer. If it is decided to wait until winter, assemble the pipe on the ice, and lower it beneath the surface through a slot cut in the ice, the duration could be much shorter. In effect, the method has changed and there is a distribution of durations different from that originally planned. Clearly, the two methods should not be considered to have the same time distribution.

Activity duration distributions must also be the natural result of the application of a fixed set of resources. For example, a duration for a pavement breaking activity has been estimated assuming that a single pavement breaker will be used. The addition of another breaker will greatly reduce the assumed duration. The time distributions, although similar, are not the same because the activity has been redefined by the increase in resources.

The second assumption made about activities in the PERT system is that there are three estimated times of completion which can be determined for each activity. These are the most likely, optimistic, and pessimistic durations. The most likely time is represented by the letter m and is referred to as the modal time. If all goes well, it can be expected that the duration will be short. This optimistic duration has by custom been identified as time a. When the activity is beset by inefficiencies and delays, the duration can be expected to be long and this pessimistic time is identified as time b.

Because the optimistic, most likely, and pessimistic times cannot be determined exactly, these durations may be considered random variables and the estimated values, a, m, and b are taken as the mean values for the three distributions.

The reliability of these three time estimates is greatly influenced by the manner in which they are derived. Historical data give the most reliable determinations, but their availability usually is limited to the most likely time. In the construction field it is difficult to obtain sufficient time data about any given activity from historical records, and the scheduler must rely upon direct inquiry of the field forces for time estimates.

When the values a, m, and b are obtained by direct inquiry there is a tendency for the optimistic and pessimistic times to be biased toward the modal value. This is a natural tendency. Asked to give the most optimistic duration for an activity, a respondent will probably shade the answer toward the high side to avoid censure for poor performance. The same respondent asked to provide the most pessimistic duration will shade the answer toward the low side to avoid being criticized as a lazy employee.

To minimize the effect of the bias when determining an extreme time, the respondent may be asked to give the usual, or most likely, time to accomplish the operation. Then several probable conditions that could affect the extreme are presented, and the respondent is asked to give the shortening or lengthening from the most likely value. This interval is then subtracted or added to the modal time to obtain the desired extreme. For example, a questioner might use a phrasing such as "Suppose one of your crew is not feeling well, your front end loader has a flat tire, and your haul trucks are arriving late. How much more time than usual will your loading of the material take?" The extra time is then added to the usual time to get the pessimistic duration.

Interaction between the questioner and respondent identifies most of the probable conditions surrounding the operation. The respondent becomes a part of the process, not merely an information source, and does not feel threatened. Thus, good, reasonable extreme values may be established.

Activity time values may also contain a systematic bias caused by the questioner. In communicating with a respondent the questioner may use words, inflections, or gestures which signal the respondent to reply according to what might be perceived as the desired answer. To overcome this bias in any of the values it is suggested that the questioner plan in advance of the questioning the exact wording to use, especially for the modal value. There is less likelihood of this type of bias if the question is actually read from a written statement.

The third activity assumption is that all varieties of duration distributions can be converted to a common distribution. Construction operations, although similar in nature from job to job, are basically nonrepetitive, and it is therefore almost impossible to obtain sufficient data to define a duration distribution. As far as is known, no studies have been made to definitely establish a type of time distribution of any kind of activity. Consequently, with only three time estimates available, one type of distribution must be chosen as being most representative.

Clark,[12.4] one of the originators of PERT, has this to say about the choice of a common distribution given the most likely time and extremes.

> With this information it is necessary to convert the estimated mode and range of a distribution into an estimated expected value and variance. The author has no information concerning distributions of activity times; in particular, it is not suggested that the beta or any other distribution is appropriate. But the analysis requires some model for the distribution of activity times, the parameters of the distribution being the mode and the extremes. The distribution that first comes to the author's mind is the beta distribution. However the beta distribution still has a free parameter after its mode and extremes are designated. Suppose we select one-sixth of the range as the standard deviation (the normal distribution truncated at ± 2.66 has its standard deviation equal

to 1/6 the range, and we feel that this truncated normal distribution is an appropriate simple model for specifying the ratio of the standard deviation to the range). Then a beta distribution is determined, and one can convert the mode and extremes into the expected value and variance. This conversion requires computations, including the solution of a cubic equation, which are ponderous relative to the reliability of the results. By empirical numerical manipulation one can observe that the results obtained from the suggested beta distribution analysis can be closely approximated by use of a simple formula. This approximation is that the expected value is the weighted arithmetic mean of the mode and the midrange, the mode carrying two-thirds of the total weight. This together with the use of one-sixth of the range for the standard deviation are accepted as the PERT estimates of the expected value and standard deviation of an activity time.

The two assumptions made by Clark can be put into mathematical terms. Let the symbol, t_e, be the expected value of the distribution and σ be the standard deviation. The resulting equations are then

$$\sigma = \frac{b-a}{6} \tag{12.6}$$

$$t_e = \frac{a+4m+b}{6} \tag{12.7}$$

Moder and Rogers[12.8] suggest that the original assumption that the standard deviation is one-sixth the range should be increased. It is argued that the original range from the zero to one-hundredth percentiles should be changed to the fifth to ninety-fifth percentiles because the latter are more representative values for wide varieties of distributions. If this assumption is adopted, the standard deviation becomes

$$\sigma = \frac{b-a}{3.2} \tag{12.8}$$

Although Moder and Rogers' arguments are convincing the most popularly used equation for PERT standard deviation is Equation 12.6. This equation will be used throughout the rest of this chapter together with the equation for expected value, t_e, given by Equation 12.7.

12.4 NETWORK ASSUMPTIONS

There are three significant assumptions made about PERT networks that merit consideration here. They are based upon the probability concepts of Section 12.2 and influence the reliability of the calculations to be discussed later.

The first of these assumptions is that any PERT path along which calculations are to be made must contain enough activities to make the central limit theorem valid.

As in CPM network, activity durations are added to obtain the length of the path measured in time units. But instead of a single time duration for each activity these additions in PERT are equivalent to adding distributions. Any conclusions drawn are based upon the normal distribution and hence there must be a sufficient number of various types of distributions added to ensure the normal tendency. Moder[12.9] indicates that the minimum number of activities required is four. Miller[12.7] gives the number as ten. Whatever the minimum number, it is clear that in most construction networks there will be a great enough number available at any milestone event of importance.

The second of the network assumptions is that the mean, TE, of the distribution of the early event time is given by the maximum mean of the duration distributions of the paths entering the node.

In a CPM arrow network if there were two or more paths from the initial event to a given node, the one with the greatest duration established the early event time. The assumption above implies the same choice even though mean values of the distributions, t_e, are being added instead of the deterministic activity durations, T. It ignores the possibility that the path with the greatest sum of t_e values could actually have a length less than any of the parallel paths to the node.

The third network assumption is that the PERT critical path is long enough in time so as to be longer than any other path in the network. Not only must the choice of the longest path be made as in the second assumption, but there can be no overlapping of the distributions. The distributions are assumed displaced as in Figure 12.5a.

MacCrimmon and Ryavec[12.5] and Clark[12.3] have made studies of this bias and conclude that the error between the true duration and the PERT duration increases as the number of merging paths increases. This error also increases as the path lengths approach each other and as the standard deviations of the merging paths increase. In practice, this merge bias may be ignored if the longest path is greater than one or two standard deviations greater than any other path.

It sometimes happens that there are two or more critical paths through the network. In these instances the path with the largest square of the standard deviation, or variance, should be used.

Because of merge bias it may be said that the event times computed under the PERT assumptions will tend to be less than their true values and that the variances of these event time distributions will tend to be greater than their true values. Corrections could be made, of course, but considering the initial uncertainty of the estimated activity time values in construction systems, they usually are not needed in practical applications.

12.5 PERT DIAGRAMS

Because PERT is a critical path technique it can be expected that the network diagram will closely resemble a CPM diagram as presented in Chapters 6 and 7. This similarity often causes confusion to those who might be unfamiliar with the details of the system.

In preceding chapters a project was broken down into work activities each of which was to be accomplished within a given time period. In general, the titles of the activities implied, or had expressed, an active verb such as obtain, build, erect, install, construct, and so on. CPM can thus be said to be activity oriented.

In a PERT network the breakdown is focused on the events to be met in the performance of the project. An event was defined in Chapter 6 as the start or finish of an activity, and in PERT the time for finishing an activity is the one usually emphasized. This event orientation leads to titles being placed on the events and not the activities. Such titles commonly have the past tense of a verb implied or actually expressed. Obtained, built, installed, constructed, and so on, are some of the words that may appear in them.

To make the above distinctions clear, consider Figure 12.6 where a portion of the network for the remodeling of the chemical laboratory is represented by each of the three diagraming techniques.

Figure 12.6a depicts the CPM diagram in precedence notation from Figure 7.12. No true events are shown but the linkages between the activities represent the interactions taking place.

In Figure 12.6b the same set of activities is presented using the arrow diagraming notation. The events are clearly expressed and numbered, whereas the activities and their durations are labeled on the arrows.

The PERT diagram is shown in Figure 12.6c. Note that the events retain the same numbers and are labeled. The activities are still represented by the arrows between events even though they are not identified.

Particular attention should be paid to Events 6 and 8. At these events the labels contain two notations, one for finishing an activity and the other for the start of the succeeding activity. Event 10 is also double labeled to show the finish of the repairs of the walls, ceiling, and floor. This procedure is adopted to avoid confusion as to which arrow corresponds to which activity. If such a technique is not used, it is possible to lose an activity entirely in the representation.

The most common misconception about the PERT diagram is that it is the same as in the precedence notation. The vertical lines in the sketch are to emphasize that this is not so. In both cases the nodes are labeled but the networks are entirely different.

To simplify the computations of the various activity and event functions, it is customary to number the events in the PERT network so that the event at the

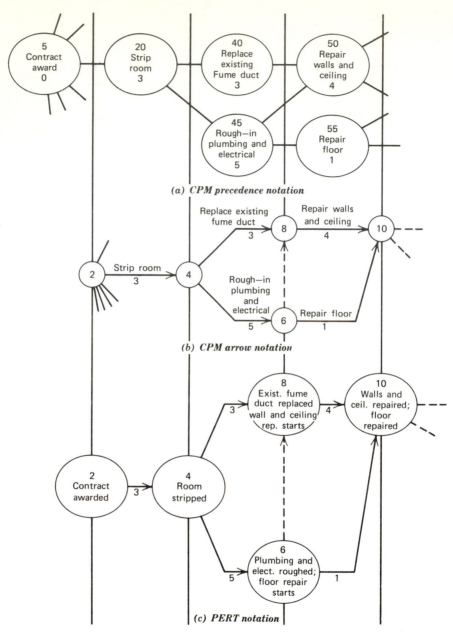

(a) CPM precedence notation

(b) CPM arrow notation

(c) PERT notation

Figure 12.6   Network comparisons.

tail of the activity arrow has a smaller number than the event at the head of the arrow.

12.6 SCHEDULE COMPUTATIONS

Although the activities in PERT are assumed to have random distributions for their durations, the network computations are performed in a deterministic manner. As in the CPM arrow network each event in the system has two time values associated with it, the earliest that the event can take place, *TE*, and the latest that the event may happen, *TL*. Slack values, corresponding to CPM floats, are calculated with the CPM interfering float becoming more important and named "event slack." Critical events and critical links are identified and the critical path or paths are comprised of the critical links in the same way as in a CPM arrow network. To examine these relationships, use will be made of the simplified PERT network shown in Figure 12.7.

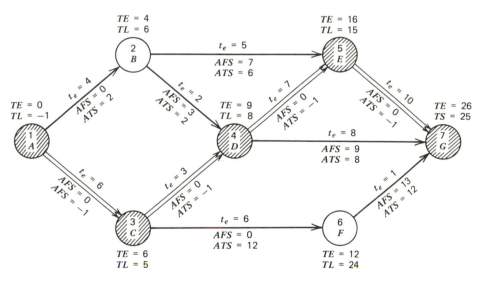

Figure 12.7 Simplified PERT network.

Early Event Times

Early event times, *TE*, may be determined by a forward pass computation similar to that done in Chapter 6. The PERT system assumes that all activity durations can be represented by their mean values, t_e, calculated by Equation 12.7. These t_e quantities are added along a path from the initial event to obtain the value of *TE* for any given node. When more than one such path merges at a node, the largest sum is taken as the *TE* in accordance with the second network assumption discussed in Section 12.4.

There must be one event in the entire system which establishes the start of the project. In most construction networks this is the signing of the contract or the notice to proceed. When an updating situation is met, this initial event may be identified as the time of updating. Whatever the particular identification, this single event must begin the network diagram and serve as a start for all the subsequent calculations.

The *TE* of the initial event, TE_0, must be assumed. Ordinarily this assumed value is zero, but it may be assigned any other value. For example, it might be day 30 in an updating computation. To this initial *TE* is added the mean duration for the first link to obtain the *TE* of the next event. The process is then repeated for the subsequent links until the terminal event is reached. As stated above, the larger value is chosen at merge events. These conditions can be expressed mathematically as follows:

$$TE_0 = \text{an assigned value} \tag{12.9}$$

$$TE_j = \underset{\forall i}{\text{Max}}\left(TE_i + (t_e)_{ij}\right) \tag{12.10}$$

The symbol $\underset{\forall i}{\text{Max}}$ is to be interpreted as the maximum sum for all links ij merging at node j.

In Figure 12.7 the events are numbered such that the event at the tail of the arrow always has a smaller number than the event at the head of the arrow. The letters represent the full descriptions of the event. The individual duration times, a, m, and b are not shown but the mean values, t_e, are given along the arrows.

In the figure TE_1 has been assigned the value zero according to Equation 12.9. The value of *TE* for Event 2, TE_2, is then found by adding the mean duration for Activity 1–2, thus,

$$TE_2 = TE_1 + (t_e)_{1-2}$$
$$TE_2 = 0 + 4 = 4$$

Similarly, TE_3 is determined to be 6.

At Event 4 the *TE* is calculated by Equation 12.10. There are two activities merging at Event 4 and each must be considered. The computation is therefore

$$TE_4 = \text{Max}\left[\begin{array}{c} TE_2 + (t_e)_{2-4} \\ TE_3 + (t_e)_{3-4} \end{array}\right]$$

$$TE_4 = \text{Max}\left[\begin{array}{c} 4+2=6 \\ 6+3=9 \end{array}\right] = 9$$

The *TE* values for all the other events have been calculated in the same manner and their values are shown near the nodes. It should be remembered that these *TE*s are the means of assumed normal distributions and not deterministic values as was the case in the CPM arrow network.

Late Event Times

The computation for the late event times for each node are determined in a manner similar to that in Chapter 6. These late event times must begin with a single event that marks the close of the project. It may be final acceptance by the owner, start-up of the facility, or just the completion of all the activities comprising the work. This last event will be called the *terminal event*.

The latest that the terminal event can take place is assigned by the scheduler. Frequently, this assignment will be the same as the early event time already established for the node. However, because the *TE* is only one possible value from a distribution it can be expected that this assignment can actually be some other reasonable value. It often happens that this assignment is determined from outside conditions surrounding the need for project completion and will bear no direct relationship to the early completion date. Hence, the assigned *TL* for the terminal event, TL_t, is commonly termed the *schedule time, TS*.

The late event times, *TL*, are dependent upon the assignment made for the terminal event. They can be found by backing through the network and subtracting the t_e values from the *TL* values already computed.

Because the longest path from the terminal node is sought, a choice must be made at any burst node. To be consistent with the choice made in the forward pass, the smallest of the *TL* quantities will be taken as the event's *TL*.

If these concepts are expressed mathematically, the following equations result.

$$TL_t = TS = \text{an assigned value} \tag{12.11}$$

$$TL_i = \underset{\forall j}{\text{Min}}\left(TL_j - (t_e)_{ij}\right) \tag{12.12}$$

The symbol $\underset{\forall j}{\text{Min}}$ is to indicate that the minimum value of the equation is to be used considering all links ij that burst from node i.

In Figure 12.7 the scheduled time for the completion of the project is 25 days. This may be assumed to have been established in advance of the forward pass computation from outside data about the project.

The *TL* for Event 5, TL_5, is found by subtracting the t_e for link 5–7 from TS_7. Thus,

$$TL_5 = TS_7 - (t_e)_{5-7}$$
$$TL_5 = 25 - 10 = 15$$

In a like manner TL_6 has been determined to be 24.

At Event 4 the TL_4 may be calculated from Equation 12.12 as follows:

$$TL_4 = \text{Min} \begin{bmatrix} TL_5 - (t_e)_{4-5} \\ TL_7 - (t_e)_{4-7} \end{bmatrix}$$

$$TL_4 = \text{Min} \begin{bmatrix} 15 - 7 = 8 \\ 25 - 8 = 17 \end{bmatrix} = 8$$

Late event times for all other activities in the network have been similarly computed and are shown near the nodes in Figure 12.7.

When the other late event times in the network have been determined it will be found that in this case the initial node has a negative TL. Again recall that all the subtractions have involved mean values of distributions and that this TL is the presumed mean of a distribution of TLs.

Activity Free Slack

Activity free slack is a term used in the PERT system, and corresponds with the free float in a CPM network. It is defined as the expected time interval in which an activity may be expected to terminate and not delay the start of any of its following activities. The expected time that any one of the following activities is likely to occur is the early event time of the j node of the activity or TE_j. The expected finish for the activity is the early event time for the i node plus the expected duration of the activity or $TE_i + (t_e)_{ij}$. The activity free slack, AFS_{ij}, can then be written as

$$AFS_{ij} = TE_j - TE_i - (t_e)_{ij} \tag{12.13}$$

Activity free slack is a function of the activity itself and is derived only from the early start schedule. As such, it can never be less than zero.

As was the case in the CPM arrow network, every event, TE, except the initial event, must derive its value from an addition to the expected activity duration, t_e, according to Equation 12.10. Therefore, every event must have at least one activity entering it with an activity free slack equal to zero. Conversely, for every event with only one activity entering it, that activity must have an activity free slack equal to zero.

To illustrate these conditions, consider Activity 1–2 of Figure 12.7. The activity free slack for this activity is calculated by Equation 12.13 as follows:

$$AFS_{1-2} = TE_2 - TE_1 - (t_e)_{1-2}$$
$$AFS_{1-2} = 4 - 0 - 4 = 0$$

This result is as anticipated because Activity 1–2 is the only activity entering Event 2. Similarly, the activity free slack for Activity 2–4 is found to be

$$AFS_{2-4} = TE_4 - TE_2 - (t_e)_{2-4}$$
$$AFS_{2-4} = 9 - 4 - 2 = 3$$

Thus, Activity 3–4 must have the zero activity free slack because Event 4 must have had its TE_4 derived from either Activity 2–4 or Activity 3–4. The reader can readily validate this value by substitution in Equation 12.13.

Each activity in the network has had its activity free slack computed in the same way and these values are shown beneath the activity arrows in Figure 12.7.

The calculated activity free slack is, of course, an expected value, or mean, of a distribution of free slack because all the terms in the equation represent mean values of distributions and the central limit theorem is assumed to be operative.

Activity Total Slack

Another term often used in PERT computations is activity total slack. This value corresponds to the total float of an activity as used in Chapter 6. Activity total slack can be defined as the expected value of the time span in which the completion of the activity can be expected to terminate and not extend the expected project duration. The latest that the j event of an activity ik can be expected to occur, TL_j, establishes the late limit for the time span. The early limit is the expected early finish of the activity. This is the same time as used in the activity free slack and is the early event time for the i node plus the expected duration of the activity or $TE_i + (t_e)_{ij}$. Activity total slack may then be expressed mathematically as

$$ATS_{ij} = TL_j - TE_i - (t_e)_{ij} \tag{12.14}$$

The ATS_{ij} is the expected value, or mean, of a distribution of activity total slack because all the terms on the right side of the equation are means of distributions.

The calculation of activity total slack for Activity 2–5 in Figure 12.7 is chosen for an example. It is made using Equation 12.14 by substituting the previously determined values of TE, TL, and t_e as follows:

$$ATS_{2-5} = TL_5 - TE_2 - (t_e)_{2-5}$$
$$ATS_{2-5} = 15 - 4 - 5 = 6$$

All the other values of activity total slack have been computed using Equation 12.14 and these have been shown beneath the activity arrows in Figure 12.7.

Activity total slack is a function of the activity. It is also a function of a chain of activities as long as that chain is not compounded by other activities entering or leaving any intermediate node in the chain. To illustrate, consider the two activity chain comprised of Activities 3–6 and 6–7. The activity total slack for each of these activities is 12 because no compounding takes place at Event 6. On the other hand, the chain comprised of Activities 1–2 and 2–5 has different activity total slack values for each activity because this chain is compounded by the emergence of Activity 2–4 at Event 2.

Event Slack

Probably the most often used term in PERT other than the early event time and late event time is event slack, or simply slack. Event slack is the time interval between the latest that an event can be expected to occur and the earliest that it can be expected to happen. It is calculated simply by taking the algebraic difference between the TL and TE of an event. The mathematical expression for event slack, ES, is

$$ES_i = TL_i - TE_i \qquad (12.15)$$

where the subscript i serves to identify any particular event.

Event slack corresponds to the interfering float of the activities immediately preceding the event as computed for a CPM arrow network. It is different in the PERT system in that event slack is the expected value, or mean, of a distribution of slack because both the TL and TE are means of distributions.

Because the TL for an event depends upon an assigned value at the terminal event, TS, it may or may not be directly related to the TE for that event. In fact, TL may actually have a calculated value less than TE at any given event. In such cases the event slack will have a negative value.

Table 12.2 gives the value of event slack for each event in the network of Figure 12.7. It will be observed that in this instance there are only two positive values of event slack.

TABLE 12.2

Event Slack for Sample Network			
Event	TE	TL	Event Slack
1	0	−1	−1
2	4	6	2
3	6	5	−1
4	9	8	−1
5	16	15	−1
6	12	24	12
7	26	25	−1

Critical Events

At the terminal event the event slack is given by the difference between the scheduled time and the early event time. In equation form it is

$$ES_t = TS - TE_t \tag{12.16}$$

Because the terminal node is always critical it can be shown that to avoid delaying the scheduled duration of the project, no event must have a lesser event slack than the terminal event. Also every event having the same slack as the terminal event must be critical. The proof of these statements follows.

Equation 12.15 states the general conditions for event slack.

$$ES_i = TL_i - TE_i$$

Equation 12.12 gives the generalization for the late event time.

$$TL_i = \operatorname*{Min}_{\forall j} \left(TL_j - (t_e)_{ij} \right)$$

Now consider any link ij where j is the terminal event, t. No minimization is needed because of this singularity so

$$TL_i = TL_t - (t_e)_{i-t}$$

and because $TL_t = TS$

$$TL_i = TS - (t_e)_{i-t}$$

Substituting this value of TL_i in the equation for ES_i results in

$$ES_i = TS - (t_e)_{i-t} - TE_i$$
$$ES_i = TS - (TE_i + (t_e)_{i-t})$$

Recall that Equation 12.10 gives the generalization for the early event time as

$$TE_j = \operatorname*{Max}_{\forall i} \left(TE_i + (t_e)_{ij} \right)$$

Applying this to the terminal event, the equation becomes

$$TE_t = \operatorname*{Max}_{\forall i} \left(TE_i + (t_e)_{i-t} \right)$$

If the link chosen is the one that maximizes the right side of this equation, then

$$TE_t = TE_i + (t_e)_{i-t}$$

and by substitution

$$ES_i = TS - TE_t = ES_t$$

Hence, because the value of $TE_i + (t_e)_{i-t}$ is the maximum value, ES_i cannot be smaller and further, because ES_t is the event slack of a critical event, ES_i must also be the event slack of a critical event.

This analysis could be carried further to those nodes immediately preceding this particular event i to establish a preceding critical event slack. It can be repeated as many times as necessary until the event slack of the initial node is found. It can then be concluded that every event having the same event slack as the terminal node is a critical event.

In Table 12.2 the terminal event, Event 7, is critical and has a slack equal to -1. Events 1, 3, 4, and 5 all have a slack equal to this value and are also critical events. No event has a lesser value than -1. These events have been shaded in Figure 12.7 to indicate their critical nature.

Critical Activities and the Critical Path

As in a CPM arrow network the PERT critical path is comprised of those critical activities forming a continuous chain from the initial to the terminal event. There are two ways to identify these critical activities. One way is to compare the expected duration of each activity with the difference in the early times at its head and tail events. The other is to evaluate the activity total slack for each activity and compare this value with the event slack of the terminal event.

Before computing the activity total slack and activity free slack, an activity may be found to be critical if its expected duration is equal to the difference between the early event time for its j event and the early event time for its i event. This can be demonstrated in the following manner.

The general expression for early event time given by Equation 12.10 is

$$TE_j = \operatorname*{Max}_{\forall i} \left(TE_i + (t_e)_{ij} \right)$$

If it is assumed that the j event is a critical event, there must be at least one activity ending at the j node which establishes its early event time. This activity must then be the one that maximizes the right side of the above equation. To satisfy this condition the i event must also be a critical event and the equation can be written

$$TE_j = TE_i + (t_e)_{ij}$$

or by rearrangement

$$(t_e)_{ij} = TE_j - TE_i \quad (i \text{ and } j \text{ critical}) \tag{12.17}$$

In Figure 12.7 both Events 5 and 7 are critical. The difference between TE_7 and TE_5 is $26 - 16$ or 10. The expected duration of Activity 5–7 is also 10 so this activity is a critical activity. In contrast, both Events 4 and 7 are critical. The difference between TE_7 and TE_4 is $26 - 9$ or 17. The expected duration of Activity 4–7 is 8 and, therefore, this activity is not critical even though it is connecting two critical events.

If Activity 1–2 is considered, it will be seen that the difference in the TE values is 4 as is the expected duration of the activity. This activity is not critical because only one event, Event 1, is a critical event.

Each activity has been similarly evaluated and it will be seen that Activities 1–3, 3–4, 4–5, and 5–7 are the critical ones and comprise the critical path. These activities have double arrows to emphasize the critical path.

When it is convenient to compute the activity total slack, the activities having this quantity equal to the event slack of the terminal event are critical activities. This can be demonstrated by the following procedure.

The general expression for activity total slack is given by Equation 12.14 as

$$ATS_{ij} = TL_j - TE_i - (t_e)_{ij}$$

An application of Equation 12.15 to event j results in

$$ES_j = TL_j - TE_j$$

Rearranging these terms and substituting in the equation for activity total slack gives

$$ATS_{ij} = ES_j + TE_j - TE_i - (t_e)_{ij}$$

The last three terms of this equation are equal to the activity free slack as given by Equation 12.13. The expression can then be written

$$ATS_{ij} = ES_j + AFS_{ij}$$

or by rearrangement

$$ATS_{ij} - AFS_{ij} = ES_j \tag{12.18}$$

Equation 12.18 is always true for any activity.

It will be recalled that the activity free slack is determined with the condition that the expected completion of the activity within its time span will not delay the expected start of any succeeding activity, and that its minimum value is zero. Assume also that the j event is a critical event. For a critical activity Equation 12.18 must then be

$$ATS_{ij} = ES_j$$

Because the j event is critical, the event slack, ES_j, is equal to the event slack of the terminal event, ES_t, hence at criticality,

$$ATS_{ij} = ES_t$$

In Figure 12.7 it can be observed that the critical activities, Activities 1–3, 3–4, 4–5, and 5–7 all have a value of -1, which is the event slack for Event 7. As before they comprise the critical path through the network.

12.7   PERT COMPUTATIONS, TABULAR FORMAT

In the discussion of PERT computations in Section 12.6 the basic mathematical relationships were developed and specific calculations of the various quantities were made directly on the network shown in Figure 12.7. The calculations could have been made using a table instead of the network diagram should this procedure be more convenient.

To illustrate this tabular format procedure, a more extensive project will be used. Assume that as a contractor you have obtained the contract to construct a series of fast food outlets. The owners wish to have an analysis made of the construction program to give some reasonable idea as to the probable length of time required to build a typical outlet. You have established 15 basic activities needed to perform the work and have estimated the optimistic, most likely, and pessimistic durations for each. In addition you have prepared a PERT diagram of a typical project. This diagram is shown in Figure 12.8.

The 15 activities and the required three dummies have been listed in Table 12.3 in ascending order of i event numbers and subascending order of j event numbers. Opposite each activity the three activity durations, a, m, and b are entered. The value of the expected duration for each activity computed from Equation 12.7 is entered in the column headed t_e.

The next four columns are used to calculate the early and late event times and the expected duration of the project. The values in the column headed TE_i all are early event times of the i event for each activity, and those in the column headed TL_j all are late event times of the j event for each activity.

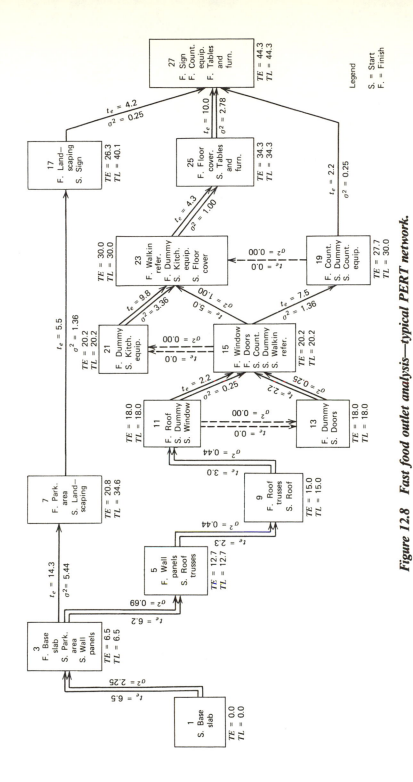

Figure 12.8 Fast food outlet analysis—typical PERT network.

343

TABLE 12.3

Typical PERT Computations Fast Food Outlet Analysis

CP	Event i	Event j	Activity	Durations (Days) a	m	b	t_e	TE_i	$TE_i + t_e$	$TL_j - t_e$	TL_j	σ^2	AFS	ATS
*	1	3	Base slab	3	6	12	6.5	0.	6.5	0	6.5	2.25	0	0
*	3	5	Wall panels	4	6	9	6.2	6.5	12.7	6.5	12.7	0.69	0	0
	3	7	Parking area	6	15	20	14.3	6.5	20.8	20.3	34.6	5.44	0	13.8
*	5	9	Roof trusses	1	2	5	2.3	12.7	15.0	12.7	15.0	0.44	0	0
	7	17	Landscaping	3	5	10	5.5	20.8	26.3	34.6	40.1	1.36	0	13.8
*	9	11	Roofing	1	3	5	3.0	15.0	18.0	15.0	18.0	0.44	0	0
*	11	13	Dummy	0	0	0	0.	18.0	18.0	18.0	18.0	0	0	0
*	11	15	Windows	1	2	4	2.2	18.0	20.2	18.0	20.2	0.25	0	0
*	13	15	Doors	1	2	4	2.2	18.0	20.2	18.0	20.2	0.25	0	0
	15	19	Counter	3	8	10	7.5	20.2	27.7	22.5	30.0	1.36	0	2.3
*	15	21	Dummy	0	0	0	0.	20.2	20.2	20.2	20.2	0	0	0
	15	23	Walk-in refrigerator	2	5	8	5.0	20.2	25.2	25.0	30.0	1.00	4.8	4.8
	17	27	Sign	3	4	6	4.2	26.3	30.5	40.1	44.3	0.25	13.8	13.8
	19	23	Dummy	0	0	0	0.	27.7	27.7	30.0	30.0	0	2.3	2.3
	19	27	Counter Equipment	1	2	4	2.2	27.7	29.9	42.1	44.3	0.25	14.4	14.4
*	21	23	Kitchen equipment	4	10	15	9.8	20.2	30.0	20.2	30.0	3.36	0	0
*	23	25	Floor coverings	2	4	8	4.3	30.0	34.3	30.0	34.3	1.00	0	0
*	25	27	Tables and furnishings	5	10	15	10.0	34.3	44.3	34.3	44.3	2.78	0	0

Calculations begin with the assignment of zero for the early event time for the initial event, Event 1. To this is added the t_e for Activity 1–3, which is 6.5. This sum is then entered in the column headed $TE_i + t_e$. The next activity, Activity 3–5, derives its TE_3 value from the sum just determined or 6.5. The t_e for Activity 3–5 is then added to give a sum of 12.7. The process continues on down the table until all TEs have been computed.

Particular note should be taken of the TE for Event 23 associated with Activity 23–25. The sum, $TE_i + t_e$, for Activity 15–23 is 25.2. For Activity 19–23 the sum is 27.7 and for Activity 21–23 it is 30.0 which, according to Equation 12.10, is TE for Event 23. This then becomes the TE_i for Activity 23–25.

The TE_i for Event 27 is not specifically listed in the column headed TE_i because there is no activity following this event. Were there to be such an activity, the TE_i value would be the greatest of the $(TE_i + t_e)$ values for the activities merging at Event 27, Activities 17–27, 19–27, and 25–27. From the table this greatest sum can be seen to be 44.3, which is therefore the TE_{27}.

The backward pass begins by assigning TL_j for Event 27, the terminal event. Because no outside information is stipulated, this assignment has been taken as 44.3, the value of TE for Event 27.

The last activity listed in Table 12.3 is Activity 25–27. With the TL_{27} established, its $(TL_j - t_e)$ is determined by subtracting the t_e of the activity, 10.0, from the 44.3, giving a value of 34.3.

The next-to-last activity in the table, Activity 23–25, will derive its TL_j value from the $(TL_j - t_e)$ just calculated, or 34.3. Again the subtraction of $(t_e)_{23-25}$ results in 30.0 which is entered in the $(TL_j - t_e)$ column. This process continues up the table, activity by activity, until the initial event is reached.

In determining the TL_j for Activity 15–19 the minimum of the $(TL_j - t_e)$ values for Activities 19–23 and 19–27 has been used in accordance with Equation 12.12. Similar decisions have been made in determining the TL_j values for Activities 13–15, 9–11, and 1–3.

The column headed σ^2 is the variance for the distribution assumed for each activity. It is computed by squaring the value of σ from Equation 12.6. For the first activity listed, Activity 1–3, it is

$$\sigma^2 = \left[\frac{12-3}{6}\right]^2 = 2.25$$

All the other variances have been computed in the same way and are tabulated.

Activity free slack is calculated by using Equation 12.13. This equation requires the difference between two early event times, TE—one for the j event and the other for the i event. Both of these are found in the TE_i column. The TE_j is opposite any activity whose i event has the same number as the j event of the activity for which the free slack is being determined. For example, consider Activity 1–3. The TE_3 is found opposite either Activity 3–5 or Activity 3–7 and is 6.5. The TE_1 is found opposite Activity 1–3 and is 0.0. The activity free slack can then be determined as follows:

$$AFS_{1-3} = TE_3 - TE_1 - (t_e)_{1-3}$$
$$AFS_{1-3} = 6.5 - 0.0 - 6.5 = 0.0$$

The rest of the free slack values are determined in a like manner and they have been tabulated in the column headed AFS. It may appear that this computation fails for the last activity, Activity 25–27 in the table, but it should be recalled that TE_{27} is derived from Equation 12.10 and is 44.3 even though there is no listing for an activity beginning with an i number of 27.

Activity total slack, ATS is calculated from Equation 12.14. The TL_j and TE_i values for each activity appear opposite the activity in their respective columns unlike the TE values used for activity free slack. As an example, consider the calculation of total slack for Activity 3–7. TL_7 is 34.6 from the TL_j column and TE_3 is 6.5 from the TE_i column. Substituting in the equation, the activity total slack is

$$ATS_{3-7} = TL_7 - TE_3 - (t_e)_{3-7}$$
$$ATS_{3-7} = 34.6 - 6.5 - 14.3 = 13.8$$

All the other total slack values are determined similarly and are tabulated in the ATS column.

Critical activities are those that have the same activity total slack as the event slack of the terminal event. In the table the event slack for Event 27 is the difference between the TL_{27} and TE_{27}. TL_{27} is tabulated but the TE_{27} must be derived from Equation 12.10 as the maximum of the $(TE_i + t_e)$ values of the activities ending at Event 27. This was previously determined to be 44.3, the same value as the tabulated TL_{27}. The event slack for Event 27 is therefore zero, and all activities with a zero activity total slack are critical. These activities are starred in the column at the left headed CP, for critical path.

It can be observed that these starred activities form a continuous chain from Event 1 to Event 27 and become the critical path. Note that both Activities 11–13 and 11–15 are critical and, in fact, there are two critical paths through the network. One goes through Events 9, 11, 13, and 15. The other goes through Events 9, 11, and 15, bypassing Event 13.

The critical path has also been transferred to the diagram of Figure 12.8 where it is indicated by the double arrows between the events.

12.8   PROBABILITY OF MEETING A SCHEDULED DATE

A question often asked of a construction manager is how sure are you that this project will be finished when you say? Usually, the answer (given with some

hesitation), is that we think it will be finished on the day proposed unless
_____. Unless what? A strike, the weather, a failure of a supplier to deliver, or
a slipup in management? Seldom can a definite qualifier be given that is, in fact,
truly accurate. There are simply too many opportunities for delays on each
activity that cannot be foreseen. One way to resolve this dilemma is to apply
PERT concepts to the project and obtain an estimate of the probability of
completion.

On large projects the construction planner is faced with the same type of
question in regard to milestone events in the network. As the milestone usually
marks the conclusion of a number of subnets and the start of new work, the
need arises to estimate, with as much certainty as possible, when the new work
can actually be scheduled to begin. High-quality project control depends upon
such milestone decisions, and a PERT measure of the probability of meeting the
milestone date greatly enhances the planner's decision-making ability.

It has been previously stated that the early event time, TE, for any event,
whether it be the terminal one, a milestone, or any other, is the expected value,
or mean, of a distribution of TEs. It has also been assumed that this distribution
is normal if an adequate number of activities have been involved so that the
central limit theorem is operative.

By repeated application of Equation 12.10, based on the central limit theorem,
it can be seen that the value of TE at any event i is the greatest sum of the
activity t_e values along a chain from the initial event to event i. Each activity in
this chain has its own standard deviation computed from Equation 12.6. Furthermore, each has a variance equal to the square of the standard deviation. The
addition of these variances results in the variance of the distribution of TE
values at event i by the central limit theorem. Expressed mathematically,

$$\sigma_{TE}^2 = \Sigma \sigma_{ij}^2 \qquad (12.19)$$

In summary, the distribution of TE values has a mean equal to TE and a
variance equal to σ_{TE}^2.

Now assume that at event i there is a scheduled time, TS. For the terminal
event, or even for milestone events, this time may be determined from considerations outside the project details, but it may be assumed to be equal to TL for
intermediate events. The difference between this value and the TE value for
event i is the deviation of the scheduled time from the mean time of the
distribution of TE values at event i. This deviation is, of course, in the same time
units as the TE.

The probability of occurrence of a value in the distribution of TE being less
than or equal to TS is represented by the area beneath the curve from minus
infinity up to TS. With only the mean and variance given above, this probability
is not easily determined. On the other hand, if the distribution is standardized so
that the mean is zero and the variance is one, the probability may be easily
evaluated.

The deviation of the scheduled time from the mean, $TS - TE$, may be put into the standardized form by dividing by the standard deviation of the distribution of TE values. This deviation is now expressed in standard deviation units and is identified as Z. In equation form

$$Z = \frac{TS - TE}{\sigma_{TE}} \tag{12.20}$$

where σ_{TE} is $(\sigma_{TE}^2)^{1/2}$ or $(\Sigma \sigma_{ij}^2)^{1/2}$.

With this value of Z the probability of meeting the scheduled time or being earlier can be estimated from the areas under the standard normal probability curve given in Figure 12.4 or can be accurately determined from tables found in references 12.2 and 12.9.

To illustrate the determination of the probability of meeting a date, the PERT network for the Fast Food Outlet Analysis shown in Figure 12.8 and the tabulated data in Table 12.3 will be used. Assume that you have been asked by the Fast Food Chain to state the chance that a typical outlet will be finished in 45 days. Your computations already show that the expected duration of one of these projects is 44.3 days. The deviation of the projected schedule, 45 days, from this expected duration is then 0.7 days. The value of Z is computed as

$$Z = \frac{TS - TE}{\sigma_{TE}} = \frac{45 - 44.3}{3.35} = 0.22$$

Figure 12.9a represents the expected distribution of the TE values and the above scheduled time. The quantities shown below the curve are given in days, whereas those above are given in the standardized form.

An estimate of the shaded area of Figure 12.9a, the probability, can be made by taking 0.22 times 34.1 percent and adding it to 50.0 percent for a total of 57.13 percent. If a reference table is used, the more accurate value is found to be 58.71 percent. In short, there is a 57 or 58 percent chance that an outlet could be completed before 45 days.

To illustrate further, suppose that the question had been for a finish in 40 days. The calculation of Z would be

$$Z = \frac{TS - TE}{\sigma_{TE}} = \frac{40 - 44.3}{3.35} = -1.28$$

Figure 12.9b represents this case. Note that scheduled value is less than the mean by 4.3 days. In standardized form this is $-1.28\sigma_{TE}$ units because the standardized mean is assumed to be zero.

An estimate of the probability given by the shaded area can be made by subtracting from 50.0 percent, which is the area up to the mean. The deviation is 0.28 more than one standard deviation so the amount to be subtracted is 0.28

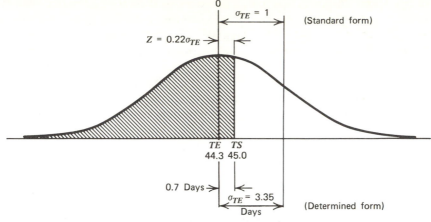

(a)   *Forty-five-day schedule: p ≅ 57%*

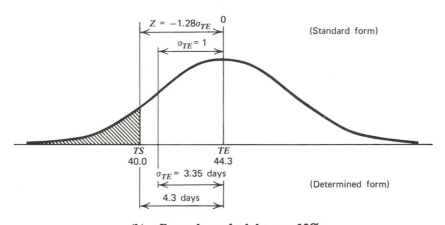

(b)   *Forty-day schedule: p ≅ 12%*

Figure 12.9   Fast food outlet analysis—probability of meeting 40- and 45-day scheduled durations.

times 13.6 percent plus 34.1 percent or 37.96 percent. The area up to the value of *TS* is therefore approximately 12.04 percent. If a reference table is used, the probability is found to be 10.03 percent. As before, the chance of completing an outlet in 40 days or less is only 10 or 12 percent.

The reader may note that the approximate values of probability differ from those in the reference tables. This is because simple proportions of the areas between the standard deviation divisions of the probability curve have been used and the actual shape of the curve has not been considered.

It may also be observed that when the scheduled time was greater than the mean, the error was toward the low side. When the scheduled time was less than the mean, the error was toward the high side. In other words, the error between the approximate and accurate values is biased toward the mean of 50 percent.

Another observation to be made is that the greater the value of Z, the greater will be the error between the approximate procedure and the accurate value.

In dealing with construction projects the initial three time estimates for each activity contain a considerable amount of subjective evaluation and they may be in error by considerable amounts. As a consequence, great refinement in the calculation of the probability of meeting a date seems unwise, and the approximate procedure will give results that appear to be well within the range of error of the initial input data.

12.9 PROBABILITY OF EVENT SLACK

Sometimes the emphasis of a PERT analysis shifts from the need to meet a scheduled date at an event to the desire to know the chance that a certain event slack will be achieved. It may appear to the construction manager that there is a possibility of failure to complete an activity within the time interval represented by the slack, yet given a day or two more time, the completion could be accomplished. The manager then wonders what the probability of being finished is. This question can be answered by the application of the same principles used in Section 12.8.

Realizing that the TE and TL for an event are both measures of distributions of early and late occurrences, it is then clear that the event slack also has a distribution. Although the mean of this slack distribution is the difference between the means TL and TE, in the course of the conduct of the work values of TE and TL could occur which may be larger or smaller than these means.

Should the event slack turn out to be the difference between a TL larger than the mean and a TE smaller than the mean, the value of this slack would be larger than the mean of the slack distribution. Conversely, should the difference be between a TL smaller than the mean and a TE larger than the mean, the slack value would fall less than the mean slack.

Figure 12.10 represents a distribution of such an event slack with a mean value identified as ES. The standard deviation of this distribution can be computed and will be identified as σ_{ES}.

The event slack is a distribution obtained by the addition of the distributions of late event times and the negative of the distribution of early event times under the assumption of the central limit theorem. The variance of the event slack distribution is, from the same theorem, the sum of the variances of the TE distribution and the TL distribution. The standard deviation of event slack is the square root of its variance. The mathematical expressions for event slack

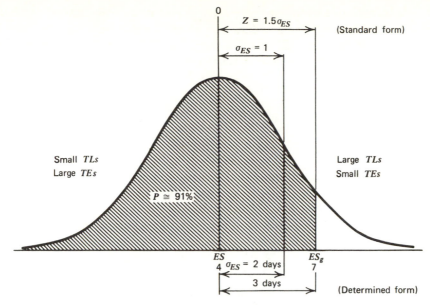

Figure 12.10   Probability of event slack.

variance and standard deviation can be written as follows:

$$\sigma_{ES}^2 = \sigma_{TE}^2 + \sigma_{TL}^2 \tag{12.21}$$

$$\sigma_{ES} = \left(\sigma_{TE}^2 + \sigma_{TL}^2\right)^{1/2} \tag{12.22}$$

At any particular event in a network the variance of the *TE* distribution, σ_{TE}^2, is found by summing the variances of the activity distributions along the chain of activities from the initial event as given by Equation 12.19. These are the activities whose means, t_e, have been added to give the mean, *TE*.

Similarly, the variance of the *TL* distribution, σ_{TL}^2, is found by summing the activity variances of the activity distributions from the particular event to the terminal event. These distributions are those whose means, t_e, have been subtracted from the assigned terminal event's *TL* or *TS* to give the mean, *TL*, for the particular event.

Assume that it is desired to determine the chance that an activity slack will be equal to or less than some given value of event slack. Call this given value ES_g. Its deviation from the mean, *ES*, can be written as $ES_g - ES$. This deviation is in the time units used in the network.

The probability of meeting the given slack is represented by the area beneath the distribution curve up to the value of ES_g. It cannot be readily evaluated because the units are in terms of time. The evaluation can be obtained if the mean and standard deviation are expressed in standard form. That is, the mean is set equal to zero and the standard deviation is made one. As was done in Section 12.8, the deviation, Z, between the values ES_g and ES can be standardized by dividing by the standard deviation of the distribution, σ_{ES}. Thus, Z in standard deviation units is

$$Z = \frac{ES_g - ES}{\sigma_{ES}} \tag{12.23}$$

As an example, consider that for the distribution of event slack in Figure 12.10 the ES has been determined to be four days and the standard deviation has been found to be two days. If the probability of an actual event slack for this event being equal to or less than seven days is desired, the value of Z in standard form is found as follows:

$$Z = \frac{ES_g - ES}{\sigma_{ES}} = \frac{7-4}{2} = 1.5$$

An approximation of the desired probability is found from the probabilities given in Figure 12.4 by multiplying 13.6 percent by 0.5 and adding 50.0 percent and 34.1 percent. The result is 90.9 percent, or say 91 percent. These quantities are also shown in Figure 12.10, both in the form determined and in standard form.

Probability of Negative Slack

In complex PERT networks the events have various values of slack, some of which may be large and some small. Also, some may have large variances and some small. It is natural therefore to attempt to rank these events as to their probable criticalness.

As discussed earlier, those events with the minimum amounts of slack are said to be critical events. It is tacitly assumed in this statement that the event slack is positive. The probability that event slack is positive however, can be determined by finding the probability of negative slack and subtracting it from one. The probability that an event will have negative slack can be easily obtained from the principles previously discussed in this section.

The probability of negative event slack is tantamount to finding the probability that the slack is equal to or less than zero. Thus, the given event slack, ES_g, can be assumed to be zero and by substitution into Equation 12.23 the deviation of this value, Z_0, from the mean, ES is derived as follows:

$$Z = \frac{ES_g - ES}{\sigma_{ES}}$$

$$Z_0 = \frac{0 - ES}{\sigma_{ES}} = -\frac{ES}{\sigma_{ES}} \qquad (12.24)$$

To illustrate the application of Equation 12.24 consider the slack of Event 19 in the Fast Food Outlet Analysis network of Figure 12.8 whose computations were made in Table 12.3. The TL for this event is 30.0 days and the TE is 27.7 days. The event slack for Event 19 is then the difference in these numbers, or 2.3 days.

The variance for the distribution of TE is found by adding the variances of Activities 1–3, 3–5, 5–9, 9–11, 11–15, and 15–19, which were the ones that established the TE for Event 19. Thus,

$$\sigma_{TE}^2 = 2.25 + 0.69 + 0.44 + 0.44 + 0.25 + 1.36$$

$$\sigma_{TE}^2 = 5.43$$

The variance for the distribution of TL is found by adding the variances of Activities 19–23, 23–25, and 25–27, which established the value of TL for Event 19. Thus,

$$\sigma_{TL}^2 = 0.00 + 1.00 + 2.78$$

$$\sigma_{TL}^2 = 3.78$$

The variance for event slack is the sum of these two variances and the standard deviation is the square root as given by Equations 12.21 and 12.22. Thus,

$$\sigma_{ES}^2 = \sigma_{TE}^2 + \sigma_{TL}^2 = 5.45 + 3.78 = 9.21$$

$$\sigma_{ES} = \left(\sigma_{TE}^2 + \sigma_{TL}^2\right)^{1/2} = (9.21)^{1/2} = 3.03 \text{ days}$$

The value of the deviation between the event slack for Event 19 and zero is then given by Equation 12.24 as

$$Z_0 = -\frac{2.30}{3.03} = -0.76$$

The approximate probability that this event will have a slack equal to or less than zero is then 50.0 percent less 0.76 times 34.1 percent, or 24.1 percent, which can be rounded to 24 percent.

Figure 12.11 represents the probability distribution for event slack at Event 19 together with the deviation of the event slack from the given value of zero and the standard deviation in customary time units. Above the curve the value of Z_0 and the standard deviation are given in standard form. The approximate probability of negative slack for this event is shown by the shaded area.

In this Fast Food Outlet Analysis example all the critical events had an event slack equal to zero. Their values of Z_0 all are equal to zero and the probability of negative slack for each is 50 percent.

By similar computations to those for Event 19 it can be shown that Events 7 and 17 each have a slack equal to 13.8 days and a standard deviation of event slack equal to 3.05 days. Their value of Z_0 is found to be -4.52 standard deviation units, and hence, their probability of having negative slack is virtually nil.

These negative slack values have been tabulated in Table 12.4 under the column headed $TS_t = 44.3$. It may be seen that the events can be ranked in criticalness with those having 50 percent probability of negative slack being the most critical, and those with little chance of negative slack being the least critical.

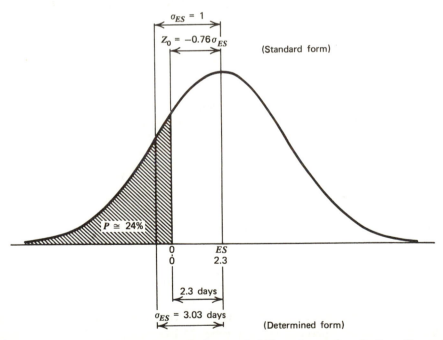

Figure 12.11   Fast food outlet analysis—probability of negative slack at Event 19.

TABLE 12.4

Negative Slack Probabilities Fast Food Outlet Analysis

Event	Probability of Negative Slack		
	$TS_t = 44.3$	$TS_t = 45$	$TS_t = 40$
1, 3, 5, 7, 9, 11, 13, 15. 21, 23, 25, 27	50%	42%	88%
7, 17	Nil	Nil	Nil
19	24%	16%	73%

In the computations made in Table 12.3 the assignment for TS at the terminal event, TS_t, was taken as the earliest that this event could occur, or 44.3 days. It was later postulated that this assignment could be 45 or 40 days. The value of event slack for each event if TS_t is 45 days would be increased by 0.7 days and if TS_t is 40 days, would be decreased by 4.3 days. The values of the standard deviations for the event slack distributions would not be affected, however, because the same activity chains would be used to establish the individual TEs and TLs.

As an example, consider Event 19. The slack for this event if TS_t is equal to 45 days is 3.0 days. The Z_0 is -0.99 and the approximate probability of negative slack is 16 percent. If TS_t is equal to 40 days, the slack is -2.0 days, and Z_0 is $= -0.66$, giving an approximate probability of negative slack equal to 73 percent. These and other probabilities of negative slack have been shown in Table 12.4 under their respective column headings. It will be seen that even though these values for each event differ, the ranking as to criticalness does not change.

REFERENCES

12.1   Anonymous, *PERT Summary Report, Phase I*, Special Projects Office, Bureau of Naval Weapons, Department of the Navy, Washington, D. C., July 1958.

12.2   Beyer, William H., *CRC Handbook of Tables for Probability and Statistics*, Chemical Rubber Co., Cleveland, Oh, 1968.

12.3   Clark, Charles E., "The Greatest of a Finite Set of Random Variables," *Operations Research*, Vol. 9, No. 2, March–April 1961, pp. 145–162.

12.4   Clark, Charles E., "The PERT Model for the Distribution of an Activity Time," *Operations Research*, Vol. 10, No. 3, May–June 1962, pp. 405–406.

12.5   MacCrimmon, K. R. and C. A. Ryavec, "An Analytical Study of the PERT Assumptions," *Operations Research*, Vol. 12, No. 1, January–February 1964, pp. 13–37.

12.6   Malcolm, Donald G., John H. Roseboom, Charles E. Clark, and Willard Fazar, "Application of a Technique for Research and Development Program Evaluation," *Operations Research*, Vol. 7, No. 5, September–October 1959, pp. 646–669.

12.7   Miller, Robert W., *Schedule Cost and Profit Control with PERT*, McGraw-Hill Book Co., New York, 1963.

12.8   Moder, Joseph J. and E. G. Rogers, "Judgment Estimates of the Moments of PERT Type Distributions," *Management Science*, Vol. 15, No. 2, October 1968.

12.9   Moder, Joseph J. and Cecil R. Phillips, *Project Management with CPM and PERT*, Reinhold Publishing Corp., 1964 (Second Edition, Van Nostrand Reinhold Co., New York, 1970).

12.10   Moroney, M. J., *Facts from Figures*, Penguin Books, Inc., Baltimore, Md, 1967.

EXERCISES

12.1   A certain project contains Activities A, B, C, E, F, G, H, K, and L. It has the following network logic. Construct the PERT diagram for this project. Label the start and finish nodes for each activity.

Activities A and K begin the project.

Activity B depends upon the completion of A.

Activity C depends upon the completion of B.

Activity E depends upon the completion of G and L.

Activity F depends upon the completion of B and H.

Activity G depends upon the completion of K.

Activity H depends upon the completion of A and K.

Activity L depends upon the completion of K.

When Activities C, E, and F are complete the project is finished.

12.2   The activities of a PERT project are given below together with their optimistic, modal, and pessimistic duration estimates. Set up a table and calculate the activity free slack and activity total slack for each activity. Identify the critical path and the project's mean duration.

			Duration Estimates (Days)		
i	*j*	**Activity**	*a*	*m*	*b*
1	2	AB	5	6	10
1	3	BU	4	8	12
2	5	CT	4	9	11
2	8	DS	15	17	19
3	4	ER	2	4	6
3	5	FQ	2	3	6
4	5	GP	4	9	10
4	6	HO	15	17	28
4	7	IN	9	11	14
5	6	JM	2	4	6

			Duration Estimates (Days)		
i	j	Activity	a	m	b
5	8	KL	3	6	9
6	9	LK	4	5	6
6	12	MJ	2	4	5
7	13	NI	3	5	7
8	9	OH	4	6	7
8	10	PG	2	3	6
8	11	QF	3	4	5
9	11	RE	2	4	8
10	13	SD	2	5	6
11	14	TC	5	6	8
12	13	UB	4	7	8
13	14	VA	5	7	9

12.3 The activities of a PERT project are given below together with their optimistic, modal, and pessimistic duration estimates. Construct the PERT diagram and compute on the diagram the activity free slack and activity total slack for each activity. Assume that the scheduled project duration is 50 days. Identify the critical path.

			Duration Estimates (Days)		
i	j	Activity	a	m	b
1	3	THIS	5	11	14
1	5	FIRS	1	5	7
3	7	DUM 1	0	0	0
3	9	IS	4	5	7
3	13	SUB	8	12	20
5	7	DUM 2	0	0	0
5	11	PRO	8	14	16
7	17	CON	3	6	9
9	15	A	6	11	16
11	15	LINK	2	4	6
11	19	TWO	4	9	10
13	17	PATH	7	10	11
13	21	ONE	14	16	18
15	17	PERT	4	8	9
15	19	SIX	6	12	18
17	21	NET	5	7	14
19	23	LAST	2	4	10
21	23	WORK	2	7	8

12.4 An activity in a PERT network has a duration mean and mode of 10.5 days. If its duration variance is 0.25, determine the lower and upper bound values of its duration.

12.5   A certain PERT network has event slack means and variances for its events as shown below. Determine the critical events and the variance of the critical path.

Event	Mean Slack	Slack Variance
2	−0.5	1.5
4	0.0	1.9
6	1.5	1.7
8	−0.5	1.5
10	0.0	1.9
12	1.0	0.9
14	−0.5	1.5
16	−0.5	1.5

12.6   Data for a simplified PERT network are given below. In addition, the value of TE_1 is zero and TE_{10} is 45. Also the variance for the project duration is 3.17. All times are in days.
(a)   Determine the mean and standard deviation for Activity 4–8.
(b)   Determine the range of the early project finish which meets a probability range of 16 to 84 percent.

i	j	Activity	t_e	σ
1	3	A	10.5	1.50
1	2	B	2.0	0.50
2	4	C	7.5	1.33
2	5	E	12.0	4.50
3	4	F	11.0	1.67
4	7	DUM	0.0	0.00
4	8	G	?	?
5	6	H	8.7	0.80
5	7	K	6.3	2.68
6	10	L	12.6	1.67
7	9	M	10.2	1.50
8	9	N	9.2	1.00
9	10	P	7.3	1.33

12.7   The activities of a PERT project are given below together with their optimistic, modal, and pessimistic duration estimates.
(a)   Determine the PERT critical path and the project mean and project standard deviation.
(b)   Estimate the probability of completing the project in 30 days or less.
(c)   Estimate the probability of reaching Event 8 in 19 days or less.

			Time Estimates (Days)		
i	j	Activity	a	m	b
1	2	A	2	3	5
1	3	B	2	4	6
1	4	C	2	5	14
2	5	D	4	8	12
3	5	E	8	10	15
3	6	F	3	3	6
4	6	G	6	9	12
5	7	H	2	7	9
5	8	K	1	3	7
6	8	L	2	6	10
6	9	M	4	7	10
7	10	N	6	8	13
8	10	P	4	5	9
9	10	R	3	5	7

12.8   The activities shown below are for a PERT network. Each is listed by i and j number with their computed PERT expected value and standard deviation shown.
   (a)   Determine the estimated probability of completing the project in 30 days or sooner.
   (b)   Determine the date for the terminal event that meets a probability of being finished with the project at or less than 84 percent of the time.
   (c)   Determine the date for the terminal event that meets a probability of being finished with the project more than 16 percent of the time.

i	j	t_e	σ
1	2	5.33	1.00
1	3	10.33	2.50
2	4	4.67	0.70
3	4	8.67	1.80
3	5	6.67	0.60
4	5	9.50	1.00
4	6	7.00	1.33
5	6	2.50	0.50

12.9   Use the data for the PERT network of Exercise 12.7 and determine the following:
   (a)   The estimated probability of negative slack at Event 10 with a scheduled project completion of 30 days.
   (b)   The estimated probability of negative slack at Event 6 with a scheduled project completion of 30 days.
   (c)   The estimate of the probability of having an event slack of three days at Event 6 with a scheduled project completion of 29 days.

12.10   The activities for a PERT project are listed below together with their optimistic, modal, and pessimistic estimates of duration. Rank the events of the network according to their probable criticalness based upon their probabilities of negative slack.

i	j	Activity	Duration Estimates (Days)		
			a	m	b
1	2	A	7	7	13
1	3	B	1	2	3
1	9	C	1	2	3
2	5	DUM 1	0	0	0
2	10	D	4	8	12
3	4	E	2	3	4
3	6	F	2	3	7
3	8	G	6	8	16
4	5	DUM 2	0	0	0
4	6	DUM 3	0	0	0
5	7	H	2	3	4
6	8	I	2	4	9
7	9	J	1	4	7
7	10	K	2	5	5
8	10	L	3	7	11
9	11	DUM 4	0	0	0
9	12	M	1	2	6
10	11	N	1	3	5
11	12	P	1	4	4

OVERLAPPING NETWORKS

13.1 INTRODUCTION

Early attempts to apply critical path techniques did not fully meet the needs of construction project planners. These deficiencies stemmed from three conditions. The early networks were constructed using the arrow diagramming procedure, and arrow networks were difficult to draw because it was necessary to use dummy activities to properly express the logic. Furthermore, the number of dummies in the network added considerably to the total activity list. Under the basic assumption given in Section 2.2 that every activity must be complete before any successor can start, the number of activities that had to be divided into parts increased the amount of work and was time consuming and expensive. These difficulties were especially pronounced when large projects were being planned, but they existed in relatively small projects as well.

Large projects, in the technical sense, are those that have more than about 10 or 12 activities. Exact solutions to such small projects can be obtained by applying the procedures of operations research, but most construction projects are comprised of more than 10 activities and cannot easily be solved by these methods. Therefore, virtually all construction projects fall in the classification of "large projects."

By today's standards, large construction projects are those that by nature take a long time to construct and that have many activities. Most of them are "phased"; that is, construction is proceeding on some parts while others are being designed. In general, all design-construct projects are considered to be large.

In 1961, Fondahl[13.2] introduced the circle-and-connecting-line technique which is now known as precedence diagramming. This advance met the first of the deficiencies in that it was easy to construct. It also eliminated the need for dummy activities and reduced the number of activities required. It did not address the required division of the activities, yet it recognized this need. Fondahl states:

> Since the completion of an operation must signal the start of some other related operation, it is not possible to have overlapping, related operations as are frequently indicated on conventional bar charts. Where such a condition exists, the operations must be divided further.

Later efforts to overcome the constraints imposed by splitting the activities were made by the H. B. Zachry Company of San Antonio, Texas, in cooperation with the IBM Corporation.[13.3, 13.5] Much of this work has been credited to J. David Craig by Archibald[13.1] and descriptions of this work appear in references 13.1, 13.4, and 13.5. Ponce-Campos[13.6, 13.7] extended the method to include all possible overlapping relationships and has since simplified the presentation of the diagrams and the computer algorithm for their solutions. Most of the material in this chapter will follow Ponce-Campos' model.

Currently, most commercial software programs for CPM permit the use of precedence diagramming and the overlapping of activities as well.

13.2   ADVANTAGES OF OVERLAPPING

At this point it may be well to examine some of the reasons frequently given for constructing CPM networks that have overlapping activities because this seems to be so important to the constructor. The most obvious advantage would appear to be that overlapping permits a more realistic modeling of the project. It has long been recognized that if the scheduling system being used does not represent the actual performance of the work, it fails; for the computed times for beginning activities do not meet the requirements of practice and the schedule quickly becomes outdated and unmanageable. The better the input, the better will be the resulting schedule.

Another equally obvious advantage is that overlapping permits the planner to reduce the overall time duration of the project. Because there are great economic benefits derived from shortening schedules, any system that can allow the project to be accomplished in a shorter time increases the probability for greater profit to the user.

Reference was made to the need for planning and control of phased projects. Much of today's construction is being performed under these conditions for economic reasons, yet the planner of such projects does not have complete plans and specifications to follow. Overlapping networks can be of real aid in phased projects because overall durations of major activities can be estimated with a fair degree of precision from past experience even though the detailed network cannot be drawn. Detailed networks can be created as more detail in plans and specifications becomes available.

Top echelons of management do not require the same level of detail in a project schedule that the operating levels do. Upper supervision must know the general progress of the work but does not need the exact details. In collecting the numerous detailed activities, overlapping becomes a necessity. Bar charts have this overlapping property and continue to serve the industry in the presentation of these summary schedules. When a network of overlapping operations is prepared, the result, whether in network form or bar chart form, is more accurate and informative for management personnel.

For those projects that are to be bid on a lump sum basis, there usually is not time nor money to prepare a detailed network for the purpose of setting a target duration for the project. Also, for phased projects, an approximate schedule is invaluable to both the owner and contractor if it is established early in the life of the project. A general summary schedule will aid in both these instances.

Overlapping networks also permit the network to be kept to a manageable size. When dealing with projects that may extend over a long period, it is difficult, if not impossible, to establish network logic and duration times for portions of the work that are to occur months away. Detailed networks containing about 200 to 300 activities and covering a short time period can be constructed with a fairly high degree of accuracy and can be processed in a relatively short time. These detailed networks can then be summarized together with the less accurate operations that are yet to be developed, and still have a summary network that contains not more than about 300 items. In fact, one of these summary networks can represent several thousand activities in a very large project.

Although the above discussion certainly does not identify all the advantages of overlapping networks, it may give the reader a sense of them through which others that may be of particular value may be identified.

13.3   LINK RELATIONSHIPS

In Section 7.2 it was pointed out that there are four relationships that link the start and finish dates of two consecutive activities in a precedence network. In the scheduling model described in Chapter 7 only one of these relationships was used, namely, the finish to start linkage. Also, no overlapping was permitted in that model. Overlapping of finish to start links will now be considered together with the other three relationships.

Finish to start, *FTS*, linkages imply that the finish of the first, or predecessor, activity will determine the start of the second, or successor, activity. The second link relationship permits the start of the predecessor to set the start of the successor. This will be called the start to start, *STS*, linkage. The third relationship allows the finish of the predecessor to establish the finish of the successor, a finish to finish, *FTF*, linkage. The fourth permits the start of the predecessor to determine the finish of the successor and is identified as a start to finish, *STF*, linkage. These four linkages are illustrated in Figure 13.1.

It should be realized that the activities are considered to be continuous, that is, if the successor start is set, the finish is found by adding the activity duration and if the finish is found, the start is determined by subtracting the duration from it. The activity is therefore considered as a single entity and not divided into several parts.

It should also be understood that if one of the start or finish times is set for the successor, the other time bears no direct relationship to the predecessor and

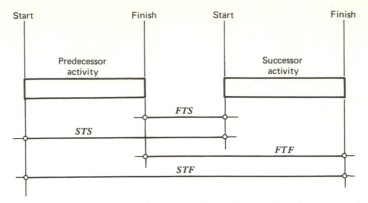

Figure 13.1   The four-link relationships for overlapping networks.

overlapping may be achieved. In the development of the model it is expected that these facts will become clear. A familiarity by the reader with the single relationship model of Chapter 7 is anticipated.

13.4   FINISH TO START RELATIONSHIP

It will be recalled that in Chapter 7 it was shown that once the early start date of an activity is found, the early finish of the activity is computed by adding the activity duration to it. The resulting equation is

$$EFD_I = ESD_I + T_I \tag{13.1}$$

Similarly, once the late finish date is found, the late start date is determined by subtracting the activity duration and

$$LSD_I = LFD_I - T_I \tag{13.2}$$

These equations are previous Equations 7.3 and 7.6, respectively. They are illustrated graphically in Figure 13.2.

As an example of a finish to start relationship consider the two activities "Form and Cast Wall" and "Strip Wall" depicted in the bar chart in Figure 13.3*a*. Note that there must be a delay between the casting of the wall and the stripping of it to allow for the curing of the concrete, a common occurrence in most construction projects. In the single relationship model of Chapter 7 the proper representation would require three activities, the third being the cure of three days as shown in Figure 13.3*b*. In the overlapping model the same information can be given with only the two activities plus the lead time for the curing shown on the start end of the link between them as in Figure 13.3*c*.

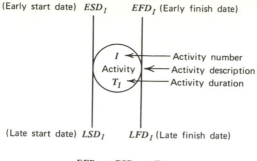

$$EFD_I = ESD_I + T_I$$
$$LSD_I = LFD_I - T_I$$

Figure 13.2   Early and late start and finish values for an activity.

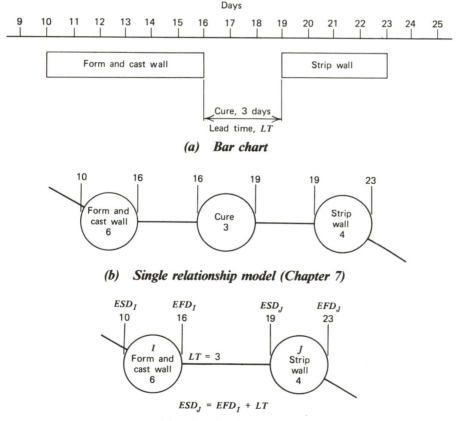

(a)   Bar chart

(b)   Single relationship model (Chapter 7)

$$ESD_J = EFD_I + LT$$

(c)   Overlapping model

Figure 13.3   Example of finish to start relationship.

For computing the early starts and finishes for the activities, assume that the *ESD* of the *I* activity, Form and Cast Wall, has been determined to be 10 days. The *EFD* of this activity is found by applying Equation 13.1, giving 16 days. The *ESD* of the second, or *J*, activity, Strip Wall, is computed by adding the lead time to the *EFD* if the first. This can be written

$$ESD_J = EFD_I + LT \tag{13.3}$$

Applying this equation, the *ESD* of the Strip Wall activity becomes 19 days. Again, Equation 13.3 is used and the *EFD* of the activity becomes 23 days.

This process is repeated for all the finish to start links in the network whether the lead time has a value or is zero. It may be observed that the *ESD* and *EFD* values for each activity are consistent with the start and finish days shown in the bar chart in part (a) of the figure.

13.5 START TO START RELATIONSHIP

In many construction projects a site, such as a parking lot, must be cleared before the foundations of a new structure can be built. This clearing need not be complete before the foundation work is started but enough must be done so as not to impede the new activities. This situation is illustrated in the bar chart portion of Figure 13.4. It has been estimated that two days of the demolition activity must pass before the foundations can commence and the two activities are overlapped. The two-day wait to start the foundation activity is the lead time in this case.

If the single relationship network were drawn to show this overlap, it would appear as in Figure 13.4*b* where the activity "Start Demolition" is added to depict the part of the total demolition activity that has been split off.

In Figure 13.4*c* the same logic is shown with just the two activities and the lead time. In order to identify that the link between the two activities is a start to start one, a small box is placed on the link at the *I* end, the end near the activity that has been split, and the lead time of two days is written above it. This representation is simple and easy to remember.

Computations on start to start links follow the same procedure that was used in the finish to start links. If it is assumed that the *ESD* of the *I*, or Demolition, activity is 10 days, then the *EFD* of the activity is found by the application of Equation 13.1 to be 18 days. The *ESD* of the *J*, or Foundation, activity is computed by adding the lead time to the start of the *I* activity. The expression is then

$$ESD_J = ESD_I + LT_I \tag{13.4}$$

The symbol LT_I has been used to emphasize that it is the *I* activity which has

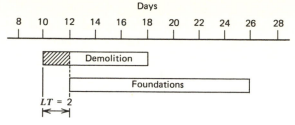

Days

| 8 | 10 | 12 | 14 | 16 | 18 | 20 | 22 | 24 | 26 | 28 |

Demolition

Foundations

$LT = 2$

(a)   Bar chart

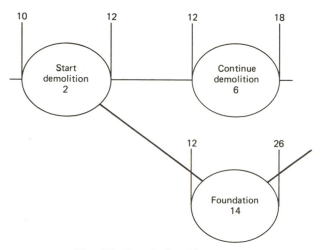

| 10 | | 12 | | 12 | | 18 |

Start demolition
2

Continue demolition
6

| 12 | | 26 |

Foundation
14

(b)   Single relationship model

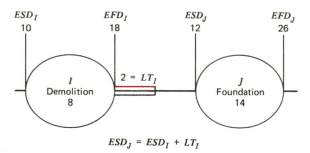

| ESD_I | EFD_I | ESD_J | EFD_J |
| 10 | 18 | 12 | 26 |

I
Demolition
8

$2 = LT_I$

J
Foundation
14

$$ESD_J = ESD_I + LT_I$$

(c)   Overlapping model

Figure 13.4   Example of start to start relationship.

been split. The result of this computation gives the *ESD* of Foundations as 12
days. Again using Equation 13.1, the *EFD* is found to be 26 days.

Every start to start link in the network can be computed in the same manner.
The lead time being used may take on any value from zero up to that of the time
duration of the *I* activity. The start and finish of the two activities in the
example are again consistent with what was expected by observation of the bar
chart in part (a) of Figure 13.4.

13.6   FINISH TO FINISH RELATIONSHIP

Figure 13.5 represents the model relationships for finish to finish activities. The
example that has been chosen for this purpose involves the two activities
"Repair Walls" and "Install Wall Cabinets." It may be assumed that a chemical
laboratory is being remodeled and that after the removal of the present furnishings, the wall along one side of the room must be replastered before new wall
hung cabinets are put in place. It has been estimated that it will take three days
to place the cabinets along this wall but that other wall hung units can be
installed on the other walls as soon as they are received from the manufacturer.
A bar chart of the two activities is shown in Figure 13.5*a*, indicating the
overlapping nature of the work.

The single relationship model of Chapter 7 has been pictured in Figure 13.5*b*.
It will be noted that the Install Wall Cabinets activity has been split to
accomplish the overlapping.

The overlapping model has only the two activities and the lead time, or split,
shown on the connecting link.

Again, the computations follow the same pattern as before. Since the *ESD* of
the *I* activity, Repair Walls, has been determined to be 10 days the *EFD* of this
activity is found by the application of Equation 13.1 to be 14 days. The diagram
defines a finish to finish linkage and the finish of the *J* activity, Install Wall
Cabinets, is found by adding the lead time to the finish of the *I* activity, giving a
result of 17 days. This can be written

$$EFD_J = EFD_I + LT_J \tag{13.5}$$

The symbol LT_J is used to show that the *J* activity is the one that has been split.
The *ESD* of the *J* activity is then determined by subtracting the time duration of
the *J* activity from it, using the relationship of Equation 13.1. As before, the
resulting values are consistent with those shown in the bar chart on the figure.

13.7   START TO FINISH RELATIONSHIP

A number of construction operations have their linkages arranged in such a way
that the finish of the successor activity is determined by the start of the

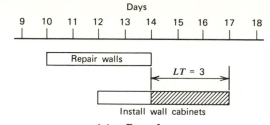

(a) Bar chart

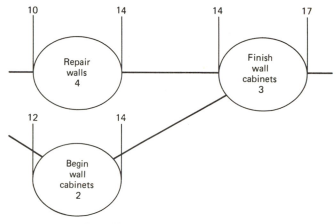

(b) Single relationship model

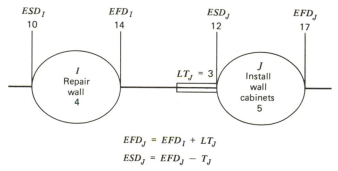

$$EFD_J = EFD_I + LT_J$$
$$ESD_J = EFD_J - T_J$$

(c) Overlapping model

Figure 13.5 Example of finish to finish relationship.

369

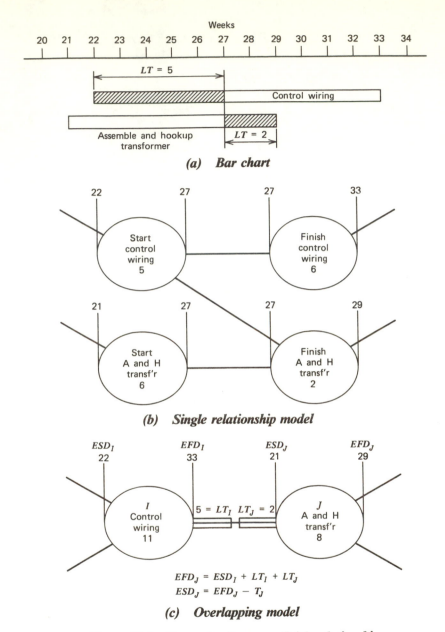

(a) *Bar chart*

(b) *Single relationship model*

$$EFD_J = ESD_I + LT_I + LT_J$$
$$ESD_J = EFD_J - T_J$$

(c) *Overlapping model*

Figure 13.6   Example of start to finish relationship.

370

predecessor activity. This is especially true in large projects. An example of such a relationship is shown in Figure 13.6.

A large transformer is to be assembled and hooked up to a control wiring system. It is estimated that five weeks will elapse before the wiring is far enough along to allow the actual hookup process on the transformer to begin. It has also been decided that there must be two weeks allowed to complete the hookup operation. These overlapping situations are shown in the bar chart of Figure 13.6a.

If this set of activities were expressed in the single relationship model, the diagram would appear as in Figure 13.6b. There would have to be two extra activities added to reflect the split in each of the main activities.

In the overlapping model the activities are not split, but the lead times are indicated on the connecting link near the ends of the link connected to them.

As the name of the linkage implies, the start of the I activity sets the finish of the J activity. The start of the I activity, Control Wiring, has been determined as 22 weeks as shown in Figure 13.6c. Its finish is found from Equation 13.1 as 33 weeks. The finish of the J activity, Assemble and Hookup Transformer, is computed by adding both the lead times to the ESD of the I activity. The general expression is

$$EFD_J = ESD_I + LT_I + LT_J \qquad (13.6)$$

Carrying out the computation gives an EFD for the J activity as 29 weeks. The ESD of the J activity is then found from Equation 13.1 as 21 weeks. The values just computed for the early start and finish of the activities are the same as those anticipated in the bar chart, as can be seen by comparison with Figure 13.6a.

13.8 COMPOUND RELATIONSHIPS

One of the most common conditions in construction projects develops from the need to begin an activity at some time after a previous one has started, but to have time remaining to complete the activity after the first has been finished. Thus, there are both the start to start and finish to finish linkages between the activities.

An example of this condition may be represented by the paving and striping of a parking lot. It is assumed that the paving activity has a total duration of 16 days, whereas the striping activity can be completed in 8 days. Figure 13.7a shows the single relationship network for these two items. After four days of paving the striping on that portion can begin and paving can proceed while the striping is going on. When the paving has finished it is estimated that it will take two more days to finish up the painting of the markings. As can be seen from the figure, the total time to do the two activities is 18 days.

In Figure 13.7*b* the four parts are charted in bar graph form. The start of the striping activity begins as soon as possible and extends from day 14 to day 20. At this point the striping must stop and wait until the paving has been completed. The finish part then starts on day 26 and ends on day 28. This six-day delay, or discontinuity in the activity, may or may not be an acceptable

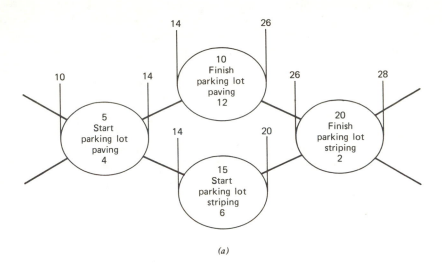

(a)

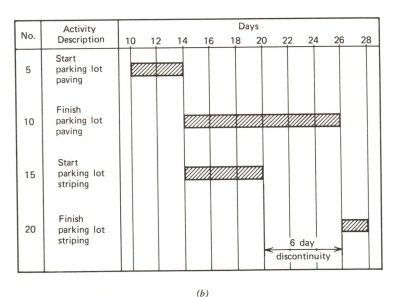

(b)

Figure 13.7 Compound relationship in a single relationship network.

model for the work. This assumption that the activity can be separated is often referred to as a time-discontinuous assumption.

The same set of activities represented as an overlapping network is shown in Figure 13.8a. In this diagram the two linkages, start to start and finish to finish, are each shown with their respective lead times. In computing the early and late starting dates for the striping activity each linkage is computed independently. The start to start link gives an *ESD* for Activity 15 of 14 days and an *EFD* of 22 days. The finish to finish link results in an *ESD* of 20 days and an *EFD* of 28 days. Because the maximum time is set by the finish to finish link, the chosen set of values are those determined from this relationship.

In Figure 13.8b each link relationship for Activity 15 is depicted, the chosen one being outlined with the solid lines. Note that Activity 15 is now scheduled to start at day 20 and finish at day 28 and is shown as though it were to be performed in a continuous manner. This will be referred to as the time-continuous assumption.

It can therefore be inferred that when the overlapping network is used assuming time-continuous conditions, the early start of some of the activities

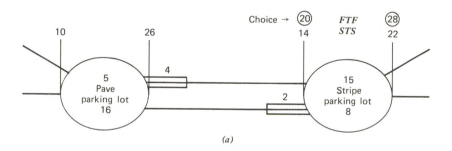

(a)

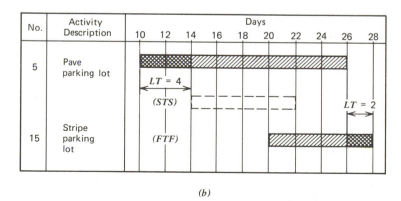

(b)

Figure 13.8   Compound relationship in an overlapping network.

may be later than it would be under the single relationship model. It may appear that this time-continuous assumption could become troublesome in project planning. Experience has shown that this is not so in the majority of cases because it merely delays the start of the activity. It also has the advantage of maximizing the utilization of the resources applied to it by avoiding the awkward interruption of the work once a crew has begun.

13.9   OVERLAPPING NETWORK TECHNIQUES

In the previous five sections of this chapter, basic link computations were made without considering the interactions of other links that might enter or leave the activity nodes. A network is now presented that demonstrates the techniques for dealing with these interactions. Computations are made to determine the early start and finish dates, the lags, the critical path, the free float, the total float, and the late start and finish dates.

Early Start and Finish Dates

The demonstration example to be used for the early start and finish dates is shown in Figure 13.9. The project consists of seven activities named with letters A through G and numbered from 5 to 35 in increments of five. These activities together with their duration times are shown in the circles on the figure. The various link relationships and the respective lead times are also given. As in Chapter 7, the *ESD* and *EFD* values are placed at the left and right above the circles, respectively.

To start the computation, the *ESD* of the initial activity must be an assigned value. In this instance it has been chosen as zero, but it could be assumed to have another value if the diagram were for a subnetwork within a larger project. The *EFD* of the initial activity is found from an application of Equation 13.1 and has been determined to be 10 time units.

The link between Activities 5 and 10 is a start to start one with a lead time of 3. The *ESD* for Activity 10 is calculated as 3 units from Equation 13.4. The *EFD* of Activity 10 is then found to be 11 units.

The link connecting Activities 5 and 15 is shown as a finish to finish relationship. Equation 13.5 requires that the lead time of two units be added to the *EFD* of Activity 5 resulting in an *EFD* for Activity 15 of 12 units. Applying Equation 13.1 gives an *ESD* for Activity 15 of −8 units. This negative time means that this activity should have its start 8 units before the start of the project, which is an impossibility. A correction must be made so 8 time units are added to the *ESD* of Activity 15 changing it to zero and also to the *EFD* making it equal to 20 units. In effect, this adjustment implies an added start activity preceding both Activities 5 and 15 with finish to start linkages. This

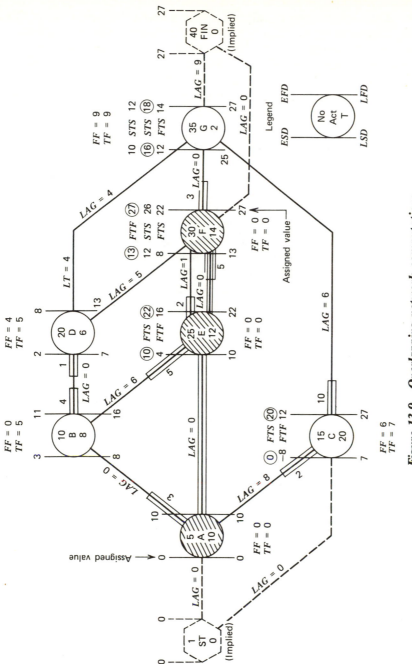

Figure 13.9 *Overlapping network computations.*

375

implied activity with its links is shown in dotted lines. For convenient reference for the reader, the two sets of values are shown above Activity 15 with *FTF* and *FTS* indications to show which link produced which set. The chosen pair has its values circled. The implied activity and links are not shown in usual network computations. Instead, only the corrected *ESD* and *EFD* values are given. Note that the *ESD* and *EFD* of Activity 5 are not affected by this adjustment because it is assumed throughout that each activity is to start as soon as is possible.

Examine the linkage between Activity 10 and Activity 25 next. This relationship is a finish to finish condition and the *EFD* for Activity 25 has been determined as 16 units and the *ESD* has been found to be 4 units. When the link between Activity 5 and 25 is considered. the *ESD* and *EFD* of Activity 25 is found to be 10 and 22 units, respectively. In this case the 10 and 22 are the chosen set and have been circled. The reason for making this choice is that the longest path through the network is sought, as was the case for single relationship networks of Chapter 7. The maximum set of *ESD* and *EFD* values is always chosen at a merge to insure that the longest path has been found.

The link between Activities 10 and 20 is given as a start to finish mode. An application of Equation 13.6 calculates the *EFD* of Activity 20 as 8 time units by adding both the lead times to the *ESD* of Activity 10. The *ESD* of Activity 20 is then easily found to be 2 units.

There are three linkages to Activity 30 even though there are only two predecessor activities because the predecessor Activity 25 bears a compound relationship to Activity 30. As before, all three pairs of activity dates are shown for clarity. The finish to start link from Activity 20 provides an *ESD* for Activity 30 of 8 units and an *EFD* of 22 units. The start to start link from Activity 25 gives the *ESD* of Activity 30 as 12 units and the *EFD* as 26 units. The finish to finish linkage gives the *ESD* for Activity 30 as 13 units and the *EFD* as 27 units. The maximum pair is the latter and this has been circled for reference.

The last activity of the network is Activity 35 and it has three predecessors, Activities 15, 20, and 30. The finish to start link from Activity 20 sets the *ESD* of Activity 35 as 12 time units by the application of Equation 13.3. The *EFD* of the same activity was calculated as 14 units. The start to start link from Activity 30 gives the *ESD* of Activity 35 as 16 units and the *EFD* as 18 units. When the start to start link to Activity 15 is used, the *ESD* is 10 units and the *EFD* is 12 units. The pair determined from the 30–35 link is the chosen set and has been circled as before. It may be observed that the early finish date for Activity 30 is larger than the early finish date for Activity 35, indicating that the actual finish of the project, the project duration, is 27 time units.

Link Lag Calculations

After the early start and finish dates for the activities have been computed, the next step is to determine the lag values for each link in the network. The link lag represents the time interval that exists between an activity's early status and the early status of the following activity to which it is linked. In the single relationship model of Chapter 7 these lags were calculated by subtracting the early finish date of the I activity from the early start date of the J activity, because the finish of the I activity and the start of the J activity represented the early state of each.

In the overlapping model the general definition of the lag remains the same but the early status of the I activity is identified by either its start or finish date, and the early status of the J activity is identified by either its start or finish date. There are therefore four equations for lag computation that need to be developed to correspond to the four link relationships.

In the finish to start relationship the early start status of the J activity is identified by the ESD_J. The early finish state of the I activity is the EFD_I plus the lead time. The lead time may be thought of as a correction to the independent variable EFD_I. The lag for FTS links can thus be expressed mathematically as

$$LAG_{IJ} = ESD_J - (EFD_I + LT)$$
$$LAG_{IJ} = ESD_J - EFD_I - LT \qquad (13.7)$$

This relationship is shown diagrammatically in Figure 13.10a.

If the link relationship is of the start to start type, the early status of the J activity is again identified by the ESD_J. The early finish status of the I activity takes its identity from the ESD_I plus the lead time for the I activity. The lag expression for STS links is then

$$LAG_{IJ} = ESD_J - (ESD_I + LT_I)$$
$$LAG_{IJ} = ESD_J - ESD_I - LT_I \qquad (13.8)$$

Figure 13.10b shows this relationship diagrammatically.

In the third link relationship, finish to finish, the early start status of the J activity is identified by the EFD_J minus the lead time for activity J, LT_J. The early start state of the I activity is the EFD_I and the lag expression for FTF links becomes

$$LAG_{IJ} = (EFD_J - LT_J) - EFD_I$$
$$LAG_{IJ} = EFD_J - EFD_I - LT_J \qquad (13.9)$$

This can be seen diagrammatically in Figure 13.10c.

The start to finish relationship, STF, is similarly derived. The early finish status of the J activity is again the EFD_J minus the lead time, LT_J, and the early start status of the I activity is the ESD_I plus the lead time, LT_I. The mathemati-

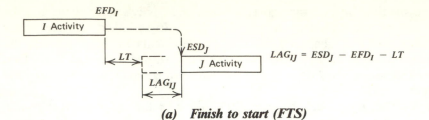

(a)   Finish to start (FTS)

$$LAG_{IJ} = ESD_J - EFD_I - LT$$

(b)   Start to start (STS)

$$LAG_{IJ} = ESD_J - ESD_I - LT_I$$

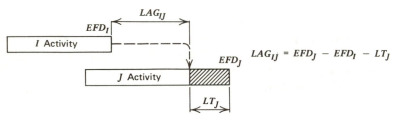

(c)   Finish to finish (FTF)

$$LAG_{IJ} = EFD_J - EFD_I - LT_J$$

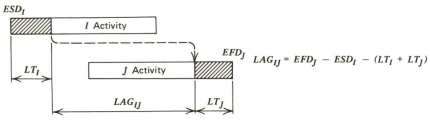

(d)   Start to finish (STF)

$$LAG_{IJ} = EFD_J - ESD_I - (LT_I + LT_J)$$

Figure 13.10   Link lag relationships.

cal expression for *STF* links is

$$LAG_{IJ} = (EFD_J - LT_J) - (ESD_I + LT_I)$$
$$LAG_{IJ} = EFD_J - ESD_I - (LT_I + LT_J) \qquad (13.10)$$

As previously, the condition is diagrammed in Figure 13.10*d*.

In the overlapping network example of Figure 13.9 the first link of the finish to start type is link 5–25. The lag for this link is computed from Equation 13.7 as simply the ESD_J less the EFD_I because the lead time is zero, or 10 minus 10 equal zero. In the case of link 20–30 the difference between the ESD_J and the EFD_I is 5, and this has been shown on the link. Link 20–35 has a lead time of 4 so the lag is 16 minus 8 minus 4 or 4.

Start to start link 5–10 requires the application of Equation 13.8. The lag is therefore 3 minus zero minus 3 resulting in a value of zero. In link 15–35 the computed value turns out to be 6 and in link 30–35 it becomes zero.

Link 5-15 is a finish to finish one and the two finish dates are used in Equation 13.9. The EFD_J is 20, whereas the EFD_I is 10. Taking the difference between these and subtracting the lead time of 2 results in a lag of 8. In a like manner the lag for link 10–25 is found to be 6.

There is only one start to finish link in the network, 10–20. The computation using Equation 13.10 begins with the EFD_J of 8 and subtracts the ESD_I of 3 and the two lead times 4 and 1, resulting in the lag value of zero as shown.

In the compound linkage 25–30 there are two lags to be calculated, one for the start to start linkage and one for the finish to finish linkage. Equations 13.8 and 13.9 are used and the lags are 1 and zero, respectively.

The Critical Path

It may be noted that all the lags are positive of zero. Also, each of the activities has at least one zero lag link entering it except the two activities 5 and 15 which start the project. This will always be so because every activity in the network must be preceded by some other activity that sets either its early start or early finish date. The longest path through the network therefore must be the path, or paths, having zero lag links entering the terminal activity. In this instance the terminal activity is Activity 30. The critical path is then comprised of Activities 5, 25, and 30 with their connecting links. This is represented on Figure 13.9 by the triple lines of the links and the shading of the activities.

Free Float

In a manner similar to that for the single relationship model, the

> **free float of an activity can be defined as the time span in which the completion of the controlling date of an activity may occur and not delay the termination of the project nor delay the early status of the following activity.**

In the definition, the late time boundary of the free float time span is the early status of the following activity. It was shown in the discussion of link lag and in Figure 13.10 that this early state could be identified as either the early start date or the early finish date less the lead time, depending upon the type of link relationship. However, the added condition that an activity must not delay *any* following activity requires that the minimum value be used if there is more than one link to following activities.

The free float definition further states that the completion of the controlling date of the activity represents the early time boundary of the free float time span. The controlling date of the *I* activity was also shown in the link lag discussion and Figure 13.10 to be the early finish date plus the lead time, if any, or the early start date plus the lead time. The equation for free float can therefore be developed as follows:

$$FF_I = \begin{bmatrix} \text{Minimum early status} \\ \text{of Activities } J. \end{bmatrix} - \begin{bmatrix} \text{Early controlling date} \\ \text{of Activity } I. \end{bmatrix}$$

$$FF_I = \underset{\forall J}{\text{Min}} \begin{bmatrix} ESD_J, \\ EFD_J - LT_J \end{bmatrix} - \begin{bmatrix} EFD_I, \\ EFD_I + LT, \\ EFD_I + LT_I \end{bmatrix}$$

The expression above can be expanded to identify the four linkages and to include the terms in the right brackets within the minimization. The early state terms within the brackets may be included because for any activity, *I*, they may be considered as constant values.

$$FF_I = \underset{\forall J}{\text{Min}} \begin{bmatrix} ESD_J - (EFD_I + LT) & \Rightarrow FTS \\ ESD_J - (ESD_I + LT_I) & \Rightarrow STS \\ EFD_J - LT_J - EFD_I & \Rightarrow FTF \\ EFD_J - LT_J - (ESD_I + LT_I) & \Rightarrow STF \end{bmatrix}$$

Rearranging terms gives

$$FF_I = \underset{\forall J}{\text{Min}} \begin{bmatrix} ESD_J - EFD_I - LT & \Rightarrow FTS \\ ESD_J - ESD_I - LT_I & \Rightarrow STS \\ EFD_J - EFD_I - LT_J & \Rightarrow FTF \\ EFD_J - ESD_I - (LT_I + LT_J) & \Rightarrow STF \end{bmatrix}$$

The expressions within the brackets are recognized as the several values of the lag previously determined. The free float expression can then be written as

$$FF_I = \underset{\forall J}{\text{Min}} \, LAG_{IJ} \qquad\qquad (13.11)$$

This is the same equation as was given for the single relationship model of Chapter 7, Equation 7.8.

Although Equation 13.11 applies to most activities, two situations in overlapping networks must be handled as special cases. The first of these is the determination of the free float for the terminal activity. The free float for this activity is the difference between its early finish date and the assigned late finish date. It is usually assumed that the early and late finish dates for this activity have the same value. This may not always be true, especially if the network is a subnetwork of a larger project where the late finish date is assigned by the main network.

In Figure 13.9 the terminal activity is Activity 30. Assuming the usual condition, the free float of this activity has been given a value of zero.

The second situation occurs when an activity has an early finish date less than the project duration and follows the true terminal activity, as Activity 35 in Figure 13.9, or when an activity is linked to such a following activity, as Activities 15 and 20. In these cases the value of the free float must never be greater than the difference between the early finish date of the activity and the late finish date of the true terminal activity.

Although it may seem that Equation 13.11 is inoperative in this situation, there is an implied terminal activity with finish to start linkages from the activities involved in the situation, such as Activity 40 in the figure. Ordinarily, the implied activity is not diagrammed, and the correct free float values are computed as the difference and entered directly on the diagram.

The free float for Activity 35 has been computed as 27 minus 18 or 9 time units. For Activities 15 and 20 the differences are greater than the lag already computed, and the free floats are simply the minimum lags as determined by Equation 13.11. The reader can easily find the other free floats using Equation 13.11. These values have been entered on the diagram near the activity nodes.

Total Float

The definition of total float for the overlapping model differs slightly from that for the single relationship model.

> **Total float may be defined for overlapping networks as the time span in which the completion of the controlling date for an activity may occur and not delay the termination of the project.**

Notice that the completion is the controlling date and not the finish of the activity. It can be shown, however, that the use of the controlling date permits the development of a general expression for total float that involves the link lag and is the same as that used in the single relationship model.

In the discussion of the link lag relationships and the illustrations of Figure 13.10, it will be recognized that there are only two conditions that involve the controlling dates of the *I* activity. These are diagramed in Figure 13.11.

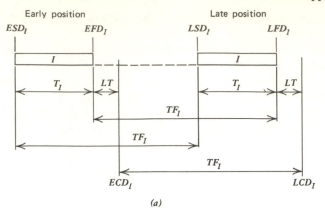

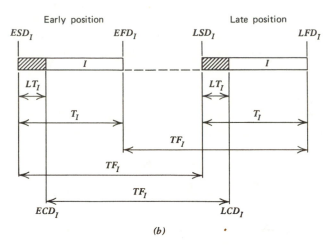

Figure 13.11   Total float relationships.

The finish to start relationship is shown in Figure 13.11a. This can also be considered equivalent to the finish to finish relationship if the lead time is set to zero. The I activity has been shown in both the early and late start positions in the diagram. If the activity is not to delay the termination of the project, the late finish of it must establish the latest time boundary that it may have. The earliest that the activity may start is the early start date and the difference between the two values represents the maximum time available in which to perform the activity. When the duration of the activity is subtracted, the remaining leeway must represent the total float. Thus

$$TF_I = LFD_I - ESD_I - T_I$$
$$TF_I = LFD_I - (ESD_I + T_I)$$

Substituting for the term in parentheses gives

$$TF_I = LFD_I - EFD_I \qquad (13.12)$$

Subtracting the time duration from each of the above terms gives

$$TF_I = (LFD_I - T_I) - (ESD_I - T_I)$$

and by substitution

$$TF_I = LSD_I - ESD_I \qquad (13.13)$$

When the lead time is added to each term of Equation 13.12, the result is

$$TF_I = (LFD_I + LT_I) - (EFD_I + LT_I)$$

The terms in the parentheses are recognized as the activity control dates previously identified with the activity in the early and late start positions. Designating the early control date as ECD and the late as LCD, the expression can be written as

$$TF_I = LCD_I - ECD_I \qquad (13.14)$$

Figure 13.11b is a diagram of the second of the two conditions for the I activity referred to above. It applies to the start to start and start to finish relationships. By a similar line of reasoning it can be seen that Equations 13.12 and 13.13 also hold true in this instance.

When the lead time is added to the terms of Equation 13.13 the following is obtained

$$TF_I = (LSD_I + LT_I) - (ESD_I + LT_I)$$

Again, the terms in the parentheses are the control dates for the I activity, and the equation is identical to that found for the first condition.

$$TF_I = LCD_I - ECD_I \qquad (13.14)$$

There are also two conditions involving the control dates of the J activity, as can be observed in Figure 13.10. The reader may wish to prove by a similar analysis, using the J activity in its early and late positions, that Equations 13.12, 13.13, and 13.14 will be valid.

In the above definition for total float the late time boundary is the termination of the project. This implies that the J activity must be in its late state, which is identified by its late control date. In overlapping networks there may be more than one link from an activity to following activities. If more than one link exists for the J activity, the late time boundary of the total float time span becomes the earliest of these late control dates for the following J activities.

As in the free float definition, the early time boundary of the total float time span is determined by the early status of the I activity.

The equation for computing the total float can then be developed from these conditions as follows:

$$TF_I = \left[\begin{array}{c} \text{Minimum late controlling} \\ \text{date of Activities } J \end{array} \right] - \left[\begin{array}{c} \text{Early controlling date} \\ \text{of Activity } I \end{array} \right]$$

$$TF_I = \operatorname*{Min}_{\forall J} LCD_J - ECD_I$$

Equation 13.14 may be solved for the late control date of the J activity and substituted in the above.

$$TF_I = \operatorname*{Min}_{\forall J} (ECD_J + TF_J) - ECD_I$$

$$TF_I = \operatorname*{Min}_{\forall J} ((ECD_J - ECD_I) + TF_J)$$

The ECD_I value may be included in the inner parentheses because it may be considered a constant for any Activity I.

The appropriate values of the control dates may be substituted in the expression to represent the four possible link relationships.

$$TF_I = \operatorname*{Min}_{\forall J} \left[\begin{bmatrix} ESD_J - (EFD_I + LT) & \Rightarrow FTS \\ ESD_J - (ESD_I + LT_I) & \Rightarrow STS \\ EFD_J - LT_J - EFD_I & \Rightarrow FTF \\ EFD_J - LT_J - (ESD_I + LT_I) & \Rightarrow STF \end{bmatrix} + TF_J \right]$$

Rearranging terms gives

$$TF_I = \operatorname*{Min}_{\forall J} \left[\begin{bmatrix} ESD_J - EFD_I - LT & \Rightarrow FTS \\ ESD_J - ESD_I - LT_I & \Rightarrow STS \\ EFD_J - EFD_I - LT_J & \Rightarrow FTF \\ EFD_J - ESD_I - (LT_I + LT_J) & \Rightarrow STF \end{bmatrix} + TF_j \right]$$

The expressions within the inner brackets are recognized as the several values of the lag previously determined. The total float expression can then be written as

$$TF_I = \operatorname*{Min}_{\forall J} (LAG_{IJ} + TF_J) \qquad (13.15)$$

This is the same equation as was developed in Chapter 7 for the single relationship network and identified as Equation 7.11.

Because the general expression for the total float contains the value of the total float for the *J* activity, the computations must begin at the terminal activity. As was the case with free float, the terminal activity's total float must depend upon the difference between the early finish date and the late finish date. It is usually assumed that the late finish has the same value as the early finish, and the total float is then zero. Should the late finish date be different than the early finish date, the total float for the terminal activity is equal to the difference between the two and the critical path becomes the path through the activities that have this total float.

In Figure 13.9 the terminal activity is Activity 30 and the total float is zero because the late finish date has been assigned as 27 time units.

Activity 35 follows Activity 30. As was the case with the free float the total float must never be greater than the difference between the early finish of the activity and the true terminal late finish date. The total float for Activity 35 is therefore calculated as 27 minus 18 or 9 time units. Note that if the implied Activity 40 is considered as the terminal, then the total float of Activity 35 is in agreement with Equation 13.15.

In a similar manner Activity 15 has a total float of 7 time units, the difference between the early finish date of 20 and the true terminal late finish date of 27 even though the lag in link 15–35 is 6 and the total float of Activity 35 is 9 for a total of 15.

Equation 13.15 applies to all the other activities in the network, and the computed values have been shown on the diagram beneath the free float amounts. For example, the total float for Activity 20 is the minimum of 4 plus 9 from the 20–35 link or 5 plus zero from the 20–30 link. The latter is then the total float for Activity 20.

Late Start and Finish Dates

The late finish date of the true terminal activity has already been discussed in connection with the total float determination, where it was pointed out that it is an assigned value. All other late start and late finish dates can be obtained by solving Equations 13.12 and 13.13 as follows:

$$\text{From Equation 13.12} \quad LFD_I = EFD_I + TF_I$$
$$\text{From Equation 13.13} \quad LSD_I = ESD_I + TF_I$$

It therefore follows that once the total floats of the activities are found, the late dates may be determined by a simple addition.

In Figure 13.9 the late start date and late finish date for each activity have been shown at the left and right, respectively, beneath the activity nodes of the network.

13.10   REDUNDANCY

It was demonstrated in Chapter 7 that when links in a single relationship network formed a triangle, the link connecting the activities on the earliest and latest sequence steps was redundant. In the overlapping model this may or may not be true depending upon the kinds of link relationships that exist along the sides of the triangle.

For a link to be declared redundant, the early start date of the activity occurring on the latest sequence step must *always* have its value determined by the links that form two sides of the triangle. It must not be determined by the linkage between the activities on the earliest and latest sequence steps.

Figure 13.12*a* is a portion of the project network from Figure 13.9 consisting of Activities A, B, and E with their respective linkages. Below it in Figure 13.12*b* is shown the same set of activities in bar chart form. In accordance with the statements above, the early start of Activity E must be the maximum of either

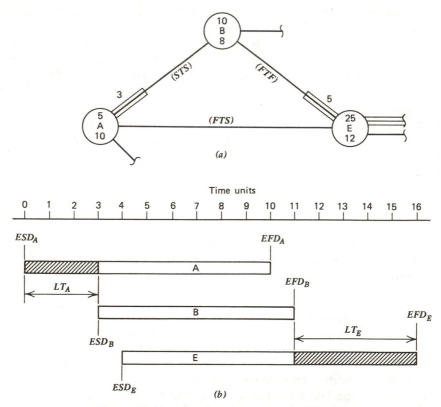

(a)

(b)

Figure 13.12   Overlapping network triangle.

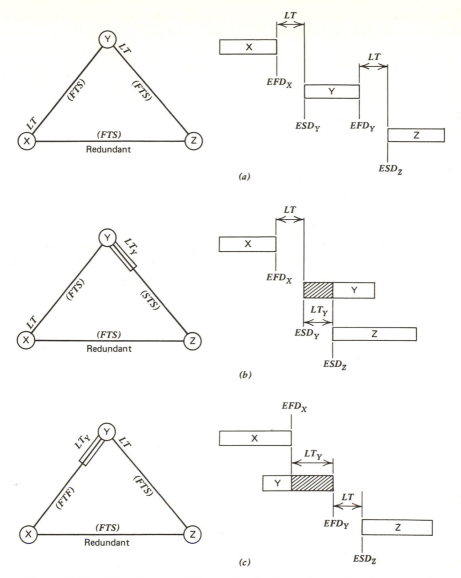

Figure 13.13 *The three conditions of redundancy in overlapping networks.*

the early finish of Activity A or the value computed along the chain A-B-E. Referring to Figure 13.12b these two alternatives can be seen to be

$$ESD_E = EFD_A$$

or,

$$
\begin{aligned}
ESD_E &= EFD_E - T_E \\
      &= EFD_B + LT_E - T_E \\
      &= ESD_B + T_B + LT_E - T_E \\
      &= ESD_A + LT_A + T_B + LT_E - T_E \\
      &= EFD_A - T_A + LT_A + T_B + LT_E - T_E \\
ESD_E &= EFD_A + (T_B - T_A - T_E + LT_A + LT_E)
\end{aligned}
$$

Hence, for redundancy to occur the quantity within the parentheses must be equal to zero or be greater. This is not a likely occurrence, and the link between A and E must remain in the network and be computed along with the others. The link between A and E is therefore said to be a meaningful link.

If the respective values are substituted in the last expression for ESD_E, the equation is

$$ESD_E = 10 + (8 - 10 - 12 + 3 + 5) = 4$$

This is the same value as determined earlier by direct computation. In this instance, for redundancy to occur the sum of the two lead times would have to total 14 time units or more.

There are three situations in overlapping networks where the link between the first and last activity of a triangle always gives a smaller or equal value for the ESD of the last activity and can be declared redundant. These three conditions are shown in Figure 13.13. By an analysis similar to the one demonstrated above for the A-B-E triangle it is easily seen that the ESD_Z always is determined from the linkage to Activity Y and not from the link to Activity X even when lead times are zero. These redundant links can therefore be removed from the network.

13.11   CHARTING

Overlapping networks have many advantages such as computational efficiency and accurate project modeling. They do have disadvantages in their communication ability, especially to the lower levels of management and production personnel. The project bar chart drawn from the computed results of the overlapping model overcomes most of these difficulties.

Figure 13.14 is a bar chart of the sample project used in this chapter to describe the overlapping model. Although there is no unique presentation of the

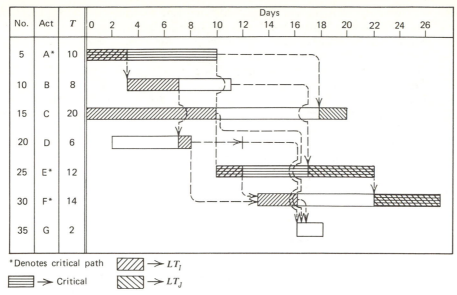

Figure 13.14 Overlapping network bar chart.

bar chart, the one here contains the most important points and is suggested as a practical display of overlapping information.

In Chapter 8 it was suggested that the critical path be presented at the top of the chart. In overlapping models this is not a satisfactory plan because critical activities may not be entirely critical and the link relationships between the activities are not of a single type. It is therefore suggested that the activities be plotted in sequence step order.

The chart of Figure 13.14 also indicates the link relationships by the dotted lines. These could be omitted at the option of the planner. In fact, if the bar chart is to be a summary one for the use of upper-level management personnel, only the bars in their proper location need to be diagrammed.

Bar charts drawn for overlapping networks can be used to control the flow of the work as well as to communicate the schedule information. The reader is referred to Chapter 9 for a discussion of project control.

REFERENCES

13.1 Archibald, Russell D. and Richard L. Villoria, *Network-Based Management Systems (PERT/CPM) (Appendix B)*, John Wiley and Sons, Inc., New York, 1967.

13.2 Fondahl, John W., *A Non-Computer Approach to the Critical Path Method for the Construction Industry* Technical Report No. 9, The Construction Institute, Department of Civil Engineering, Stanford University, Stanford, CA, 1961 (Second Edition 1962).

13.3 Anonymous, "Construction Project Management Control System at the H. B. Zachry Company," IBM Data Processing Division, IBM Corporation.

13.4 Moder, Joseph J. and Cecil R. Phillips, *Project Management with CPM and PERT*, Second Edition, Van Nostrand Reinhold Co., New York, 1970.

13.5 O'Brien, James J. (ed.), *Scheduling Handbook* McGraw-Hill Book Co., New York, 1969.

13.6 Ponce-Campos, Guillermo, "Extensions to the Solutions of Deterministic and Probabilistic Project Network Models," Ph.D. Dissertation, The University of Michigan, Ann Arbor, 1972.

13.7 Ponce-Campos, Guillermo, *Precedence Network Based CPM—An Introduction*, Training Manual, Townsend and Bottum, Inc., Ann Arbor, Mich., 1970.

EXERCISES

13.1 The activities and their overlapping relationships for a small building project are given below. Construct an overlapping precedence diagram for this project.

Activity Number	Description	Duration (Days)	Relationships
5	Demolition and underground service	3	Begins the project.
10	Concrete work	6	Activity 10 can begin after two days of Activity 5 have elapsed. Also once Activity 5 is finished three days of Activity 10 remain to be done.
15	Exterior walls	6	Activity 15 can begin after three days of Activity 10 have been completed.
20	Roof construction	4	Activity 20 can be started as soon as Activity 15 is complete.
25	Carpentry	3	Activity 25 can be started as soon as one day of Activity 15 has been done.

Activity Number	Description	Duration (Days)	Relationships
30	Interior walls	3	Activity 30 can start after two days of Activity 25 have been completed.
35	Plumbing	7	Activity 35 can start after two days of Activity 20 have been done and after Activity 30 has been completed.
40	Electrical work	6	Activity 40 can start after two days of Activity 20 have been done and after Activity 30 has been completed.
45	Floor finish	2	Activity 45 can begin after Activity 20 and Activity 30 are done.
50	Ceiling	3	Activity 50 can start after Activities 20, 30, 35, and 40 are done.
55	Finish work	7	Activity 55 can start as soon as Activity 45 is done but there must be three days remaining after Activities 25, 35, 40 and 50 are done.

13.2   The activities and their overlapping relationships for a sewage pumping station
       are given below. Construct an overlapping precedence diagram for this project.

Activity Number	Description	Duration (Days)	Relationships
5	Excavation and under-ground services	3	Begins the project.
10	Incoming sewage lines	5	Activity 10 can start after one day of Activity 5 has elapsed.
15	Foundations	5	Activity 15 can start as soon as Activity 5 is completed.
20	Transformer and main power lines	6	Activity 20 can start at the same time as Activity 5.
25	Outfall line	6	At least four days of Activity 25 should be left after completion of Activity 10.
30	Floor slab	7	Activity 30 can start after four days of Activity 15 have been done.
35	Concrete block walls	10	Activity 35 can start after four days of Activity 15 have elapsed.
40	Installation of grates and racks	7	Activity 40 can start after six days of Activity 30 have passed. There must remain at least five days of Activity 40 after Activity 25 is finished.

Activity Number	Description	Duration (Days)	Relationships
45	Roof and roof finish	4	Activity 45 follows four days of work on Activity 30 and after the completion of Activity 35.
50	Install and test pumps	8	Activity 50 follows the completion of Activities 40 and 45; but four days must be left in Activity 50 after Activity 20 is finished.
55	Electrical work	3	Activity 55 must have two days of work remaining after Activity 45 is finished. Also Activity 55 must follow the completion of Activity 35.
60	Mechanical work	4	Activity 60 follows the completion of Activity 35 and after two days of work is done on Activity 45.
65	Finishes	2	Activity 65 can start after two days have elapsed from both Activities 55 and 60.
70	Start-up	1	Activity 70 starts as soon as Activities 50 and 65 are completed.

13.3   Decide on the overlapping relationships for the bus stop project of Exercise 1.3 and construct the overlapping precedence diagram.

13.4   Decide on the overlapping relationships for the one-story commercial building project of Exercise 1.4 and construct the overlapping precedence diagram.

13.5   The activities for the construction of highway grade separation bridge are given below with their estimated durations in working days. Decide on the overlapping relationships for these activities and construct the overlapping precedence network. Assume the project starts on the first working day of March for the current year.

Activity Description	Duration (Days)
Set up traffic detour.	2
Order and deliver piles	45
Excavate for Abutment A.	10
Excavate for Abutment B.	10
Drive piles for Abutment A.	9
Move pile driver to Abutment B.	1
Drive piles for Abutment B.	8
Construct footings for Abutment A.	20
Construct footings for Abutment B.	20
Construct Abutment A.	45
Construct Abutment B.	48
Place backfill for Abutment A.	10
Place backfill for Abutment B.	12
Order and deliver bridge railing.	20
Order and deliver guard rail.	15
Fabricate structural steel.	65
Erect structural steel.	10
Construct concrete bridge deck.	22
Erect bridge railing.	10
Erect guard rail.	4
Construct concrete curb and gutter.	20
Place backfill for approaches.	40
Set up paving train.	4
Pave approach roadways.	4
Delay seeding of slopes until April 1.	—
Seeding must be done before June 30.	—
Seed approach slopes.	10
Final inspection.	1

13.6   For the overlapping precedence network whose data are given below draw the equivalent single relationship (*FTS*) network. Label each activity with its proper number, name, and duration.

Activity	Duration	Depends upon	Type of Link	Lead Time
K	4	—	—	—
L	5	K	*FTF*	2
M	7	K	*STS*	2
P	5	L	*FTS*	0
Q	6	L	*FTS*	3
Q	6	M	*STF*	2,3
R	4	P	*STS*	2
R	4	P	*FTF*	1
R	4	Q	*STS*	2

13.7 Data for a single relationship (*FTS*) precedence network are given below. Construct the overlapping precedence network for this project. Label each activity with its proper number, name, and duration.

Activity	Duration	Depends upon
A	2	—
Start B	3	A
Continue B	2	Start B, Start C
Finish B	6	Continue B
Start C	8	A
Finish C	2	Start C
D	4	Continue B, Finish C
Start E	4	Finish B, Finish C
Finish E	1	D, Start E
Start F	3	D, Finish B, Start H
Finish F	5	Start E, Start F
G	4	Finish E, Finish F, Finish H
Start H	2	D, Finish K
Finish H	4	Start H
Start K	3	Start C
Continue K	3	Start K
Finish K	4	Finish C, Continue K

13.8 Data for a small overlapping precedence network are given below. Construct the diagram and compute the early start and finish dates for each activity, the link lags, the free floats and total floats for each activity and show the critical path.

Activity	Duration	Depends Upon	Type of Link	Lead Time
A	4	—	—	—
B	5	A	STS	2
C	6	A	FTS	0
D	7	B	FTF	4
D	7	C	STF	3,2
E	4	B	FTS	0
E	4	C	FTS	0
F	3	D	STS	5
F	3	D	FTF	3
F	3	E	FTS	3

13.9   Data for a small overlapping precedence network are given below. Construct the diagram and compute the early start and finish dates for each activity, the link lags, the free floats, and total floats for each activity and show the critical path. Also compute the late start and finish dates for each activity.

Activity	Duration	Depends upon	Typs of Link	Lead Time
A	4	—	—	—
B	4	A	STS	3
C	10	A	FTF	5
D	10	B	STF	1,3
D	10	C	FTS	0
E	10	B	FTS	0
E	10	C	STS	2
E	10	C	FTF	6
F	2	D	STS	3
F	2	E	STS	4

13.10   Use the overlapping network developed for the small building project in Exercise 13.1 and determine the early start and finish dates. Compute the free and total floats and identify the critical path. Also determine the late start and finish dates.

13.11   Use the overlapping network developed for the sewage pumping station in Exercise 13.2 and determine the early start and finish dates. Compute the free and total floats and identify the critical path. Also determine the late start and finish dates.

13.12   Use the overlapping network developed for the one-story commercial building in Exercise 13.4 and determine the early start and finish dates. Compute the free and total floats and identify the critical path. Also determine the late start and finish dates.

14

SELECTED APPLICATIONS

14.1   INTRODUCTION

The preceding chapters have detailed the basic techniques for applying critical path methods to construction projects. The examples used in those chapters were academic and selected to illustrate particular points of the process. In this chapter, material has been selected from *actual* projects to illustrate the use of the technique in practice.

It is the intent of these examples to not only bridge the gap between theory and practice, but to illustrate some of the variations that schedulers use to meet the particular needs of their projects. From an examination of these samples, the reader should be aided in making a proper and efficient use of critical path methods.

These examples have been chosen to illustrate how several techniques are used as well as to show the types of projects to which the methods apply. Because of the limitations of this volume, the samples chosen are small; but the firms using these techniques also apply them to their larger projects.

Assistance in preparing the examples in this chapter has been provided by persons from several firms. Mr. Joe E. O'Neal, President of O'Neal Construction Company has aided in the presentation of the Restaurant Addition Project. Mr. Harry L. Conrad, Jr., President, and Mr. Phillip V. Frederickson, Vice President for Construction Management, both of the Christman Company have made available the material for the Construction Management Project of Section 14.4. Mr. Ben J. Mescher, Field Service Engineer of the Power Generation Service Division of Westinghouse Electric Corporation has been helpful in providing information for Section 14.5, the High Pressure Turbine Inspection Project. Without the aid of these persons and their companies this chapter could not have been written.

14.2   A HIGHWAY RECONSTRUCTION PROJECT

A highway contractor obtained the contract to reconstruct five miles of State Highway located 150 miles from home base. In planning the project, concern developed as to whether the specification for seeding the raw embankment and side slopes could be met.

The particular specification limited seeding to a period between July fifteenth and October fifteenth. If construction would not permit seeding during this period, the contractor would be forced to wait until the following April. Upon initial evaluation it appeared feasible to complete all embankments and cuts before the end of the year leading to a probable final payment the following June. On the other hand, if the total contract could be completed by the first of November, final payment could be received in December. A fairly large sum of money was involved and the six month difference for receiving payment would greatly influence the contractor's operations. Hence, it was decided to construct a critical path diagram to determine the feasibility of complying with the specification.

As a result of the analysis, it was determined that the project could be finished in time for the seeding to be done. In addition, it became apparent that the number of trucks required could be minimized, the scrapers could be continuously employed, and a record could be established showing the actual construction performance.

The project's general terrain was gently rolling and the present highway had a profile that rose and fell with it. The final grade to be achieved was relatively flat. An examination of the plans showed that the western one and a half miles and the eastern two miles required excavation to lower the grade. The middle one and a half miles required the placing of an earthfill to cover the existing roadway embankment.

The western end of the project began at the edge of a small village. About one half mile from this end was a small stream over which a new bridge was to be built. The contractor planned to subcontract the bridge construction.

The village had a storm sewer that crossed beneath the highway and discharged a short distance downstream from the new bridge. This sewer was to be reconstructed as a part of the contract.

The plans called for keeping the existing pavement up to the bridge. This pavement was to be widened on each side and then covered with a bituminous wearing surface.

Figure 14.1 is the initial arrow diagram. Each of the activities has the duration in working days shown beneath the label. The project was scheduled to begin on April fourth and the time interval from this date to each of the specification limits for seeding was found to be 90 days and 165 days. These times appear as durations for the Restraints 2-75 and 2-22.

The excavation was to be done using scrapers. These machines were presently in use and the contractor elected to delay sending them to the job site for six weeks. Because the planned work week was six days long, 36 day restraints were entered on the diagram preceding the excavation activities. These appear as Activities 2–18 and 2–36 on Figure 14.1.

The information taken from the diagram was punched into computer cards and preliminary schedule values were obtained. The results indicated that the

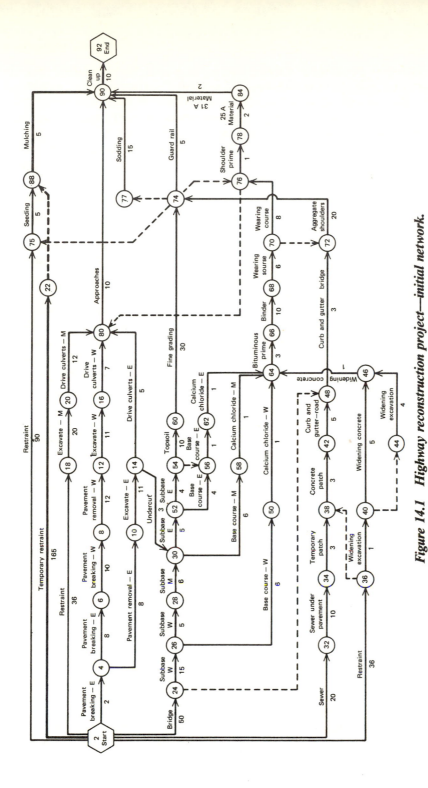

Figure 14.1 *Highway reconstruction project—initial network.*

399

critical path was comprised of Activities 2–22, 22–88, 88–90, and 90–92. Because Activitiy 2-22 was the 165 day restraint for the completion of seeding, it was clear that all seeding could be accomplished within the specification limit.

The schedule and diagram were next reviewed for errors in logic. The contractor's plan was to begin excavation in the eastern portion, shift the equipment to do the western end, and then construct the embankment in the middle part. An examination of the computer printout revealed an overlap in the excavation activities for the western and middle segments. A dummy, Activity 16–18, was added to insure that these excavations were sequential. Three additional dummies, Activities 16–25, 24–25, and 42–64, were also added to make certain similar logic relationships were maintained.

Figure 14.2 is the modified diagram. The restraint on the finish of the seeding operation, Activities 2–22 and 22–88, has been removed and the logic dummies have been added.

The subsequent computations established the critical path through the bridge, subbase, base course, wearing surface, shoulders, and sodding. This path was essentially the one originally expected and appeared satisfactory.

The plan was again reviewed to assure that the application of equipment was acceptable. The contractor planned to haul subbase and base course material with the same trucks. As shown on Figure 14.2, Activity 52–54, Subbase-E, and Activity 52–56, Base Course-E, both appear on the critical path. The computations set a proposed schedule for them to be done from day 81 to day 85. Activity 52–54 required five trucks and Activity 52–56 required six. Thus, eleven trucks were required on only these four days. Nowhere else would more than than five trucks be needed.

These two activities were re-evaluated to remove this resource conflict. Although the subbase operation might use the full four days, there was a good chance that it would be completed early on the fourth day, thus releasing the trucks to haul the base course material. The base course operation was also judged to be somewhat long. By starting the hauling of this material early and working overtime if needed, the duration of the base course activity could be reduced to two days. Further, the base course hauling could be accomplished with only four trucks of slightly larger capacity instead of the six initially anticipated. It was therefore decided to place the two activities in sequence and increase the project duration by two days. The contractor elected to assign five larger trucks to the project instead of the six smaller ones. By doing so, hauling costs were clearly reduced.

Figure 14.3 shows the above adjustment. This diagram was accepted as final and became the target plan. The subsequent computations resulted in a project duration of 153 working days and set the project finish date as October first, far earlier than the contractor had anticipated.

According to this target schedule, the excavation on the eastern portion is scheduled to be performed on days 11 through 21. The excavation on the

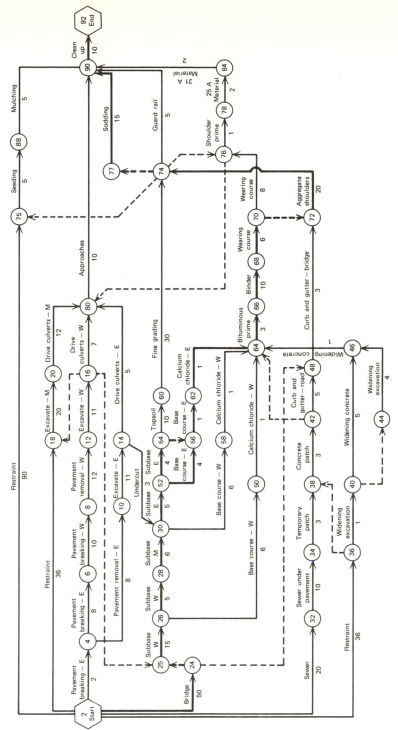

Figure 14.2 Highway reconstruction project—modified network.

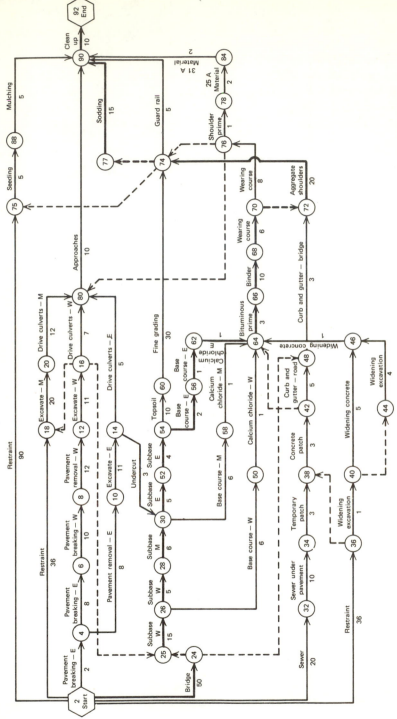

Figure 14.3 *Highway reconstruction project—final network.*

402

western part is to be done on days 33 through 43. The eleven working days between these two activities was judged unsatisfactory by the contractor. Three scrapers were to be assigned to the excavation activities and because of the distance from the contractor's home base, extra expense would be incurred to store the scrapers and provide for the crew. It was agreed to begin the excavation on the east end on day 22 so that once the scrapers and crews were on the site, the excavation operations would be continuous. Considerable cost was saved by this action.

It will be noticed in Figure 14.3 that Activity 14–30, Undercut, and Activity 14–80, Drive culverts-E, were scheduled to begin as soon as the eastern excavation was completed. These two activities were therefore delayed by the same eleven days. Because each of them had computed free float greater than this amount, no difficulty existed in making this adjustment.

Because of the successes already achieved, the contractor decided to control the project by measuring actual performance against the target schedule. The information given by the computations was expressed in the form of a bar chart on which actual progress could be marked.

A portion of this bar chart is shown in Figure 14.4. It shows the status of the project on April twentieth, or working day 15. The percentage completion of each activity is shown by the cross hatching on the bars and the actual start and finish of each is indicated by the letter S or F beneath the small arrow on the appropriate day. Activities crossed by the vertical shaded bar should have been underway while those entirely to the left should have been finished and those to the right were not scheduled to begin.

It will be observed that the pavement breaking and removal activities were progressing faster than expected. Initially, the contract required traffic to be maintained over the highway during reconstruction and the contractor planned to operate one pavement breaker on one side of the roadway to keep the other side clear for travel. As the time for construction approached, the State arranged for a detour so that traffic would be eliminated. The contractor then decided to send two pavement breakers to the site. The breaking times were therefore reduced to half their planned values.

Because of the increase in activity on the eastern part of the project, the sewer reconstruction was not started. Work should have begun on this activity because 15 days of its float had been used, although there were still 46 days of total float remaining.

The subcontract work on the bridge was also behind schedule with only 14 percent of the work completed instead of the targeted 30 percent. Overall, it appears that the project was generally on schedule. Activities that were ahead of the target were offset by those that were lagging. The contractor immediately initiated actions to speed up the bridge work because it was a critical item and continued low performance would delay project completion.

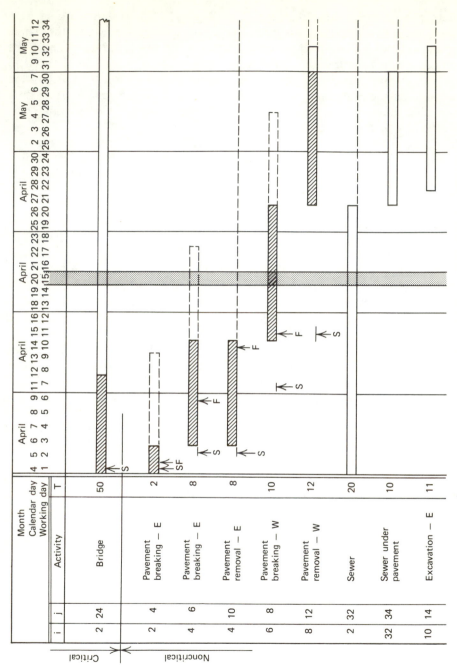

Figure 14.4 Highway reconstruction project—part of bar chart.

404

The contractor continued to monitor the project in the manner just described. As excavation proceeded on the eastern portion, a spring was opened and two days were lost coping with the resulting excess water. Several other unforeseen conditions developed but the plan permitted them to be overcome with minimum delay. The project was actually completed by October fifth and final payment was made in December.

14.3   A RESTAURANT ADDITION PROJECT

A well-known restaurant chain operates a first class restaurant in conjunction with a nationally recognized motel in a major city. Because of recent increases in business volume, the restaurant management decided to expand this facility by the addition of two areas on opposite sides of the present building. One addition was designed to increase the present banquet area and the other was to provide three smaller meeting rooms.

A contract was signed with a local contractor and work on the project began in August 1977. It was expected that the work would be finished by February 1, 1978.

In Ocotober, the restaurant obtained a tentative agreement from a professional group to hold an annual convention immediately after Christmas. To accommodate this group along with the expected holiday increase in patronage, the restaurant management desired the use of these new additions. A new target date of December 20, 1977, was proposed and the contractor was asked to expedite the work as much as possible.

The contractor restudied the schedule plan to establish new priorities and to assess the feasibility of meeting the new completion date. A critical path network was developed and analyzed and the results showed that the additions should be substantially finished by December 13, 1977, or about one week before the proposed target date.

Because of the extensive shortening of the project, the contractor became concerned about its effect on construction costs. A bar chart was prepared from the CPM schedule and the projected expense for each activity was established. These costs were summed for each day of the project and a plot of their daily cumulative values was made. From this plot the contractor determined that, even though the expenditure rate was high, the new financial demands could be met without undue hardship.

The banquet room extension was a one story concrete block structure with a built-up roof over steel joists. The end wall of the present banquet area was to be removed and replaced with a moveable partition and the new area was also divided in half with a like partition. The addition also included an extension of the main corridor from the present building, a new serving pantry, a storage area, and two additional rest rooms.

The new meeting room area was of similar construction to the banquet rooms. The design provided for three rooms with moveable partitions between them to permit their use as one large room. Access to each one of the three rooms was through a new doorway cut through the present corridor wall. There was also an associated storage area at one end of the addition.

In replanning the work, the contractor established the first day of work on the new schedule as October 26, 1977. A precedence network was assembled and the projected completion derived from this plan was about two weeks later than the proposed deadline.

A meeting was called by the contractor at which representatives of the subcontractors and the owner reviewed the network in detail. This review provided further refinement in the activity durations and some adjustment in the logic relationships to more fully integrate the responsibilities of the subcontractors. The resulting network is reproduced here as Figures 14.5(a), 14.5(b) and 14.5(c).

The general plan adopted for this network arranged the work so that activities in the meeting rooms followed similar activities in the banquet rooms. For example, Activity 1021, Facia Framing in the Banquet Rooms, shown on Figure 14.5(a) was followed by Activity 2021, Facia Framing in the Meeting Rooms, shown on Figure 14.5(b). This cross referencing is indicated by the activity numbers in the elongated circles on the respective sheets.

It will also be observed that some of the activites in Figures 14.5(a) and 14.5(b) are overlapped in the manner indicated in Chapter 13. This overlapping helped greatly to reduce the final duration of the project. The revised completion time was 33 working days from October 25, 1977. Thus, the new date for scheduled completion was December 13, 1977. This schedule was subsequently adopted by all concerned as the new target plan.

Once the feasibility of meeting the owner's proposed delivery date had been demonstrated, the contractor shifted attention to the costs to be incurred. A bar chart was prepared with each activity positioned according to its early start date, *ESD*, and early finish date, *EFD*.

Labor and material costs for each activity were reestimated with recognition given to the revised activity durations. The estimated cost for each was divided by the duration to obtain an expected daily rate of expense and every activity on the bar chart was labeled with this daily rate. For each project day, the daily rates of the activities on which work was scheduled were added to give an estimate of the day's probable expense. The total of all these daily costs equaled $138,402 and was the contractor's expected cost.

Curve A of Figure 14.6 is a cumulative plot of the daily costs. The apparent discontinuity at Work Day 13 marks the end of the rough construction and the beginning of the finishing work. Two periods can be seen to have high rates of increasing cost. The first, from Day 3 to Day 8, has a approximate average rate of $8800 per day. The second, from Day 13 to Day 18, has a rate of about $7500 per day.

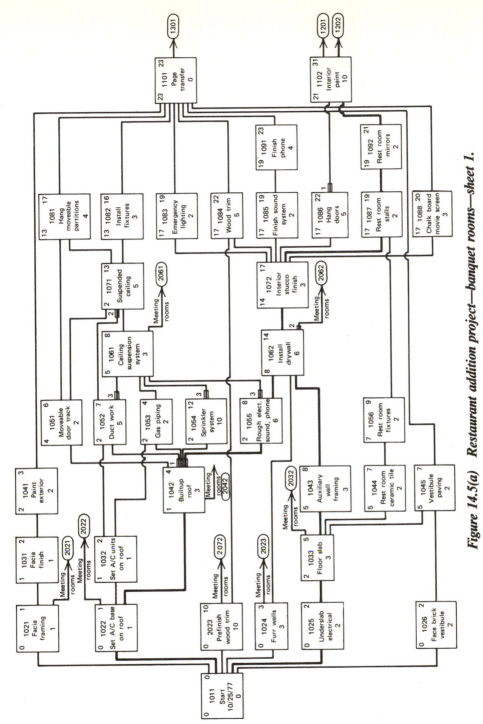

Figure 14.5(a) Restaurant addition project—banquet rooms—sheet 1.

407

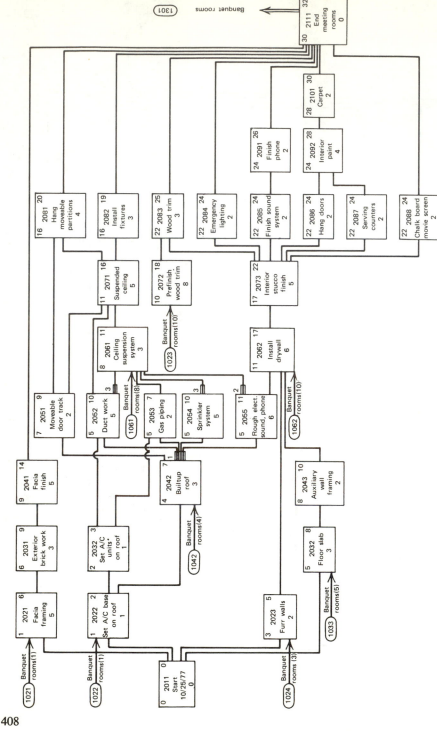

Figure 14.5(b)   Restaurant addition project—meeting rooms—sheet 2.

Calendar

Date	10/26	10/27	10/28	10/31	11/1	11/2	11/3	11/4	11/7	11/8	11/9	11/10	11/11	11/14	11/15	11/16	11/17	11/18
Working day	1	2	3	4	5	6	7	8	9	10	11	12	13	14	15	16	17	18

11/21	11/22	11/23	11/24	11/25	11/28	11/29	11/30	12/1	12/2	12/5	12/6	12/7	12/8	12/9	12/12	12/13
19	20	21	H	H	22	23	24	25	26	27	28	29	30	31	32	33

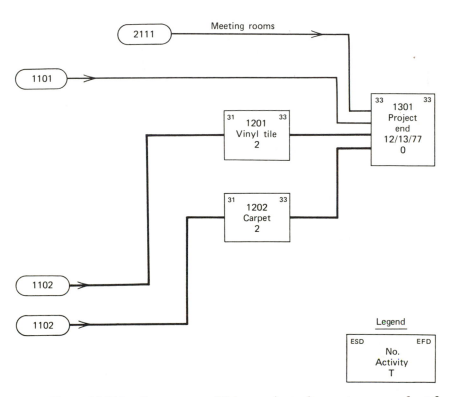

Figure 14.5(c)   Restaurant addition project—banquet rooms—sheet 3.

409

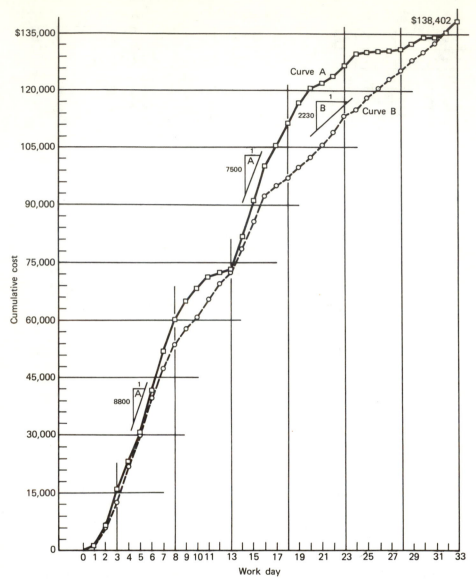

Figure 14.6   Restaurant addition project—cost curves.

Because of these high cost rates and the abrupt change at Day 13, the contractor decided to examine the schedule further to improve the daily cost demands. The cost rates were therefore leveled following the procedures of Chapter 11 and the results were plotted as Curve B of Figure 14.6. Not much change occurred in the first half of the project but significant gains were made in the second half where the approximate cost rate during this period averaged $2230 per day. The leveling also had the effect of almost eliminating the discontinuity at Day 13.

The effect on the work because of these changes was to significantly relieve the pressure to complete the duct work, gas piping, installation of fixtures, installation of the suspended ceiling, and the preparation and installation of the wood trim. These activities were consequently allowed to be performed at a slower pace.

Even though the cost rate during the early part of the project remained high, the contractor was able to meet these demands because they extended over only three weeks and involved relatively high material costs whose payment could be delayed until the end of the month. It should be pointed out that this was a very short duration project and that in a longer project such delays might not be feasible.

No attempt has been made here to consider the projected rate of income. This contractor was able to accommodate these adjustments using working capital, but this might not always be the case. In a more extensive project the ratio between the material and labor costs would play a significant role in overall cash flow considerations. Some other factors relating to income that would need to be evaluated are the intervals of billing and payment and the percentage of retainage given in the contract. The number of subcontractors and the size of their contracts, the relationship between the amount of subcontract work and general contract work, and contract provisions governing the obligations of the signatory parties would also need to be determined for a complete cash flow analysis.

14.4   A CONSTRUCTION MANAGEMENT PROJECT

A contractor signed a contract as a Construction Manager for the erection of a ten million dollar home office building for an insurance company. The contract required the Construction Manager to be closely associated with the owner and an Architectural/Engineering firm from the earliest beginnings of the project until final acceptance and occupancy. Because the many elements of the planning and design stages must interlock under this type of contract, a critical path network was developed to serve as a control for the entire process.

The plan developed permitted contract documents to be prepared, contracts let, and construction to be accomplished. The techniques used enhanced communications between the Construction Manager, the owner, and the Architect-/Engineer. They also shortened the delivery time of the structure to the owner.

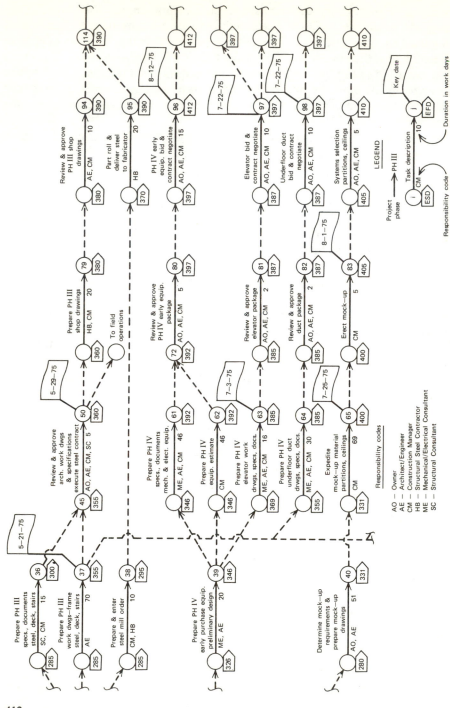

Figure 14.7   Construction management project—part of network.

As Construction Manager, the contractor was required to provide a cash flow forecast for the owner. The CPM network allowed the contractor to satisfy this need by using the IBM Job Analysis System 32, JAS/32, for the necessary computations.

The network prepared was an arrow diagram based on the independent activity approach discussed in Chapter 3. The contractor elected to retain all the relating dummies and to assign numbers to the head nodes of the activity arrows unless the tail node was a merge node, in which case, a number was also assigned to the tail node. Figure 14.7 shows a portion of the diagram. The entire network contained approximately 570 activities and covered seven 24 inch by 36 inch sheets. The project was scheduled to begin in mid-December 1974 and to be completed in May 1977, for a total duration of 615 working days.

The part of the network shown in Figure 14.7 is devoted mainly to the preparation of drawings, specifications, and contract documents. It is taken from the first sheet of the seven indicated above and has been chosen to illustrate the type of information made available to all parties.

For each activity in the figure, the contractor has computed the early start date, ESD, and the early finish date, EFD. These values are shown immediately below the activity's start and finish nodes and represent the number of working days elapsed since January 1, 1974. Because the planned work week was five days long, key activities have had their EFD values converted to key dates as shown on the small flags at the heads of their respective activity arrows.

In some instances the ESD value does not seem to be consistent with the EFD of the previous activity. This is because all the ESD and EFD values are target quantities and the contractor has chosen to float the activity for reasons other than just the maintenance of an early start schedule. Note, for example, Activity 39–63 which has a 16 day duration and is scheduled to start on Day 369 rather than Day 346, thus providing a target date of July 3, 1975.

The project as conceived was divided into phases and work packages for which separate contracts were to be awarded. This information is shown as a part of the appropriate activity descriptions.

Under a Construction Management contract the responsibility for the execution of many of the activities is shared by several contracting parties. To insure that all these parties are aware of these shared responsibilities, codes have been entered on each activity to clearly show these relationships. Such information is essential if confusion and delay are to be avoided during the conduct of the project.

14.5 A HIGH PRESSURE TURBINE INSPECTION PROJECT

Turbines in power plants must undergo periodic inspections and maintenance to avoid unexpected shutdowns. This project depicts a typical fall inspection of an operating turbine in a major power plant.

The inspection program involves the disassembly of the unit, evaluation of each unit by visual and mechanical means, performance of needed repairs and adjustments, and reassembly. These operations are under the direct supervision of a representative of the turbine manufacturer. The time required for this work is to be kept to a minimum so that service to the utility's customers is not interrupted owing to an excessive downtime for the turbine.

Although the exact amount of work to be done on the turbine cannot be determined until disassembly takes place, it is possible to plan a reasonable shutdown period by using critical path techniques. A critical path network can be assembled to provide a close control of the activities using estimates of time derived from previous inspections.

In this particular project an initial precedence network and bar chart were created for planning and control by the field engineer of the turbine manufacturer. Even with some unexpected changes to the prepared plan, it was possible to complete the necessary work and to have the turbine operating again on the proposed date.

This diagram is shown in Figures 14.8(a), 14.8(b), and 14.8(c). The project was to be carried out by working two shifts each day. Therefore, the work shift was used as the time unit and all activity durations were expressed in these terms.

As can be seen in Figure 14.8, the early start and finish times for each activity were computed and entered in the upper corners of the rectangle enclosing the activity name and the late start and finish times were also determined and entered in the lower corners. These computations were made manually because the network was small. From these values the total float for every activity was obtained, the initial path identified, and the project duration was found to be $52\frac{1}{2}$ shifts.

The field engineer next prepared a bar chart from the network data to be used for control purposes; it is shown in Figures 14.9(a) and 14.9(b). The time headings at the top of the chart show the month and the date. Beneath each date is found a D and an N to identify the day and night shifts. The continuously increasing numbers at the bottom of the heading represent the number of shifts from the start of the project.

The project was scheduled to begin on September 19, 1977. Its duration of $52\frac{1}{2}$ shifts set the project's end on October 15, 1977. It should be noted that work was to be performed every calendar day throughout this period.

The general arrangement of the chart places the critical activities first followed by the noncritical ones in early start order. The total floats of the noncritical items are shown by the dashed lines extending from the open bars. The open bars are the originally planned positions of the activities and the cross-hatched bars show the actual performance on each activity.

Several significant changes on the critical path in the original plan are worthy of mention. Activity 170, Improvement work rotor blades, was work that the manufacturer proposed to bring the turbine up to current performance standards. This activity was delayed and when it was performed it took somewhat

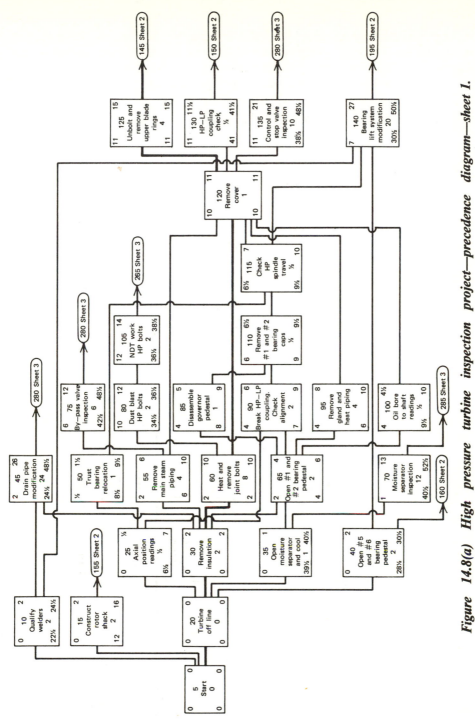

Figure 14.8(a) High pressure turbine inspection project—precedence diagram—sheet 1.

415

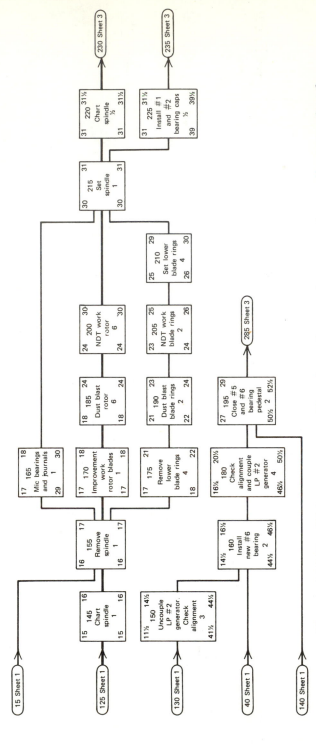

416

Figure 14.8(b) High pressure turbine inspection project—precedence diagram—sheet 2.

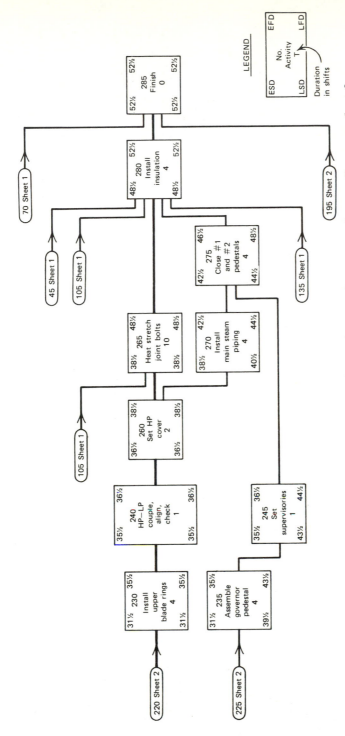

Figure 14.8(c) High pressure turbine inspection project—precedence diagram—sheet 3.

417

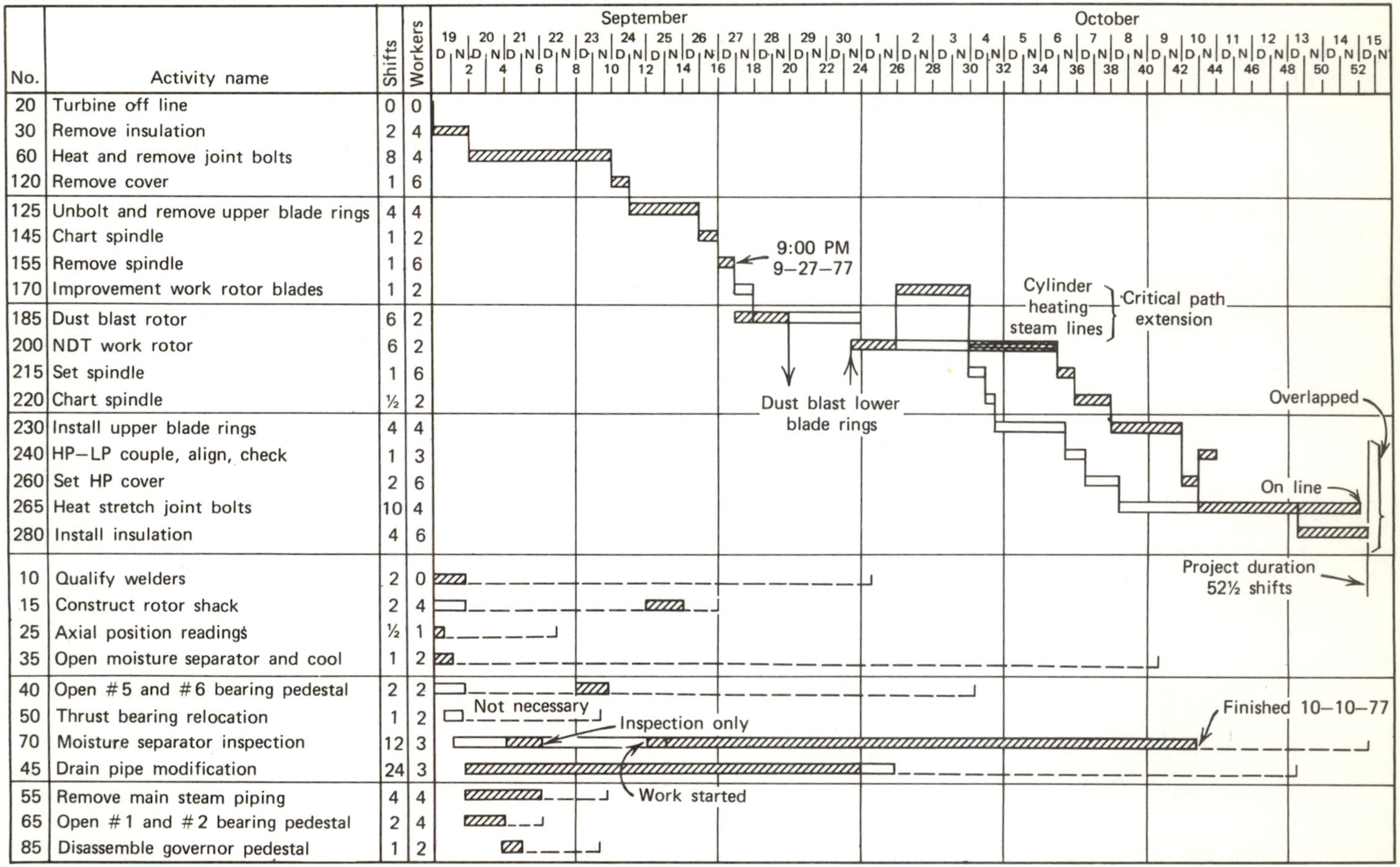

No.
Activity name
Shifts
Workers
September
October
19 20 21 22 23 24 25 26 27 28 29 30 1 2 3 4 5 6 7 8 9 10 11 12 13 14 15
D N D N D N D N D N D N D N D N D N D N D N D N D N D N D N D N D N D N D N D N D N D N D N D N D N D N
2 4 6 8 10 12 14 16 18 20 22 24 26 28 30 32 34 36 38 40 42 44 46 48 50 52
20 Turbine off line 0 0
30 Remove insulation 2 4
60 Heat and remove joint bolts 8 4
120 Remove cover 1 6
125 Unbolt and remove upper blade rings 4 4
145 Chart spindle 1 2
155 Remove spindle 1 6
170 Improvement work rotor blades 1 2
185 Dust blast rotor 6 2
200 NDT work rotor 6 2
215 Set spindle 1 6
220 Chart spindle ½ 2
230 Install upper blade rings 4 4
240 HP–LP couple, align, check 1 3
260 Set HP cover 2 6
265 Heat stretch joint bolts 10 4
280 Install insulation 4 6
10 Qualify welders 2 0
15 Construct rotor shack 2 4
25 Axial position readings ½ 1
35 Open moisture separator and cool 1 2
40 Open #5 and #6 bearing pedestal 2 2
50 Thrust bearing relocation 1 2
70 Moisture separator inspection 12 3
45 Drain pipe modification 24 3
55 Remove main steam piping 4 4
65 Open #1 and #2 bearing pedestal 2 4
85 Disassemble governor pedestal 1 2
9:00 PM
9–27–77
Cylinder heating steam lines
Critical path extension
Dust blast lower blade rings
Overlapped
On line
Project duration
52½ shifts
Not necessary
Inspection only
Finished 10–10–77
Work started

Figure 14.9(a) ***As-built bar chart—high pressure turbine inspection—sheet 1.***

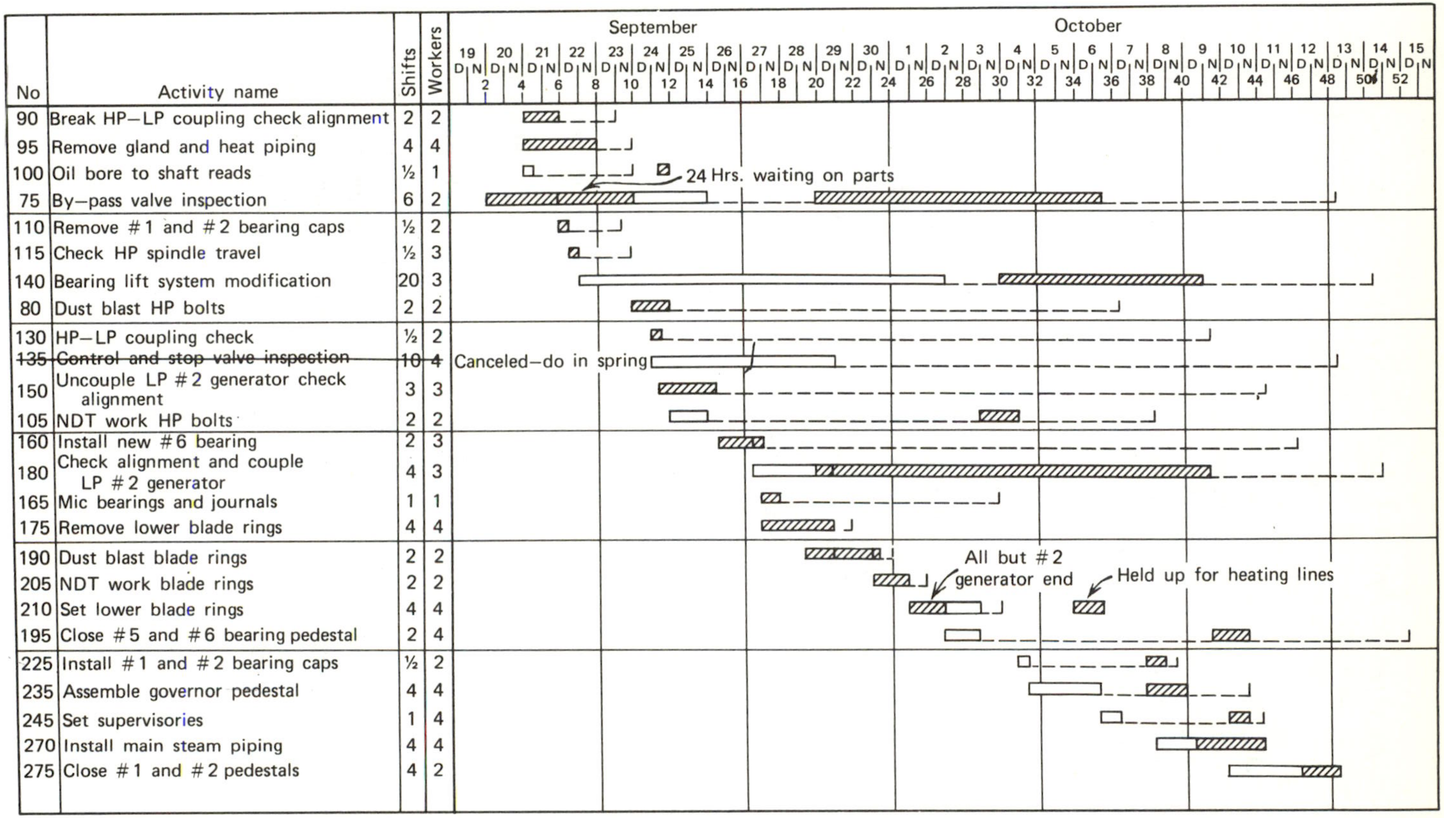

No	Activity name	Shifts	Workers
90	Break HP–LP coupling check alignment	2	2
95	Remove gland and heat piping	4	4
100	Oil bore to shaft reads	½	1
75	By-pass valve inspection	6	2
110	Remove #1 and #2 bearing caps	½	2
115	Check HP spindle travel	½	3
140	Bearing lift system modification	20	3
80	Dust blast HP bolts	2	2
130	HP–LP coupling check	½	2
135	Control and stop valve inspection	10	4
150	Uncouple LP #2 generator check alignment	3	3
105	NDT work HP bolts	2	2
160	Install new #6 bearing	2	3
180	Check alignment and couple LP #2 generator	4	3
165	Mic bearings and journals	1	1
175	Remove lower blade rings	4	4
190	Dust blast blade rings	2	2
205	NDT work blade rings	2	2
210	Set lower blade rings	4	4
195	Close #5 and #6 bearing pedestal	2	4
225	Install #1 and #2 bearing caps	½	2
235	Assemble governor pedestal	4	4
245	Set supervisories	1	4
270	Install main steam piping	4	4
275	Close #1 and #2 pedestals	4	2

September   October

24 Hrs. waiting on parts

Canceled–do in spring

All but #2 generator end — Held up for heating lines

Figure 14.9(b) As-built bar chart—high pressure turbine inspection—sheet 2.

419

longer than expected. Activity 185, Dust blast rotor, was begun as soon as the the spindle was removed. It took less time to complete than planned so the dust blasting shifted to the lower blade rings. In effect, this placed Activity 190, Dust blast blade rings, on the critical path.

Activity 200, NDT work rotor, was started on schedule. However, the nondestructive testing revealed some difficulties with the heating steam lines to the cylinder. It was therefore necessary to add a five day extension to the critical path to correct this difficulty. This correction was placed on the chart as a lengthening of Activity 200's bar and the following critical activities were moved to the right by the five days.

To recover this lost time, extra effort was applied to Activity 260, Set HP cover, resulting in a one shift performance instead of the planned two shifts. Also, Activity 280, Install insulation, was started before the heat stretching of the joint bolts, Activity, 265 was completed. This overlapping of four shifts permitted the project to be completed on time.

Among the noncritical activities there were also several changes of note. Activity 50, Thrust bearing relocation, was found to be not necessary, thus releasing two workers to begin other tasks. Activity 70, Moisture separator inspection, was originally expected to take 12 shifts to complete. First inspection revealed more work on the moisture separator than expected, resulting in further detailed planning. Corrective work actually began on Shift 13 and was finished on Shift 43 for a total time of 34 shifts spent on this one task.

Activity 75, By-pass valve inspection, was actually started early but inspection revealed an unexpected need for parts and 24 hours was lost while waiting for the delivery of these parts. A further delay occured because of a lack of personnel, so actual corrective work began on Shift 21. Work on this activity was finally completed during Shift 35.

Activity 135, Control and stop valve inspection, was canceled and rescheduled for the spring inspection schedule because it was decided that this task was not of a critical nature. Also, Activity 210, Set lower blade rings, was partially delayed because of the difficulties with the heating lines.

Undoubtedly, had not a schedule plan been prepared and used for control, this inspection and maintenance project would have overrun its expected four week duration. Unexpected conditions were revealed as the turbine was disassembled but the schedule allowed the field engineer to predict the effect of these difficulties on the project's duration and to take corrective action.

INDEX